PRAISE FOR *LETTERS TO MY FATHER*

In *Letters to My Father* Kathleen Balgley treats  ng
people, places, and cross-cultural encounters, st
Jewish origins in Eastern Europe. An epic of soι 's
to My Father is an intimate look at how our l d
generations—timely in its account of immigra. ..., and outcasts, lost souls
and soul survivors—including second and third generation Americans. Balgley is a
candid participant-narrator whose Chekhovian observations take us behind the surface
of things to the untold inner-dramas within them. Narrated with enchanting verve,
humor, and intelligence, *Letters to My Father* is an inspiring journey of the spirit, very
moving and very wise.

> Robert L. Inchausti, Ph.D.
> Professor Emeritus, California Polytechnic University, San Luis Obispo
> Author of *Thomas Merton's American Prophecy*; *Subversive Orthodoxy*; and *The Ignorant Perfection of Ordinary People*

In this beautiful, keenly observed, and evocative book, Balgley takes us on a journey
to find her origins, and as with all good literary journeys, this one is rich in history, in
characters large and small, in revelation and heartache. Balgley's writing is thick with
everyday life, reclaimed and honored. And Balgley succeeds on another front: reading
her quest stirs the desire to explore our own history, excavating the events that we
know shaped us and, possibly, events we have yet to uncover.

> Professor Mike Rose, Ph.D.
> Graduate School of Education and Information Studies, UCLA
> Author of *Possible Lives*; *The Mind at Work*; *Lives on the Boundary;* and *Why School: Reclaiming Education for All of Us*

"I had gone to Poland to learn hard truths and rescue hope," writes Kathleen Balgley,
an American literature professor, the daughter of an Irish Catholic mother and a Polish-
Jewish father who distanced himself from his Jewish lineage. Balgley's desire to
reclaim that lost history propels her, as a Fulbright scholar, into the looking glass world
of 1980's communist-era Poland. Her soulful remembrance of that sojourn and her
attempt to recover her family's story—at a time in Poland when discussion of Polish-
Jewish relations and Polish anti-Semitism were taboo—is honest, nuanced, haunting,
at times hilarious. *Letters to My Father* is a rigorously researched, beautifully written
tale about identity and belonging.

> Louise Steinman
> Author of *The Crooked Mirror: A Memoir of Polish-Jewish Reconciliation*

Balgley's *Letters to My Father* is probing and panoramic. Her hunt for identity takes the latest descendant of a brilliant Jewish family back to the old country. Balgley's genius is literary, and her evocative poetic prose transports the reader back to the old country with her. The hospitality, the Soviet-era bureaucracy, and the blinkered national narratives among both Poles and Jews form the canvas on which Balgley wrestles across decades and continents. Her inner eye for detail and deft use of plush language invite you to read aloud as she conjures worlds and refines relationships from the rich ore of heritage.

Rabbi Shai Cherry, Ph.D.
Congregation Adath Jeshurun
Elkins Park, PA
Author of *The Torah Through Time*; *Introduction to Judaism: the Great Courses*; *Coherent Judaism: Constructive Theology and Halakhah*

At a historical moment when racial, ethnic, and women's movements exploded the myth of American cultural homogeneity, Kathleen Balgley set out on a quest affirm what her father had suppressed. Like Art Spiegelman, author of the graphic novel *Maus,* she was motivated by an avid interest in family history and indignation at being denied knowledge about her connection to European Jews, most of whom had been exterminated in World War II. But while many American writers pursued family roots in Eastern Europe, none have done so with such determination and for as long as Kathleen Balgley.

Dominika Ferens, Ph.D.
Professor Wrocław University, Wrocław, Poland
Author of *Edith and Winnifred Eaton: Chinatown Missions and Japanese Romances*; and *Ways of Knowing Small Places: Intersections of English Philology and Ethnography since the 1960s*

A gripping personal narrative, the author of *Letters to My Father* construes her role as the traditional "candle child" of the family, one who takes responsibility for preserving stories and heritage for the benefit of past and future relatives. Along with accounts of meeting sought-out family members, the book includes a rich collection of documents and photographs accumulated with a professional scholar's ingenuity and persistence. On a larger scale her historical research bears witness to the annihilation of European Jewish communities leading to the foundation of the state of Israel. On this level, the purpose of her quest "to rescue hope" is realized in her travels in Israel, where she finds relatives eager to host her and experiences the despair and renewal prompted by passing through Jerusalem's Yad Vashem Holocaust Memorial museum.

Steven Marx, Ph.D.
Professor Emeritus of English and Environmental Studies, Cal Poly University, San Luis Obispo
Author of *Youth Against Age: Generational Strife in Renaissance Poetry*; *Shakespeare and the Bible*; and *Cal Poly Land: A Field Guide*

Kathleen Balgley's *Letters to My Father* is an account of the author's rediscovery and reclamation of part of her identity: her father's, and hence also her own, suppressed Jewish self. Like Ezriel, the protagonist of Isaac Bashevis Singer's *The Estate*, Balgley's father turned away from his Jewish heritage (following his immigration to America from Poland). In *The Estate*, Ezriel rediscovers his Jewishness following a visit to the eastern edges of pre-World War II Poland; in *Letters,* Balgley rediscovers and reclaims her father's, and her own, identity on the eastern edges of today's Europe during a journey that takes her across time, continents, and political systems.

Part autobiography, part narrative, part memoir, part travelogue, part reportage, and part research report (replete with photographic and documentary evidence), the account is a personal archaeology—an excavation and examination of an "inherited sense of a larger, metaphoric displacement." Lifting the veil of her father's secrecy about his past leads Balgley behind the veil of the Iron Curtain, as well as behind the multiple silences that surround this still troubled and contentious aspect of recent Eastern European history.

Cezar M. Ornatowski, Ph.D.
Professor, Department of Rhetoric and Writing Studies
San Diego State University

A profound and deeply moving quest to find her father's hidden Jewish history.

Ruth Behar, Ph.D.
Professor, Department of Anthropology, University of Michigan
Author of *An Island Called Home: Returning to Jewish Cuba*; *The Vulnerable Observer: Anthropology That Breaks Your Heart; Letters from Cuba*

The text springs from a conflicting double bind regarding the author's father's repudiated inner life: In a double bind commensurate with Greek tragedy, she finds out that she should leave him and his inner world alone, though doing so would be tantamount to depriving herself of her own history, and of that gnawing desire to meet an unknown part of herself encrypted in her father'story. Isn't "truth" or the hallowed "know-thyself" a fundamental imperative, as demanding as the respect owed to others' privacy and intimate secret?

In leaving Poland in 1920 at the age of 8, Kathleen's father was ridding himself of "Middle Europe's" centuries of turmoil, ridding himself of his Jewish identity, and ridding himself of Polish-Jewish history and barbaric pogroms. Not the trope of the "self-hating Jew," he no longer wanted to address that part of his past identities. His Jewishness was enmeshed in the bleak history of that "Middle Europe" which he was fortunate to have left behind, to start a new life, to be given the American second chance, ahead of the horrors of the Nazi years, WW2, and the Shoah. Thus one might talk about his profound omission or "suppression," or even about a repudiation of his Jewishness, albeit not of "repression" since he never forgot that he was Jewish. He opted to no longer talk about it.

With a daughter's inchoative curiosity, Kathleen implodes the domestic drama, morphs into detective mode, then veers into a Moebius interweave with the geopolitical.

Frustrated by the ubiquitous débris, she is slowly determined in her deconstruction of the family's accepted silence and narrative, and slowly pieces together the mosaics of her vast extended family diaspora, photo-by-photo, document-by-document, letter-by-letter, relative-by-relative, tombstone-by-tombstone, country-by-country. She keeps finding still another missing piece, another lost or dead family member, whose presence in her puzzle never quite completes her interminable quest for a truth which seems to always elude her. As a Fulbright postdoc, she dared stay for two years in the land from which her father escaped, and returned for further research several years later. In late Œdipal confrontation with her internal paternal figure, as well as in symbolic appropriation and therapeutic reframing of the contextualization with which she had grown up, she sludges through the cobblestones, the cold, the snow, the buses and trains of today's middle Europe. Now she focusses upon the massive migrations of European refugees and the seismic turbulences of the history of Jews, along with the geopolitics of the 20th and 21st centuries. Over centuries, her father's native Brest-Litovsk kept shifting national appartenance as the maps of Belarus, Poland, Lithuania, Ukraine, have been dizzyingly reconfigured multiple times.

The deeper her search and research into her father's chiaroscuro of rejected origins and history, the more moved the author feels by the Jewish part of herself which had been occulted throughout her childhood and adolescence. In that process, she appropriates and repairs the broken parts of her father's mindset. This leads her to two spectacular epiphanies amongst the many epiphanies scattered throughout the text. One of them is a visit to Yad Vashem in Jerusalem where she is overwhelmed by the horror of the Shoah, its shattering unthinkability, while feeling awed by the stark dedication in Yad Vashem to the name of the dead (some of her father's relatives are included into those millions) therein exposed and consigned to a forever memory.

The other epiphany I'd like to undescore is that of her thought out decision to "convert." She disrobes and walks into the purifying waters, as prescribed by the Jewish *Mikveh* ritual. Separated by a screen from her father and husband who attend the ceremony from behind that screen, she is now fully inheriting the jewishness her father had denied. There's something mystical in this conversion, —as there would be in an alchemical conversion into gold. As she espouses her father's past perceived and well-defended vulnerability, she transforms it into a source of strength for herself and for him in mirrored reverberation. In so doing, she configures a sort of mystical union with her father whom she has reconciled with his past, with himself, and with herself. Crossing then willingly the threshold of Jewish identity under her father's gazing mind, she dissolved her own initial double bind. By "writing" it, she now dissolves it a second time.

Alain J.-J. Cohen, Professor of Comparative Literature & Film Studies, UC San Diego & Psychoanalyst, Member of SDPC, APsaA and IPA

For Jennifer
With warm wishes
Kathy

Letters to My Father

Excavating a Jewish Identity in Poland and Belarus

A Memoir

KATHLEEN A. BALGLEY

Preface by Dominika Ferens

Bashert Press

Bashert Press
Box 406
4653 Carmel Mountain Road, Suite 308
San Diego, CA 92130

Grateful acknowledgement for permissions:

Adam Gopnik, *Through the Children's Gate: A Home in New York*. Vintage Books, A Division of Random House, Inc., New York, 2007, permission granted by Random House.

Patricia Hampl, *A Romantic Education*, W. W. Norton and Company, 1999, permission granted by Patricia Hampl, 12.2021.

Adrienne Rich, "Split at the Root", *Bread, Blood, and Poetry: Selected Prose 1979-1985*, W.W. Norton, 1986, permission granted by W.W. Norton and Company.

Adrienne Rich, *Diving into the Wreck: Poems 1971-1972*, W. W. Norton, 1973, permission granted by W. W. Norton and Company.

Doreen Carvajal, "In Andalusia, in Search of Inherited Memories, New York Times, August 21, 2012., permission granted by Doreen Carvajal, 2.2022.

Rebecca Goldstein, *Betraying Spinoza: The Renegade Jew Who Gave Us Modernity,* Schocken Books, 2006, permission granted by Nextbook Schocken.

Text design by Mike Gates
Cover design by Gelila Yoseph

Cover illustration: Image *Allégorique*, oil on canvas by Jacob Balgley, 1917. Courtesy Balgley Family Archive

Printed in the United States of America

For John and Emily
and all the Balgley Family living or dead,
known or unknown

We can write about *the* world only by writing about *a* world, and that world the one we think, at least, we really know. Journalism is made from the outside in; but writing is made from the inside out ....The metaphors of experience each writer finds in his own backyard, or air shaft, or palace gardens, have, of necessity, different colors—some are gold and some are green and some merely gray—but in the end, the shapes we know are all the same: the arc of desire and disappointment, the rising half circle of hope, the crescent of aging, the scribble of the city or the oval of the park, or just the long, falling tunnel of life. Each of these shapes is to be found in any life lucky enough to have any shape at all.

ADAM GOPNIK, *Through the Children's Gate: A Home in New York*

Looking repeatedly into the past, you do not necessarily become fascinated with your own life, but rather with the phenomenon of memory. The act of remembering becomes less autobiographical; it begins to feel tentative, aloof. It becomes blessedly impersonal. The self-absorption that seems to be the impetus and embarrassment of autobiography turns into (or perhaps always was) a hunger for the world. Actually, it begins as a hunger for *a* world, one gone or lost, effaced by time or a more sudden brutality. But in the act of remembering, the personal environment expands, resonates beyond itself, beyond its "subject," into the endless and tragic recollection that is history.

PATRICIA HAMPL, *A Romantic Education*

I came to explore the wreck.
The words are purposes.
The words are maps.
I came to see the damage that was done
And the treasures that prevail.

ADRIENNE RICH, *Diving Into the Wreck*

Contents

Preface

Letters to My Father doubles as a quest and a family saga in the form of a memoir. While the quest is a linear narrative, the family saga mostly unfolds in reverse, as Kathleen Balgley follows trails of archival documents back to the nineteenth and early twentieth century. This astounding finely-crafted narrative sprung out of a young American literature scholar's puzzlement with and resistance to her immigrant father's denial of his Jewish roots. But while conceived by a young woman, it is the cumulative effect of her lifelong work of piecing together the history of one extended family scattered across three continents.

In 1988, at a historical moment when the racial, ethnic, and women's movements exploded the myth of American cultural homogeneity, Kathleen Balgley set out on a quest to affirm what her father had suppressed. Not unlike Art Spiegelman, author of the graphic novel *Maus*, she was driven as much by an avid interest in family history as by indignation at being denied knowledge about her connection to European Jews, most of whom had been exterminated in World War II. Many Jewish American writers have pursued their roots in Eastern Europe, but none, I think, have done this with such determination and for as long as Kathleen Balgley.

Interest and indignation guided Kathleen Balgley's career choices. Having earned a Ph.D. in Literature from the University of California, San Diego, instead of immediately seeking a tenure-track job, she applied for a Fulbright Fellowship to teach in communist Poland, and then requested an extra year to better understand the country of her father's birth. Interest and indignation still burned with great intensity twenty years after she returned to California. It drew her back to Eastern Europe at great personal cost, to dig through Belarusian archives, wrest genealogical knowledge from haughty historians, tramp across snow-covered fields, and wade knee-deep in leaves in search of distant relatives' gravestones in Poland. To write the family saga she had to overcome language and alphabet barriers (Polish, Belarusian, Russian, Cyrillic, Hebrew), mountains of human indifference, as well as sheer physical limitations. A recurrent motif in the text is lugging suitcases full of books and photocopies (also in times when suitcases did not have wheels) up and down stairs. Where others would have thrown up their arms and gone home, she sought out allies among strangers: taxi drivers, amateur guides and interpreters, strangers on trains, professional genealogists – kindred spirits.

Not everyone has the means and strength to go on such an arduous quest. By researching and recording the history of the Balgleys for her father, siblings, daughter, and relatives scattered on three continents, Kathleen Balgley has, in a way, quested on behalf of all those people who need to understand why their parents and grandparents concealed their Jewishness or some other stigmatized identity, or else discounted its importance. I am one of those people, a Polish student of Kathleen Balgley's, who did not know she was half-Jewish. Had Kathleen Balgley not insisted that her students reflect on the Holocaust and read Adrienne Rich's "Split at the Root," I, who grew up in communist Poland, in a "don't ask, don't tell" regime, would never have questioned my father and he never would have volunteered the information that his Jewish ancestors had converted to Catholicism and passed for ethnic Poles at least since the 1930s.

Today there are enough academic publications on Polish-Jewish history to fill a library; Polish children go on school trips to the grand Polin Museum of the History of Polish Jews in Warsaw; mainstream newspapers regularly revisit the history of antisemitism and address ethnic Poles' indifference to the plight of Jews as well as the active engagement of some in the Holocaust. But in 1988, when Kathleen Balgley first came to Poland, Polish-Jewish history did not exist as an academic field, while those who had first-hand knowledge of the Holocaust and postwar pogroms (as both victims and perpetrators) were silenced. Consequently, while questing for knowledge Kathleen Balgley found herself prodding Poles out of their ignorance and complacency. As her memoir poignantly demonstrates, prodding strangers, friends, fellow-teachers, and students to think about the role Polish antisemitism played in the absence of Jews in Poland caused her much discomfort. She performed this emotional labor because, as she would later write, "at every turn, I was struck by how the hiddenness of Polish complicity and responsibility echoed the hiddenness of my father's and my Jewish identity."

Many episodes in the memoir depict encounters with Poles and Belarusians who are unhelpful, patronizing, rude, unfeeling, or downright hostile, yet Kathleen Balgley did not allow these characters to congeal into stereotypes because she interpreted their behavior with reference to historical, social, and economic contexts. "Always looking to understand, I saw each day in Poland as part of a journey I had chosen. The stakes were high. The time was limited. I had to attend to every detail so I could learn as quickly as possible, take everything in, try to fit my understanding to what I had learned. The intensity was exhausting, but it held meaning at every turn. Nothing was dispensable. Everything was to be heeded." While single-mindedly pursuing family history, she attended to the material circumstances of the everyday lives of Poles and

Belarusians. She asked endless questions and reflected deeply – though not uncritically – on the answers.

Conversely, on returning to the US, she became more aware of the history of American antisemitism: the enrolment quotas which prevented her father, Ely Balgley, from studying medicine at Harvard, the way her Catholic Irish-German mother supported his decision about hiding his Jewishness with "Shhh," afraid with him that it would jeopardize his corporate chemical career, and the nonchalance of US government officials who took 17 years to issue Ely Balgley a Certificate of Citizenship, which he should have received automatically, as a son of a naturalized citizen. No less matter-of-factly, Kathleen Balgley exposes the anti-Polish prejudice of American Jews, who winced during her lectures on her Polish experience, and called her out: "So what are you then? Catholic or Jewish? What's your point?"

The point – articulated more than once in the memoir – is that sometimes people like herself, positioned between conflicted ethnic groups or classes, take on the role of mediators. And particularly "in families affected by cataclysm and traumas, families which dispersed and never looked back on the disaster, there are those who do look back, who care deeply, and who feel compelled to go back to find whatever shards remain of family history." Such people inherit "a sense of a larger, metaphoric displacement" which pushes them to seek ways of restoring wholeness, if only in symbolic ways. A key discovery Kathleen Balgley made while writing *Letters to My Father* is that moving on and never looking back is as legitimate a survival strategy as is claiming one's heritage and preserving the memory of beloved people and places. This discovery tempered her initial indignation at her father's passing for white in an era when Jews were seen as racial others, and at the fact that he continued to do so long after the need to pass had ceased.

Letters to My Father is, first and foremost, an important contribution to Jewish self-writing, one that allows us to eavesdrop on an intimate conversation between the living and the dead. But it should also be recognized as part of a number of other literary traditions. One is the prominent strand of American autobiography and autobiographical fiction that thematizes the emotional impact of concealed family histories. As such, it should be read alongside Maxine Hong Kingston's *The Woman Warrior*, Joy Kogawa's *Obasan*, Cynthia Kadohata's *The Floating World*, and Sigrid Nunez's *A Feather on the Breath of God*, to name but a few. No less importantly, it is a story about one man's ethnic passing to build a corporate career and provide for his family. African American passing narratives, such as the semi-fictional *Autobiography of an Ex-Colored Man* by James Weldon Johnson or the more recent *Caucasia* by

Danzy Senna, are more familiar, but there are equally poignant stories about men and women of other races.

Letters to My Father is an exemplary text for anyone interested in reconstructing family history, for it shows not only a complex approach to doing such work through interviews, correspondence, ethnography, and archival research, but also the wealth of historical knowledge that can be found and sophisticated ways of interpreting it. Lucky coincidences happen throughout this memoir: an exhibition of art by a Jacob Balgley is held just before Kathleen Balgley's visit to Belarus, the Balgley family name pops up on plaques in unexpected places, a relative supplies a missing piece of the puzzle, rumors questioning Barack Obama's citizenship provoke the author's father, Ely Balgley, to finally reveal the file documenting his struggle for citizenship. None of those coincidences would have happened, however, without Kathleen Balgley's lifelong commitment "to find whatever shards remain of family history."

Finally, as a Polish reader I particularly value *Letters to My Father* as an account of an American's two-years in late-communist Poland, a period that feels like distant history now that the economic and cultural distance between Poland and the West has shrunk. Like Thomas Swick's *Unquiet Days: At Home in Poland*, it covers a time of food shortages and ration cards, of almost unlimited state power and "internal emigration" (the retreat into private life) as a form of resistance, of travel restrictions for Poles and single-entry visas for foreigners, and does so from the perspective of a woman who claims, "I stood apart. I was an interested observer," yet goes out of her way to make friends with Poles from all walks of life and social classes, and listens to what they have to say.

Dominika Ferens
Professor, Wrocław University
Wrocław, Poland

Introduction

My father died on October 4, 2014. He was 102 years old. My three siblings, Michael, Janie and Lisa, were at his bedside. I was not. I was in Europe. Somehow over time my father and I had exchanged places; I was regularly in the Old World from which he had come, he in the New. I realized it was a risk to be out of the country given his age, but so much of my life had been influenced by my father that I told myself I should go ahead with my plan to be in Europe anyway. Still. It was strange I shouldn't be there, the daughter who had spent so much of her life seeking out his story so that her own could also be told.

And his story, veiled as it was, revealed a life began as a Jew in Poland in 1912, a shtetl existence of extreme poverty, hunger and the absence of a father. The arduous journey he, his mother, and three siblings made to the US was in 1920; he mercifully escaped the Shoah, though many of his family did not.

Not long after his arrival, he made a decision to turn his back on his Jewish identity. Later, he sought even to bury the place of his birth, responding with, "New York," when asked. Some argue it's understandable, an American story of assimiliation, a reasonable choice given the danger he had experienced and from which he wanted to protect himself and his family. But the abandonment of his true story, the erasure of his history, exacted a price, and that price became the heart of my conflict with my father.

From as early as childhood, I was compelled to recoup that history. That drive felt fueled by forces unbidden, forces I could not even explain. I call it *"bashert,"* the Yiddish term variously translated, often as one's destined soulmate, I invoke as "destiny."

Even as a child, I was following in his footsteps with my enchantment with music. Even then, I was drawn to "otherness" in people, "everyday exoticisms" in my local neighborhood, before I knew such was in him, and in me. His silences were a mystery, and troubling to me. His sudden emotions about certain events, like the murder of the Israeli athletes in Munich, when he told my mother in my presence, "If the world is like this, I don't want to live in it!" And her horrified look, that told me this was not the first time she had heard reactions like this from him. I felt his tottering—on the one side, taking joy in his music and his science, yet on the other, not too far from giving up on the world. His dark view would flicker in and out of his enthusiasm for Chopin, Shakespeare, Einstein.

I had gone to Poland to learn hard truths, but maybe especially because of his ambivalence towards life, also to rescue hope. He had not approved initially of my going, yet he was ultimately game, coming to visit me in Poland with my mother. His trip surprised him; I surprised him: I shook him at points out of his denial and pessimism, but it needs saying I also inherited those traits. The closest he and I touched on this shared ambivalence was when he smiled with understanding as I told him I had heard a saying, "There is nothing so whole as a broken Jewish heart."

The "candle child" phenomenon, the idea that one child in a family is designated and unbidden becomes the receptacle for history lost, the source of light for forgotten or repressed memory, fit my role in the family, the one member moved by forces uninvited to retrieve what had been lost. A role even hardwired.

Such retrieval requires a search, a dredging up, from the well of requisite forgetting often attended by shame. I intuited my father's shame, his disdain for his past. Given the pathos of his (and my) family story and the stories of Jews worldwide, this seemed a crime to me.

It was the drive to rescue what my father had left behind that sent me to Poland on a Fulbright for two years just before the fall of the Iron Curtain, and then later to his birthplace now in Belarus, to search the stories and fates of the Balgley family in archives there. Later I found my relatives living in Israel and Germany, and some in the United states whom I had not known existed. I wanted to bring back the story to my father and to my siblings, to share a history of which we should be proud, a story at once powerful and fragile.

Maybe my father and I had our closure before he died. It was a St. Patrick's Day. We were in California at a place called "The Abbey Pub" where we each had a beer, he by now in a wheelchair, me by his side. He pondered silently for a moment, and then remarked on the strange miracle that his long-discarded Jewishness should come back to him in the form of his second daughter. When he said, "You are a lot braver than I ever was," an entirely new door opened for me.

I

Early Places 🌳 Noticing and Remembering

Everyday Exoticisms
Dearborn, Michigan, 1958

Our "hi fi" or Victrola, as we called it, was in the dining room, a beige box on a black stand with a built-in, front-facing speaker. It is 1958 and I am 6. Although I was a verbal kid, often expounding at length on various subjects monopolizing conversation at the dinner table to the exasperation of my parents, I now understand that music was my first language, a fluency and love inherited from my father. I spent hours sitting in a chair next to the machine sifting through records, reading and rereading album covers, playing records by taking care to see that the needle was in place so not to scratch the vinyl. My parents had given me a set of Leonard Bernstein LPs for children. These were designed to educate about various instruments in the orchestra, and I especially remember Bernstein's voice describing the "licorice stick" in such a playful and inviting fashion that it seemed possible I could pick up a clarinet and make it sing. I loved to look especially at the covers of my father's record collection. I understood that I was not allowed to play these records on my own—these were family treasures and not to be taken lightly. The thickness of Wanda Landowska's *The Well-Tempered Clavier* fascinated me particularly: the spine was black and silver and the cover showed Landowska in black and white at the piano with an expression on her face that at the time I could only associate with the faces of people praying in church.

However, my fascination with the exotic really began with my child's copy of Alexander Borodin's *Dances of the Polovetski Maidens* from his opera, *Prince Igor*. The 45 was a transparent red, and before, after and at intervals listening over and over again to the music, I would take the record from the old-style turntable, hold the disk up to the light, and peering through the transparent red of this most prized 45 record, I felt the dining room transformed and imagined what I was seeing was the world from which the music came.

This red world was also an escape from the hues of everyday life, particularly the solemnity of the atmosphere of that quiet house. Maybe it was because my siblings and I were separated by enough years to make our worlds quite apart from one another's—my sister was a teenager by then and my brother was off to college—that the house felt very still and quiet much of the time. My mother was always busy with household tasks, and I had a good deal of time by myself. This is not to give the impression that the house was

joyless or that I was ignored by my mother; indeed, the sounds of her working in a nearby room were soothing and reassuring: I felt that we were both at our separate but parallel tasks.

Occasionally I would link the two worlds, the red exotic one with the neutral tasteful tones of our house, by asking my parents to be seated in the living room as an audience while I put on the red record. Garbed in anything I could find that made me look what I imagined a Polovetskie maiden should look like—I remember silk scarves and one time adding absurd angles to my eyebrows with a retractable white and gold fleur-de-lis makeup pencil I found on my mother's dresser—dancing across the dining room and adjoining living room, leaping and turning with great seriousness to transmit to my parents the significance of this other, red world. From my earliest memory, there was always an automatic attraction, a pull to the "other," to a world different than my own, to the exotic. I couldn't know at the time, but the instinctive draw in me towards the "exotic," this "other," would lead me to find a personal identity I could not have predicted.

The neighborhood was a third world, of another color, one separate from the neutral tones in the house and the red of my imaginings. Both the fields and outdoor spaces in which we children played, but also the interiors of the houses of my friends. Our house was on a cul-de-sac, at the south-east intersection of Cherry Hill and Robindale Court. The house number was "1," that is to say "One," and the neighborhood was full of girls my age, in particular the dark-eyed' D'Angelos, the Italian family of five daughters, one of whom, Maria, became my best friend. The family spoke Italian in the home, and on weekends male relatives in hunting attire and muddy boots tromped into the house and dropped piles of dead pheasants on the modern kitchen floor. The mother, Mary, of the pale-complexioned Italian type with hair so dark it was blue-black, I never saw without an apron, her body in constant motion, her voice a constant patter in Italian (she did not know English), would pick up a bird by the neck, and placing each one by one in her deep double sinks, efficiently defeather the entire pile in under an hour. Mary's kitchen was enormous, with two ovens, a freezer, and two refrigerators. On the counter stood Mr. D'Angelo's juice machine, the daughters' nemesis, because every night before bedtime each of the five girls had to drink a glass of carrot juice brimming with bitter carrot scum. When I was there I was given a large glass and expected to drink it down too. The other evening ritual consisted of the two youngest girls who were my age—5 and 6—running around the house in only their underpants. This was thought to be healthy, and like the carrot juice, it probably was.

Mr. D'Angelo owned grocery stores, and thinking about the family's habits now, I realize he was an early health food and exercise advocate. But then, those rituals were simply strange, hence mysterious, and thus for me allured by the "exotic" to begin with, magical and enchanting. I was under the spell of this enchantment, this everyday exoticism whenever I was in the D'Angelo home. The house was always filled with enticing smells from the kitchen. I remember seeing Mrs. D'Angelo's cookies laid out to cool one day— filigreed slices of powdered sugar and air—and thought they were somehow connected with the lace tablecloths and doilies throughout the house. The living room was dark, movie-theatre dark when the thick velvet drapes were pulled. We girls pretended we were going to the movies. Borrowing the older sisters' pocketbooks, we filled them with a pink crayon (for lipstick), and fresh, raw almonds (plentiful in the Italian home where buttered popcorn was not), and settled in to "watch the movie"—whatever was on television. One time, in the darkness reaching into my purse for my "popcorn," I instead found the pink crayon, and mistaking it for an almond, took a large bite, chewed and swallowed, and then let out a cry of surprise and revulsion. Poor Mrs. D'Angelo ran to me not knowing what had happened nor understanding what

I was saying, got me to the bathroom where I made a scene of throwing up pink—which Mrs. D'Angelo first thought was blood—until her daughters, exclaiming in Italian and digging into their own purses to show their "lipstick," allowed their mother to at last comprehend that I was not going to die.

The odd ways of this foreign country were challenging enough for Mrs. D'Angelo, but we girls added to her panics. Another time we decided to build a fort with bricks scattered about the vacant lot on the cul-de-sac. The lot belonged to a Mr. Demonoff, a Russian or perhaps Ukrainian immigrant, who entered his property ceremoniously every week, wearing a pith helmet, round wire-rimmed spectacles, and a khaki uniform of shirt and oversized Bermudas, belted at the waist. A corpulent man, Mr. Demonoff came at intervals to walk around in his lot, inspecting the small crop of corn he had there. Wild strawberries grew there and these we ate fresh from the dirt while sitting in ragamuffin groups making plans to disrupt the predictable. We were afraid of him because I think we felt that the wild theatricals and make-believe games we played there beyond our parents' view and judgment, somehow left traces in his field, enough so that he knew we had been up to something so untamed it felt erotic, though none of us could have named it so.

The day we decided to build the fort, we were hunkered down inspecting a worm under a brick we had just lifted, when suddenly a sound we could not identify begin to rise up as if from under the earth. Then we were in the middle of the sound and it engulfed us: we had unknowingly interfered with a beehive, and the swarm we disturbed created a black cloud around us, stinging us over and over again. Without any words among us, we all ran screaming in the separate directions to our houses—me, dancing up the street because bees had gotten inside my sun suit and had already stung one of my eyes, and the D'Angelo girls running to their mother, who could not understand what had occurred, and seeing her girls rolling dementedly on their beds as if possessed by the devil, phoned her husband at his grocery story, wherein he directed her to put them into a bathtub of cold water. It was not until my mother, after stripping off my sun suit in the backyard and releasing the angry bees, ran down to the D'Angelo house and was able to make Mary understand that we had been attacked by bees, that Mrs. D'Angelo believed her girls had not been visited by Satan himself.

One summer Mr. D'Angelo decided the family would go for an extended trip to Italy, to the village of his birth. I was already mourning the girls' absence when Maria told me the family would be driving to Italy. I checked with my parents who explained that this would not be technically possible. But on the morning of their departure, all five girls and their parents were sitting in their long wood-paneled white station wagon, preparing to pull out of their driveway and, as I was told again by Maria, drive to Italy. My parents and I along with some other neighbors were there to see them off, and it turned out that, yes, in fact, Victor D'Angelo had arranged that their station wagon be shipped to a port in Italy where he, along with his six females, would retrieve it. Mr. D'Angelo explained that morning that he felt he should have his own automobile in Italy, the better to get around his home village and its environs. My parents smiled at this because of course Victor could have arranged to rent a car there. It was a mystery to me then how a car could drive across an ocean—would the station wagon sprout wings or a rudder and sail? But today I think that perhaps Mr. D'Angelo wanted his American car in his birthplace in order to demonstrate his success in America to the locals. It was hard to say. Mr. D'Angelo was a man of distinct opinions—who knew why he had made this extravagant choice? Whatever the answer, I was sure he knew what he was doing, and my best friend was safe in his hands.

At the middle point of the cul-de-sac, the furthest from the main street, sat the Gronkowski house, just two houses away from the D'Angelo's, but it could have been another country. Two girls close to my age lived there, the Gronkowski sisters of cornflower blue eyes and straw-colored hair—the photo negative of the D'Angelo girls. What set these girls apart from the rest of us was that they had no mother. We never knew if she had died or what had happened, but they had only their father, who seemed to us much older than our own parents. When he appeared, which was seldom, he looked sad and weary. I never saw him without a cigarette in his hand, a faraway look on his face, dark circles under his eyes. He worked and thus was away all day, and although there seemed to be an old aunt in the house during the daytime as a sort of babysitter to the girls, we never saw her. The D'Angelo house was home base and —we could run in and out of there without being questioned. But the Gronkowski house always seemed locked up, locked away even from the two girls who lived there, so that when we did venture in from time to time, it was as if the girls were breaking into their own house. The place was dark and cold, I remember, and as we tried to creep silently across the floor, I once caught a glimpse of the old aunt, if she were indeed a relative at all, sitting in the dark living room during a sunny day. She was entirely motionless, seemingly lifeless, a frozen mannequin in a white wig wearing clothes from another century—a sort of Bates Motel tableau. Scary as it was, this household, too, was exotic, just in a different way than the D'Angelos.

I had scraped my leg badly on the D'Angelo's teeter totter one day, and the oldest Gronkowski girl, Peggy, insisted she knew the medicine I should have. We entered the Gronkowski house from a door in the garage and crept in. Reaching the bathroom with fingers pressed to her mouth to remind us to keep silent, Peggy produced a jar from the medicine cabinet. She was whispering that the old aunt had been a nurse and thus Peggy knew about such remedies. Indicating I should sit on the toilet seat, Peggy slathered a large glop of the stuff on my open scrape. I let out a whimper, but Peggy, always the commander of our pack, shoved her hand over my mouth to keep the aunt at bay. We got out of there fast. I forget the exit, but I had a moment to glimpse the medicine jar. It read: HEET. Later I had to concoct a story for my mother which explained the ripening red welt on my leg.

There were, though, two principal attractions of the Gronkowski lot. The first was a life-sized cement deer that sat in the middle of the front yard. The equivalent of a lawn jockey, the deer had antlers and a surprised look on its face and was painted to look actual. We loved it, and took turns sitting on it and riding. The second feature of the lot was that its location at the apex of the cul-de-sac made it the only house on our street that backed up to empty land—meadows with flowers, a creek, and a big willow tree which hung out over the water. We were not exactly prohibited from going there, but our parents from time to time would remind us not to "go too far." Under Peggy's command, though, we did go too far. She devised games and contests for the rest of us who were younger than she, the most memorable of which was seeing who could shit first in the open field. The D'Angelo girls and I sensed this was not right, but Peggy cleverly explained that whoever won would get the prize of her black cowgirl hat with red trim. She wore it all the time, and I thought it spectacular—especially the way she wore it with the red and black strings hanging loosely down her neck. I tried to win but failed. As I recall, no one accomplished the feat, though we all tried at Peggy's bidding, dropping our shorts and our underpants in the bright sun with everyone circled around and watching, especially Peggy who leaned over to have better look at our progress, and telling us, "Almost, almost."

We, all the D'Angelo girls and the Polish Gronkowski girls, went to the local Divine Child Catholic church, and one time when I saw Peggy come out of the confessional, I wondered if she had told this story as a sin. I had not had the courage to confess my part in it.

There was one other girl on the cul-de-sac who sometimes played outside with us; her parents were of German descent, I recall, strict, so that Sharon was too proper for our games. When we practiced tying each other to trees and running away, Sharon would not consent to play, and went back inside her house. Even Peggy shied away from her more outlandish proposals when Sharon was around. There was a childless older couple, possibly of Scandinavian background, who lived across the street from my family's house. Both were white-haired, tidy and fit, always in tennis whites, their matching neat coiffures matching their neat lawn. That house and its inhabitants were of no interest in the least to my band of girls. I was always running, either sweating in the sun or slightly chilled at dusk, but never slowing up until I was forced to come inside and eat and finally to bathe. Sound, motion, activity, movement—freedom.

When my baby sister was born with a congenital birth defect that threatened her life, this blur of activity and motion halted. Though some attempts were made to describe the situation to me, I only remember my sister who was seven years older than me, sobbing the nights my mother was in the hospital, hearing my father's voice speaking quietly and gently to her after I had gone to bed, trying to comfort her, and the vast stillness of the house with my mother gone. I could not imagine the baby or its problem, but I felt that my mother was in danger and would never return to our home or to me. The house was enveloped in silence and even though I still ventured outside, sound and motion had disappeared from the air. The pace palpably slowed. Quiet long hours. No movement. Quiet. I realize now it was as a funeral would be, or a long, extended wake of the solemn type. I cannot say if my parents were funereal about the situation—it is possible that when my mother and little sister returned from the hospital, the house quieted because a baby was sleeping. Though I felt it had to be more than that. The day the older D'Angelo sisters came over to see the baby for the first time, bringing with them delicate lace baby bibs from Italy, they paraded silently in single file into my parents' bedroom where the baby slept, and peered in to the crib as if into a casket. They had become mourners to my child's eyes. I could not know then that in time to come this little baby would become the treasure of our family. But at the time there was a small circular portrait of Pope John XXIII framed in clear transparent plastic resembling a snowflake which hung on the wall over my baby sister's crib, and I remember that this gesture of my mother's made me understand that all would be alright.

Pictured on my baby sister's, Elise's, baptism day. Left to right: My mother Margaret, my sister Janie and my brother Michael (godparents) and myself. Courtesy Balgley Family Archive.

Cranford, New Jersey, 1960

I had worried in Dearborn, Michigan, that my mother would never return to me or to our house there. And in a sense, she never did. My father accepted another job; our three years in Dearborn were over and we were moving east again.

The house on Woods Hole Road in Cranford, New Jersey, was white and wood and spacious just like our old house on the Dearborn cul-de-sac, but the boogey man lived there, and I spent a terrorized year of nights hiding from bedtime, shrinking from the zombie backlit from the hall light nightly at my bedroom door. His menacing form was so real, even today I am able to believe he was actually there. I *saw* him.

My domain had shrunk. At Woods Hole Road there was no crowd, no reliable mob of children at the ready. The quiet that had developed in Dearborn inside the Robindale house traveled with us and laid itself over the inside and outside of the house in Woods Hole Road. Even on sunlit spring days, the neighborhood had about it the stillness of mute houses during a gentle snowfall—the air cushiony, static, deserted. So all my energy moved inside myself, all the Robindale exertion stopped dead, the centrifugal force that had flung me out of doors at Robindale reversed itself sharply to the tight centripetal coil to the center of self. Even when I sought out my old outside domain in the woods that ringed our yard, I walked into the thicket, not running, and alone found a spot deep in the woods, a clearing dappled by sun, and listened to the minute noises of the woods, the only conversation out of doors in that neighborhood.

That time marked my discovery of trees. At Robindale a tree was a utilitarian thing, shade for the pack, hiding spots in games. Trees were props of the social, outdoor life. Here in the slowed time, unpeopled gardens, trees assumed personality, and as such were witness to history, my own and those before me—even ancient, I pondered. I was stunned by this abrupt change in the feeling of existence. I felt it to be mysterious and thought more and more it had to do with movements and transactions residing well beyond my comprehension, transactions begun somewhere and some time before my birth, impersonal forces which had shifted and by accident reshaped my little world. I suppose some might recognize this as the discovery of God or fate or mortality or all three as one trinity. I suppose I had become an ascetic, no more physical battles or wild plans to fight enemy bands of kids as at Robindale. No naughtiness or forbidden imaginings. Reflective and quiet, the wild child had become penitent and still.

This cul-de-sac had only one family on it with girls, and only one of my age, Patty, who organized the kids in school against me for a time, likely because I was the new kid, and over-popular with the boys. I remember four boys on bicycles visiting my house as a group or in pairs to ask me to be their girlfriend, and news of that making a ruckus at school, being noticeable like that. Being popular with boys that early on never brought me any self-regard; if anything, it made me feel strange because I could not understand it. I primarily saw their attention to me as slightly dangerous, though I cannot now say why I thought that, although there did seem to be a relationship between the number of boys' bikes parked in my front yard after a school day and the amount of razzing I got the following day walking home from school, "You think you're a movie star, you walk that way just to swing your hips! You think you're a princess!" I was prepubescent at eight years of age, obviously, all the kids were, but there was some erotic energy in those taunts.

The classroom itself offered no solace. Third grade, Brookside School, my teacher Miss (or was it Mrs.—I got wrong each time I addressed her, and she corrected me with a frown each time) did not particularly like children. My only memory of her classroom was having to leave for hurricane practice, and then not for practice one day when *Donna* thundered through our town, my former Midwestern orientation wondering how a tornado could be so big, you could not see it at all.

During that year of transformed space and time, the dining room table revealed itself as a long, shining life raft in the traumatic turmoil of my soul—not for the regular meals taken there—with a few exceptions, these I do not remember vividly perhaps because my older sister was a high schooler now entrenched in the teenaged world, and my older brother, still away at college back in the Midwest, and my younger sister was still a baby. Rather that table, the raft, or the island, was the place I did my school work at night after dinner, the chandelier above the table bright; it was where I remember writing my first poem (it was "published" in the third grade student section of my elementary school's newspaper), a place where I felt the same quiet as in the woods, but with a new medium—writing—that allowed me to give shape to the new feelings inside me. Also, the dining room I associated entirely with my mother—its pale sea green and powder blue colors were her. Her collection of teacups of the thinnest porcelain were delicate like her skin and made me think of her hands and the fragrant tea she served with them to me on Sunday afternoons, letting me choose each time which tea I preferred and which teacup.

In that dining room resides the first vivid memory I have of feeling the otherness of my father's origins. Sora-Feyge Slomiansky Balgley and Israel (or Srul) Balgley came to Cranford from their apartment in Brooklyn. What separated that day out from others at its start was the nervousness I sensed in my mother—we had guests from time to time, and she was a very good cook and an organized, confident hostess, wife and mother. But that day as I followed her about from kitchen to dining room readying the table, I felt her unease. My paternal grandparents seemed different and strangely out of place in this airy, sunny dining room with the breeze coming through the open windows. I was later to reflect on how without realizing it, I was right about them being out of place when I met them in their own home. But that story comes later. For now, their foreignness did not fit in that bright place. Not only was the dining room the place where special family meals and celebrations were held, but also this was the place that had become that private sanctuary, like the woods, where I was alone with my thoughts and my writing. Most of all it was their accents, particularly my grandmother's, and I was at once drawn in and afraid in this formerly familiar place.

As the meal progressed, I remember that I went to my mother who was seated at her customary place at the opposite end of the dining room table from my father, hesitantly sidling up to whisper in her ear, not wanting to be noticed, but apparently needing to check in with her in some way about these people who were in our private world of our home but whom I did not know. I must have thought my whisper to my mother would go unnoticed because I felt very shy and remember keeping my head lowered. But it was not to be. I whispered to my mother, "Why do they talk that way?" Suddenly the conversation at the table that I had counted on continuing without noticing me, suddenly halted, as my grandmother's head and imposing upper body turned to my mother and me, and smiling, said, "Oh, the little girl has something to tell her mama." I was mortified. I must have known that it was impolite to whisper about people in their presence, but I was worried, I was intrigued, and yes, I must also have been repelled.

Before the dinner, in our family room, I remember that our traditional family hors d'oeuvres had been set out—I only recall that there was pepperoni, always considered an exotic and special treat by me, and as I recollect the scene today, I think how touching my mother's efforts were to make her in-laws welcome, and yet how out of touch she was (and my father, too) to imagine my grandparents would eat such a sausage! I did not know that at the time, of course, but I recall my grandfather's efforts to win me as a playmate and conspirator in mischief. So as my grandmother continued to generally orchestrate the social interactions and conversation with my parents (she never included my grandfather in this, except to suddenly gesture to him, and say, "Ah, he doesn't do anything!" or something amounting to that).

My grandfather pretending that it was a secret between us that no one else could see, surreptitiously placed the coin of pepperoni into my hand, closing my fingers, and putting his finger to his lips. How touching, I now think, how charming, that my grandfather tried to reach out from his foreignness to the new world granddaughter he hardly knew. And what did I do? I left the room, went into the downstairs bathroom, opened my hand, examined the pepperoni for a moment, and then flushed it down the toilet. I thought his hands had somehow contaminated it. But more, I was at once afraid and drawn in. Who are they? What are they to me? It shames me to tell these things now. And what did it mean? It was in its way a typical child's fear, but even then I knew it was more: their strangeness was akin to the exoticism of the D'Angelo's, and I knew without understanding, that in this case, I was part of that. This was my first brush with the exotic that had to do with me, and the suggestion of this was powerful enough to both repel me and draw me in.

The last detail of the afternoon dinner: my mother kept her beautiful china teacups in a china closet in our kitchen. Apparently, the other such "valuables" like my sister's and my china coin banks in the shape of playful cats, were also stored there. Each cat wore a gaily-colored china ribbon around its neck, and on this ribbon a lock was attached connecting the cat's head and torso. We made a big deal out of keeping our coins in these banks, and the banks were locked. The tiny keys that would open the lock and decapitate the cat-bank were stored in two of the teacups in this cupboard. I remember that I liked the cupboard because its glass front made it possible for me to look at what I perceived as family treasure any time I came through the kitchen. My mother served tea that day—my favorite ceremony at the close of more formal meals. That day after my mother cleared the cups from the table, and as my grandmother was continuing to hold the floor in the dining room, in the kitchen my mother, hand on her forehead, turned to me gasping as she looked into my grandmother's empty teacup and saw the tiny silver key lying at its bottom. I was my mother's only confidant in this.

Long Island, 1960

From our house in Cranford, it was not too far to get to my mother's family, all of whom lived on the east coast. And this was important as my mother had been geographically separated from her siblings and her mother when our family moved to the middle of the country, to Dearborn, Michigan. The O'Haras were a close family, and they saw my father as inarguably one of their large Roman Catholic brood. Surprising, really, given their provincial upbringing and the anti-Semitism to which they were likely exposed. I

My maternal grandmother, Mae, with her son, my Uncle Art. Courtesy Balgley Family Archive

credit my mother's mother with her children's lack of bigotry. Grandma Mae had been widowed in her early 30s when her husband died in 1918 in the Spanish flu pandemic, and raised five children on her own in a town called Sparrow Bush, outside of Port Jervis, in New York State where the Pennsylvania and New Jersey borders meet. Her background was German Catholic. I do not know why, but she had not an ounce of prejudice in her, and my mother was consistently progressive in her politics and her deep sense of social justice. Surely, had it been otherwise, she would not have married a Jew in 1940 outside her church. Her whole family came to the ceremony conducted in a chapel adjacent to St. Teresa's Church at Sterling Place in Brooklyn. The main church was being used for a mass because depending on your point of view, either ironically or triumphantly, their wedding day was on Good Friday, the day, of course, that historic anti-Semitism in the Catholic Church pointed to and explained to parishioners when "the Jews crucified our Lord."

My father seemed relaxed around my mother's family, and my parents in the summer would pack us up and make the drive from our home in Cranford to Long Island, where my mother's sister and her family lived. My mother's sister, my Aunt Marion had married into an immigrant Italian family, the Catanzaros. My Uncle Augie from the region in Italy of the same name, came of age like my father in New York, and played the clarinet in the orchestra where my father was the pianist. They were therefore colleagues and friends in music and family, even though their ethnicities were miles apart from one another, and so were their politics. Uncle Augie was a working-class Republican who blamed his difficulty in getting jobs on American prejudice against Italians. As a Jew, my father arguably had more reason to feel ostracized in America, but he had achieved success through his remarkable intellect, diligence, and talent.

From his immigrant beginnings, my father had proven himself a piano prodigy and mastered English in less than a year, winning prizes at his elementary school in Brooklyn. By the time I was born in 1952, he had already been translating dissertations on science and writing abstracts of them for DAI (Dissertation Abstracts International), and he had established himself in executive positions in corporations, so we lived in upper-middle class neighborhoods. Our Cranford was green, blue and white, the Cranford house a New England-style white house. This was the land of large and well-cared front lawns, wooded backyards, sidewalks, where yellow school buses stopped at the corners of tree-lined streets, sprinklers in summer, skating ponds in winter. It was the Garden State, as license plate monikers proclaimed, a bird sanctuary (for which the state is famed), and a sanctuary for many a New Yorker, my parents included. When we headed for Long Island, while it was not the City itself, it was close enough to it, and far enough from Cranford to make me feel this was a slightly dangerous and foreign land.

And in fact the gatherings at my aunt and uncle's house were more truly foreign than I could have then immediately comprehended. Uncle Augie had come to America with his parents, a brother and sister from Italy some years before. Augie's father, always referred to by my parents as "old Mr. Catanzaro" as if he had always been old, had died before I was born. The son, Augie's brother, Moe, had married and moved "away"—a term freely used to describe anywhere from the other side of town to the other side of the world. Both were equally "not here," not with the family, the family always denoting not one's own offspring and mate, but parents and siblings of the "true family." That's at least how it was in the Catanzaro family, and I remember Uncle Augie proclaiming at the dinner table one night that "blood is thicker than water," a gesture towards his mother and sister who lived with my aunt and uncle, and a sort of statement of principle and warning to my aunt. Thus, Augie's mother, Mrs. Catanzaro (my middle-aged parents deferentially only used that formal way of addressing her or speaking of her) lived with my aunt and uncle, and I remember her vividly, sitting at the opposite end of the long dining room table from my Uncle Augie. The matriarch in my aunt's house, Mrs. Catanzaro's position at the table reflected her dominant role in the household, and my Aunt Marion's place at the side of the table, and even that changeable, revealed the precariousness of her status. Somewhere I must have seen a photograph of Mrs. Catanzaro in her youth, for I remember thinking that as an old person she had become the living negative of that snapshot: the black hair gone to snow, the delicate pale of the skin turned to a deep walnut, ridged and lined like that fruit. The generous lobes of her ears were pierced and held tiny silver rings which seemed not so much adornment as an organic part of her person—it was unthinkable that these would ever be removed. She shared the head of the table with Molly, her daughter, Augie's sister, and in the parlance of the day, "spinster" sister, a quiet and gentle person who could have been 35 or 55. The two sat together on what seemed to be a piano bench, though there was no piano in the house, and while this placement might have seemed to bestow on Molly equal rank with her mother, her place there only underscored her dependent role, like a child who sits next to a mother at meals for help. Molly sat there, very small next to her mother. The two spoke Italian to each other quietly, and Augie would (much more loudly) address his comments to them in that tongue. Molly spoke some English, and she spoke it to me, in the same, soft way she spoke her own language, but I never heard Mrs. Catanzaro speak anything but Italian.

My cousins seemed not to notice or be affected by this at all. Two of them had the Mediterranean look of my uncle, his sister and mother, but they were so entirely American in manner and speech that, if anything, they seemed out of place in this setting. The dining room was the center of that house, and the meals were served and consumed with all the ceremony closely approximated by the rituals of my Roman Catholic experience, with Uncle Augie the officiating priest. The other rooms of the house were studies in light and dark in my memory, static and still. When no one was in those rooms, they seemed quieter than quiet, like paintings of rooms and not the rooms themselves. Compared with the capacious dining room, the kitchen was tiny. Though Molly had a job in a glove factory, on her return home she joined Mrs. Catanzaro in the kitchen. Her mother worked most of the day to prepare food for the big evening meal. Cooking was life there, I concluded. My mother, a good cook, and the preparer of all our meals at home, stayed away from that kitchen. My aunt was part of it, but she was often pushed aside. It was Molly's and her mother's domain. Along a shelf just above the sink, there stood a line of jars filled with mushrooms, which looked foreboding to me, embryo-like or mysterious embalments, sharing from one jar to the next only one thing, a silver dollar, which by its change of color would reveal whether or not the mushrooms were poisonous. Snails were regularly cooked in a pot, and one time my aunt in a rare moment in the kitchen, thinking to tease or scare me, I do not know which, lifted the lid with a mischievous glint in her eye, and showed me steaming shells attached to the inside of the pot's lid. She said to me, "Your mother is going to *eat* these." When Mrs. Catanzaro and Molly carried the food out on large platters to the dining room table, they carried them high like gifts, treasure to be admired and consumed, like a chalice before communion.

The summer my parents sent me there on my own, I ate so much no one could believe it. My mother had told them I was a picky eater. At the dinner table I listened to my Uncle Augie's tirades every night on different subjects which he delivered with the same anger. My own father led the talk often at our dinner table, and he too could become emotional about certain topics, but he did not rage in soliloquy like this. My father expected a response. Augie did not. He spoke and everyone had to listen and no one was to speak back. From the beginning of my stay there, I knew dinner time was not to involve a dialogue. I felt my uncle slightly dangerous because of this, but more for the fact that sometimes he would speak to me at length separate from the rest of the crowd at family gatherings. I felt he wanted something from me, maybe desired me in some way that was not right, a sort of surrogate to take him to a better time he had left behind. But in later years reflecting on those moments, I have concluded that what he wanted in talking to me was to plumb the mystery of my father's brilliance, of his success. Maybe talking to me was simply a way to capture Augie's past, the glory of it—to feel the excitement and ardor of his days as a musician. I remember one time his telling me the story of the first time he met my father: "We (by that he meant the band he was playing in) had advertised for a piano player, and here comes this little kid, wearing knickers, for Pete's sakes, and a cap on his head. He said he was there to audition. We looked at each other and said, 'What, this little guy thinks he's ready to play in a band?'"

Then my uncle went on to relay his astonishment at my father's musical virtuosity, his shock that "this little kid" could play above and beyond all the other musicians in the band. This was Augie's story, but in fact as I later learned, the truth was, it was my father who got Augie the job playing clarinet and saxophone in the band, but Augie needed to reverse the power in his telling. I think he admired my father but was also confused by and envious of his genius, and felt himself judged by the superiority he readily granted to my father. This he could not in any way broach with my father, his brother-in-law and friend, but he might unlock the mystery by unburdening himself in telling his friend's daughter of his own incredulity of that friend's accomplishments.

One day I recall visitors coming to the Catanzaro home—all family —I do not believe the Catanzaros cultivated friends like my generation did and does, so those people would have been alien to the home, outsiders to the family. The still rooms came alive then, crowded with relatives on both my uncle's and aunt's sides, spilling onto the backyard, a place my cousins and I thought of as ours, a play place where adults whose business in life was work, would rarely have reason to appear. It was disorienting to see Mrs. Catanzaro outside the house sitting on a lawn chair in the yard. And not only her. My mother's and aunt's side included all of us and several of their brothers—the O'Haras— whose Irish presence changed the Mediterranean dark of the Italian home to a sort of springy daytime vitality. My mother's brother, my Uncle Dick O'Hara, came with his wife, my Aunt Anne, who reminded me not to say "aunt" before her name because, as she explained, the assonance was unpleasant to her ear. Perhaps that had to do with her own sense of the English language and its felicities, she herself having learned it after her native Spanish in Argentina where she had grown up before coming to the United States. Anne brought her mother, a tiny woman we called "Mita," in a black lace mantilla, who smiled and nodded, but understood probably very little of the English we spoke to her. Uncle Augie's nephews, his brother Moe's, kids, were there in identical outfits, white shirts and black trousers, black hair slicked back and shining with pomade for the occasion. My mother's youngest brother Charlie had married a Jewish girl, Aunt Debbie, and they were there with their children, my cousins all. I was all of these, I thought, and these were all part of each other. Mita and Mrs. Catanzaro, the matriarchs, could not have communicated easily, but sat together nonetheless, as if groupings by age surpassed any other segregation like country of origin or language spoken. The yard mingled silver-haired, blue-eyed O'Haras with the dark Italians and South Americans. Someone collected all of us cousins to pose for a photograph and in the photograph I seemed the figure who connected the two opposites—light brunette and green-eyed with an olive skin, I could have been on either side—or on neither.

Still, somehow, I belonged. We ran hard in the yard, stopping only when an adult physically pulled us from the fray to come eat. We were the freest people there—free to run in and out of adult conversations, free to run to a world of our own making in the corners of the yard, beneath trees where we built stories and lives to fit into them. As I ran from the clusters of adults back to the children, I brought with me the stuff for my play; the strand I reeled in behind me as I left the adult company, which I then wove into my imaginary world with my cousins, so that there never was a clean break between the two. In this way I think I learned to make places in my imagination for the real, making real the imaginary.

It was rough play we cousins played—physically rough and attended by a playful meanness that lent a sense of psychological danger to our games. Each of us improvised on a story that took shape among us. Any actor was a director and could change the shape of the story any time. One quick turn of improvised plot could make one of us the pariah in the story or maybe the heroine. You never knew what could happen. And those stories, even after official play had ended, could stretch into our actual lives, giving us roles we could not easily shed.

*A large multicultural gathering of my young cousins
at the Catanzaro home on Long Island.
Courtesy Balgley Family Archive.*

When my parents agreed to leave me at the Catanzaros without them, any remnant of the privacy and decorum of Cranford life vanished. Baths could be communal ones with cousins lined up ready for the cement set tubs in the Catanzaro basement. I never got entirely used to such proceedings, but since no one else seemed to mind, I regarded it as a rite of passage and true proof I belonged among them. But I had to earn this passport over and over for some length of time. It was weeks before my initiation was over and I could take at least a few things for granted. Days had established a contour of their own, and my place in those days and among my cousins shaped up and consolidated itself while I was not paying attention. We were a pack by then, wild, but still wily; we knew what not to let the adults in on. And my cousin closest to my age, the youngest daughter of Marion and Augie, stopped making me the pariah in and out of the plays.

My parents were due to return to pick me up from my stay with the Catanzaros, and though I looked forward to their arrival, I wondered if they would be able to see the semi-feral self I had become by virtue of running with a pack. When they did arrive, the Catanzaro home seemed quieter, less chaotic, but I realize now that had to do with the turning of my attention away from the pack and toward my parents, toward the familiarity of my ways and routines with them. My cousin Barbara must have seen this and resented it--her power over me had been diluted when I cared to please anyone but her, especially my parents.

Brooklyn, 1960

An uncharacteristic bath in the middle of the afternoon, and upstairs in the Catanzaro house, not in the usual basement set tub. A scratchy, fancy nylon ensemble—what we children derisively called a "dressy dress." These marked something unexpected one day after my parents arrived. My cousin looked up at me descending the stairs from the bathroom, and said in her best snotty voice, "Where do you think *you're* going?" I did not know, that was the thing. I only knew that I was to be clean and dressed up as on a holiday. From the familiar set tubs and dining room of the Catanzaro house that had now become like a second home to me, I only was told I was going to a place called Brooklyn.

The trip from my mother's family on Long Island to Brooklyn, the home of my father's parents, might as well have been from one planet to another—along the Belt Parkway, past the ships in Lower New York Harbor, past Fort Hamilton, glimpsing the bridge connecting Brooklyn to Staten Island, and Manhattan's lower skyline which boasted the famous aquarium in the Battery. Away from Catanzaros and O'Haras, away from rooms of Catholic icons, Celtic crosses and miniature shrines of serene Italian white china madonnas—to a place entirely new and mysterious for me.

You park in a crowded urban street, but one lined with remarkably large trees. You walk to the porch of the old Brooklyn brownstone apartment building. You do not walk in yet, but wait for the heavy door to seemingly unlock itself, and find my dark, mustachioed grandfather, the "super" of the building and, I later learned, its owner. Just behind him—but not for long—my grandmother followed, an imposing presence who clearly ruled the roost. Appearing much larger than my grandfather, she greeted us. With the sound of her voice, I had a memory of their visit to our Cranford home and I blanched at the memory of what I had done with the pepperoni that day. I was also transfixed. She turned to my grandfather and in quick Yiddish directed him to open the door of their bottom-floor apartment (we were in the building's hall), and as we entered, there before me was the heavy wooden furniture, in a darkened room, ostensibly to keep cool from the bright afternoon. As my eyes adjusted, objects coming into focus—a burnished samovar, an old silvered menorah, small rooms, large furniture (they had lost another bigger home in the Depression and these must have been remnants from its day), a profusion of newspapers, a table already set with steaming food, and the directive, "come, eat," delivered not once, but punctuating many times the duration of our stay, long after I thought mealtime had finished. Then my grandmother led the way to another room where sunlight fought through nearly closed louvered doors. The shuttered door opened, the heat hitting us first, blinded by the sun—then eyes adjusting once again: there it lay—my grandmother's magnificent garden—lush in the middle of a cement enclosure, vegetables and flowers mixed together with no prejudice for one or the other. She grasped my mother's arm, and in that deeply, differently cadenced English observed, "Don't we live on the smell of pepper plants, feel we could eat the daffodil?" Many years later I learned that she and her four children relied for survival almost entirely on the food she grew in a garden in Brest on the Polish-Russian border.

Unlike the visits to my mother's family which were typically protracted, unbounded by the clock, more like time spent at home where one did not have to hurry, since bags were unpacked and toothbrushes were in the medicine cabinet, here there was already in the air the sense of departure, of a set period of time now concluding. Formal, unfamiliar, odd. Like before with the pepperoni, but this time a new unexpected emotion roiled inside me: enchantment. But in place of the pepperoni that had repulsed me, as we prepared to depart, a silver dollar was pressed into my hand by my grandfather. I did not recognize it as money; it instead seemed akin to the golden-wrapped chocolate-covered cherries that sat in a silver bowl on the table in the darkened dining room. Like the D'Angelos and the Catanzaros, my grandparents were exotic, yes, but with the other families, I stood apart. I was an interested observer. But here, now, this was about me. That feeling was new and it overtook me suddenly. In an uncanny way, during that visit, I remembered what I had never seen. I said nothing to my parents about that sensation, but I knew something had happened. I cannot actually explain it today, but it was a mysterious transformation. I was in an unknown place that I somehow knew. Although I knew I could not comprehend it, that experience began the discovery of my own exoticism, my own otherness, and because it was mine, unlike the D'Angelos and the Catanzaros, it hit me with remarkable force.

I could not know then that I was beginning a journey that would take me to the villages of my grandparents' and father's birth. I could not know then that my father had early in his life abandoned his Jewishness, shed not only his religion, but also his Jewish identity--kept it hidden. And I was to hold it against him, my sense of his not owning himself, and thus my ignorance of my own identity, my inherited sense of a larger, metaphoric displacement. Later in my life, I was to feel the full force of *bashert* (a Yiddish word variously translated as destiny or kismet, among other definitions), a word I could not have known as a child in my grandparents' Brooklyn apartment, and in a dramatic way I could not have predicted then.

My father's Jewish identity was confirmed for me at the same moment I learned the facts of life. It was a hot summer day and my father was going to take me to a local swimming pool. I wanted my mother to go with us, and I kept begging her, until she sat me down alongside her at the kitchen table and explained what menstruation was, and how babies were made. Naturally, I was appalled at the latter especially, and declared I would never do anything like that. But the intimacy of that moment with my mother led me to ask about another topic so veiled in the family that it felt akin to these facts of life. "Is Daddy Jewish?" I asked her, still trying to name the uncanny connection I felt during the visit to my grandparents in Brooklyn. My mother leaned in towards me, gently taking my arm, her gesture at that moment was burned indelibly into my memory: fingers to lips, she pronounced, "Shhhhh." "But why?" I asked. "Why is it a secret?" I recall she answered kindly, but sadly too, "It would hurt your father in business." At that moment, then, without understanding why, I knew that the connection I felt to my grandparents included my father, included me, and was for an unknown reason, dangerous. As I got older, this "shhh" took on greater implications. What did this prohibition to speak about my father's Jewishness, and by extension, my part in it, say about my parents? How could it be that such people of their caliber and mindset would make such a decision? They had always taught me to stand up for my beliefs in school, anywhere, unpopular or not, and I had watched them stand up for theirs in the various communities in which we lived, among people who were bigoted and narrow-minded. I was still too young to understand the sort of world where such information could be so harmful. This "shh" frightened me—what was so unspeakable?

In her essay, *Split at the Root*, the poet Adrienne Rich wrote:

> For about fifteen minutes I have been sitting chin in hand in front of the typewriter, staring out at the snow. Trying to be honest with myself, trying to figure out why writing this seems to me so dangerous an act, filled with fear and shame, and why it seems so necessary. It comes to me that I have to claim my father, for I have my Jewishness from him and not from my gentile mother; and I have to break HIS silence, HIS taboos; in order to claim him I have in a sense to expose him. And then I have to face the sources and flickering presence of my own ambivalence as a Jew; the daily, mundane anti-Semitisms of my entire life. These are stories I have never tried to tell before. And yet I've been on the track of this longer than I think.[1]

On the track of this longer than I think. That was the *bashert*, the uncanny kismet, destiny, inexplicable recognition I had experienced at my grandparents' home in Brooklyn. But I still could not understand what had happened there—how it was I knew a place I had never been.

Displacements

While I was troubling myself over what I perceived as a contradiction in my parents' characteristic ethics, and the meaning of my identification with my grandparents, another force was at work—our regular moves from one part of the country to another. My father, an ambitious and successful scientist, was always ready to move his family when he advanced in his work. So although I was an east coast kid, born in Fair Lawn, New Jersey, my parents from New York, I came of age in the Midwest, and moved back and forth between the east coast and the Midwest more than once. Displacement was in me, just as my father's first dramatic displacement had been for him. He was never "placed" after that, not really, despite his affiliation with his first and longstanding Brooklyn home. He was ready and willing to move almost anytime and anywhere if the opportunity was a good one. Those frequent displacements bred into me a heightened awareness of regional, ethnic and cultural differences among people. To live in Dearborn, Michigan, and befriend the neighborhood Italian D'Angelo sisters was an exercise in everyday exoticism for me. I was mesmerized by their "otherness," the specialness of their rituals, their food, their language. The same was true for the Italian family my mother's sister had married into, the Catanzaros in Baldwin, Long Island. As a grade school child, I spent so much time among those Italian families, my parents told me I would come home speaking Italian without really knowing it.

The exposure to such everyday exoticisms in my childhood made for a particularly intense search for my own identity, and brought me to reflect: who am I? This larger sense of displacement, beyond the literal truth of the moves, made me hyper-aware of memories, even the idea of memory itself, as an anchor, a place to permanently reside. Thus, noticing and remembering became instinctive to me. To find myself, I regularly looked out; if I wanted a self, I had to find a place. My father's sense of no-placeness, his denial of his history, made him, his story, the locus of my own search for self. Moving so often, gazing out at so many woods in so many backyards in various parts of the country, I turned my attention to the ways my father connected to the places we lived. He looked closely—at a leaf in our yard as if it were a miniature map of the universe, or conversely, from a great distance, as a philosopher surveys his culture. Always either microscopically or telescopically. But beyond his position in the companies where he worked and which weekly took him to other cities, he didn't engage much in the towns where we lived except for a high-intentioned and admirable run for a local school board once (his ideas were innovative and brilliant, but the locals did not follow the words he used to describe what he had in mind), and he lost the election. While he knew the tiniest detail of Manhattan, he was lost in the various local downtowns of the cities to which he had moved us.

But one consistent aspect of every house we lived in were the woods surrounding each home. The houses my father chose for us (and two he had built) were situated among trees. These woods provided a continuity in the frequent displacements. No matter how exotic a new region of the country seemed to me, as a child I conjured a vast, unbroken, familiar, universal forest which flourished outside any window of a room I occupied. I had always associated my father with trees, their dignity, their silent and unknown history, unspoken recorders of time passing. We always lived among trees—a woods met the perimeters of our symmetrical green backyards, civilized gardens bordering a wild thicket into which I would frequently venture alone, if only to stand noiselessly next to some woody monolith, in its leafy shadow, as if in a church. Because my father wanted always to live close to these forests, he finally built our last family home in the midst of a woods—no longer a space between yard and forest—all was one now.

One year my father assigned me a project of identifying and mapping each tree in these woods which constituted our yard. He instructed me to chart those trees, plot them on a makeshift map, and look up each variety, identify each tree. It would be like naming new children, inaugurating new relationships, finding the friends there that as a new kid I lacked elsewhere, as if, finally in identifying the trees, I would know something of myself. If my father meant for me to make this connection, he was right. I held the lime green osage orange in my hands, felt its knotty, ridged texture—it was anything but an edible fruit—a misnomer, out of its place, like me, I pondered, yet finding a place to flourish nonetheless. I consulted botanical books lying open on the ground, their glossy illustrations, diagrams of deciduous and conifer, dappled with sunlight from the canopy over my head. I remember noting about the fruit of the osage orange tree: "lime green in color, like an ancient relative to the Florida orange, with a scaly, bumpy, reptilian skin, like the skin of old people's hands." This connection between the fruit and my grandmother, really between the tree and me, confirmed something, I could not say what. But somehow I knew then that everything in the world was connected, that displaced as I felt, there was a larger connection that I had not yet discovered. This feeling had ripened from the earlier childhood days in the forest in Cranford where, removed from Dearborn and my wild child freedom, I had turned into myself.

Now the forest had accreted more significance for me, though I still could not name what it was. It was years later when my father told me of the forests of his birthplace, when I learned about the lyrical significance of the Białowieża forest in Poland, and the murderous meaning of the Bronna Góra forest close to my father's birthplace where 50,000 Jewish inhabitants of Brest were shot over open pits in less than six months, and when years later he and I met in Poland and he broke down telling me that the only lovely thing he recalled from his impoverished boyhood home in the shtetl on the Polish-Russian border was a glorious white flowering tree on the town's perimeter, the only place to which he cared to say some sort of a farewell when his family began their journey across Europe to the United States, how years after his departure, during the Nazi terror, the woods of my father's origins became the hiding place for Jews and the organizing spot for the partisan armies.

Noticing and remembering

I had learned to look closely, and to remember the details of what I saw in the forest. This noticing and remembering carried over to the details of my parents' stories—what they told and what remained untold. In his *Landscape and Memory*, Simon Schama explains that the concept of landscape is a human invention, from *landschaft*. "But why did we need to invent it?" he asks. We needed to anchor ourselves, he suggests, to characterize place in such a way that allowed us to form a relationship with it. We personify place. I quickly, efficiently personified the places we lived because time was short. Landscape, woods, trees are one part of the quotient of self; the other may be the houses we live in. It is no accident that years later my doctoral studies took the theme of houses and landscape in literature as edifices of values. Architecture and landscape are the reflection of belief. A house's structure and its landscape reveal and shape the selves of those who occupy it. So I wrote about Fanny in *Mansfield Park* who must preserve the original style of the house and its landscape; and *Middlemarch*'s Dorothea who must integrate her house and its landscape with the coming land reforms in England; and the Schlegel sisters in *Howards End* who must reconcile their inherited country farm house and its meadows with the encroaching Beau Brummelism of London. Intrusion on the landscape and the house violates self in these novels. Later still, trees and the forest reverberated for me and continued to accrete personal significance in my travels to Poland.

But that was much later; then I was a child making a map of trees of our house's landscape for my father.

Music: A first language

My own enchantment with and such observation of detail, and the vivid and explicit memory of such detail, I realize now, was what had made music my first language. A piano student of my father's, I readily memorized difficult pieces, could "play music" in my head and hear its complexity accurately at will. But his instruction was old school, strict like the instruction he had experienced, and at 13, I could not keep apace with his requirements to practice two hours a day. So one Sunday morning when we had our lessons, frustrated with what he saw as my lack of guts and true commitment, he fired me as a piano student. I was simultaneously bereft and relieved. I loved music, but I was a kid in 1965, a different time than 1927 when he was 15 and his Juilliard professor told him he had mastered the piano. I felt a failure compared with him, and looking back, I guess I was, if that meant giving up all other interests for the piano. I lacked the grit he had possessed and I could not go the distance and he told me so. I remember he took the pale yellow Schirmer's Library of Classical Music edition of Chopin's Preludes (one area where I had not disappointed him, having mastered several of them), and bonked me over the head with the volume at our last lesson, as if to say, "You foolish kid, you're not serious enough for this."

I felt very serious about music, I loved it, but it did not translate every week in my performances at our lessons, and so he, exasperated, quit on me. The relief came only because I knew I would not have to face his disapproval again—at least not in piano performance. Only many years later, when he related the story of how his parents had taken the violin away from his older brother—a boy who loved the instrument but failed to impress a virtuoso auditor as to future greatness—did I connect my story with my uncle's. But that story will wait for now.

After the music, my "first language," was silenced, I turned once more to my former language: writing. It had always been there from the time I remembered in Cranford, ten years before the piano lessons were stopped, when I would have been 8 years old. But from the beginning, writing had seemed more "natural," not something I needed to practice. Now, more and more cognizant of my father's and my mother's own stories of literal displacements, noticing the details of their stories, remembering these as I had readily remembered musical pieces, writing became a way to store and try to make sense of my own literal displacement in the moves my family made, as well as the metaphoric displacement concerning my own identity, the "split at the root" aspect of my origins which I had confronted first at my grandparents' Brooklyn home and shortly after with my mother's cautioning "Shhhh…".

After that momentous experience for me during the visit to my grandparents, we returned to my mother's family in Long Island, and then to our house in Cranford, the house where my interior life had begun. We only stayed in that Cranford house for one year. My father was always in search of a better position; by now this move meant my third elementary school in four years. I was the perennial new kid at school and in the neighborhood.

Decatur, Illinois, 1961

The forces that had drawn me into myself now abated because West Forest Avenue, the new place in Decatur, Illinois, where we had moved after the one year in Cranford, had kids on the street once again. But though my sense of freedom, of physicality had been restored, I never lost the change that had come over me the year before. There was always now an interior life, a faculty that automatically picked up on the unspoken, the nuance, the underlying significance of everything I experienced. You might be able to say I had begun to think metaphorically, symbolically: images, events, words held possibility beyond their literalness. The threat of losing my baby sister had passed, but the fear that we might lose her, and also lose my mother, had carved out a space in me where even the smallest thing had significance, was somehow serious, or at least noteworthy.

Seriousness is not quite the right term, but now there was a sense of the significance in how I spent the moments of my day. More accurately, perhaps the attitude I brought to my work—and even my play. Ice skating with my father, for example. The spot was an outdoor frozen pond, always better than an artificial rink. This pond was called "Dreamland," and as corny as the name was for a smallish body of water in small town America, the name fit. Evergreen surrounded the pond and banks of snow cleared from the ice were piled along the perimeter, so that the place had the appearance of just happening to be there, not man-made, just part of a natural landscape. The pond had finally frozen so that at last we could put on our skates in the cracking, cold air. My father put on his black leather skates first—the type with longer blades I associated with expert skaters. And he was an excellent skater. How he had learned to skate so well, I did not know, but I wondered if his experience dated from his childhood in Poland where lakes and ponds and streams were frozen more days than not. But because my Uncle Morris, my father's older brother, had told me that the family ate bread "moistened with the juice from a herring, but never the herring itself," I did not imagine they could have afforded ice skates. My father knelt over my feet and laced up my skates—too tightly—and the sky was opaque, gray. I was 9 and uneasy. It seemed like the outing should be joyful and full of laughter. But it was somber: he laced up my skates exactingly, but they were too tight. I did not want to complain, though, or displease him or have him think of me as a baby. Mostly, I wanted him to approve my skating, to be proud that I did not complain about the cold or the pain in my ankles. I saw my father, somber, determined, a fine skater, against the gray sky, clouds moving behind and over him. Perhaps that cold, dark frozen day took him back to his forcibly forgotten and repressed memories of the Jewish town on the Russian-Polish border where he had been a boy—back to a time and place of deprivation, of hardship, certainly of cold. Maybe that day at the Dreamland Pond, he was really dreaming— remembering harsh boyhood winters in the Old World in a house with just a fire for heat, and an earthen floor. Maybe he did not see me that day—I do not know. I do remember he held my hand as we skated round and round, yet his face looked directly forward, not down at me by his side. He was far away, it was cold, and my heart as well as my feet ached. Wherever he was, the play of ice skating seemed serious—significant to me.

The memory of that icy day recalls another memory in Decatur, but that one conjures the sweltering heat of a summer day. I am 9. The atmosphere was steaming, it was hot, near suffocating. My father was outside in our backyard, shirt off, gardening or maybe just pulling crabgrass—the picture is not entirely clear. His back was to me as I sat in a wicker chair on the backyard patio. There was no respite from the heat on the patio, no umbrella. I watched my father's sunburned back move up and down as he worked in the blinding sun. It was still and silent, except for an unbroken, high-pitched, unending buzz that often accompanied such Midwestern heat—cicada, I reckon. Into the yard came young Peter, a neighbor boy, a year older than me, who regularly followed my neighborhood girlfriends and me around. We never wanted him there. He was a know-it-all who often provided in-depth information on subjects we cared little about. If he had been really an expert, it might have been different, but while we girls niftily climbed up to a tree house to be together and away from him, he would clumsily follow and impose himself on us with an arrogant lecture about climbing and tree houses.

One time, holding forth on some subject, he fell from the tree house, a dangerous distance, breaking his arm when he hit the ground. The cast he had to wear for several weeks became a badge of his general ineptitude and intrusiveness. We would have felt sorry for him, I suppose, had he been less of a show-off. There was an incident that occurred when we girls were gathered around in a neighbor's yard when he suddenly pulled down his trousers and underwear in a movement so rapid the genitalia he exposed appeared a blur. A mother saw this performance for us from her window overlooking their yard, but Peter had already run away from us.

On that day of relentless heat as I watched my father work in our yard, I might have been happy to see Peter. It was so hot and uncomfortable, I wanted any diversion and was alone except for my father who seemed drawn into himself while he worked. Peter was intelligent, that I knew. And he often singled me out from the crowd, if he could, to discuss "higher issues" with me alone. This earned me the teasing of the other girls who said that Peter was in love with me. Although that idea was repellant to me, I did sometimes see a reflectiveness in his face, an adult sort of awareness that set him apart from my lord of the flies gang of girls. His parents were from Germany, and both spoke with heavy accents. His father was a pediatrician, my pediatrician, and I remember one time when he playfully held me upside down in his examination room so that I could walk on the ceiling, my mother laughing along with him. He wore thick glasses and was very pale, but had a shock of dark hair that fell across his forehead and a fit physique which made him seem younger than other adults I knew. The mother, Peter and his younger sister, Gabriele, went to our local Catholic church. I would see the three of them at Mass, the father never with them. The two children looked like the father—pale skin, even the eyelashes seemed blonde, so that the father and children had a kind of naked look to the eyes and brow. The mother, on the other hand, had a burnished complexion and dark gold short hair, always a kindly expression on her face, different from the father and children whose faces appeared intelligent but somehow malevolent. My mother always had nice things to say about their mother—that she was very gracious and kind. My mother's mother, Grandma Mae, had been a German Catholic, and I wonder if there was some sense that these were good people, not like the "other Germans." Peter sometimes wore short pants to Mass, dressy, tasteful ones, like good lederhosen maybe with suspenders, but this made him look all the more sissified.

He launched himself in a crooked way into our backyard that day, appearing like a little white ghost on the perimeter of the yard, scanning the territory for a moment with his blonde gaze and seeing me, darted furtively in my direction. I do not remember what the talk was that led us to this topic, but we had moved from the patio to the shade of a large tree in the yard, and my father continued to work in the heat. Peter exclaimed, "The Jews are barbarians, don't you know that!" As I look back, I do not know what information or family influence I was drawing on, but I fought back. "No, they're not, stupid! You don't know anything! That's not true!"

In his usual way, Peter was gesturing and pointing, and now shouting since I was telling him he was wrong. I did not hear my father walk up behind me, my back was still to him, and Peter became aware of him before I knew he was there. He had seemed so distant in his work, so uninvolved with us that it surprised me to see him standing near. What I saw when I turned around gave me an unforgettable shock: the heat could explain it, but my father's incandescent appearance was otherworldly—it did not come from the sun that day, but from a fury that radiated from somewhere inside him. His eyes were burning coals, wide open in a truly frightening way—a monster at high noon. He took no notice of me whatsoever but stared at Peter. The boy became catatonic, suddenly stuck in mid-gesture, stunned to silence in mid-sentence by fear. Slowly my father raised one arm, and in a voice too quiet for regular conversation, said to Peter, "Get….off….my….property." Peter took little faltering steps backward first, and then nearly falling, turned and ran like I had never seen him run before—off my father's property. I stood still looking back between my father who appeared like a statue afire and the fleeing figure of Peter. Seconds passed. The boy was out of sight. I looked at my father, to my father to help me understand. But he never looked at me, and instead turned around and walked back to his work.

My father had sayings that had become family legend: "Life is real; life is earnest," or another version I found bleaker, "Life is a series of compromises."

My father had survived poverty and hunger in shtetls, Kobrin and Brest Litovsk, variously governed briefly by Germany, Russia and Poland when he lived there for the first eight years of his life in the early part of the twentieth century. Less than a decade later, now a young man living in New York, he lived through the Great Depression. He was a true democrat, a believer in the civil rights of every person, a citizen of the world, a free thinker. He could even be thought an idealist when he talked about the place of ethics in our society, and about his still shining, if tarnished, version of the American dream. But it would always happen when I came to him in my adolescence with a tale of painful disillusionment—hardly significant compared to his experiences, but still—like the time my best girlfriend in high school organized a mini-war against me because I fraternized with the Black kids at my school. It would happen that while he would sympathize, commiserate, I could never escape the resignation that showed in his face at these tellings: "You know, life is real, life is earnest."

II

Their Beginnings ❧ Shtetl, Meadow, City

Brest-Litovsk, Polish-Russian border, 1920

In 1918, Brest-Litovsk had become (again) part of Poland, having over the years been governed variously by Germany, Poland and Russia. They had survived a killingly cold winter in 1920—the family, four children under the age of 11 and their 30-something year-old mother. Their dwelling in Kobrin, a shtetl on the eastern edge of Poland and neighboring Russia, was a single room, a wooden structure. Raised platforms made of the same wood filled with hay and fastened to the walls served as beds. The walls were wooden slats and the winter wind found its way through these into the beds and into the bones of the children. Their garments were ragtag, but carefully mended as the mother was a gifted seamstress. She had once acquired a horse blanket from which she planned to stitch warmer clothing for her children, but she was accused of stealing it, and she had been whipped in punishment and the blanket taken away. Shoes were a problem. Mostly the children wore oversized shoes, someone's castoffs, and these they handed down to one another as they grew. They kept their shoes on in winter when they slept. Some warmth was provided by a large iron pot in a space adjacent to their room which divided their dwelling from the family's next door, an anteroom just large enough to accommodate the pot and room around it just wide enough to allow the inhabitants to enter the doorways into their separate homes. The wood fire beneath the pot was regularly stoked, but during the night the fire would burn low and the cold would set in. At holiday the pot held *cholent*, a stew that consisted mostly of vegetables from the garden the mother maintained —the garden that was the family's primary source of food—with a small meat bone for flavor. More typically, though, the family ate the conserved summertime vegetables in jars, with bread. The bread was hung by strings from the ceiling of the room to prevent the mice from eating it.

The father, my grandfather, had left seven-and-half years before for America, promising to send passage for the other five. But no word had come since he had departed. Maybe, the mother wondered, he had decided to abandon them? Certainly that was not unheard of in the shtetl. But even if he had not done so, it would be nearly impossible for him to get word to his family: World War I had broken out and the youngest, my father, an 8-year-old boy, had seen his town occupied consecutively by Germans, Russians, and Poles, all in his short lifetime. The boy had been born in the summer of 1912. The father was planning his journey after his son's *bris*, the requisite seven days

33

after the boy's birth, in the early fall so that the weather would not be an additional obstacle. The boy thus had no memory of his father whatsoever and could hardly believe in his existence, feeling more vulnerable than the other boys in the shtetl because of his fatherless status.

Example of my father's childhood dwelling in present-day Belarus, but part of Poland when my father was born before World War II. Courtesy Balgley Family Archive

Besides the cold, the other problem was hunger. They did have the garden, but that was a meager source of nutrition for the children. All of them showed signs of rickets, with their legs already bowed from lack of vitamin D. The mother's parents had disapproved of her marriage, and though the children's maternal grandfather owned apple orchards, no help was coming from those quarters. The father's family lived a short distance from Kobrin in Brest-Litovsk, but the father had many brothers and a sister, so help could not be expected from that source, either.

One day in the heat of late summer 1920, a horseman arrived at the family's home. He asked for Sarah Feyge Slomiansky Balgley, my grandmother, indicating he had a letter for her from America. The letter was from her husband, Israel Balgley, who wrote from New York City where he had established a hardware business and had become an American citizen. Enclosed with the letter were five tickets for passage to New York on the vessel *La Lorraine* which departed from Le Havre, a major port in the northern French province of Normandy. None of the family had ever seen the sea, but they had a sense of it; the mother had traded some of her conserved vegetables for light cotton fabric and began to hand sew sailor suits for the three sons, and a sailor dress for the eldest, a daughter. The family began preparing. A wagon, horse and driver would be needed for the trip across Poland. The destination would be Warsaw where Israel had relatives and the family could stop there for rest.

It would be fall before the five would be able to set out on the journey. Before departure there was one significant goodbye to be said. Aaron Slomiansky was the children's maternal grandfather, he who had disapproved of his daughter's marriage to Israel. Like his daughter, Aaron was a master gardener. In his case it was the apple orchards he relied on for his living. Sarah and her children went to take leave of Aaron, and the boy, young as he was, knew this was a permanent farewell. Yet there was little emotion expressed. The boy and his siblings view the luxuriant apple trees, but only through a grille at the entrance to the orchard, as their grandfather did not want his trees disturbed by children walking among them. Aaron and his apples make an indelible impression on the boy. He remembered the grandfather's red beard and the ripening red of his trees and the matter-of-fact, forever goodbye.

The family had few possessions to begin with, and what they did have would have been of little use on the journey. Once the horse and cart were arranged, the main task was loading the cart with hay and a blanket so the children could sleep. There was hardly room for even four in the cart, so Sarah decided to sit in front on the bench with the horse driver. It was September now and the air had become crisp. Although a current map of today's highways will show Kobrin to be less than four hours away from Warsaw—280 kilometers or about 175 miles—the route in 1920 meant unpaved dirt roads most of the way to the Warsaw outskirts. The family's conveyance would travel approximately three to four miles per hour, and the physically strenuous ride would allow at most five hours of travel each day. So the journey to Warsaw would have likely taken nine days under the best of circumstances.

Name of Passenger	Residence	Arrived	Age on Arrival
1. David Belgley	Cubrin, Russia	1920	11
2. Ilie Belgley	Cubrin, Russia	1920	7
3. Moses Belgley	Cubrin, Russia	1920	9
4. Rachel Belgley	Cubrin, Russia	1920	14
5. Sarah Belgley	Cubrin, Russia	1920	34

From La Lorraine passenger manifest, my father's first and surnames are misspelled as "Ilie" and "Belgley," with his three siblings and mother.
Courtesy JewishGen

My father's passenger record on La Lorraine, shows names misspelled as well as ethnicity, "Beb" should read "Heb" for Hebrew. Age should also read 8y. Courtesy JewishGen

Name:	Belgley, Ilie
Ethnicity:	Polish Beb.
Place of Residence:	Cubrin, Russia
Date of Arrival:	September 13, 1920
Age on Arrival:	7y
Gender:	M
Marital Status:	S
Ship of Travel:	La Lorraine
Port of Departure:	Le Havre, Seine-Inferior, France

The ground over which the family passed had seen more than its share of strife.* (See Appendix). In September 1920 when my father and his family set out, the Polish-Soviet War, an aftermath to World War I, was underway from February 1919 to March of 1921. The Battle of Warsaw was happening as they approached the city and pogroms had taken place in Brest only fifteen years earlier in the wake of the 1905 Bolshevik Revolution, and continued to occur near Brest and Kobrin. Although it was not geographically close, the pogrom at Kishinev in 1903 had brought world attention to the situation of Jews in that part of the world. In 1906 there had been a pogrom in the Polish city of Siedlce. This was the dangerous situation prevailing for Jews at the time my father and his family left Brest and Kobrin by horse and cart to cross Poland to Warsaw, then on to Paris, and finally from Le Havre to sail to New York.

The youngest boy remembered that the family stopped at least once at an inn—and in 1920 Poland, Jews were the primary innkeepers, even if their clientele were primarily gentile. In the dark of night, the exhausted family in peasant dress came upon gas-lit windows with movement and music behind them. They wearily entered and saw merry-makers made merrier by a plentitude of vodka. Jews were also the tavern keepers and liquor distributors of the day, while again their customers were mostly gentile. The customers look up from their glasses at the five and regarded them with some surprise, as they were not typical night-time visitors. As their driver saw to the food and water for the horse outside, Sarah arranged for a room above the tavern where she, the children and possibly even the driver (though he may have slept the night in the cart of hay) might find some comfort for the night.

The La Lorraine

ADD TO YOUR ELLIS ISLAND FILE

Associated Passenger
Belgley, Ilie

Date of Arrival
September 13, 1920

Port of Departure
LE Havre

Built by Compagnie Generale Transatl
Nazaire, France, 1899. 11,146 gross t
(bp) feet long; 60 feet wide. Steam tr
expansion engines, twin screw. Servi
knots. 1,114 passengers (446 first cl;
second class, 552 third class).

Built for French Line, French flag, in 1
named **La Lorraine**. Le Havre-New Y(
Served as an armed merchant cruiser
World War I as LORRAINE II. Resume
New York service in 1919. Scrapped ir

Photo: Richard Faber Collection

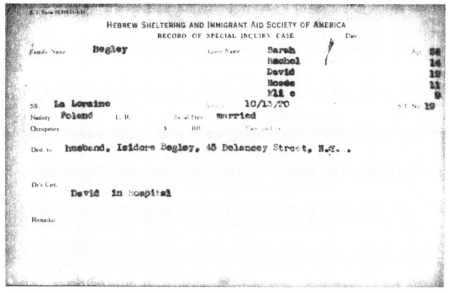

Hebrew Sheltering and Immigrant Aid Society of America (HIAS) document indicating my grandfather's acceptance of his family's arrival to the United States. Grandfather's first and surname misspelled. They should read "Israel Balgley" not "Isidore Begley." His home address, however, is correct. Note that David, my father's brother, was detained at hospital. Courtesy JewishGen

Other nights were spent on the road, as inns were too expensive to use regularly, and besides, the travelers were anxious to get on with the journey and to keep stops as brief as possible. The boy slept in his clothes in the cart, of course, and kept his cap on his head for warmth. He remembered mornings being awakened in the hay by the rising sun, which gradually found its way under the brim of his cap.

Warsaw, Poland, September, 1920

The five arrived in Warsaw and found the home of Israel's family.[2] It was lavish given their experience. The large home was one of the fine old apartments in a well-appointed building with a gated courtyard attended by a gentile Pole. It seemed that the three or four other large apartments in the building were Jewish homes, as well. There was a place where Jews are not impoverished, the boy thought. But more, in the city the family saw paved streets, opulent buildings and streetcars. And a streetcar's mirrors. They had not seen a mirror before. The dress of the city dwellers, the noise of traffic. The family had never met these relatives, and their arrival was met lukewarmly. The boy sensed that these relatives accept them grudgingly and looked forward to the five's departure.

Paris and the Crossing, September, 1920

Of the famous city of lights, the boy remembered only this: that his older brother became so fascinated by a puppet made of feathers which danced on the Parisian streets on strings, that the mother had to tear him away. And that the mother bought a fur stole. With what money, no recall.

Then a train to Le Havre, but no memory of which train from Paris. The ship they boarded was *La Lorraine*. Because the messenger on horseback had delivered purchased passage, the five sailed in comfortable conditions, not the steerage typically associated with immigrant voyages. The four children, then on board, wore the sailor suits handsewn by Sarah Feyge at the shtetl. An artist on board sketched the four together and wrote at the bottom, "Bolsheviki," his satirical commentary on that threat. The family was presented with lobster for the first time in the ship's dining room. Since they had never seen or heard of such a creature, it's hard to say if they would have known eating its flesh violated *kashrut*. But they sent away the lobster with the French waiter, and asked for something else. I do know, though, that this began my father's appreciation not just for lobster, but for fine foods generally, for the rest of his life. That bread, as I wrote earlier, "moistened with the juice of the herring, but never the herring itself" was replaced by herring as an appetizer before every family Sunday or holiday meal throughout my childhood. But Jewish foods, simple ones, like pickled eggs in beet brine, for example, like my grandmother would have prepared in his boyhood, he always enjoyed.

Whatever other delicacies they may have been exposed to, those stories, like what he experienced when he first saw the sea, I never could fully extract from him. But one day when he was nearly 100 years old, we were casually discussing a recent trip I had made to New York City, referring to the by then stereotypical images of the arriving immigrant looking out from the deck of a ship, I almost jokingly asked him if he remembered the first time he had seen the Statue of Liberty. He surprised me with a sudden turn of his head to face me directly, and said emphatically, "Why, of course, I do." What did I know? He had for so long been so unsentimental about his origins, acting as if the details of that story were nothing particularly noteworthy or special, that I only was able to get the story, and that in fragments, over time. The memory clearly seemed important to him, yet at the same time, his general attitude about his beginnings he gave no special significance to, no drama, and most of all no self-importance. This was a classic example. It took asking him specifically about his memory of the Statue of Liberty to get an answer.

And it was more than just that one-sentence answer. He smiled, but it was a smile turned inward, as if just remembering this for the first time, or perhaps revisiting an old forgotten scene. Since he had been born in July of 1912, and his father had departed for America in 1913, arriving in the United States on June 15, 1913, he had no memory of his father. He told me he considered himself a fatherless boy, and one day he unexpectedly related to me the story of how two older girls in the shtetl had taken him by the hand, led him to a darkened barn, and while one kept watch at the sunlit crack at the door opening, the other, as he put it, "Fooled about with my genitals." He shrugged as he told the story, and commented matter-of-factly, "They thought, how about him, he has no father, let's take him."

What struck me at the telling was the complete lack of self-pity in his tone, a tone that masked a pain that had to come with the vulnerability he recognized in his situation. But it was nearly self-mocking, as if to say, "Well, what would you expect? Life is real; life is earnest." That attitude was one I had seen before when he talked of any difficulties he experienced in his adult life.

U. S. DEPARTMENT OF LABOR
NATURALIZATION SERVICE

BUREAU OF
NATURALIZATION
RECEIVED CATE

No. 91402

D. 187- 167

A. NOV. 20

UNITED STATES OF AMERICA

DECLARATION OF INTENTION

Invalid for all purposes seven years after the date hereof

State of New York,
County of New York, } ss: In the Supreme Court of New York County,

I, __Israel Balgley__, aged __29__ years,
occupation __Grinder__, do declare on oath that my personal description is: Color __white__, complexion __dark__, height __5__ feet __3__ inches, weight __130__ pounds, color of hair __black__, color of eyes __brown__, other visible distinctive marks __none__

I was born in __Litovsk, Russia__ on the __5th,__ day of __August__, anno Domini 1 __885__ I now reside at __141 Division Street__, New York City, N. Y.

I emigrated to the United States of America from __Triest Austria__ on the vessel __Panonia__; my last foreign residence was __Litovsk, Russia__

It is my bona fide intention to renounce forever all allegiance and fidelity to any foreign prince, potentate, state, or sovereignty, and particularly to __Nicholas II,__ __Emperor of all the Russias__, of whom I am now a subject; I arrived at the port of __New York__, in the State of __New York__, on or about the __15th,__ day of __July,__, anno Domini 1 __913__ I am not an anarchist; I am not a polygamist nor a believer in the practice of polygamy; and it is my intention in good faith to become a citizen of the United States of America and to permanently reside therein: SO HELP ME GOD.

Israll Balgley

Subscribed and sworn to before me in the office of the Clerk of Court at New York City, N. Y., this __26th,__ day of __September__ anno Domini 191 __4.__

[SEAL]

WILLIAM F. SCHNEIDER
Clerk of the Supreme Court
DEPUTY
Special Clerk

My grandfather's application for naturalization in the United States.
Courtesy JewishGen

My grandfather's World War I draft card. Courtesy JewishGen

Grandfather Israel in his World War I American service uniform, showing his rank as sergeant. Courtesy JewishGen

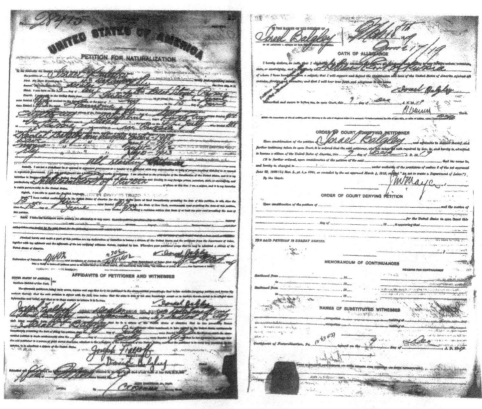

Grandfather Israel Balgley's certificate of arrival, petition for naturalization, and oath of allegiance, documents that were ultimately misplaced.
Courtesy JewishGen

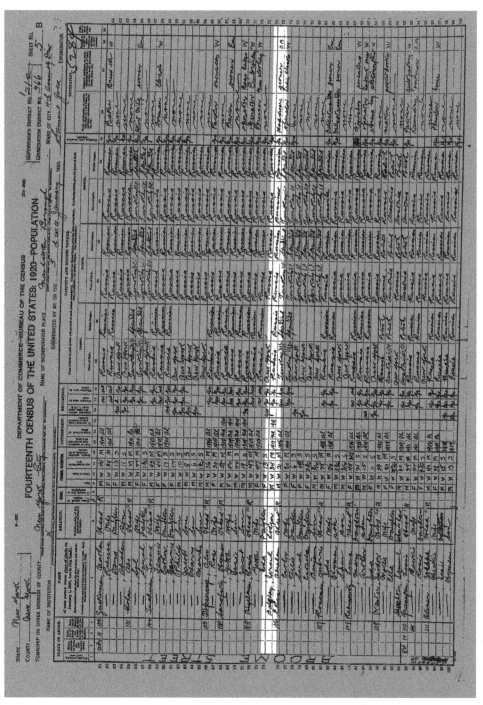

1920 Census sheet. Courtesy JewishGen

Israel Balglay in the 1920 United States Federal Census

NAME:	Israel Balglay [Israel Balalay]
AGE:	34
BIRTH YEAR:	abt 1886
BIRTHPLACE:	Russia
HOME IN 1920:	Manhattan Assembly District 4, New York, New York
STREET:	BROOME STREET
RACE:	White
GENDER:	Male
IMMIGRATION YEAR:	1913
RELATION TO HEAD OF HOUSE:	Lodger
MARITAL STATUS:	Married
FATHER'S BIRTHPLACE:	Russia
MOTHER'S BIRTHPLACE:	Russia
NATIVE TONGUE:	Russian
ABLE TO SPEAK ENGLISH:	Yes
OCCUPATION:	Hardware
INDUSTRY:	owner
EMPLOYMENT FIELD:	Own Account
NATURALIZATION STATUS:	Naturalized
NEIGHBORS:	View others on page

HOUSEHOLD MEMBERS:	NAME	AGE
	Louis Bigelman	47
	Yetta Bigelman	47
	Ida Bigelman	13
	Israel Balglay	34

Source Citation
Year: 1920; Census Place: Manhattan Assembly District 4, New York, New York; Roll: T625_1192; Page: 5B; Enumeration District: 366; Image: 383

Grandfather Israel's 1920 census record details. He must have lodged with the Bigelman family up to the time that my father and family arrived in September 1920. Courtesy JewishGen

1930 Census sheet. Courtesy JewishGen

Israel Balgley in the 1930 United States Federal Census

NAME:	Israel Balgley
BIRTH YEAR:	abt 1885
GENDER:	Male
RACE:	White
BIRTHPLACE:	Poland
MARITAL STATUS:	Married
RELATION TO HEAD OF HOUSE:	Head
HOME IN 1930:	Brooklyn, Kings, New York
MAP OF HOME:	View Map
STREET ADDRESS:	Rodney St
WARD OF CITY:	Pt 4th AD
BLOCK:	M
HOUSE NUMBER IN CITIES OR TOWNS:	101
DWELLING NUMBER:	96
FAMILY NUMBER:	267
HOME OWNED OR RENTED:	Owned
HOME VALUE:	15, 000
RADIO SET:	Yes
LIVES ON FARM:	No
AGE AT FIRST MARRIAGE:	23
ATTENDED SCHOOL:	No
ABLE TO READ AND WRITE:	Yes
FATHER'S BIRTHPLACE:	Poland
MOTHER'S BIRTHPLACE:	Poland
LANGUAGE SPOKEN:	Yiddish
IMMIGRATION YEAR:	1913
NATURALIZATION:	Naturalized
ABLE TO SPEAK ENGLISH:	Yes
OCCUPATION:	Hardware
INDUSTRY:	own store
CLASS OF WORKER:	Working on own account
EMPLOYMENT:	Yes
HOUSEHOLD MEMBERS:	**NAME** **AGE**

Israel's census record details from 1930. 101 Rodney Street is the address my father remembers coming to on his and his mother's and siblings' arrival. Courtesy JewishGen

"But his hat blew off"

Yet at the memory of his first seeing the Statue of Liberty, his tone was different; this was reverie. "We drew closer and disembarked at Ellis Island. I don't remember a long line, but I recall that although I had never seen him, I realized this was my father waiting for us. He wore a suit and a tie. There was a fence or gate separating the five of us from him at first, but then we all united." I asked if this was an emotional scene—was there kissing and embracing— were there tears? He only nodded affirmatively at this, but gave no details, save one: "My father appeared organized and ready to receive us. He was ushering us out of the hall, but his hat blew off." *But his hat blew off.* My father stated this with a smile but a smile that said, "Too bad that happened." That my 8-year-old father recalled this detail struck me as remarkable, especially the "But" of the statement: "***But*** *... his hat blew off."* His father had made a fine impression, a powerful savior, but the memory of the hat caught in the breeze and taken from his father's head stayed with the boy: there were many things this potent man could control, but a great deal he could not. Nature, the wind takes his hat, what else can it take? What other forces can take more than a hat? The vulnerability of the boy in the shtetl barn was not erased, and it was remembered by his 100-year-old self. He also recalled, as if for the first time, that his brother, Dave, just two years older, had been detained on Ellis Island, as the boy reportedly had some sort of a rash on his face. The officials said the 10-year-old boy would have to be quarantined, that he could not go with the rest of the family. I only know from photos and descriptions of the quarantined cabins what they must have been like, especially for a little boy in a strange new land without his family-- dark and isolated. How long Dave was there, my father could not remember. But he did tell me that after that time and for the rest of his life, Dave suffered from severe stuttering.

My father reported that before he arrived in America he had "never held a pencil in his hand," as he put it. How that was the case I have never learned. Nor did he understand why he had never gone to school. Brest-Litovsk before and after 1912 had Jewish schools for children. Why had he not attended? But perhaps more crucially, why had his older siblings not attended either? His sister, Rachel, was the eldest, and she would have been a teenager by the time the family made the journey to America. I think of her often, of her particular situation, of how much more difficult immigration would have been for her than for her three younger brothers. In a family photo of the six of them taken in New York a few years or so after their arrival, Rachel, or Rose, as they called her, looks like an aspiring flapper, dressed in the costume, her dark

Semitic looks reminiscent of Hedy Lamarr, but with her eyes uncomfortably averted from the photographer's lens, whereas her younger brothers, along with their parents, appear confident and self-possessed.

In contrast to his seldom-made references to his brothers, which seemed at least loving, my father never talked about Rachel (in America, called "Rose"), though one time he commented, "She wasn't so swift upstairs." I took that in, and then objected, "But it was so much more difficult for her than you and your brothers. She was older; she knew only Yiddish and maybe some Polish—imagine her put into an American high school—literally fresh 'off the boat' to find her way among American teenagers! How much more easily you would learn English than she. And a girl! Your parents would not have placed much academic hopes in her anyway. What with their Old World outlook, a girl should only marry well, if possible." My father nodded, but it was as if he had never considered any of this before. And I thought how self-absorbed this little eight-year-old could have been, likely scared, but at the same time young enough to be enthralled by this new setting, with no time to consider how his older sister got along.

As it turned out, the parents' hopes for their boys soon became focused on my father, their youngest. He took to his American school so readily, that by 9 he was fluent in English with no trace of an accent. Apparently his written English was so advanced, and not just for fluency, but for the ideas expressed in his early essays, that within his first year in elementary school he had won the award for English. But mathematics and science were his passions. He told me how as a young boy, alone, he regularly visited the American Museum of Natural History, because it was his entertainment. So quite soon, his teachers advised that he skip grades in elementary school. By the time he entered Brooklyn College, he was likely 16 years old, a mere eight years had passed since he first saw the Statue of Liberty.

My father and his brothers, David and Morris, at various times in their lives.
Courtesy Balgley Family Archive

At the same time, his parents, like many Jewish parents, felt that a musical education was essential for their children. A piano was purchased, and lessons apparently were begun for Rose, but she was reportedly unable to make the grade, as it were. Lessons began for all three boys. As it turned out, the oldest of the three brothers, my Uncle Morris, had an affinity for the violin, and so he was allowed to forsake the piano for the violin. My father reported that Morris loved the instrument, loved playing, even practicing, and so, apparently to find out if their eldest son had real talent, the parents brought in an accomplished adult violinist to hear the boy play. My father recalls that the outcome was a case of "thumbs down." "He'll never be a virtuoso," the auditor judged. Immediately, the violin was taken from the boy. The instrument was likely sold. My father shook his head, but I did not see emotional handwringing at this, so much as an attitude of "Life is real; life is earnest."

I do not know, and it was never mentioned, how my father's piano lessons led to an admittance to The Juilliard School in New York at the age of 10. The school was only seventeen years old itself at that time, and the practice in those early years was to assign a student to one teacher—a version of the Renaissance apprentice training for painters. My father remembers his teacher well, an Italian professor, whom he described as gifted and fair. There was never any mention of him being demanding or difficult. The only story my father ever told about the tough requirements of the piano were that when neighbor boys would come to the door and ask for him to play stickball, his mother would send them away with, "Ely is practicing."

Although he never stated it outright, I got the impression he never learned to play stick ball, or any sport. He didn't know how to ride a bicycle until he was a young adult playing in his band at the Eddy Farm. He once related a story to me about a Brooklyn neighbor, a family, who had recently moved, their home lying temporarily empty. Somehow the house was left open, and the three boys went inside to look around. There they found some extraordinarily strange objects which intrigued them. My father paused in the telling, and smiling to himself, a philosophic expression on his face, stated, "We later realized these must be toys."

The family did have a dog for a while, but in another story, I learned that my grandmother, deciding it was much too much trouble, boarded a street car with the pet, and travelling a good distance from their home, simply dropped the animal off, and was done with it. I looked at my father to detect some disapproval or even a trace of recalled sadness, but he shrugged, again sort of smiling, seem to say, "What can you do!" Though he was likely not witness to it, I thought of the horsewhipping of his mother in the shtetl for the alleged crime of taking a horse blanket to sew winter clothes for her children, and concluded that for my father, suffering is relative.

When my father was 15, the Italian professor told him his instruction was complete, that he had mastered the classics and could play anything. The lessons had lasted only five years. It was 1927 and my father was eager to make money for his family. He told me how he went immediately to a movie house to apply for a job as an accompanist to silent films, as was the practice in those days, only to learn in that very year that talkies had made their debut, meaning he was out of luck.

But there were other opportunities to make money with his musical ability. My father, the "young kid" whom my Uncle Augie described in his false history of who hired whom, became the leader of the band he joined. The band members agreed the band should be named for him. He demurred. Later I learned he suggested instead that another band mate's name be used. The name he wanted was pure WASP, and though he would never admit it—to me or even to himself—this was again another example of his deep ambivalence about his origins, which were foreign and Jewish and suspiciously "un-American."

One day sitting with my father not long before he died in 2014, at 102 years of age, he recalled an event he said he had forgotten. Forgotten or repressed, I cannot say, but when he told me, he told me as a sort of confession, a true regret. Not long after he had finished at The Juilliard School, and was by then respected by his family and neighbors as a significant talent, his own father asked him if he would play for a group of the older man's associates. This was to be at a synagogue, perhaps a club meeting, the details were not clear. My father reported that he asked his father what amount he would be paid for this performance. His father admitted it would be for free. Hearing this, my father turned down his father's request. Imagine, a 15-year-old with such cheek, I thought. How conceited and insensitive this little genius must have been! In his telling, my father lowered his head and said, "Why couldn't I just have played? Why didn't I? And after all, he had bought the piano for me in the first place and paid for my music books. I could have played for him. But I didn't."

This story provided me with a picture of my father I might not otherwise have had. Yes, he was dutiful and serious and brilliant, but he was early on hardened in his own way. I wondered if his refusal had had anything to do with the fact that the performance was to be for a religious group, since he, even at that early age, had turned away from Jewishness, from the entire idea of religion. Even though music, romantic as it is, was the article of exchange, my father had a mercantile consciousness about it. "If I play, I am paid." That attitude reminded me of the story of his parents' termination of his older brother's violin study, and of the abandonment of the family dog. These people had survived much, and they were not about to be impeded by sentimentality.

There was a moment at another time in the life of my father and in my own where that feeling resonated with me. I had invited my father to visit the Jewish school where I was teaching. He was already nearly 100. We had agreed that as part of his visit he would play the piano for my teenaged students. He was happy to come. And he did play. Afterwards, the students were given the opportunity to ask him questions. A particularly sweet male student whom I knew was sensitive and introspective, asked, "How did you deal with anti-Semitism as you grew up?" Here my father was, a person who had passed for much of his life, and here was I, the daughter who had queried him, but never had the courage or heart to accuse him directly. It was a tense moment for me, and I suspect, for my father. Here he was faced with innocence, with vulnerability, and a responsibility to answer, at least I felt it was a responsibility, to answer as honestly as possible. A beat and then the answer came thus: "I was interested in other things—science and music." I suppose it was a sort of an answer, given my father's personality and viewpoint on religious affiliation, but then it was not an answer at all.

My father played for income steadily from the time he finished The Juilliard School, bringing money home to his parents, paying for his undergraduate education when he entered Brooklyn College at 16, having skipped previous grades, and graduating from Seward Park High School. He remembered playing at fraternity dances and later at posh hotels in Manhattan, riding the subway back to Brooklyn in the early hours of the morning, at 3 a.m. or so, and needing to rise before 7 a.m. to get to his scheduled laboratory classes. Uncle Augie recalled that people commented at the clever tricks of the piano player who, although seeming asleep as he played, would switch tunes without a hitch, never losing the orchestra's pace. "The truth was," Augie recalled, "There were no tricks, he really was asleep."

Even after my father had gone on from his undergraduate years at Brooklyn College and graduated in chemistry from New York University, had married my mother in 1940, was employed by General Electric in Pittsfield, Massachusetts, had two young children (my older brother and sister), he continued to play, moonlighting nights at a place in the Berkshires called The Springs in New Ashford, Massachusetts. His playing became such an asset at the elegant place that the owners ran an advertisement in *The Berkshire Eagle* extolling his ability and inviting others to "come and hear him."

His boss at GE unfortunately saw the advertisement and summoned Ely to his office, indicating to him that he would either have to quit this night job or lose his elite day job at GE, as it was not "seemly" to have a moonlighting musician at the company. This is how The Springs lost their pianist. I visited the place in 2016, taking the route from the family's home in Pittsfield to the restaurant. The distance was about twelve miles. I learned my father navigated the family's Pontiac there at night along the darkened mountain Route 7, snow-covered in the winter.

But before that time, and before entering New York University to study chemistry, my father's true desire was to attend medical school. When I was ill as a child, or had injured myself, his style of diagnosing the problem and then caring for it, was always informed and scientific. More memorable

At

The Springs

New Ashford, Mass.

Ely Balgley

playing the piano

Come and Hear Him

Every Wednesday and Saturday

Tel. Williamstown 661-W2

A press advertisement promoting my father's regular musical performance at the Springs, New Ashford, Massachusetts, published in The Berkshire Eagle on December 5, 1947. Courtesy Balgley Family Archive

though was his manner in such instances: gentle, calming, his characteristic sternness disappearing in those cases. He gave the impression of a natural healer.

Cutting the mustard

When I queried him about how it was he decided not to study medicine, his reply was at first just curious, then ultimately misleading. Apparently, he felt that Harvard Medical School was the only option. Why he thought this is inexplicable, especially seeing that he was a resourceful person. Would he not have known better, known that there were other schools, other options? But he only applied to Harvard. And he was rejected. I knew his grades were top, and so I pushed the question further. How was it he was denied entrance to Harvard Medical School? His answer stays with me: "I guess I didn't cut the mustard."

I thought then and I know now this was an evasion. My niece, Tracy, who had finished a doctorate at the University of California Los Angeles (UCLA) in Higher Education had the research ready to hand: Jews applying to medical school in this period were subject to a harsh quota system, the infamous *numerous clausus*. In *Time to Heal: American Medical Education from the Turn of the Century to the Era of Managed Care,* Kenneth Luderer explains how the 1920's saw the growth of a nativist sentiment in the country: immigration restriction legislation combined with intense prejudice against admitting to medical schools Catholics, Italians, Jews, and additional religious and ethnic minorities, made for quota systems for all. But Jews, because they had had success in education and in society in general, faced the most rigid quotas. Many young Jews were seeking admission to college and medical schools. One official of Harvard Medical School stated that the school was "overwhelmed by the number of Jewish lads who are applying for admission." The Jewish population in the United States from 1880 to 1925 had grown from 200,000 to 4,000,000. Most of the Jewish applicants were from Eastern Europe, rather than Germany, and school admissions committees shared the same fear as the rest of the country of this so-called new wave of immigrants. The first quotas began in elite private schools, but not long after, quotas showed up in graduate schools, including medical schools. This trend continued and by the late 1930's and early 1940's, tight quotas were everywhere in American medical schools. Three out of every four non-Jewish students were accepted; one out of every thirteen Jewish students were accepted.[3]

Once again, in keeping with his absence of self-pity, his refusal to think himself special in any fashion, and his non-acknowledgement of his Jewish identity, my father only shrugged at my question, and held to his explanation of not being smart enough, of not "cutting the mustard," in his words. It was just this sort of passivity, or deference, or at worst, denial in such matters that, especially in contrast to his views on social justice, disturbed me and made me sense he felt a threat so deep that it could not even be acknowledged. In truth, though, it ignited and continued to fuel my anger with him.

Sparrow Bush, New York, 1933

One momentous summer, when my father was 21, he and his orchestra had an offer that was more attractive than any other they had ever had: a summer job to perform nightly at The Eddy Farm, a resort on the Delaware River in the small town of Sparrow Bush, New York, near the city of Port Jervis, located where the Delaware and Neversink rivers meet. The area was a natural rural paradise, especially compared to the urban life to which my father was accustomed. The Eddy Farm was named for the eddying river which had been an important conduit for shipping lumber and other goods that helped develop cities like Philadelphia and Trenton. The town of Sparrow Bush where the resort was located was pristine. Less than three miles from the city of Port Jervis where New York, Pennsylvania and New Jersey meet, Sparrow Bush was a place of meadows filled with wild rhododendron, fields of daisy, hollyhock and sunflower, intermittent streams for swimming. The orchestra performed at dinner and in the evenings, so the days were free. The job included room and board, so the band members had essentially the same experience as the guests.

In Sparrow Bush lived a family of six—a widowed mother and her five children. The second to the youngest was my mother, Margaret O'Hara. Her father had died at 32 in the 1918 Spanish Flu pandemic when she was 2 years old. Another child had died an infancy. At 17, Margaret, and her sister, Marion, two years older, both stunningly beautiful and resourceful girls, took summer jobs as waitresses at The Eddy Farm. The resort was within walking distance

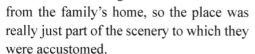
Ely's Orchestra: Front row, second from left, my father, Ely, third from left is my Uncle Augie. Courtesy Balgley Family Archive

from the family's home, so the place was really just part of the scenery to which they were accustomed.

It was there then, where my parents met— a Jewish city boy from an immigrant family, and a "country girl" from a Catholic Irish-German family. Their courtship necessarily had to last for some years, as my father was finishing school and working in the city, and my mother was still very young. They married seven years later, on March 20 of 1940, Good Friday. Given the national attitude at that time, the marriage of a Roman Catholic and a Jew was considered an interracial marriage.

My father's family—not just his parents, but even his in-laws, particularly the wife of his oldest brother, my Uncle Morris, vociferously condemned the courtship and the marriage. For the golden boy of the family, marriage to a gentile was the worst fate they could imagine. My father, by now an educated sophisticate, reared up against their prejudice, thinking they were hypocrites duplicating the kind of religious persecution to which they had been subjected.

My mother related to me an incident that occurred before their marriage when she had uncharacteristically been a guest in my father's family home.

It was morning and my father had already departed for class. My mother was with her future mother-in-law alone, and as the older woman prepared to leave the house for the day, she instructed my mother to wash the floors before she herself departed. My mother told this story without a trace of anger, but with obvious sadness. I asked her what she did. "I washed the floor before I left." Another time when discussing my father's family's reactions to her, my mother, again regretfully sighed and stated,

"I wish they would have given me a chance. I could have been such a good daughter-in-law to them." I was continually struck by her absence of anger, but it was not her way.

Perhaps more surprising was my mother's family's reaction to my father. There was never a trace of objection, of disapproval, and this in a family provincial in many ways, and very likely exposed to anti-Semitism. My father was fully embraced by them. He chose my mother's youngest brother, a devout Catholic, as his best man, and until the end of his life, my father would comment on how remarkable it was that this family accepted and even loved him. Although he had already discarded his sense of his being Jewish before he knew my mother and her family, it is reasonable to believe that this acceptance made it easier to abandon his own family, and his identity as a Jew.

My mother's lack of prejudice, her lack of anger at her in-laws' failure to welcome her, her desire to be a part of my father's family—all this makes her heroic in my memory. And it makes me have to question why I was nonetheless ultimately called to my Jewish half, the Jewish self that felt truer the more I examined it, rather than the Catholic upbringing I had through my mother. It bears saying, however, that despite my mother's observance of her faith, she became deeply alienated later in her life by the Catholic Church's refusal to honestly investigate the widely reported child sexual abuse among the clergy. I have never forgotten that on her deathbed in the hospital in June of 2006, when presented with a form where she could enter "religion," she wrote in large capital letters: "NONE." I wonder today if her ultimate rejection of her religion would have affected her opinion of my connection to my Jewish "half" over my Catholic "half."

The pastoral feel of Sparrow Bush my mother brought to all the houses in which we lived over the years; no matter that she had left her first home, the colors of those meadows came with her. The flower gardens she planted in all our homes were spectacular—peony, rose, forsythia, crocus, bachelor button, violet, rhododendron, and more. Taking my hand as a child, she would walk me through these gardens and point out to me their first spring appearance.

Even her person was imbued with that first place: the sage and azure colors of her dining rooms, for example, and her apparel, her physical self—blue green eyes and olive skin, and finally silver hair like cloud. But it was also her manner—calm and patient, as if she were an extension of the grace and quiet of those meadows. Her Catholicism was made of the same stuff: I was a religious little kid, or at least spiritual, because being with her at Mass, honoring any of the traditions, celebrating the religious holidays, she modeled for me some sort of transcendent way of being in the world as accepting and kind. Her political views were as strong as my father's, her views passionate about social justice and the bane of prejudice. She had told me a story about her teenage years working at The Eddy Farm when the Ku Klux Klan (KKK) would burn crosses on Point Peter, the mountain that overlooked Port Jervis, visible from the resort. She was still anguished decades later at the memory of the Black cooks with whom she worked at The Eddy Farm who were terrorized by the sight. And she also related how Catholics in her region, like her and her family, were also targeted by the KKK.

The area was working class for the most part, and despite an atmosphere of friendliness, Port Jervis had a history of racial violence. In the summer of 1892, an African American man named Robert Lewis was lynched on Main Street in Port Jervis. He had been accused of an assault on a white woman. Nine people were indicted for the crime. The incident became the seed of the novelist Stephen Crane's novella, *The Monster,* written in 1898 when Crane had lived in Port Jervis. By the time my mother and the cooks at The Eddy Farm saw the burning crosses, the KKK had experienced an early twentieth- century resurgence throughout the nation. She never forgot the effect on her fellow workers —and her own family's fear as Catholics. My father had grown up among the intellectual Jewish left in his neighborhood and college, so it made sense that he would hold those views. Hers seemed to spring from something inborn, constitutional in her, and obviously verified by her experience, and never contradicted by her family who similarly held no prejudices.

My parents' courtship was glamorous. They had the Eddy Farm in the summers, but Sparrow Bush was a mere eighty miles from Manhattan, and when my father returned there for work and school in the fall, my mother would take a train to visit him there. A musician, my father knew all the ballrooms and hotels in the city. They frequented The Waldorf Astoria, among other places, which in the 30s were palaces. My Uncle Augie, who continued to be in the same orchestra with my father, used to make fun of this "country kid," as he called my mother, "Look at this girl with hay in her hair—she knows all the best places in New York!" Eventually, at 21, she moved to the city with a girlfriend. They shared an apartment, and my mother worked as a secretary

My father, Ely and my mother, Margaret. Courtesy Balgley Family Archive

at Foremost Ice Cream Company located just under the Brooklyn Bridge. It's still there, in fashionable DUMBO, now a gourmet candy operation.

I visited Sparrow Bush and Port Jervis years after my mother's death. The town brought to mind the town in the film *The Deer Hunter.* There was something innately heartbreaking about the place with its hardworking, honorable people, living in simple houses where Missing in Action (MIA) and Prisoner of War (POW) flags hung from porches, one after another. I went to the cemetery where my grandmother and many of her relatives were buried—a Catholic cemetery filled with Irish and German names, and on many of the tombstones, inscriptions indicating in which war the dead had served or had died serving. Miniature American flags festooned the graves. My mother's background, disadvantaged economically with significant consequences, nonetheless seemed filled with family love and pleasure. Where my father seemed to be all reason, she was all romance. Of course, this is not perfectly true; when he played his music, it was obvious that it came as much from his heart as from his practiced hands. And my mother experienced a hardscrabble early life. By the time I was born, they had made a success of combining the two.

My parents, photographed on a train journey. My mother is looking forward with anticipation, while my father looks characteristically skeptical about the innocence of the world. Courtesy Balgley Family Archive

Outbound aboard the S.S. Acadia to Bermuda honeymoon, 1940.
Courtesy Balgley Family Archive

Return from honeymoon in Bermuda aboard the S.S. Acadia.
Courtesy Balgley Family Archive

III

Forward into the Past ❄ The Fulbright Stories

The Reading Life

In my early life books provided a wider territory for my childhood habit of noticing and remembering and naturally fed my writing. The urgency of my search for my identity found a home in my fascination with the identities of characters in literature and their struggles. By the time I was finishing my undergraduate studies in literature and creative writing at University of Illinois, Urbana, among the other characters I studied, I was introduced to Leopold Bloom, the fictional, famous Jewish Irishman in James Joyce's *Ulysses,* his ultimate outsider status drawing me in, his person combining my own mixed identity. With the encouragement of my professors, most notably, the teacher of the Joyce seminar, I went on to a doctorate program in literature at the University of California in San Diego.

Trees grow in southern California, that cultivated desert, but the trees there, the imported eucalyptus and palm, were not the ones from my youth, and for a time I felt cut off from the forests I had known. Literature replaced the forest as the place where I was alone and free, became the sanctuary the trees had once provided.

By the time I had completed my PhD in literature in 1986, I had been reading extensively about the Jewish experience in Poland from its beginnings in the tenth century to the present, from the early time when King Casimir is said to have invited the Jews to Poland, through times of relatively peaceful coexistence between Jews and Poles. More and more I read about how Polish policies kept Jews from full citizenship; I read of the pogroms committed by Poles against their Jewish neighbors from early centuries right up to pre-World War II years, and then after the war when surviving Jews attempted to return to their homes. But I also read of the remarkable (and successful) efforts gentile Poles made to hide or otherwise aid their Jewish countrymen. At risk of their immediate execution, the now named "righteous" Poles saved some Jews from Nazi annihilation. I was immersed at this time in discussions with Poles I was meeting in America who vociferously denied the charges of anti-Semitism in Poland. These Poles were not bigoted or stupid or callous—they really believed this. But the history I was reading was not false. That the issue of Polish anti-Semitism was so divided and so emotional drew me back to my personal story, a story, like this issue, that had at its heart, denial and obfuscation.

The confusion I had felt during my childhood about what I then thought of as my father's "passing," and the *bashert* I had experienced in meeting my grandparents, planted in me a need to understand this split in opinion, this split within me. It's possible this search began with the earliest "shhh" from my mother when I asked about my father's Jewish identity, and then morphed into the feeling of Adrienne Rich's "split at the root." It surely was fueled by the burning outrage I felt at the Polish friend in California who denied any Polish anti-Semitism. But it finally culminated in a deep need to go to Poland and to see what I could learn. And without being conscious of it at the time, I went also to rescue hope.

First Look: Poland, 1984

In 1983 I had met and fallen in love with the person who would eventually become my spouse. John, intellectually and politically astute, physically handsome, his athletic life (and genes) had given him an Adonis physique, was an enormously gifted visual artist who had a Polish surname, grandparents born in Poland, a father born in Chicago and raised in the Polish town of Hamtramck, near Detroit, speaking Polish. Despite that legacy, a "Bohemian" in the newer sense of that word, John did not identify with his Polish heritage. He felt more Californian than anything else and was not inclined to support nationalism wherever it showed itself. And then he met a Polish painter, Natalia Witkowska, who by marriage to one of John's teaching colleagues, ended up, oddly, in Southern California, having been born and raised in Warsaw and Paris. I say oddly because Natalia's character and personality had been shaped by her life as a "Mitteleuropean," with all the culture, romance and tragedy of that part of the world. Also, she had received a brilliant art education in Warsaw. John met Natalia, and though he had been making art since he was a boy, exposure to Natalia and her work offered him a trajectory for his own art. They were colleagues and formed a mentorship that helped both. It was Natalia who encouraged John to take his work to Poland for exhibition. That was 1981, the year of martial law in Poland. John stayed in a flat where a painter had formerly lived—a painter who reputedly had committed suicide. It may be an apocryphal story, but I understood that the rope he had hanged himself with was still in place when John moved in. A tragicomic beginning for an American to the world behind the Iron Curtain. John stayed for four months and made many friends and art colleagues. He was interviewed on Polish television (Roman Polanski was scheduled for an interview on that show, but their paths did not cross). It is difficult to say if John felt any ethnic connection to the country at that point. The Poles certainly greeted him as a "countryman," a connection he ducked away from. But he was in the land of his forebears, and the history he was absorbing, the impressive Polish art he was seeing, and the experiences he was having could not have failed to influence him and perhaps make him feel part of the story of that country. He had been raised Roman Catholic and had eschewed that long before, so the devoutness of the country did not draw him in, though he did see how the Polish Church stood as a bulwark, an oasis for Poles against the repressive communist regime at that time.

One day leaving his flat in the morning in late May 1981, he found the normally busy street deserted, emptied of its usual pedestrians. He proceeded to walk towards the Opera House *(Teatre Wielki)* and saw a large crowd gathered. Without warning, armed police with batons and shields appeared, marching toward the crowd. He heard gunfire, and he, along with the rest of the crowd, began to run. He had seen other demonstrations, but this was different—the police had new orders and lives were in jeopardy. He got to the American Embassy where he was told it was best for him to leave, to cut his planned trip short. They also told him they could get him out in forty-eight hours. He asked after his artwork. The press club gallery where his art was hanging was shuttered, and the American Embassy officials told him they could be of no help. He went to the Canadian Embassy and was told they would collect his work from the gallery. The Canadians were good for their word. The work was retrieved and brought to the Canadian Embassy where John packaged the twenty-five pieces which he then hand carried onto a train out of Warsaw headed to Świnoujście, a Polish port in the north where he boarded a ship for Sweden, and made his way back to California after visiting American friends in Denmark.

When John and I talked about Poland, we shared the same opinions about the problems wrought by Polish nationalism and the Church, and admiration for Polish courage throughout the years. John and I had a good deal in common—an interest in literature, art, music (the Blues in particular—he had illustrated a book about the American Blues in Poland) -- and we had both been raised Roman Catholic. His father's heritage was Polish, mine, too, in a different sense. Our mothers shared a Celtic background. His interest in Poland, though, had really only bloomed when he met Natalia, and naturally grew exponentially when he went there to show his own work in 1981.

But my connection was different than his. Fueled by my own (as yet unexplored and hidden by my father) Jewish Polish identity, I always veered to my specific agenda--the history of the Jews of Poland, the question of Polish collusion with the Nazis, the then current state of Polish acknowledgement of its responsibility for the destruction of its former and annihilated vital Jewish presence. I was well read on the early and recent history of the Jews of Poland, I knew about the Cossack Bohdan Khmelnytsky 1648 massacre of the Jews in Poland (now modern Ukraine), through to the infamous Kishinev pogrom in 1903, the Shoah and its aftermath, and into the present day. And I had met a Polish friend in California who vehemently denied the existence of Polish anti-semitism. Yet despite our different connections to Poland, we both had the journeyer's instinct, so when John invited me to travel there with him in 1984, I did not hesitate.

It was John who introduced me in 1984 to Poland and the friends he had made in 1981. That was a special opportunity. I did not have the standard tourist's introduction to Poland. Instead, I met individuals who shared their views on the regime, the actions of Solidarity, the trade union that had become the lightning rod for change in Poland. While there I absorbed their ideas about art and music. Yet my desire to know more about the former Jewish presence in Poland was not fed in those conversations. These were educated and enlightened Poles, and though their brows furrowed in empathy at the mention of Polish Jews, they really were not that informed about the past or present Jewish story in Poland.

By 1983 I had met my future husband John, whose family were of Polish origin. Pictured here in Kraków, Poland. Courtesy Balgley Family Archive

John and I went to the Warsaw Ghetto memorial, but I learned that the Poles I was meeting had not ever visited the spot—at least not on purpose. It was as if the "Jewish question" had just evaporated from the daily lives of Poles in the 1980s. Jewish history in Poland was for those Poles a footnote only to Polish history, and to the current siege their government had imposed on them during that time. This disturbed me, but it brought to mind the question of how many educated and progressive Americans focused on the history of slavery and the legacy of racial discrimination in America. There were those who cared, but the subject would not have been on the tips of their tongues when meeting a foreign visitor. Nonetheless, that silence in Poland on the Jewish past was an empty echoing chamber for me that only served to fuel my need to know more, and to know how it was exactly that Poles had forgotten or repressed such a powerful story.

One day John and I were at the Sukiennice in Kraków, the medieval "Cloth Hall" with stalls offering Polish silver and amber jewelry, fabrics and other

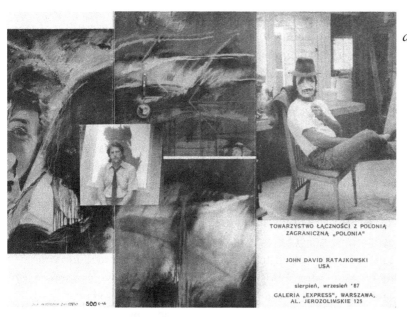

Pamphlet accompanying John's exhibition in Warsaw. Courtesy Balgley Family Archive

souvenir gifts, when I saw a table not in the hall itself, but outside, a cheap card table with a pile of antiques mixed in with some cheap *tchotchkes*. I nearly walked away when in the pile I saw a beautiful silver menorah of the type that had been in the "Precious Legacy" exhibition of Judaica rescued from the homes of annihilated Jews. Buried under some plastic toys, I was stunned to see it. I pulled it from the jumble, and asked the single Pole manning the table, *"Ile to kosztuje?"*—"How much does it cost?" The salesman immediately recognized that my Polish was not native, and eyeing me in an unfriendly manner, replied in his accented English, "Twenty-five dollars." This monetary quote made clear the merchant had a fairly good idea about with whom he was dealing, and his scowl confirmed his distaste. Who knew if he even recognized what he had there? But he straightaway understood that this tourist had no sense of the Polish economy. At that time, twenty-five dollars would have been the equivalent in złoty for a university professor's monthly salary. The man scored hugely when I handed him the cash in dollars. I knew by Polish standards he was fleecing me, and I was only too happy to comply. Today I regard this wondrous menorah as the most precious thing I own. When a fire threatened our Southern California neighborhood some years ago, and there were only minutes to take something from the house, I took the menorah. I use it every Hanukkah and keep it in a place where I and others can see it every day. I think of the hands which held it, the home that sheltered it, and the fact of its survival in a junk heap on a card table in 1984 Poland.

The Fulbright stories (1987–1989)

That was a brief introduction to Poland, and I knew I would have to return there somehow. I got the opportunity when I was awarded a Fulbright Professorship to teach American literature to Polish university students three years later. The Fulbright award is a program of competitive, merit-based grants for international educational exchange founded by United States Senator J. William Fulbright in 1946. The program's stated purpose: to increase mutual understanding between the people of the United States and other countries.

From the very first moment that I was notified of my Fulbright award, it was laden with ambivalence, since my family had never spoken openly of my father's Jewish identity and we had never discussed Polish anti-Semitism. Nevertheless, my father's reaction was not neutral. "Why go to POLAND?" he queried. "Why compliment these people by learning their language and taking your talents THERE? Why not, instead, choose England or France for your Fulbright?" This last suggestion I bristled at since France's Vichy government had openly welcomed and collaborated with the Nazis, but even today escapes the degree of blame leveled at Poland, a country that famously fought the German invasion despite knowing they would be destroyed. "Well," my father

The menorah discovered in a pile of tchotchkes at the Sukiennice Cloth Hall in Kraków, I rescued from oblivion and brought for safekeeping to my home in San Diego. Courtesy Balgley Family Archive

replied, "I can't imagine you would want to go there, but you are young, so maybe you will find something of interest for you."

From my point of view that statement was an ironic understatement. My father's concealment of his Jewishness and thus my own Jewishness was the veil I had lived with my entire life, and it was the need to pull back that veil which sent me to Poland. And another veil moved me, when serious-minded, intelligent Poles I met in America adamantly denied Polish anti-Semitism, blaming the proliferation of that idea on the communist regime's desire to discredit any form of nationalism. In the broadest sense I was going behind a veil, behind a wall, *the* wall, dividing communist from free Europe.

I felt I needed to go to the heart of darkness, the epicenter of Jewish suffering and the suppression of the fact of that suffering to have at least a chance to see what lay behind the vehement disagreements, and the meaning of my own dual identity. I had become highly involved in discussions about Polish anti-Semitism, had heard furious, passionate arguments on both sides, I, the daughter of a Polish Jew who had hidden his origins, I, raised by my mother as a Roman Catholic, who even as a child in my Jewish grandparents' Brooklyn apartment had been powerfully and uncannily drawn to my veiled Jewish half, I was now going to a Catholic country, former home to the largest annihilated Jewish population in the world. Yes, I felt certain I would "find something of interest" living and teaching in Poland. My father wished me luck, but added, "Your mother and I will meet you in Paris or London, but not in Poland."

Ania
Los Angeles, 1987

But the Fulbright began even before I left for Poland. After I learned I was granted the award, I was offered the opportunity to study the Polish language at the University of California, Los Angeles (UCLA) in an eight-week intensive program. It turned out that the program was offered every summer, alternating from an east coast university to a west coast university. I was fortunate: that year it was the west coast, and at UCLA, where I had been teaching, so it was easy for me to arrange to live in the dormitory on campus reserved for all academics going on Fulbrights to Slavic countries studying the language of their assigned country.

We were a curious crowd. Young academics from all over the United States, suddenly living together in an undergrad-style dormitory gave rise to all sorts of peculiarities. For one thing, we had been abruptly demoted from professor to novice and almost none of us had any previous training in the language we were to study, so we were no longer the experts but instead lowly beginners. This suited me fine. I always liked being a student even more than being a teacher—much more exciting and much less responsibility.

Our living conditions underscored our new status. Thrust back to our early days as students, we shared a single room with a roommate and we would walk down the hall to use the communal loo and showers. Again, I liked the simplicity of the arrangement, with no apartment or household to worry about, and no need for an automobile, as our classes were held on campus a few minutes' walk from the dormitory. Unlike teaching, unlike adult life, the assignment was singular and simple: get up at least by 7 a.m to eat the soggy dorm breakfast and sit only with those in your language group. And from day one: speak Polish! Get to the four-hour class with your professor and speak Polish! Return to the dorm for lunch and repeat the breakfast scenario, but this time your teachers will join you, so you cannot cheat and ask for the mustard to be passed in English. As with any beginner, you were invited to make a fool of yourself, and most people understand that any attempt when you are a beginner is a courageous one. Think learning to ride a two-wheeled bicycle. But we were a group of academics, nice enough people, but people so accustomed to defending their academic prowess (with good reason—constant professional review, tenure wars, university politics and low salary), that all combined could over time transform hardworking scholars and teachers into defensive egomaniacs. So began the non-stop criticism of our professor of Polish. We had quizzes every day at the start of class. These were returned to us with typically flunking marks. The professor's point was to keep at it—flunk but learn for next time. The truth was our professor was an immensely talented speaker of Polish and Russian, though she was an American. A Polish friend of mine who met her later outside the classroom told me that the professor's Polish was indistinguishable from a native speaker's. Poor woman. What a bunch of brats she inherited. My fellow students were not willing to extend to her any professional courtesy, and the complaints they voiced were exactly the clichéd ones our own students would register against us. If the complaint was not a cliché, then it was wrapped in the language of pedagogical theory and attempted to damn her with a more sophisticated and supposedly erudite criticism. The *ad hominem* attack was not resisted, so her hairstyle came under discussion. The point was we were all struggling. It was grueling work, and we had grown unaccustomed to the rigor and failure the neophyte must endure.

There was one student in the class who had Russian, and so she was ahead of the game in comparison to the rest of us. She could understand and answer quickly in class, and she mastered the grammar efficiently enough to score well on our quizzes. It happened she was my roommate, and I admired and coveted her success. However, I was soon to learn that what we saw in class was merely a sliver of her identity. She explained she was from the northeast United States, but her English had an odd sound to it—perfectly grammatical, properly pronounced, but absolutely from nowhere a native American speaker could recognize. At all hours, she would leave our room, and from time to time if I happened to be headed to the lobby of the dormitory, as I came down the old wide burnished curving staircase, I would be surprised to see her locked into a phone booth on one of the landings, talking animatedly. True, there were other students in the program—one studying Serbo-Croatian—who did not rush to cover up the fact that he had studied at the Monterey School of Languages as part of his CIA training. I really did not want to give in to the notion that my roommate was a Russian spy, but she became stranger and stranger as the eight weeks went on. It was possible to lock the closet assigned to us, but no one ever did. This was before computers, so there was little we had that someone else might want. But my roommate always ceremoniously locked her closet upon leaving our room. I never knew what became of her—it was not clear to what Polish city she had been assigned, and no one in the program whom I knew had ever learned what she did after the language program finished. However, at least five or more years later, a friend of mine from San Diego, an American attorney who had a Latvian background, reported to me that he and his wife had been touring Russia, and through getting to know their guide better, it was, amazingly, discovered that this person had been my roommate at the UCLA Polish language program. I wonder today if she had been an earlier version of the convicted Russian agent Maria Butina.

But before the language classes even began, we future Fulbrighters were first met by native Polish speakers, most recent emigres to the United States living in California. Many of those people were then teachers of language and had been employed to address us about Polish culture and history. I was lucky enough to be assigned to Ms. Ania Goldblum. My first visual impression of her was of a willowy honey-colored reed—her dark gold hair fine and silky falling out of a demure chignon, soft bangs falling across her forehead and a demure dress, drapey but fashionable. Her eyes occupied most of the space of her heart-shaped face—dark and wide set. Her manner mimicked her appearance: soft-spoken, unobtrusive, yet poised and confident. Her English was excellent, but charmingly accented—she was foreign in all the interesting ways in my mind. She stood in front of our assembled group and rather than formally begin her lecture on Polish culture with a teacherly voice, instead she moved her eyes about the room without a word and quietly brought us to attention. She was unremittingly elegant. Because I am now so familiar with Poland's history and culture, I cannot recall the specific content of the lecture. I only knew then that her very manner anticipated the charm of what I was to experience in Poland.

Months, later, living in Poland, I was to think of her again and again, reminded of her by some small detail like the beautiful old silver on Polish dining tables, or the smell of dill in Polish homes, or the formal manners of even a taxicab driver. She embodied what I later found so attractive in Poland. But my memory of meeting her that day is marked by something more profound which I have never been able to forget and which haunted me then and continues to do so now.

After her lecture and the following question and answer discussion period, I had a chance to speak to her on my own. She had talked about Polish pronunciation and used Polish surnames as some examples. I asked her about her own surname which could not serve as an example for Polish pronunciation. I recognized it as German at first, and then realized that it must be Jewish. With pleasant anticipation I approached Ms. Goldblum and said, "Your surname—lovely—I think it must be Jewish?" I cannot now recall if I added "like mine," but I do remember that the impulse was in me to assure her it was a friendly, warm question. When her already huge eyes opened even wider and complexion blushed so deeply, I was stunned: she was unmistakably both embarrassed and afraid. I hardly knew how to react. Apology came to mind, but that could not have been right, as I was asking out of admiration and interest. Her reaction caught me entirely off guard. Today as I recall the incident, I realize how naïve I was about the "Jewish issue" in Poland. My own reading and my own history had given me an in-depth, sophisticated, advanced understanding of that "issue," and I was soon to learn how ignorant Poland, the United States and the rest of the world was about the history of Poles and Jews— how the issue had been pushed underground in Poland, and how loaded the entire subject was. I believed I was asking a question of a colleague in this, someone who may not have had a scholarly background in the subject, but even better, a person who had grown up Jewish in Poland after the war. Her facial expression made me understand she was unprepared for such a question, that it was impertinent, even rude. I stood silent for a moment, and then added quietly, "Because my own family is Jewish from Poland and that's the main reason I'm going on the Fulbright."

She slowly nodded and said, "Yes, the name is of Jewish origin." Not "my name," not "is Jewish," or "I am Jewish." I was shocked at her reaction, and even more distressed that I had upset her. Her presentation to us had been so charming and she appeared so innocent and fresh. I felt like I had darkened the optimistic, bright view she had provided about her home country, that I had unnecessarily ruined her experience that day. But if I had, it was my own innocence that caused it. It never occurred to me that she would be ashamed of being Jewish. This was the first of many sharp lessons I was to learn as the time grew short before my departure to Poland.

Beata
San Diego, 1987

In many important ways my trip to Poland to begin my Fulbright assignment was different from my fellow Fulbrighters. For one thing, I had connections with Poles in California who themselves still had relatives and friends in Poland. Through the circle of Polish friends I had in San Diego, I met a Polish woman who had recently moved to San Diego with her two daughters. A single mother recovering from at least one bad marriage, Beata was one of the type I would later come to see frequently on the streets of Warsaw and Kraków-- strikingly attractive, fashionably attired in what can only be described as art— such handcrafted silver jewelry, such hand-painted extra-large scarves tied in crafted drapes, hair a shade of red that would never be mistaken for natural, but that so fitted the palette of the overall effect it seemed absolutely the right color. Trim but not boney or sinewy in the over-tanned California style, these Polish women seemed ageless, not young, particularly, but nor were they old. Age was not part of the quotient of their attractiveness. It was difficult to know whether a woman was "young" or otherwise, and it was not important. These women exuded a sexiness derived from their style. Their appearance made a statement about their capabilities and their experience, and that made for an intrigue that was unmistakable.

Beata was all of that. Meeting her in the California beach community where she had come fresh from Warsaw made the contrast between her mode of style and the Americans around her even stronger. Her apartment was one of the sort a Californian would select for its sunniness and proximity to the beach. But she shut all that out. Her place had the feel of a haute museum or gallery. She had painted the walls a rich tasteful slate gray and the windows were covered with angular black vertical blinds which not only kept the outside out, but created the atmosphere inside of an affluent, chic nightclub for artists. The artwork on the dark gray walls underscored this impression: a mix of fine antique Polish tapestries and large modernist abstract paintings all expertly lit demonstrated her taste and experience. Add to that the fact that Beata was a talented and trained chef. Once my eyes adjusted to the dark of her apartment, I would typically see a linen-covered table laden with dish after dish of culinary art. There were always the Polish-style offerings: half a dozen varieties of marinated mushrooms, herring, smoked salmon, snails, and cold vodka in a crystal container stuffed in a cut glass ice bucket, and excellent dark bread. But there was also the sushi she had learned to make in California, the oysters on the half shell, the champagne. She would urge us to eat, eat, eat, but I never saw her partake of her own creations. Instead she would stand to the side of her table, and like the table, dressed exquisitely, both in muted khaki linen and black, leaning slightly against a wall, one arm bent at the elbow wrapped around her waist, the other holding a cigarette. Though she would take a vodka with her company, I never saw her eat even a morsel. It was disconcerting and worrying, but we friends got used to it. An inescapable but fundamental truth about Beata was that she was unhappy. Whether this came from a disposition that would have been depressed no matter the circumstances, or whether her melancholy was a result of truly unfortunate and sad events in her life, it was hard to tell, and probably irrelevant. We friends just knew we loved her and wanted to help in any way we could. We always wondered and worried about how she could afford to entertain so expensively. We would try to dissuade her from cooking, but it was of no use. One day Beata confided in me that she needed to find work, and her hope was that she could open a dress shop. But she was short on funds, and did not know how she could do it. As it turned out, John lent her a sizeable sum of money to rent a space in a fashionable location near her home in San Diego where European-style women's clothing might have a clientele. John even constructed and physically installed a beautiful hardwood floor in the shop. I guess the shop got on for a while, but before we knew it, Beata was talking about moving, maybe back to Poland or maybe to Chicago where Polish friends had settled.

She did move and promised to write. But she disappeared with the IOU to John, the artist who had helped her, and as we came to know later on, others of our friends, as well. But before she disappeared, knowing I was going to live in Poland, Beata told me she had alerted her mother who lived in Warsaw that I was coming, and that this elderly woman was "waiting to help" me, as she put it. I was doubtful. I had no intention of wanting to intrude on this old person nor accept any return favors. But Beata insisted. She had been in contact with her mother and the lady expected me when I arrived in Warsaw for the first part of my Fulbright before I moved to the Silesian part of the country where I would be teaching. I reasoned that in any case, it would be interesting to meet the mother, and a visit to her might even be a kindness since her own daughter was far away.

Pani Zofia
Warsaw, 1987

I cannot say what I was expecting, but Beata's mother was not it. I had been given her address before I left California for Poland and told that she knew I would be coming to see her when I arrived. A phone call from me was out of the question, as she knew no English, and the Polish I had would not be sufficient to communicate with an elderly person by phone. Warsaw would be my first destination in Poland, before the requisite Kraków orientation for Fulbrighters and the final move to our assigned cities.

I found *Pani* ("Madame" in Polish, the respectful and proper address for an older person or the formality on meeting someone initially) Zofia's address on a street known for its elite status: Aleje Uzjadowskie, in an elegant pre-war building near several embassies, including the American one. I knew that part of Warsaw had been spared as the Nazi high command used those apartments for their living quarters during the occupation of the city. The façade of the building was decorated with various stylized figures, very beautiful, and in contrast, riddled in places with bullet holes. Two huge statues, male nudes in the mode of Atlas, stood on each side of the wide entry way. I walked through a curved and deep entrance to an interior courtyard in which stood a single ancient tree, the perimeter of which was surrounded by a low wrought iron fence for protection and aesthetics. Consisting of two floors only, the building's six or more apartments formed a "U" around this centerpiece, with floor to ceiling windows and balconies facing inward. Tilting my head back, I could see the sky as I stood in the center. Even with this display of old and lovely architectural design, the place showed its hard history: openings to stairways that began from this center had likely had handcrafted doors at one time, but now the entrances were more like low holes in the brickwork, so I had to look for a moment to find them. I had the number of *Pani* Zofia's flat along with the street address, so finding my way to one of these entrances, I encountered a staircase, again, a feature from another era, wide, marble with a fine wooden railing, and again the curving shape. A heavy wooden door on the first floor showed the flat number I had been given. The door was original, and was made of a fine burnished wood, but four newish ugly metal locks had been drilled into its face. The contrast was starkly representative of so much of Warsaw, where the elegant old had broken and was cheaply repaired. There was a buzzer—this looked original as well—and after I used it I had to wait only a minute before the locks of the heavy door were cranked open with alacrity from the inside; I was expected.

My first impression was toughness: steel gray hair cut short, a creased face with alert black eyes buried in a deep overhang of a forehead below a dark brow, a cigarette in her hand, a stance that suggested readiness. A quick nod and grin, at the same time crone-like and girlish, mischievous, wily. I bowed slightly as I greeted her in Polish and extended my hand. Her grip was bracing, a confident no-nonsense handshake. She stepped aside from the doorway and motioned me in with a rapid sweep of her arm. I noticed that her body, though slightly hunched, moved quickly without a trace of old age. It took only seconds to realize *Pani* Zofia was a force. I was soon to learn just how accurate this first impression had been.

The flat was an artifact, an art piece from *Stara Kochana Warszawa* (dear, old Warsaw), the phrase used by people who had known the city in its prime), that civilized and cultured Warsaw where droskeys carried people to theatres, concerts and ballet, where educated, cosmopolitan gentile Poles mingled with their assimilated Jewish friends. There were several rooms adjoining one another with large arched doorways, crème walls, high ceilings adorned with handcrafted carved plaster designs, thick carpets over fine wood parquet floors, a piano, paintings, an etched crystal chandelier, antique furnishings. In short, a picture of what elite Warsaw looked like on the inside before the war. It was undeniably romantic.

Pani Zofia showed me through the flat but did not seem particularly impressed by its grandeur and I could see she had lived there a long while. Within moments of the tour, she signaled me to sit at the dining room table. The large wooden table was covered with a lace tablecloth and stood before one of the floor to ceiling windows covered with diaphanous curtains. Thick, dark green velvet drapes hung at the edges of the transparent ones with long wooden poles to pull across the window if desired. We were managing to communicate entirely in Polish. With just brief experimentation, I quickly realized she understood not a word of English, and so hobbled as I was with my neophyte Polish (and vaguely ashamed—in her presence and in these surrounding, I felt like the least I could do was to speak properly), we were able to follow one another. She brought out an absurd amount and variety of foods: sausage, two kinds of ham, beef, horseradish, mustard, pickles, fresh bread, and did not sit down to partake with me, but rather stood watching me while smoking a cigarette, a smile on her face. I could not help but conjure the image of her daughter doing the same in California. The food was delicious. When I indicated I was finished, she asked me, *"Co chcesz zjeść?"* ("What do you want to eat?") presenting me with the choice of pork chops or roasted chicken or both. Even though I demurred, she served me a plate with half the chicken, steaming fragrant potatoes with fresh dill, and marinated beets. It made no sense to refuse, and in truth, the food was so tempting, I indulged myself, and her. She was clearly pleased that I was not a foolish American girl who did not eat enough.

I had supposed we would share the flat for the brief time I was to be in Warsaw, but after the meal, she presented me with keys—a heavy ring with a long, old-fashioned key for the main (and I guessed, the original) lock, and three smaller ones for the newer locks. She explained I could stay there as long as I liked, and at any time I returned to Warsaw from my future teaching assignment in the south of the country, the flat was mine to use. But, I queried, "Won't you be here?"

"No, I live across the city in another flat." I was flabbergasted. I realized I understood essentially nothing about this arrangement, except perhaps that John's beneficence to *Pani* Zofia's daughter had carried weight, and that I would have to just get used to surprises.

The keys to Pani Zofia's apartment in Warsaw, including keys for both old and new locks. Courtesy Balgley Family Archive

And there were surprises: some days later, I had been entertained in the homes of Poles who were friends of John's and to whom I had been introduced in Warsaw in 1984. Despite shortages and ration cards and long lines for food, when I dined at their homes—small apartments in Soviet-style block buildings—where they amazingly managed to convert a bedroom, for example, into a comfortable sitting room with a dining table, these Poles offered wine they had saved for special occasions, plenty of good food which without doubt had cost them a great deal of time, effort and expense. I wanted to reciprocate and treating them to a dinner in a restaurant was no comparison to the personal warmth I had experienced in their homes, so I thought that with a bit of research I could prepare a meal for them and have them to *Pani* Zofia's flat.

I first asked *Pani* Zofia for her permission to entertain my friends at the flat, and invited her to join us. I explained what I had in mind—a small dinner for a few friends. As soon as she caught my drift, she said, "Oczywiście!" Polish for "Of course!" a phrase I later realized was used by Poles to mean, "but naturally, how silly you would think otherwise!" I asked her for a suggestion of where I could purchase some meat. I did not realize what I was in for. She stubbed out her cigarette, threw on her coat, and giving me a gentle push, indicated we would go, yes, now, to "arrange" things. ("Arrange" in Poland at that time had several layers of connotation from the innocent simply "to plan" to "we'll manage with some work," to the darker implication "this will happen no matter who we need to bribe.") I had learned that *Pani* Zofia had been a taxi driver after the war in demolished Warsaw; the photographs of the city in ruins are well known, and it was nearly impossible to imagine how someone would drive in those conditions. But she had. And I pictured a younger version of her, hands on the wheel, cigarette in mouth, a permanent scowl on her otherwise impassive face, driving people and cargo through the destroyed streets and rubble of her beloved city. At that moment, she moved me quickly down the stairs to her car which was always parked in the same spot directly in front of the building. Parking was not easy in Warsaw, and I knew she must have "arranged" that this be her permanent parking spot. I never saw another car in that place at any time day or night. She still drove like the taxi driver she had been, eyes squinted, cigarette on lip, maneuvering her car, a Soviet-made *Lada*, large and heavy, with skill, but mostly through speed, intimidation, and bravery. She did not blink when we hit potholes in the street as her foot stayed on the accelerator no matter what. We plowed through the streets in a whirl. I could not even keep track of where we were headed since she took so many sudden turns and shortcuts.

At last we arrived at a large open air market. Hunched over in her characteristic posture, she walked as quickly as a teenager among the stalls with me in tow, trying to keep up. It soon became clear that she had a particular destination in mind—a meat stall, where the attendant in his bloody white apron obviously knew her. They did not greet each other, but rather he first looked from side to side, and then reaching under the counter of displayed cuts of meats, pulled out the thickest and best cut of meat I had seen in a market since my arrival to Poland. She grunted affirmatively, and he quickly wrapped the meat for her as she handed him złoty, the amount of which I could not see, so rapidly did the exchange take place. To my objections that I had intended to make the purchases for the party, she simply waved her hand and kept trudging through the market where for whatever else she wanted to buy, a similar sort of transaction took place. I was uncomfortable—both with her paying, but also that it now appeared anything I might ask her about, she felt obligated to provide. I had been a friend of her daughter's; I had helped her daughter some, but whatever Beata had communicated to her mother, it was now clear that my wish was her mother's command. I knew it was pointless to continue to object, so I followed along, feeling wrongly privileged in this struggling society.

The market experience might have been enough, but returning to the flat, *Pani* Zofia made it clear that I was not to cook anything—the meal would be prepared and I was to stay out of the way. I found myself regretting I had mentioned anything to her about entertaining a few friends. These favors were not delivered gently or kindly; quite the contrary: there was a brusqueness to her insistence that I be waited on hand and foot. Whether this came from contempt for Americans, or whether this was how she delivered all her favors to everyone, I was at a loss to know.

That night when my guests arrived, the dining table had been set, but I noticed that there was one place setting missing. Querying *Pani* Zofia, she let me know she herself would not be dining with us. Again, just like Beata, she would stand to the side and observe her guests indulge in the food she had prepared. Not the most genial scenario, but still I breathed a sigh of relief: I would be able to host my guests and serve them the meal I had been forbidden to help prepare. My guests arrived, bringing flowers and wine, typical of their consistent generosity. I thought *Pani* Zofia would excuse herself after introductions, but no, she ushered all of us, including me, to the table, and in a moment of sickening realization, I saw that *Pani* Zofia intended to be our "server for the night." My guests were nonplussed. Here was an old lady acting as waitress, quite the contrary scenario of Polish respectful attitudes towards the elderly. That was bad enough, but then when she brought out platters of hard to come by meat, and in such excess, we were all embarrassed. The evening was anything but the warm, personal gathering I had intended. Everything—from the opulence of the flat itself to the food—was such that it made my guests feel out of place, aware of the disparity between their lives and this setting. It was like an official dinner at the palace of royalty you did not particularly like. The party, it suddenly dawned on me in another wave of sickness, was for *Pani* Zofia, an opportunity to display her power and wealth. Even as I saw this truth, I was certainly not in a position to blame her. Behind that creased face and those black eyes, who could guess which part of history compelled her to behave like this? It was possible she had no idea how gauche her behavior was. I had asked her for help and I got it in spades. Like my guests, I sat like an obedient child and ate the food she presented like gilded treasures on a silver platter. And like such gold treasure, all of it, the food, the night, the situation, was difficult to swallow.

This preliminary time in Warsaw was coming to an end. The orientation for Fulbright professors was soon to begin in Kraków, and I needed to get there in time to move into the dormitories at Jagiellonian University, which were reserved for American Fulbrighters. I planned on taking the train south. It would be a bit of a challenge, primarily because I needed to take the year worth of luggage I had brought to Poland with me. I explained to *Pani* Zofia that I would be leaving soon, and why. Fortunately, I had already booked my ticket on the train, so when she indicated she would see to that, I was able to tell her I had already taken care of it. Maybe I rose a tiny bit in her estimation. I wasn't as helpless as she thought.

Early in the morning I was to depart the flat for *Warszawa Centralna* to board my train. *Pani* Zofia uncharacteristically spent the night at the flat with me, and I soon learned that she would not hear of me taking a taxi to the train station, but that she herself would be driving me there. When it came time to move my luggage downstairs, she insisted on doing it. Imagine my discomfort, an elderly person schlepping the heavy bags, and me, princess-like, walking unburdened behind her. After she had carried down my luggage, the same scenario took place as she threw open the trunk of her car. Moving me aside, she hefted the bags herself. This cannot go on, I thought, and told her so. Cigarette dangling from her bottom lip, eyes squinted, she looked over at me in the front seat and smiled. Was this authentic maternal kindness or was it just another victory over me, again?

She revved her vehicle's engine and we tore through the streets of Warsaw. When we arrived at the station, without a moment's hesitation, she drove up on the sidewalk and parked, getting as close to the station as possible. As it turned out, *Warszawa Centralna* was teeming that morning; the crowd was so dense, it was difficult to just walk normally, much less tow bags. It became clear quickly that without her, it would have taken me much longer to figure out what platform I should go to. There was no "information booth," and the lines at the windows to purchase tickets wound around the station's central lobby endlessly. *Pani* Zofia got me and my bags down some stairs to the right platform next to the train I was to board. We saw instantly that the train was a nightmare, packed solidly with people standing in the aisles, so I reasoned I should have arrived earlier. I began to thank her and prepared to take my leave and hurl myself into the mob, when she grabbed my arm, and said "*Czekaj!*" ("Wait!"). Suddenly, seemingly out of nowhere, *Pani* Zofia had conjured a tall uniformed train employee. He was already bowing and nodding to her. He was immediately in her employ, although I had not seen any money change hands. It was like the day at the market with the meat. Alright, I thought, I can use some help getting my bags on the train. But no, that was not her plan. The train officer gestured from the platform outside the train through the window to a group of people inside the train and seated in a compartment. I could not imagine what was about to transpire. The group began to rise to its feet and then the officer grabbed my bags, took my arm, and led me to the compartment. I watched, stunned and open-mouthed as the train officer communicated to the group that they must move out of their seats. It turned out the group was a young family with children. I stood idiotically outside the compartment as the family filed out; they registered no complaint nor gave me or the officer dirty looks, but rather appeared resigned and did as they were told. I turned to the officer to protest, but he had already barged in, placed my bags on seats that would normally be for passengers, and extending an arm out into the aisle, gently took my arms and bowing again, indicated I would sit in the seat across from my bags: this compartment would be solely mine. All this was watched by *Pani* Zofia in her black overcoat just outside the window, smoking her cigarette as usual, with her characteristic squint. The officer had departed the compartment. I was still standing, and I looked at her through the window and shook my head, "No." She just rocked on her knees a bit, and then smiling commanded, "*Siedź*" ("Sit"). For a moment, she spread her arms to the front and sides of her body and without words indicated to me "Relax, enjoy, be comfortable." I fell back on to the seat, once again the obedient child, and suffered an embarrassment and shame the degree to which I have never known since.

In later months, when I would visit Warsaw from my isolated and bleak environment in Silesia, I would come by night train usually on a Friday after a teaching week. One night, weary from the week's work and the train travel, I reached the flat and made myself a very hot bath in the old-style large tub. Caught up in my daily responsibilities at the institute where I taught, I think now I failed to realize the wear and tear on the body and mind. Going to Warsaw was a respite. I could walk to restaurants, visit the American Embassy's commissary to get items nowhere else available, and walk the lovely parks. As I sank into the steaming tub, I heard the keys in the locks at the door, and for a moment startled, I realized it had to be *Pani* Zofia—no one else would have all the requisite keys. I wondered what brought her on a dark, rainy night to the flat. Walking towards the bathroom, she said she thought I might be there and wanted to say hello. She had never been unkind to me, but as I say, her favors always seemed delivered by obligation rather than for pleasure. But that night she came into the bathroom and seeing me in the bubbles, suddenly bent down on one knee and taking up a loofah and soap, proceeded to wash my back. I laughed, not knowing how else to respond. She just smiled at me and continued with her work, and I thought how lonely she must be, and how for this moment, it seemed like I was the daughter she once bathed now far away in California. I relaxed and enjoyed it myself. *Pani* Zofia had even put out her cigarette.

On another occasion when I visited for a weekend in Warsaw, *Pani* Zofia and I were watching television together at the flat. The program concerned the Warsaw Uprising. She glanced over at me as we watched. She pointed to the television set and lifting up her sweater, showed me a line of circular scars stretching across her back and side. She explained: "This is from bullets. I was in the streets and part of the Underground. I was captured. It was discovered I was pregnant. I told the Germans the father was a Nazi officer, so they didn't execute me. I lied, of course. I was smuggled out by the Polish Underground. The real father was killed in the Uprising." I wanted to ask dozens of questions, but it did not seem right at that moment. I only nodded and said, "*Byłaś odważna*" ("You were brave").

I never queried her about her view on Polish Jews; to be honest, I imagined what I might hear, and I did not want to hear it. It was enough that at every turn in my teaching and living away from Warsaw, I confronted the issue. Maybe she would have surprised me with her attitudes. I knew that during the Warsaw Uprising the Polish Underground had freed Polish Jews from a Nazi concentration camp in the city. Still, I stayed away from the topic with her. But every now and then, she would comment about a personality on television, and gesturing at the television, pronounce "*pedał*" (the Polish pejorative for homosexual—"fag"). I had no energy or heart to take on any additional prejudices she might have had.

In the dormitory
A guide, Mike, Judith, Pan Jakubowicz and Father Jimmy
Kraków, 1987

I made it to Kraków on that train, managed to get my luggage and myself to the dormitory where I would live with my American colleagues until we all would disperse to the various cities to take up our teaching posts.

The dormitories had been designed for students at Jagiellonian University; we were only there in August temporarily when the regular student inhabitants were at home over the summer break. I was reminded of my stay at the dorm at the University of California, Los Angeles when I was studying Polish language—again, such accommodation returned me to adolescence—which had its plusses and minuses as at UCLA: shared bedrooms and collective bathrooms down the hall, institutional meals, and so on. The difference between the UCLA and Jagiellonian dorms were just those between standard Polish and American dwellings of any kind: shortage of or complete absence of hot water; equipment that was continually under repair—like the elevators which were out of order and meant climbing many flights of stairs. I had brought with me from the United States homemade tapes of favorite music I knew I would enjoy having, and thinking that I might have use of such in the "American Culture" class I was told I would be teaching. Our rooms at the dorm had locks and keys, but within two days of my arrival, all my tapes had been stolen from my room. There had been no breaking and entering; someone likely in charge at the dorm with another key had entered and helped themselves. It was a loss, but it was not a major one, and I was not going to allow that early problem to bother me too much. What did strike me, naturally, was how those "in charge" of our well-being at the dorms were not to be counted upon, and this served to underscore my growing understanding that Polish institutions in general, like the train administration, the police, or as I was soon to learn, university departments, were like the larger regime that ostensibly governed them, and offered no recourse or protection. Indeed the institution *was* the very adversary against which one needed protection. That was not a surprise, since I could expect as much in that country, but that it operated even at the lowly level of the dorm administration, was a bit of a wake-up call. We were assigned guides of a sort, individuals who accompanied us on "field trips," and to whom we could go with questions and for assistance as needed.

One of those was a particularly intriguing young woman. Her demeanor and general personal style set her apart from the other guides and Poles I had socialized with up to that time. Instead of the openly warm behavior typical of Poles I had met, her style was sarcastic, even acerbic. She always wore a smile, but it was a sly smile, and it was not possible to tell if it was also a mocking smile when we would approach her with questions. She was dark-eyed and olive-skinned with a shining fringe of black hair. Slim and pretty, her dark looks set her apart from the other guides. When I told her my tapes had been stolen, her first reaction was a knowing grimace with a thumb gesturing towards the dorm reception below. There was no doubt in her mind that someone working there had stolen the music. She offered to make signs written in Polish to post in the dormitory asking for the tapes to be returned with no questions asked. I was surprised she bothered with this, and I saw that despite her outward appearance of indifference, she would help when she deemed the problem worthwhile. We sat at a table together while she printed the signs in Polish, and as she finished, she looked up at me with that same slyness, and smirking said, "Let's add 'May God Bless You'—that'll get 'em."

With that inclusion, she implied she was targeting the guilty consciences of Catholic Poles—and with her 'em, she set herself apart from "them." Very odd, very unusual—I liked her for it. One of us, an American Fulbrighter finishing his studies for the priesthood, suggested she worked for the Party and was "probably Jewish and hiding it." The other Fulbrighters speculated that she was Roma or Jewish, and her mocking attitude came from what bitterness she may have experienced being a member of either of those persecuted minorities in Poland. I had wondered this myself. When I first saw her, I thought, what a lovely Jewish face, and privately hoped that maybe I was right about her "origins," as Jewishness was referred to in Poland. But when I told her I had visited a synagogue in Kraków one day, the smirk returned to her face, and this time pointing her index finger straight up, remarked, "Don't the women have to sit up there? I think I saw that one time."

My thought: Good point! Yes, discriminatory, misogynist, even. She is aware. And she "saw this one time," so perhaps the student priest was right: she is Jewish and as unimpressed by Judaism as she seemed to be by Polish Catholicism.

Whatever the case, I liked her more and more, and found myself in conversation with her regularly. I told her that my father was Jewish and born in Poland, that I had been raised Catholic by my Catholic mother, and that my father had eschewed all connection to his Jewish identity. I mentioned that the only thing my father had shared with me about his shtetl was his memory of a beautiful flowering tree—pink and white. She listened with interest but did not comment at length. She told me she had a young daughter and a husband—something I would not have guessed as she looked so young and student-like.

One day she asked me if I would like to go with her and her husband for an afternoon, she could show me the kind of tree my father had told me about. I was flattered to be invited and accepted at once.

She and her husband collected me from the dorm on a Sunday—a day off for the guides. He was a tall nice-looking, soft-spoken fellow—no trace of satire in his manner. They had a small Polski Fiat usually meant only for two people, but they explained it was no problem, and insisted on giving me the passenger seat in front as their guest, while she squinched in behind the front passenger seat into what was just a cramped non-seat of a place. Off we went, her husband folding himself down to fit in the driver's seat, and me in the privileged comfort of the front passenger seat.

They took me to one of the famous Kraków Mounds. There are four of these in the city, two "modern ones," Kościuszko Mound, about 1,000 feet above sea level and completed in November 1823 by volunteers to the height of 112 feet. Inside the mound there are urns of soil from all the battlefields in Poland and in America where Kościuszko fought on the side of the American forces during the Revolutionary War. Considered a hero also in America, there is a published volume of letters between Tadeusz Kośiuszko and Thomas Jefferson. The second "modern mound" completed in 1937 is Piłsudski's Mound built to honor Józef Piłsudski, the chief of state of Poland, and eventually its prime minister during the halcyon period beginning in 1918 when Poland became the Second Polish Republic after over a century of the 1795 Partitions of Poland by Russia, Prussia and Austria. The two other mounds, Krakus and Wanda, are prehistoric mounds, the first to honor Kraków's mythical founder King Krakus, the second, the "Wanda Mound," reputed grave of Krakus' daughter. I suggested we go to the Krakus Mound, as I knew more about the history of Kościuszko and Piłsudski than I did about the legendary Krakus. We drove to the Podgórze district of Kraków and climbed Lasota Hill to the Krakus Mound. The initial purpose of Krakus's Mound is not clear. Artifacts found in the 1930s date from the eighth century. Other theorists claim the mound is older, dating from the second to the first century BCE, and suggest Celtic origins. A myth in the city says that on King Krakus's death, mourners came to the site with sleeves packed with sand and dirt to build the mountain that would see over the kingdom as King Krakus had done. Other researchers claim that Krakus Mound, like other ancient structures, served astronomical purposes. I learned from my friends that if you stand on Krakus Mound looking towards Wanda Mound at sunrise on the morning of a certain Celtic feast day, you can see the sunrise directly over Wanda Mound. As we climbed to the mound, my friend pointed me to a kasdan tree—a horse chestnut, "This is likely the kind of tree your father remembers from his village." I was all at once struck by the image of my father as a little boy standing before the glorious flowering tree amid the everyday gray of his shtetl, going to the tree to say goodbye as the family prepares to leave forever. He had told me later that it was the only thing there to which he felt an attachment.

It was a lovely sunny but cool day. The three of us walked around the green mounds and chatted. I have a photo of them from that day. The smile on her face is anything but sarcastic. She and her husband warmly embrace, and I thought to myself about the difference between private and public life in Poland. Interactions among people in Polish institutions represent nothing of the actual, true personalities of individual lives.

The projected stay for my Fulbright group in the Kraków dormitory was ten days. We took all our meals together at a cafeteria across the street from the dormitory, and during the mornings attended lectures in English on Polish history, literature, economics, and politics, given by Jagiellonian faculty. These were consistently excellent. As adult students, living, eating and learning together, I got to know some of my Fulbright colleagues quite well. One of them was a soft-spoken Jewish American from Philadelphia. Mike had been in Poland longer than any of us, having studied there as a graduate student some years before winning the Fulbright. He was engaged to a Polish woman and spoke Polish fluently. He told me how some months previously he had been in a Kraków nightclub where he was mistaken for an Arab, and after being thrown out into the street, and attacked by several Poles, he had escaped with some not insignificant injuries. He could now laugh a little about the irony of the situation: a Jew beaten by Poles who took him for an Arab. He shook his head, and said, "You can't win."

Another of our group, Judith, was a linguistics professor at the University of Pennsylvania. Her father, now living in California, was a German Jew and a Holocaust survivor. Judith was brilliant; in our Polish language class at UCLA she had picked up the language seemingly without effort and was understanding and answering our instructor quite fluently while the rest of us were still flunking our tests. She was also great company, quick-witted and funny. She never came across to anyone as superior, though as far as intellect went, she certainly was. Mike and Judith knew that I was half-Jewish and first generation, and the three of us noted how little mention there was of Jewish Poland in the lectures we were hearing. Mike knew Kraków reasonably well, and after having decided we wanted to see what we could of what remnants remained of Jewish life in Kraków, we broke one afternoon from the larger group and with Mike, as our guide, set off on foot.

Mike led Judith and me to Kazimierz, the former Jewish section of Kraków. Reminiscent of the "bad part of town" in any city, the rundown, ramshackle, decaying streets and the impoverished inhabitants were a stunning contrast to the Sukiennice, the show place part of the medieval city just a quick walk away. He showed us two synagogues in close proximity to one another, both closed up, and with no visible entrance since foliage had covered over their facades. At one site blocked by branches, we could just see a window in the shape of the Star of David and the window was broken. We climbed through brambles and overgrown grasses under a wire fence to see a Jewish cemetery, the tombstones ("*matsevot*") of which appeared to have become part of the natural landscape, so enmeshed had they become with the wild vegetation that grew there. Everywhere there was neglect. In the streets, elderly, poor people, walked, many with canes and bent over; the entire scene had the look of a photograph from another century. Some apartment windows were open and we could see some younger Poles sitting at the sills, clearly the poor of the city. We walked down a central street that opened on to a plaza (or plac) towards a stone wall where some men stood. That was the Remah Synagogue, first completed in 1557, a Renaissance-style structure named after Rabbi Moses Isserles who lived from 1525 to 1572. The synagogue took on its name as the Hebrew acronym for the rabbis's name, ReMA and pronounced in Polish as Remu.

There is some dispute about the origins of the synagogue, as one tradition claims that Israel ben Josef, the grandson of Moshe Auerbach of Regensburg, founded the synagogue for his son Moshe Isserles. Isserles was considered brilliant in his youth, and perhaps this is what made him a candidate to be named for the synagogue, but on the fountain table of the synagogue, there lies this inscription:"Husband, Reb Israel, son of Josef of blessed memory, bound in strength, to the glory of the Eternal One, and of his wife Malka, daughter of Eleazar, may her soul be bound up in the portion of life, built this synagogue, the house of the Lord, from her bequest. Lord restore the treasure of Israel." Another version holds that Rabbi Isserles founded the synagogue to honor his first wife who died at 20.

Kazimierz itself had been a Jewish community since the fifteenth century, moved from Kraków's Old Town after a fire in 1495. Although the foundation tablet states that the synagogue was built in 1553, permission had not been granted until 1556, and this after many years of obstruction by the Catholic Church. The earlier date on the foundation tablet may thus refer to the year when this permission was granted, not when construction began. Like the earliest synagogues in Poland, it is likely that the original structure was wooden and was destroyed by a fire in 1557. With new permission granted, a Renaissance-style building was constructed. Improvements were made throughout the centuries, and the building was restored in 1933. The Nazis assumed control of the synagogue during the Holocaust and stole the ceremonial objects from the interior, as well as the bimah or altar, and used the space to store firefighting equipment. Somehow the building itself escaped destruction, and in 1957 the interior was restored to a version of its pre-war look.

We stopped to talk to the men who stood there with a seeming sense of proprietorship. One of the men was Pan Jakubowicz, a man in his 60s, silver-haired, distinguished looking, strongly built and hale in his own way. He explained that he was the head of the Jewish community in Kazimierz and invited us to follow him behind the wall to the entrance of the synagogue. Here was a ghostly atmosphere, formerly beautiful books destroyed from water damage. It was as if time had stopped somehow—the quiet that follows catastrophe. He gestured and shrugged, but there was a dignity in his style. We were only able to glance at the restored interior, but even there, despite the work that had been done in the last three decades, there was an overwhelming sense of loss and abandonment. He invited us to come back, and gave us his card, indicating that we should come to the address printed there. The three of us had to get back to the dorms for our required presence at the requisite collective dinner, but we agreed that we would go to the address in a few days. We headed back towards the dormitory, and it seemed, back to the present century.

Remuh synagogue and cemetery, dating from the sixteenth century, in the centre of Kraków. Courtesy Balgley Family Archive

Top: Ancient gravestones lean forward in the crowded Remuh Cemetery in central Kraków. Courtesy Balgley Family Archive

Bottom: The neighboring "Old Synagogue" on same platz as Remuh. Courtesy Balgley Family Archive

The young American priest who was among our group living at the dormitory had made a unique impression on the rest of us. A Midwesterner, his soft-spoken way and gentle manner gave him the air of knowing much more than he said—an old man's wisdom in the body of a youthful and handsome young man. People found that they opened up to him about their personal lives without really knowing why, and without being cognizant of anything in particular he had said that made them confide in him. As we all got to know each other better, more than one person remarked that after a conversation with him, one came away knowing very little about him. It was true, he rarely offered information about himself, and so in addition to this inexplicable readiness to confide in him, there was also an atmosphere of mystery around him. Though it had not struck me on meeting him, a number of people in our group thought the priest and I were related, that I was his sister, as apparently we physically resembled each other. Once that was commented upon, I could see the resemblance, though I never once felt that I shared anything like the impression he made on everyone. If priests are ideally endowed with the quality of lifting people up, of bestowing peace and forgiveness, of understanding things before they are explained, then he, even in his jeans and pullover sweater, was priest-like. All of us remarked that in his presence we felt a strange peacefulness.

One evening he and I were chatting and we laughed at the group's supposition that we were brother and sister. He said, "Well, you know, yes, you did remind me of my sister when I met you," and reaching for his wallet took out a photograph of her to show me. Gazing at the photograph he slowly shook his head and spoke of her in melancholy terms; she had had hopes of finishing school and doing important work, but had married early and badly, had three children, and was now a single mother back in St. Louis where the family was from. She had of necessity, given up her dreams of a different future. He seemed genuinely and deeply sad about his sister. I remember thinking that she was still young and her life could change, but there was a definite quality of fatalism in the way he told her story, and I had a moment to think of his Catholic training, with its notions of the price of sin, penance, acceptance—a fatalism that would not be denied. If she was to be redeemed, his tone suggested it would not be in this life.

The girl in the photo did resemble me, and as we talked more about our families, we were surprised to learn that both of us were children of a Catholic mother and a Jewish father. He laughed, and said, "Well, maybe we're related after all!" I told him that like him, I had been raised Catholic, and had come to Poland because I felt an incompleteness in my identity—I wanted to know as much as I could learn about Jewishness in Poland, and about my own

Jewish history. I told him how my father's hiding of his Jewish identity had wounded me. Again, here I was confiding, but at least this time it was mutual. He explained that the coming Sunday he would be serving his first Mass in Kraków, and asked if I would I like to come. I was surprised and complimented by the invitation, and I later learned that I had correctly suspected he had told none of our group about this auspicious event. As I say, mysterious, even odd.

The church was a tram ride away from the dormitory; I left early to be sure I would find it and not be late. As it turned out, I found it easily, and arriving early, I entered and took a place in a pew. Within minutes, he materialized seemingly out of nowhere and was at my side in his black cassock assuring me I was in the right place, welcoming me, thanking me for coming. Even if he had appeared priest-like in his jeans, now he was transformed: the standup collar, the long sleeves, the full-length skirt of the black cassock covered all but his hands and face, and the contrast between the dark of his sober vestment and the light of his skin made his face appear radiant, his hands quiet and shining. I looked over to see him greet an older couple, obviously American visitors, but not of our group. He served the Mass but remained in his black vestment, not adding the usual colorful robe and scapular typical of a priest serving Mass on the altar. Perhaps it was to show his neophyte status. Watching him, I became unaware of time passing or even the parts of the Mass. His performance on the altar was like a ballet. His hands moved gracefully like two doves added to the one in the Trinity, rising and ascending with the chalice, his face intermittently hidden as he bowed and knelt, and then reappearing, bright and beatific as he rose. Public as the nature of the Mass is, seeing him here on the altar was like peering into his private world, so solitary and transported was he. I met the American couple after the Mass and we three congratulated him and took our leave. He had apparently already arranged to leave the dormitory before the rest of us (we never knew why), and so after that Mass I never saw him again until many years later in a different place in circumstances the inverse of that day in the church.

My fellow Fulbrighter, Jimmy (center), after he served Mass in a church in Kraków to which he invited me. On the right is an unidentified American visitor who attended the Mass Courtesy Balgley Family Archive

Mike, Judith and I later went to the address on the card Pan Jakubowicz had given us the day we met him at the Remuh Synagogue. When we set out, we were not entirely sure exactly to what sort of place we were going--was it Pan Jakubowicz's home, his office, a Jewish meeting place? We had no idea, but we took with us a bright bouquet of flowers, the sign of appreciation of one's host, traditional in Poland. We wound our way around the small corridors of Kazimierz. The day became darker and the dwellings seemed hunched over, bending towards each other across very narrow streets, forming a kind of dilapidated canopy blocking the sky. After several mistaken stops, we finally found the address—or more accurately, a single doorway with a barely legible number affixed to it. At first we knocked, but conjuring no one, we pushed the door slightly and discovered that it opened onto a tiny vestibule, so small we three could not fit in easily. From there stairs revealed themselves and we climbed them to another doorway. That door swung open to reveal a scene that immediately struck all three of us, since we did not utter a word. There before us was a scene from an old etching or lithograph: the colors gray and brown and black, the subject a dozen or so very elderly or infirm people sitting in groups of twos or threes hunched over a wooden table sitting on benches concentratedly eating. Our entrance distracted them at first, and they eyed us with a mixture of curiosity and suspicion, followed shortly by an indifferent, collective shrug, and went back to their food to which they devoted all their attention. The women wore kerchiefs on their heads, the men caps. All shared the look of suffering endured. Pan Jakubowicz was standing in the room, like a sort of shepherd to the people at the tables. He moved toward us without making a big fuss of our arrival, unlike a typical Polish greeting, and began to explain what this place was. "We make this place to feed the sick and old Jews of Kazimierz. We don't have much, some soup and some bread, but it helps. They can play at chess here, too, if they want." We listened nodding, not wanting to appear intrusive or like rich foreigners slumming. I became aware of the flowers we had brought, our intended gesture of respect and kindness now made ridiculous in this context. The huge and expensive blooms were absurd here, better we had brought food or a monetary donation. We weakly handed the bouquet to Pan Jakubowicz who briefly glanced at it for the worthless offering it was and without expression or comment set it aside. At one point in his explanation of the center's function, he stopped for a moment and looked at Judith, asking "You Jewish?" Almost as if to imply that only then could she empathize, could she care. He must have assumed Mike was Jewish—his was an unmistakable Semitic look (Poles had thought so—only they, to his misfortune, ironically took him for an Arab). Pan Jakubowicz's eyes never rested on me, and as the three of us walked back to the dormitory, both of my companions remarked upon, among other observations, the way Jakubowicz appeared to ignore me, so I realized I had not imagined it. I had felt invisible, and it was uncomfortable, as I had actually been the one in the first place to press our going to the address. Judith and Mike then engaged in a discussion about whether I seemed Jewish or not. It was comical in its own way, their debate, very Jewish itself, not mincing words. I walked along quietly between them while they gestured back and forth to each other, animatedly weighing the pros and cons of my Jewish identity. Mike unequivocally stated, "She absolutely looks Jewish," to which Judith, about whom I had become very fond, said a bit peevishly, "No, it's just what you believe a person is—I wouldn't say she looks Jewish."

I confess I felt a bit hurt, at least excluded from their midst. I was an outsider, only half-Jewish, and not even on my maternal side, so perhaps Pan Jakubowicz had his reasons not to include me in his talk. From his point of view, I would have no reason to care about the old, sad people eating their bread and soup at his center.

Our sojourn at the dormitory was coming to an end. We would all be going our separate ways to our towns and cities throughout the country to take up our duties. Some were lucky to be staying in the now familiar and beautiful Kraków. Others were off to the capital where we had spent some time as a group before coming to Kraków, so they were familiar with the city, and also home to the American Embassy. Others were going to Wrocław and Lublin. I was headed to Sosnowiec, and by everyone's measure who knew Poland at all, to the worst place in the country and the toughest assignment of the group.

My New Home
Dąbrowa Górnicza ("The Oaks") outside Sosnowiec, September, 1987

I had heard of black rain, but never experienced it. A driver, a Pole from the Polish Consulate in Kraków, had been arranged to take me to my apartment in Dąbrowa Górnicza. The late fall day was overcast as we left Kraków and darkened as we traveled south to the Silesian part of Poland. The driver, Bogdan, had only a smidgeon of English, but with effort we could make ourselves understood to one another. He registered his amazement and disapproval of our destination; he was aghast that I should live in such a part of the country. I explained that I was renting the flat from a Polish acquaintance in America, an explanation that caused him to grimace. He clearly distrusted any such arrangement and told me I should move to Kraków and commute to my teaching post in Silesia. Looking back, his suggestion might not have been unthinkable, but I could not have known that then.

The rain began just outside Kraków and picked up intensity as we neared "my" town. Bogdan continued to mutter and shake his head; he really was very pleasant and his concern for me seemed avuncular. I had already been schooled in the many reasons why where I was headed was highly undesirable: isolated, polluted, rural, few English speakers, dirty and ugly. By now, though, I was over worrying about those warnings. After all, at the first mention of my application for a Fulbright in Poland, well-intentioned people told me it was dangerous, a big mistake to go there. Citing everything from communism to Chernobyl, I was given to understand this was a bad plan. My strange roommate from UCLA Polish classes, with a somber expression, had recommended I take a Geiger counter along to check the food before I ingested it. The physician at the Washington, D.C. office of the Council for the International Exchange of Scholars, who addressed us Fulbrighters going to Eastern Europe, did so with an attitude of disapproval, mixed with contempt for our poor judgment, warning us that should we become very ill or a victim of a serious accident the only way we could receive appropriate medical attention would be with an airlift to Berlin, and this, he emphasized, we would be very lucky to procure. Thus, by the time I was a passenger in Bogdan's late model, tidy American consular car, I had already accepted that everything I had taken on—the country I had chosen, the town I would be living in, the apartment I had rented sight unseen, the hazards to my health, the university where I would be teaching—all these were entirely unpredictable and likely at best a struggle.

In a way, all the forewarning was liberating. I had jumped off a cliff by choice, and now I would just have to make the best of it. As Bogdan turned a corner into the street address I had given him, and laid eyes on the dwelling where I was to live, he groaned. He stopped the car amid the buckled and broken concrete of the building's parking lot, and swiveling his upper body around to look squarely at me in the back seat of the car (where he had insisted I sit, as a sign of deference to his chauffeur status), he nearly implored me just to turn around with him and go back to Kraków.

Together from our places in the car we surveyed the building which bore the address I had given him: a gray concrete square with long stains reaching down the concrete from its roof to the ground. There was no obvious entryway, but just around the corner of the wall facing us, we could make out a rusted wrought iron railing. Bogdan reluctantly parked his vehicle. As I stepped out into the parking area, my foot immediately found a puddle, and when it splashed, it splashed black water. The rain was coming down now, and it was hard to say whether it was black as it came from the sky or just when it struck the filthy concrete on the ground. I had on decent (black) boots, and I was wearing a wool overcoat that my generous older sister in California had lent me to bring to Poland since I had not owned a wool overcoat in some years. It was actually a beautiful white coat, and the unsuitability of it in that black rain and amid those black puddles struck me with symbolic force: perhaps I really *was* unprepared for all that lay ahead of me. But what I noticed first and remember very well to this day was the smell as I exited the car. The air reeked of something toxic, diseased, even evil—unfit for human beings. And the sky above was not just cloudy due to rain; it was an opaque poisonous green.

Bogdan accompanied me to the entrance to the building, a seven-storey Soviet bloc style structure. Walking into a tiny concrete and steel foyer, I saw the rusted mailboxes affixed to a cement wall, and surveying the numbers on the boxes, learned that my flat would be on the top floor. The building had no elevators, so Bogdan and I began the climb up the metal staircases—there were fourteen steep sets of these. We had not taken out any of my baggage yet, thinking instead to get the lay of the land first. The point of the visit was to locate the building and try the keys that had been given me in California to be sure they opened the door of the flat.

The smell inside became acrid—like dust ground into metal for many years. I turned to Bogdan once we started our ascent and told him he could wait below, I could find the apartment and see if the key worked. He would hear none of this, and though he was not young, he accompanied me up, up, up to the top, both of us making use of the rusted hand railing along the stairs. When the stairs ended, a single door presented itself—apparently, my flat was the only one at the very top. A daunting number of locks affixed to the gray-green door, I had been instructed as to what key belonged to which lock. We managed and entered. The flat had been the home of a family of four, and as such was tiny by American standards. The layout consisted of an entrance hall, with the entryways to rooms just off it. The hall ended at a tiny kitchen, a bleak gray room, which had the same acrid metallic scent of the foyer below with the mailboxes. The place was low-ceilinged and dark since windows were covered over with heavy drapes, save light that shone from a bare window at the end of the hallway. There were no beds per se, but chairs and couches that opened up to make beds—two singles and one double. If there was a décor at all, it would have been a version of 1950s America.

The place had the feel of people having left in a hurry: children's stuffed animals abounded on every chair, crystal glasses sat in a glass-fronted china cabinet, a dated newspaper left near a style of television set I remembered from my childhood. There were three small rooms off the hallway: a living room where the television sat (this would have been the couple's bedroom with a couch that converted to a double bed), and two other rooms with wide chairs that became single beds for each of the two children. There were bookshelves filled with books in one of the children's rooms—the family library—and below the bookcases, a small built-in desk. This would have been the family's den or study when a child was not using it as a bedroom. All closets, cabinets, bookcases were portable pressed veneer particle board structures with plastic high-gloss finishes that mimicked wood grain. Nothing was "built-in" as Americans might think of it.

For me, the setting was poignant. This was how a middle-class family lived in communist Poland—they made the best of it, and the careful attempts to insure a child's special place in the flat were touching. The family had managed to make it to the United States; well, good for them. The head of this family was now my landlord, the Polish friend of my Polish friend both living in the United States. To curb my sentimental outlook, I reminded myself that my Polish friend in America felt his friend was gouging me. I had not thought so until later I learned my rent (in dollars) was more than twice the monthly salary of a Polish academic. Still, the amount was infinitesimal by American standards. I was not about to object. Bogdan's eyes flitted over the place as he continued to shake his head skeptically. I noticed a bright neon orange telephone—it resembled a child's toy phone—but was an actual telephone, and I found myself wondering if it still worked.

That would be my home for at least nine months. It felt alien, strange, but I had no time to worry about that then. Having found the place and confirming that the keys worked, it was time for Bogdan to drive me to the university where I was to see where I would be teaching and to meet colleagues and supervisors.

A Shepherd

Bogdan and I traipsed down the stairs, an easier task than the reverse, and walked out into the gray outdoors. The puddles continued to splash black water—was it water, I wondered, it seemed more like gasoline. And then I noticed what I had not seen when we first approached the building: a child's swing set. Though it had the typical A-style construction, there was only a single swing and this with one broken chain so to make it useless. I looked at it for a moment trying to imagine children playing outside that block housing. I could not picture it but thought that maybe when I would be resident there, I would find out.

The drive from Dąbrowa Górnicza to Sosnowiec, the town where the Institute of English Philology was located, was important. That would be the distance I would travel each day to reach my teaching assignment. I needed to pay attention as Bogdan drove. The institute was a special branch of the University of Silesia in Katowice (*Uniwersytet Śląski w Katowicach*) which had its main campus in Katowice. I had been told that the institute was for students who had shown talent and interest in the English language; the program there was highly selective, and the students attending had likely been speaking, writing and reading in English for some years before they ended up there. I was impressed by this and looked forward to meeting them.

Bogdan pulled up to the front of the institute where a wide entrance with many doors sat in an otherwise unimpressive building. Two concrete statues stood at the margins of the wide cement steps--idealized versions of the worker in the Soviet realistic style. This entrance led into a large lobby-like room which seemed to me an odd use of space in a university, but then I reminded myself how little I knew about how academic institutions functioned in Poland—maybe this had a special use? A long counter ran along the right side of this large room, and behind the counter I saw rows upon rows of metal structure on which hung coat hangers. I read the sign above: (*"SZATNIA"*)—a coat check—the place to hang one's coat upon entering. How civilized, in its own way? But, I asked myself, is all this space necessary for students and faculty to hang their coats? Again, like wondering if children would be playing outside my block housing, I would have to wait to see.

We found our way to the department office, and there I met a taciturn young woman who was secretary or receptionist or both. She managed a smile when I introduced Bogdan and myself, but it was a cold, perfunctory smile. However, in a moment more people entered the office, my future colleagues and some students, all quite friendly and welcoming, and creating such a clamor around me, that it took me a minute or two to see a young man trying to make his way through this mini-throng around me to introduce himself. With some difficulty, not wanting to be rude to the others, and excusing himself to them as he pushed past them to reach me, he did: Piotr, my "shepherd." Smiling, soft-spoken, bowing slightly, even apologetic-seeming, he explained to me that he was responsible for helping me settle in, both at the institute and at my flat, wherever that was.

It was already late afternoon, but he explained to Bogdan that now he, Piotr, would take charge of me, and that Bogdan need not stay any longer. True to character, Bogdan peered at me anxiously—it was obvious that he was not at all convinced he was leaving me in good hands. Bogdan looked at me, smiled kindly, shook my hand, reminded me that Kraków was not very far away, gave me his card with phone number, and departed. Piotr informed me that now we would go to my flat to take the luggage Bogdan had unloaded from his car into the *szatnia.* He apologized that he had no car, but we could ask someone in the department to drive us. I demurred. I had only just met these people and the loading and carrying up the stairs would be a big favor. I convinced Piotr that I could hire a taxi to drive us and help carry my bags to the flat. By Polish standards, this would be an extravagance, but Piotr was worldly enough to imagine that for an American being paid in dollars and living in Poland, this was more than affordable. A "radio taxi" was phoned (this as opposed to waiting at a taxi stand), and the driver appeared in the lobby, and began to take my bags to the taxi. Piotr insisted on helping, and on my not helping, so even though he seemed tired from his long day at the institute, he and the driver handled the job—heavy suitcases with a year's worth of clothes, but also books and teaching materials.

We made our way to the block building in Dąbrowa, Piotr asking how it was I arranged to live there. I explained the friend of a friend situation; he accepted that, and reminded me that there was free housing for foreign faculty in Katowice, but that perhaps I would have more privacy here. However, he worried aloud that I would be isolated. Somehow or other, all the bags were carried up the many flights of stairs and deposited in the flat. Watching Piotr, now freely perspiring, schlepp up the heavy bags, I was embarrassed and uncomfortable that he should have to do this for me. At least in the case of the taxi driver, I would be paying him for his trouble. I assumed at the finish of this job, I would tell the taxi driver to take Piotr where he needed to go and pay in advance for that trip, after which I would turn to the job of unpacking. But no, Piotr explained that we would now go to his home, as his wife was waiting to meet me, and she had prepared dinner.

The day had been long and momentous, and I was exhausted myself, but there was no way to refuse. I just found myself marveling at Piotr's staying power. I thanked him and tried to give him a way out of the invitation, if he wanted one, but no, he seemed genuinely committed to making me his guest that evening. I suggested we take the taxi to his place, but he could not allow me to waste my money (again) in this way, and so the taxi driver was paid and dismissed. Piotr and I followed shortly after, and he explained that he knew the trams and would get us to his home in that way.

It turned out that a good deal of walking was in this plan, and though I needed a nap, I kept up the pace. I asked Piotr if there would be a place on our way where I could purchase a bouquet for his wife, but again, hyper-politely, he told me there was no need of that, but I insisted, and he acquiesced.

We took one tram, hopped off it at a stop, and walked a distance to a small flower stand. The day had brightened a bit in that late afternoon, and the colors of the flowers shone amidst the otherwise mostly gray surrounding. The vendor, a babushkaed tiny woman of indeterminate age, smiled a toothless grin at me. I selected a bouquet, and as I paid my zloty to the flower lady, I noticed that Piotr was purchasing a small bouquet, violets with a lace collar and ribbon hanging down. I assumed this would be his addition to my gift for his wife. So I was unprepared when, with a slight bow, and a warm smile, he presented it to me. There was a sweetness and charm about the offering that I was soon to understand as characteristic in Poland. We proceeded back to the tram, and after about an hour-and -a-half, all told, we arrived to Piotr's neighborhood. His was block housing, like mine, but a large complex, the exterior rundown and dismal. But climbing the steps to his apartment, and stepping inside, I entered Polish private life, a warm, inviting and well-cared for home, and in Grażyna, Piotr's young and pretty wife, an attorney by profession, and a genuinely welcoming hostess. This was the first of many moments like this when I experienced the striking contrast between the broken external world of Poland, and an internal world which Poles indomitably held to—a glimpse of a former Poland, a private place where the personality of a people and a bygone era were preserved intact and alive against the odds of the depersonalizing encroachment of the regime.

Interior Lives in Exterior Places

That night at Piotr and Grażyna's brought to mind the day I spent in Kraków with the "mysterious" guide from the Fulbright dormitory and her husband. Although I had not visited their private home, I was allowed inside their interior lives in the woods of the park, arguably the most exterior of places. But parks, and their wilder form, forests, have a deep symbolic resonance in Poland. I was taken back to my childhood and my father's love of trees, his only memory of his shtetl —the flowering kasdan. The forests of Poland are ancient, and once covered the whole of the country. And after my father's departure from his childhood home, and the beginning of the Nazi terror, Goebbels used the renowned Białowieża forest as his hunting grounds, photographing his pillage in the corpses of elk, deer and boar. These same forests were the hiding places for Jews and for the partisans, and regularly the killing grounds by Nazis of Jews. I thought perhaps my father as a boy, without knowing it, had learned his love of trees in his native Poland. With the Kraków couple, we had spent hours in the open space of a park talking about the trees where she had taken me to see the kind of tree to which she believed my father had bid his only farewell. So although the park the couple took me to was a public space, it felt private, and harkened back to an old Poland, like the inside of Piotr and Grażyna's flat. These spaces deep inside or "deep outside" provided an escape from a compromised daily polis and a return to the romance that had been key to Polish sensibility.

Marzena
"The Banality of Evil"

Piotr had made a point of introducing me specifically to the Polish professor who would be my office mate, and before classes even began, like Piotr, she invited me to her home. It was a Sunday morning, and though she had a car and insisted on picking me up at my flat, I explained that I could make my way to her, as I did not want to put her to the extra trouble of finding me when she had made such a generous invitation. She would hear nothing of it, so I gave the best directions I could, and stood vigil at my tiny kitchen window which overlooked the parking lot so that I would avoid keeping her waiting.

She found me and we stopped at her flat, quite spacious in an older, brick building that did not have the stained cement look of the typical block building, and on a street with large, old trees. Her neighborhood and her home I suspected, would be thought relatively elite to the average Pole. We had tea, and then she inquired, "Would you like to see my church?" Of course, I would. It turned out to be a Mass. When she saw that I knew the rituals and recognized me as Roman Catholic, her reactions to me changed. She softened and smiled and told me about her family—her elderly and infirm mother, a new baby nephew, and briefly the story of her romance with an American academic who had lived in Poland—an affair that ended, and I sensed, not well. She had never been married, and although her face was not old, her manner and style, made her seem prematurely aged, a "spinster," a stereotype I decry, but which fitted. Her clothes were drab, a severe skirt below the knee and business-style jacket, both cut in the style of the American 40s, her haircut from the same period. There was about her a sense of a sexuality that had been rubbed out before it had a chance to live. She peered at me through thick glasses behind which were very lovely blue eyes, but difficult to make out through the lenses. One of the first things she had said on first meeting me was, "A professor of American literature from California ... and a *woman*," her voice rising at the end of the sentence indicating intrigue and a bemused approval. I invited her to lunch after the Mass, indicating I would like her to be my guest. She accepted and we made our way to one of the standard government-run hotels where, though lacking in décor, served reliably good food. As she ate, she took her time; this was after all, an expensive lunch by Polish standards, and she seemed to take a kind of slow, sensuous pleasure in the meal. I was pleased she was obviously enjoying the lunch, but she did so in a melancholic sort of way—as if she had been treated to such lunches before, that this would be the only sensible way she could indulge in one. Later, after the meal was finished, she smoked, and this too, had a sensuality about it. For a time, she looked dreamily over my shoulder at nothing, as she slowly inhaled and exhaled— seemingly lost in some reverie. I liked her, I thought her kind and certainly intelligent, a survivor in Polish academia which was run by men, and sexist, despite communist claims to the contrary.

It had been decided that after our lunch she would drive me to Piotr and Grażyna's flat; again, as I was the newly arrived, they, like her, wanted to be sure I did not feel abandoned, and had invited me for supper that evening. Earlier Piotr had confided to me that she was his dissertation adviser, and that she was making his progress very difficult and for reasons he could not understand. I had forgotten about that until we pulled up at Piotr's block building, where she, Marzena, turned to me from her driver's seat, and said, "Be careful with him; his father-in-law is a communist official and Piotr is known as an informer." This was stated just as Piotr stepped out on his balcony, a welcoming smile on his face, and waving his arms to signal that he knew we had arrived. It made for an odd picture, this joyful man against the backdrop of a huge gray, stained ramshackle wall festooned with rusted balconies just like his own—an animated human figure suspended on a dead gray canvas. Marzena looked at him and lifted a hand from the steering wheel to indicate she had seen him. She then turned to me, a sour expression on her face, and sighing said, "Well, he is your shepherd, but don't trust him." There being no suitable response to this, I sat there in dumb silence, until she pulled up to an entrance in the block and exiting her car, I thanked her for the afternoon. This was just the beginning of many instances where, novice that I was, I would unintentionally stumble upon the deep distrust and suspicion my colleagues had for one another, and witness how the system encouraged this malaise for its own purposes.

Everything related to the institute had about it a subterranean feeling of secrecy—like ubiquitous fog or an underground, an only slightly discernable whisper, a just detectable incomprehensible drone. One evening I was invited to a dinner party at Marzena's home; this was to include other American Fulbright faculty in Poland who would travel from their assigned cities to attend. It was always appropriate to bring flowers for any social occasion, and though it was a dark fall evening when most flower stands were shuttered, I knew it was important, especially on this more formal occasion, to bring a bouquet to the hostess.

I walked the distance from my flat to the local taxi stand, and once underway, indicated to the driver that I would need to stop to buy flowers. My

Polish was not very good at this early stage, but I usually could make myself understood. I asked, "Please, flowers first." I pronounced "kvee aht tee" for the Polish word for flowers, "*kwiaty*." The driver shook his head in confusion. I tried again. Still more confusion. I resorted to putting my hands together to indicate a bouquet and made to hand this to him; this only further confounded the driver. I could not imagine what kept this man from understanding what I meant, until finally, I held the imaginary bouquet to my nose and inhaled with a pleasurable sigh. "Oh!" he exclaimed, and repeated the word I thought I had been saying a dozen times or more. But I noticed a slight (for me) difference in the accented syllable and a merging of the first two consonants which apparently made all the difference. He heard "*kawa*" when I should have been clearer with "kvee ah," and hence the poor man was looking for coffee. So we found an open florist, much fancier than the flower stands I typically saw, and was able to purchase a dozen spectacularly fresh yellow roses for Marzena. The taxi driver continued to shake his head all the way to our final destination at Marzena's home.

The flowers were more ostentatious than I would have liked, but at that hour they were the only ones available; Marzena furrowed her brow when she greeted me at the door, and said, "Kate, you musn't feel like you have to bring flowers every time we meet." I was a little embarrassed, but it was understandable she say this—and nice of her, too. Another American couple whom I had met before at our orientation in Kraków were there, as well as other Polish faculty. Theodore Kanski was Polish-American and not well-liked by the other Fulbrighters when we were in Kraków. His manner was arrogant generally, and being Polish-American, felt he knew much more about the country than any other of us.

That night he was expounding on the American literature courses he was teaching, and when he finished, he moved on to demonstrate his knowledge of Polish writers. As he indicated the names of well-known Polish writers, I mildly observed, "And so many of them are Jewish Polish writers." A silence descended on the gathering; people stole glances at one another. In this sophisticated group of academics, it seemed reasonable that there ensue an informed discussion of the implications of this fact. But no. As an American academic accustomed to open discussion of controversial topics, it must be said that Kanski nodded affirmatively, but he did not take up what he knew was at the heart of my observation. I could not let the silence go unremarked, so I plunged ahead, "You know, it strikes me as ironic that we Americans teach the history of American prejudice in our ethnic American literature classes to our Polish students, but we do not address the history of ethnic prejudice in their own country. I know that my family experienced pogroms before the war here in Poland. Family lore has it that a relative of mine, a physician, was killed by his Polish neighbors."

Little did I know at that time, that a book like *Neighbors* by Jan Gross which documented the massacre of Jebwabne Jews by their Polish neighbors would appear eleven years later (January 28, 2000).[4] Up to that time, I had not shared with the group that my father was Jewish and born in Poland; indeed, Marzena had taken me for a Roman Catholic when we had visited her church together. Maybe it was slightly unfair of me to shock her in this way, to reveal what had not been clarified privately earlier. But somehow that night, I cared less about that sort of fairness. I thought of the Poles I had argued with in California, their adamant denials of Polish anti-Semitism, the refusal to compromise even a little on the subject. After all, a much larger "unfairness" was up for grabs at that moment. I felt the heat rise to my face. Marzena turned to me, and said, and I can never forget her exact words: "They must have had a good reason for it." As if a murder can ever have "a good reason for it," as if to wipe clean any implication of racially motivated hatred, in spite of what she had to know about the pogroms in her country. I looked around the room where people were trying to look any place but at her or at me. And a vision of other polite, comfortable dining rooms throughout history drifted across my mind, where other polite, intelligent and supposedly civilized people socialized and tolerated the anti-Semitism that led to the Final Solution. In those parlors and dining rooms, not enough people, whether agreed or not, would have said an opposing word. Better to remain silent, not to cause a problem at a social gathering. Coincidentally, the television had been on with the sound turned off all this time. At that moment, the face of Jerzy Urban, Poland's communist Jewish Press Secretary appeared. A man much hated by anti-communist Poles, and with arguably good reasons: he had published his views on the soon to be murdered activist priest, Jerzy Popieluszko, calling him an "anti-communist Savonarola." Urban had accused the United States of knowing in advance about the installation of the 1981 martial law and betraying Solidarity and he regularly proclaimed his atheism. The group glanced over at the television; Marzena gestured at Urban's image on the screen as if to say, "Well, there you have it—this is why Poles don't trust Jews." She raised her eyebrows, and looked at me and the circle of her guests, and shrugged. True, she did not say those words, and I was no fan of Urban's. But what shocked was the ready ease with which we could slip from a story about Poles murdering a Jewish neighbor to the dislike of a Jewish communist government official. Was Marzena's meaningful shrug on the heels of her comment, "They must have had a good reason for it," a *quid pro quo*? A justification? It seemed so. I suddenly felt physically ill; the room, like all rooms in Polish homes was overheated, I had had some wine, and as I looked at the people who said nothing, I wanted to be out of that company as soon as possible. I was not prepared to be rude, to make a scene; in fact, I felt that the issue itself and my feelings about it behooved me to act with grace, so not to invite more shrugs in my absence about the "overreacting Jewess." I allowed the subject to change; I reasoned I had said enough to distinguish me from the silent ones in the imaginary picture of other dining rooms. Maybe that was an excuse to myself. But I did not have the heart or the stomach to go further with it, so I waited until my departure might not be associated with the exchange and took my leave. Marzena had called a "radio taxi" for me—the only way one could get a cab that late at night in a suburb. She walked me to the door, thanking me again for the roses. I returned the thanks for the dinner. But once I got out into the freezing night air, I felt even sicker, and I realized that the heat in the house and the wine were not the reasons I was ill.

The cab got me home to my building which seemed exceptionally ugly now, isolated, and even menacing. Sweating in the cold, I paid the driver, and went up the fourteen flights of stairs to my flat. Without taking off my coat or turning on lights, I fell face up on my pull-out bed in the dark. What I remember most was the sound of the wind howling outside the building. Suddenly everything in my flat's block seemed alien, foreign in a frightening way. I made it to the bathroom and vomited, and then stumbled back to the bed, still in my coat and scarf. I lay there for hours, staring straight up into the dark. Why had I come to this place? Who had been hunted and murdered in the woods just adjacent to my apartment? How immodest, arrogant of me to have come here at all in search of answers, to the very killing fields of my family and my people. An ignorant little girl from California who thought she could take on such questions—and alone? Was this a self-imposed exile under this filthy sky a form of penance, I wondered? And for what? My father's "passing"? My own? And more, had I insulted the memory of the murdered ones by coming here at all? And on the other side, who was I to condemn the silent ones tonight? Especially the Poles. What did I know of their experience, privileged visitor that I was? Still: it was the easy slippage of the mention of a racially-motivated murder to the dislike of a politician—that was what sickened. Hannah Arendt's phrase came to me—"the banality of evil." Yes, that explained why I was nauseous. But it was a Sunday night, and tomorrow I needed to be up early and ready to go to the institute to teach the "American Experience" in the morning.

"Completely different traditions"

The lecture hall was vast and filled with nearly 100 students. This never was my preferred teaching scenario—desks affixed to the floor, audience style, all facing the alleged "maestro" who would spout the wisdom students were to write down, rather than a seating arrangement where students could face each other as well as the professor, so that open discussion was also a part of the lecture. The subject of this course was a survey of American literature, and these were the Polish students who had not yet arrived to the level of the *"Magister"* (Masters) where they would specialize in some aspect of literature and write a thesis on that subject. These were the neophytes at the institute, very bright as their written and spoken English was so excellent it had qualified them for admission to the Department of English literature in Sosnowiec, where I had been assigned, a branch of the main university in Katowice. In many cases, these students' essays in English were superior to my American students at UCLA. Still, they were young, and beleaguered by the communist society that imposed endless bureaucratic obstacles on their lives.

On this particular day, we had been discussing contemporary American writers, and without having planned it, I brought up Jerzy Kosinski's *The Painted Bird*, a novel written by an American but one who had been born and raised in Poland and who was Jewish. I asked the students if they thought this novel felt more Polish to them than American. There were several interesting answers, and then, one young girl raised her hand and said, "But Jerzy Kosinski is not Polish. He is Jewish. And that is an entirely different tradition than our Polish one." From where I stood, it was as if the whole of the student audience lowered their heads towards their desks; there were red, embarrassed faces, which looked back at the girl who had made the comment. Dead silence in the lecture hall. She herself glanced about her, entirely unaware of any faux pas she may have committed. And what was her offense, anyway? Her bluntness, her naivete, her saying aloud what the rest of the students may have believed but would not have said, their shame for her ignorance? It is hard to say. The girl had stated this without a trace of enmity and had not intended any nuance or offense. Yet, interestingly, the entire class was embarrassed by what she said. I let there be silence. It seemed appropriate—let the issue sink in—a teaching moment. After a minute or two, I asked her and the class what it meant that the historical list of the most revered Polish writers were in large part Jews. What of Boleslaw Leśmian, Antoni Słonimski, Bruno Schulz, Aleksander Wat, Julian Tuwim, among others? I commented that as an American it was interesting to me to survey the list of famous and touted "Polish" writers and to note how many of them were Jewish. How did this bear on the young girl's statement that Polish and Polish Jewish traditions were so different? There was no answer—just a few nods of recognition of the contradiction between what the girl had said and what I now asked.

It is important to remember that in 1987, unlike today, the entire subject of Jewishness in Poland, was not one discussed openly. At every turn, I was struck by how the hiddenness of Polish complicity and responsibility echoed the hiddenness of my father's and my Jewish identity. An enormous and emotional subject—simply skipped over. The subject of Jewishness in Poland existed but behind a veil, suppressed, curtained off, shrouded. In fact, on my return trips to Poland after my Fulbright ended in 1989, I was at once taken aback by and thrilled to see the growth and finally the explosion of interest and work in Poland on Jewish subjects, including work by Poles on Polish anti-Semitism and collusion during World War II. On the one hand, visiting the renovated Jewish section of Kraków, Kazimierz, the one in 1987 when I had had to crawl under fences to get to Jewish cemeteries, the place where precious Jewish sacred texts lay rotting on the shelves of the Remuh Synagogue, the place where I met Mr. Jakobowicz, the then head of the tiny Jewish community there, who showed me the crumbling walls of the once beautiful *shul*, —built in 1557, the place where I had visited the soup kitchen for the elderly and impoverished Jews who still lived in the remnants of the destroyed apartment buildings in the district—now, I see an artificial recreation of the vital Jewish community of Kazimierz: bright-colored awnings bearing the Jewish surnames of the shops' former owners, restaurants offering Jewish cuisine, shops selling Jewish artifacts, renovated synagogues. I had to think of those Indian reservations we Americans visit where we can buy Indian jewelry and pottery, the population itself destroyed by Europeans who came to America to make Indian-owned land their own. Yet here was an opportunity for Poles like my Polish students, largely if not entirely ignorant of Jewish history, Jewish tradition, Jewish religion, Jewish custom, and more than any of these, the story of the brilliant Jewish presence in their own country and what it provided their country, a loss from which Poland has never recovered—here was a chance for them to learn.

Oskar
A Private Coachman

For the first few days of classes I managed to take the pre-war tram from a stop near my flat to the institute, but learned quickly that such form of transport was not only miserably crowded and slow, its schedule was unreliable and could easily make me late for the classes I was assigned to teach. I would arrive back home after dark when I took the tram, more exhausted from the transport than from the day's teaching. I realized I would have to find a more streamlined transportation, that as much as I had tried to resist it, I would have to succumb to the embarrassment I would inevitably feel by regularly taking a cab from the taxi stand a few blocks from my flat. The cost of a taxi commute to and from was literally pennies in American money, but there was no way I could escape the shame I felt for such a luxury, surrounded by the daily physical challenges of the average Pole. So sharp was this embarrassment that after a week or so, I would ask the driver to drop me some distance from the institute--it was unthinkable for me to pull up to the entrance in that chauffeured manner.

There was, as it turned out, a positive side to this hypocrisy. As the fall turned to a deep gray and cold winter, and I took up my usual place in the taxi line, I became a regular fixture for the drivers waiting for fares. It is possible that I was seen as a mark of sorts, a foreigner who might pay better, or one in need of changing money on the black market, a transaction regularly engaged in by taxi drivers. Whatever the case, one day while I was standing in line, a tiny man, gnome-like, stepped from his taxi and approached me in a courtly manner, gesturing with his arm to his vehicle, as if to lead me to a royal carriage. He spoke Polish only, of course, and his voice was so high-pitched and his stature so small, he seemed a miniature footman out of a fairytale—a Rumpelstiltskin of sorts. He was impeccably dressed in casual but crisply ironed clothes and groomed with the tidy slicked hairstyle out of the American 50s, still typical in Poland among working class people. His taxi was as fastidious as its driver—not new, but so clean I nearly hesitated to enter it with my wet boots. How we ever managed to communicate such relatively intricate transportation arrangements, I cannot reconstruct, but in the end, he understood that on certain days I would be going at specific and varying times to the institute. He explained that he would be able to collect me from my block building—it was not necessary I walk to and stand in the taxi line. I was to have a monopoly of his business, I understood, and though I wondered how he could arrange to be free at those particular times, I saw no reason to object. I have to confess that thoughts ranging from possible romantic designs he may have on me, to rape, robbery and murder did flit through my head. But from the very first ride, he told me about his wife and two children, indicating that his home was not very far from mine, and that one day, when it was convenient for me, his wife would be happy to have me to their flat for dinner.

So it was that Oskar became my private driver, despite my guilt and embarrassment at such (relative to Poles) extravagance. I did eventually go to dinner at his family home, and there I met his wife, the opposite number to Oskar: tall and gaunt to his short plumpness, taciturn to his jolliness, old (though she could not have been with her teenaged children) and worn out compared to his energetic child-like appearance. The dinner was taken at a small table in the single communal room in the flat. Despite the tiny space in which to work and dine, Ania served the traditional Polish dinner, replete with homemade soup first, followed by meat, potatoes and vegetable. The kitchen was a sliver of a room, and yet she managed to turn out a meal with all the trappings expected in a wealthier Polish home. The bathroom was also the laundry room with a washing machine, but no dryer, so clothes lines laden with the sheets and towels and the family's garments criss-crossed the small space and created a veritable maze, through which one would wade to use the facilities. The heat in the flat was always turned up so I would begin sweating within minutes, but I felt it was possible this, too, was a gesture of hospitality: the guest would not be cold in their home.

One morning on the way to the institute, as I sat in the back of Oskar's taxi, he began singing, a high-pitched sound that made me think of the voices of the *castrati*. And it was opera he was singing! He referred to Puccini, and as he drove, he would change hands on the steering wheel freeing one hand to gesture like a conductor or *primo uomo*. It was an astonishing spectacle, and he sang like a serious performer without a hint of self-consciousness. All I could do was offer praise when he finished, accolades he accepted like a confident, seasoned professional with a nod which resembled the bow he could not take from his driver's position. Later I purchased an expensive record album recording of *La Bohème*, a gift to thank him for all his help and hospitality. I realized too late that he had no record player, and as he opened and inspected the record album, it became clear that he had never seen such an object. He turned it over in his hands, and in order not to make a show of his ignorance, he then politely stashed the thing on a shelf. I believe it never moved from that shelf.

I regularly had to fight off his too frequent invitations to dinner. He was insistent, and regularly woke me very early in the morning (on weekend days when I could sleep later), to present me with *bułki*, a Polish bread warm from the bakery where he had just retrieved it—at about 5 a.m. One night when I accepted another dinner invitation, I realized that I had not understood he and Ania's intent. As we finished our meal and chatted, I made ready to leave. Husband and wife shared a look of confusion and gesturing to the single couch in the communal space, explained that they intended I sleep in their flat that night. When I begged off, Oskar explained that he had put his taxi away for the night, and I learned at that moment that this was a nightly ritual. The vehicle, of which he was very proud, was kept in a locked garage some distance from their block. Nonplussed, I indicated that the distance was not far and that I could walk home. Again, they exchanged glances, and finally acquiesced to my refusal to sleep the night there. But then I noticed them both bundling up in the accessories all Poles wore in the winter's cold—always a kind of elaborate ritual that I had seen in homes and public places: *szalik* (scarf), *czapka* (hat), gloves, coat, boots—they could walk me home. Again, I tried to convince them that I would do fine on my own, that I did not need to inconvenience them; after all, they would have to walk back. But this was to no avail. So the three of us set out in the cold night to walk the twenty minutes or so to my flat.

A light snow whirled about in the wind which also carried the everyday factory stench, but the sky was quite clear and black with plenty of stars. The gray block buildings erased by the darkness and all that remained was the crisp, bracing cold and starry black night--it was beautiful. They had been doing their best to be polite, to comply, but they could not really understand. So against my better judgment, given that my Polish was adequate for everyday concerns but not up to par for what would be a philosophic explanation, I thought I would try to explain. I was not at all sure that I could make myself understood, and there was always the chance that I could insult by accident. I think that somehow the quiet and cool of the walk's atmosphere inspired me to try. I began telling them how American friends had told me not to come to Poland, how dangerous it would be, citing Chernobyl and communism—at this last, they had a good chuckle, the sophistication of which surprised me a bit coming from them. As I went on to enumerate all the reasons why people discouraged me from coming to Poland, they smiled and shook their heads. I said, "What if I had listened to them? I never would have come." And then I made the connection to my capacity to walk home alone, which also made them smile, and finally, I tried for the larger point: I was an independent person, an independent woman, I liked my solitariness and my freedom to make my own choices. They should not worry about me. I cannot say whether this larger point was understood but I had been honest, and they were not offended. There was a slight but perceptible change in how they looked at me—though difficult to name, I could feel it—a kind of respect, a new awareness, a realization? I could not say. I may have got them to think about what I thought was obvious: I had made my way alone to Poland from California—should that not be evidence enough for my ability to manage my life? We said our goodnights at the rusted door to my block; mercifully, they did not insist on walking me up the many stairs to my flat. Perhaps they were ready to release me a bit---their one and only ever American friend.

Krajobraz or "The Countryside" outside Dąbrowa Górnicza
December, 1987

Ever since I had met Oskar and his wife, Ania, they had talked about "Ania's *tata*"—her father and the wonders of the place where he and Ania's mother lived. I could gather that the place was not too far away, but "in the countryside," as they put it, and at a beautiful spot which I must see. Eventually, after months of descriptions and elaborations, it was planned.

The arrangement was straightforward enough. Oskar, Ania, and their two teenaged children picked me up at my flat early on a late winter morning. There was much excitement and nervousness among the four of them—I could see how important this visit was to them. I reached for the back door of the taxi to join the teenagers there, but such a fuss was raised by the parents' insistence I sit in the front seat, I gave up without a fight. I had learned I rarely if ever won these battles, whether it was politely refusing second and third helpings of food, discouraging early morning bread deliveries (in their explanation, so that the bread was still fresh and hot), or demurring to stay overnight in their flat. So Ania squeezed in between her children, and I like some reluctant dignitary, took the front seat.

We did indeed travel outside the gray, polluted confines of the town of Dąbrowa Gornicza to enter a rural area, but it was late winter by then, and the glories of the countryside they had promised, were not in evidence. We reached the farmhouse, dark and small and set not too far away from the main road, surrounded by fields instead of other houses. As we drove up, the darkened windows were the first noticeable aspect of the house. Ania's *tata* had prematurely aged; he was a white-haired, wizened and wiry man, yet his twinkling eyes filled his face with expression. In his face I recognized Ania's angular features, which in themselves could have been handsome, but on his face too deeply creased with wrinkles, and on Ania's, made too sharp by deprivation and daily hardship. *Tata's* Polish was mumbled and perhaps even archaic. To my disappointment, I could not understand even a single word. Ania bore no resemblance to her mother who could have been any age, and in fact, given her portliness and fat peasant face, appeared younger than her gaunt daughter. The mother had lost most of her teeth, so again I could not make out her spoken Polish. Her nose may just have been pug, but it might also have been broken. Her fingers were black with soil or perhaps coal dust, her legs covered with special leggings, her head babushked, her body formless under a shift. Where the house began was uncertain; we entered a hall and at first the floor was earthen and then it was not, but the air warmed enough to be noticeable. I was directed to stand in a special room while the others stood in the kitchen—it was not clear why, but perhaps it was a polite ceremonial gesture of formality for a guest. Before I was handed through the door from that room, I caught a movement out of the corner of my eye: in a darkened corner of the room a small human being was crouched, a Mongoloid daughter, I realized. This must have been Ania's sister. No one acknowledged her and she was not introduced. *Tata* and *Mamusia* greeted me with nods and smiles and welcomed me into their house—more like a hut, low-ceilinged and dark. In that context, Oskar and Ania suddenly looked modern and out of place. Both families were poor in their own ways, and their matter-of-fact manner in greeting one another was strangely poignant to me as an outsider. The grandparents had lived through World War II and maybe even have remembered World War I, and they had the look of survivors. The way that Ania and Oskar obviously esteemed them was touching.

The house was damp and cold, though there was a peat fire burning in a corner of the room. A table had been set with the accurate number of places, but it was agreed among the group that we should first go for a walk before sitting down. There was some wan sunlight outside and we walked around the perimeter of the house and then out to some woods which were quite lovely still, even in that winter season. I speculated that it was these woods that explained Ania's and Oskar's enthusiastic talk about this long-planned visit. Ania's pride in showing me that was evident in her face. For the first time, I think I saw pleasure there. As we strolled through the forest, I wondered if some of the land was part of Ania's tata's property, so I asked Ania. She looked puzzled for a second, and then with that characteristic Polish shrug which usually meant, "it's obvious, of course!" she answered that the land belonged to "*państwo,*" translated to "the state," but also designating "the people," a term regularly used by the communist regime, what would substitute for "public" in the West, a loaded term there and then, one that most Poles despised for what they saw as its disingenuousness. In their view, "*państwo*" meant that the government owned everything; the "people" owned nothing. But Hania had answered without a trace of irony, so I understood that she had no objection to her government—her lower social and economic class likely separated her from the Polish intelligentsia and the world-renowned dissidents from the time of Solidarity (and before), and who were still very vocal. She had not had the benefit of an education, and for all I knew, she may not have been literate. The simplicity of the answer, and the way which she felt it was obvious and God-given did not surprise me. Still, Lech Wałesa was an electrician …

I looked at her parents walking ahead of us, and recognized what I had felt but not identified before: these welcoming and simple people were the same sort of people Claude Lanzmann had interviewed for his film, *Shoah*—Polish peasants who felt they minded their own business, and could not be held accountable for the boxcars that passed by their farms. But there is also an important history of the *szmalcownik*, the Polish perjorative slang term that referred to those Poles who blackmailed Jews or the Poles who aided Jews by extorting money from them in exchange for keeping their locations or identities secret. This has been widely documented in the Polish countryside. I felt myself shiver.

We returned to the house and the meal began. Bowls of steaming stew were served from a large black pot over the open fireplace and handed round the table. I was moved by their welcome and wanted to let them know I was happy to be in their midst. I complimented the home, the meal, and thanked them, smiling and friendly. Conjuring the scene now, I think my sociability stemmed in part from guilt—I was compensating for having a better life—and this thought makes me feel guilty again: who was I to say my life was better? In any case, I wanted to assure them that their efforts to entertain me were appreciated. As we conversed at the table, with me the center of attention, the day darkened to night outside the windows. I notice that Ania's sister had moved into a place where she could observe us more easily. It is Oskar who at last tells me this is Rosalia, and it is he who says, "Rosalia, *chodź* ('come')," as cookies have been laid out, and he invited her to join us and to enjoy the dessert. She did. Her mother fed her some homemade wine, and took Rosalia into her lap as if she were a small child, feeding her the sweet cookies, obviously loving this daughter, holding her close to her body, smiling and rocking her. Rosalia was likely around 40 years old.

I needed to use the lavatory, and so asked, "*Przeprazsam*," "excuse me," addressed to all. At once there was a palpable stiffening at the table; the young part of the family looked at each other, discomfited and embarrassed. I was not at all certain what was happening. But then Ania, in her characteristic commonsense take-care-of-business manner, stood, a sharp look on her face and an unceremonious gesture with an arm, led me outside into the freezing dark.

The night was so black and the route so circuitous, that I could not at first see at all where I was going. But I followed the vague outline of Ania before me until we reached the quiet of a small dark stable. At first, I sensed rather than saw the animals inside—their exhalations and their odor. Saying nothing, with a jerk of her hand, Ania pointed inside the stable. I was to relieve myself there; of course, there was no indoor bathroom. The night air was very cold by this hour, and as I hiked my skirt and lowered my tights to urinate, I saw the placid, sweet faces of the goats quietly, innocently regarding me in their animal way. As my pee hit the warm hay, it steamed, and their breaths and mine together came out in white clouds. There was something pleasant and reassuring about being with the animals there—calming, still, ancient. And then with Ania standing there, her back to me to allow me some privacy, the image of the most famous stable came to my mind, and with it, the drama of the child in the manger so central to the Polish Catholic mythos, and the thought that they inside the warm hut were not so removed from that symbolic gathering under the star of Bethlehem.

Those personal experiences with such contrasting parts of Polish society might give the impression that I had become accustomed to my new environment. But that was not the case. Despite these personal interactions, there was always a surreal quality to my days. I often felt as if I were in a dream, or as if I had traveled back in time to know people who had lived and died before I was born. Or that I was existing in an endless present outside of time and space, in a world disconnected from the one I had come from. After all, I had come to my post in deep, polluted Silesia, at a distance from major cities. I lived in a Soviet-style block under a green-gray sky in a community of miners and other workers who regularly stood in long lines for meat and other staple items. The faces of the people I would pass on the streets of my town were out of a Brueghel painting. One of the formerly most beautiful areas of Europe had been ravaged by war and polluting industry. Everyone in Silesia had a cough. I developed a cough, and finally pneumonia, from the unhealthy quality of the air. It is not very difficult to imagine how an American academic, particularly one from California, might experience the place as a foggy dream. Despite the fact that I was functioning adequately—I managed to feed myself, to find the transportation I needed, to master the language enough to do business and to socialize, to meet the requirements of a demanding teaching job, to cope with the subterranean secrets at the institute, to pay careful attention to everything around me—I could not escape the feeling that I had not awakened from the dream, penetrated the fog, had not pierced the surface of Polish society. Until one night.

"Emigracja Wewnętrzna" (Internal emigration)

It was by now late fall and the nights had grown cold and windy. In the area where I lived, and actually throughout much of Poland, nights were dark because the streetlights westerners take for granted, were far and few between there. It was often difficult to go out at night entirely safely—whether driving or walking—because of the poor visibility and terrible, even dangerous conditions of the roads. But that night I needed to go out of my rooms on the top floor and stretch my legs. It would be a walk just around my tenement block near the broken swing set. The night was black and cold, but I had my warm boots, *czapka*, *szalik*, and for a reminder of home, a good old Bruce Springsteen-style American blue jean jacket. The night was actually quite lovely, the blackness lit only by the surrounding block tenements' hundred or so windows, so that then the ugly, gray, stained exterior was removed from vision—erased by the night, with only those hundred beacons gleaming with a rose-colored light. My dilapidated neighborhood was transformed—a twinkling landscape with all scars hidden for the moment. I heard only the wind through the old trees around me and the dried leaves blowing over the playground's cement slab. And then the faint tinkle of piano music, a Chopin Prelude, coming from a flat where someone practiced.

The scene suggested a metaphor which helped me give names to the incomprehensible contradictions I had been seeing: interior vs. exterior, or in the language of linguistics, surface structure vs. deep structure. More than just the notion that things do not always appear to be what they are, though certainly that was true in Poland. Instead, I saw layers of truth, like geological strata, each having its own story to tell, its own integrity. And looking at those windows at night, Polish society had been just for a moment sliced open so that I could see a cross-section—at least two layers of truth that like an excavated chunk of earth revealed the history of the land. The innermost core, what was lit in the darkness from where I stood, the innermost layer was the shape and color of private Polish life: books, music, flowers, cuisine, art, hospitality, the power of symbol and myth, particularly as these pertain to religion, individuality, the cult of the hero—that courageous individual who stands alone against all odds for a cause, like the Polish cavalry who met Hitler's panzer division at the Baltic knowing it was a suicide mission like others before it in Polish history, whether defending against the Swedes, the Turks, the Russians, the Tatars. The Warsaw Ghetto Uprising. The Warsaw Uprising. Solidarity had inherited this trope of the hero—David against Goliath—in the person of Lech Wałesa, and millions followed. But which impulse, I wondered, was the inner reality, the refusal of the Polish friend in California to acknowledge the existence of any Polish anti-Semitism, Marzena's shrug in the face of my question about Poles killing their Jewish neighbors—or this courageous idealism? Was this courageous idealism just a form of chauvinistic nationalism? Maybe all these were not mutually exclusive. All I could realize for now was that the outer layer of life in Poland, dealings in the polis, in no way represented the inner core. And then I learned that there was a name for this phenomenon, familiar to Poles: "*emigracja wewnętrzna*," "internal emigration," The individual turns away from the polis, emigrates into him or herself. I learned that the term had been used when German writers opposed to the Nazi seizure of power in 1933 decided to stay in Germany. A controversial idea then, as some felt that those Germans who stayed and "internally emigrated" indirectly sanctioned what was happening in their country, and even benefitted by remaining there during the war. Others felt that remaining was more courageous than literally emigrating. In any case, the term was appropriated in Poland and described how Poles moved "inside," hung on to their private lives as best they could to shield themselves from the public sphere's oppression.

A Railway Rescue

The following day I had planned to board a train from my local Dąbrowa Górnicza railway station to Kraków, a daring feat as, unlike the stations in the large cities, these small-town stations relied on word-of-mouth for arrival and departure times, as well as platform designations. I had managed to learn the approximate time a train would depart for Kraków on that Saturday morning in late fall, but once I arrived by taxi to the station (I could never have found it myself—it took the cab driver, a local, numerous circuitous turns to get to the station, set deep in a wood), I discovered there was no attendant, and I could not make out the signs which might have indicated the correct platform for the Kraków-bound train. I positioned myself on a platform that afforded the best view of all the tracks, hoping at the last minute I would recognize the right train and hurry across to board it.

I stood waiting about an hour—not another soul had appeared at the station. I began to wonder if this planned trip would be aborted, when a pretty woman, dressed in urban attire not typically seen in Dąbrowa, came rushing out of the station onto the platform where I stood. I greeted her and asked if a train to Kraków was, in fact, coming, and where I should be to board it. She quickly explained that she, too, was catching the train to Kraków, that I was on the wrong platform, and that we needed to hurry to get to the right one. In the charming fashion I found among Polish women (but mainly in the city, not in small towns like mine), she hooked her arm through mine, and taking quick steps, led us both to the right place. Getting to that platform involved climbing several rickety staircases over the tracks (I had been entirely in the wrong spot), and arriving just in time to see the train, a pre-war rusty model, huffing its way towards us. She held fast to me, moving me across the gap from the platform to the train, at which point I thought she would release me. But no. The two of us pressed down the narrow outer hall of the train, she brought me to a closed glass compartment, and opening the doors there, pushed me politely into a lounge seat. Shades of *Pani* Zofia! Like her walk, her talk was much too fast for me to comprehend, but it was clear she was explaining to those seated in the compartment my need for continued help. This way of seeing a job to its finish, particularly as it regarded helping a complete stranger, I soon discovered was typical of women in Poland. As an American, that sort of caring for the stranger, took me by surprise every time it happened. In this situation, there was a comical element to the scenario. As it transpired, all the passengers in that compartment were men, seated by obvious preference at a distance from one another, caught up in reading their newspapers, and appearing not to have had any conversation with each other. Now here we were, this intent woman with her willing hostage, bursting upon them and addressing them as if they all belonged to a group, a group that needed now to work together to ensure my safety. The men, surprised, put their papers on their laps, and listened to my savior. For her part, she was polite, but firm with her auditors, and when finished with her speech, she turned to me, smiled warmly, and then threw open the sliding glass compartment door, and in a hurry, sashayed charmingly down the train hall.

At her departure, there was a sudden awkward silence, a vacuum her huge presence had left in its wake. Embarrassed by the fuss I had caused them, I nodded at my compartment mates, and they nodded back. There were three of them, all stationed in corners of the compartment (I was seated in the spot closest to the compartment door); one of them seated next to the window, was younger than the others, and he smiled and even laughed a bit in response to my own little embarrassed laugh--he knew how I felt. He was movie-star handsome without seeming to know it, his clothes a bit worn and his hair and nails, like many Polish men's, were not groomed in the way one would expect a man with his style and looks would be in America. This added to his charm.

We engaged in conversation first in my faltering Polish, and then noting this, he switched to English, and his was quite good. He reminded me of one of my students in his readiness to get the joke, but there was something about him more mature than my students. His manner was poised and self-confident. He asked questions about my teaching and about California, intelligent, thoughtful questions. I explained I needed to visit the American Consulate in Kraków, and he told me he knew it, that it was very close to the rail station—he could easily take me to it, but would I have lunch with him first? He knew a good, authentic, Hungarian restaurant nearby. I wondered at this ready familiarity, but deciding there was no risk to me involved, I accepted.

The Hungarian restaurant was tucked away on the Kraków streets—again, I never would have found it on my own. The restaurants I had frequented thus far in my stay in the country were state-run, one like the other, so this was a special treat for me. After the lunch, we traded phone numbers, and he escorted me to the consulate. At goodbye, I offered my hand to shake, but instead grasping it, he quickly bent his head low to kiss it in the traditional way aristocratic Polish men do when meeting or taking leave of a woman. As he stood, his face and upper body were framed by the American flag outside the consulate that whipped in the breeze behind him. His manner and style came from an old, bygone time, so that his person, backgrounded by the comparatively new American symbol, suddenly presented to me a tableau which symbolized all the contradictions I had been experiencing—space and time, interior and exterior, real and surreal.

A few weeks later, I did receive a phone call from my luncheon companion, Antoni. He asked if I would like to come to his family home and meet his parents and brother and sister, and a maternal grandmother who lived with them. Their home was not far from Dąbrowa Gornicza and he could arrange to use the family car and bring me to their home. He indicated in advance that he was the only one in his family who spoke English, but not to worry, he would help translate. I accepted and a date for the coming Sunday was set.

Under the Spell of Joanna

Late morning Antoni arrived at my shabby block building in an old model Peugeot. Although Antoni was 20 some years old, like most young Poles, it would be incomprehensible that he would own his own car or live in his own apartment at that age. All my students lived with their parents; even if they had the means to live in places of their own, the waiting list was absurd. That reality created a highly observable difference in the relationship between Polish parents and children of that age and their American counterparts. Although there was always the traditional Polish children's respect and deference to their parents, their physical proximity to one another made their age difference less marked. I was continually struck by the youthfulness of parents—blue-jeaned, physically attractive, hip-looking bearded fathers; sexy (often beautiful—many Polish women possessed exotic, chic appearances) mothers. The generational difference between such parents and children faded, and you would find yourself thinking you were in a group of friends rather than parents and children. This would prove to be true when I met this family.

Antoni and I made the trip to his family home from my flat, about thirty minutes over bumpy, pot-holed, unsafe roads. They lived in a small town, a village much smaller than Dąbrowa Gornicza, which had been and remained essentially agricultural. There was a town center, but very small and only sparsely populated with shops for basic requirements—meat and bread, some vegetable stands.

Antoni had told me about "his country"—the white rock of the landscape near his home. He wanted to show me this first before we went to his family's home. It turned out that the white rock was limestone, called "*jura*" from Jurassic and I was not prepared for the drama the landscape presented. Giant rock formations veined crystalline surrounded by huge boulders, bordered by meadow, created all variety of cave and crevice, a kind of inviting playground. That landscape, I learned, comprised a part of the Kraków-Częstochowa Upland which extends over a large area of Silesia and Kraków. One would not guess that such a natural drama existed in such close proximity to Antoni's village—again, the unexpected contrast between surface appearance and deep "reality." It was obvious that Antoni had been in love with this ancient landscape since childhood. Moving among the ruins of an old castle that was situated within this landscape, he guided me around the ruins as if it were an old familiar place for him, like a home, even.

We drove on to the family home and just as we approached the house by car, he turned to me and with a smile said to me, "Don't be shocked by anything you see." I was not sure what he meant by this, but he elaborated, and it became clear to me that though the house was once a beautiful country home lived in by his aristocratic forebears, it was now dilapidated. He was worldly enough to know that an American like me might be unacquainted with the way he and his family lived—with the reality of life in Poland—the reality that there was no money to repair or renovate in those times. I was touched by this "preparation" and did my best in the minutes before we were to enter the house, to show him that he could credit me with more sense and experience than to be "shocked" by deprivation. He laughed and seemed to accept this.

The family had obviously been awaiting our arrival, and I sensed we might be a bit tardy because of the white rock tour. What a stately group of people greeted me: Antoni's father, tall, a groomed mustache and beard, dressed for the occasion in a pressed and starched immaculate dress shirt buttoned to the collar, an ascot at his neck. The sister, beautiful, also tall, with long shining black hair gathered behind her neck, with dark eyes to match. The little brother, a teenager, with the dark eyes of his sister and brother, wore his glossy hair long, a shock of it falling charmingly across his brow. The maternal grandmother, with coiffed white hair, her frame slightly bent, yet dignified, and formal, wearing a suit.

But the one who captured me most was Antoni's mother, Joanna. She stepped forward to greet me like all the others, but after offering her hand as they all had, she put her arms around me and kissed my cheek. She wore a spun wool filigreed river-green foam shift adorned with an antique silver brooch on the right shoulder—uniquely Polish silver, and in the shape of a falling leaf.

Her hair, feathered away from a glowing face, was auburn like the color of the leaves on the fall trees surrounding her house. The house was hers; it had been her family home long before she ever met her husband. Her surname, I later learned, was an aristocratic family name, and it was her father and her grandfather who had farmed the fields that lay adjacent to the house. The fields still belonged to the family, leased out to farmers, but Antoni oversaw that business and was thus something of a gentleman farmer, without the wealth that is often associated with that moniker. The house had been a large stone and wood country house, a well-to-do home with land all around it. It was easily over 100 years old, so it had survived both wars. The floors were beautiful planked wood and there were many rooms, but most of them needed repair to their walls and ceilings. The bathroom was a shambles—an old bathtub and toilet with ancient plumbing that leaked water. Like the bathroom, the kitchen's plumbing was old and leaky. A wood stove stood next to a newer, much smaller gas stove. A large room functioned as a dining room, and it was outfitted that day with a wide and long table covered in a fine lace tablecloth, all the places laid with old and lovely china and heirloom silverware. A silver candelabra sat at the end of the table, and in the center a vase held dried flowers tied with satin ribbon. On a nearby antique sideboard sat a silver tea service and a samovar. The walls were covered in old paintings and photographs. Everywhere I looked there was something to see. A curtain of thick fabric hung across a portion of the dining room and cordoned off a large part of the already big room. With a glance I saw this was the grandmother's sleeping quarters. Joanna led us to the table and the meal began.

The large meal of the day for Poles is called *obiad* and is typically served between 2 p.m. and 3 p.m. Having taken the tour of the castle and the white rock, we were in fact late, and I could see that they had been waiting, since it was after 4 p.m. when we arrived.

It has first to be said that the kitchen preparation time for *obiad* takes hours. Aside from the culinary preparation hours involved, obtaining food and other necessities at this time in Poland involved standing in long lines, relying on meat ration cards and confronting shortages and absences of even the most fundamental items. Toilet paper, for example, was a luxury. Women did that work, and typically had jobs "outside the home" as well. Joanna was a social worker in the schools. Women did not usually own automobiles, so they relied on the trams, and thus it became a matter of carrying all the supplies by hand onto a crowded, outdated tram, most often having to stand, since all seats were filled. Women brought cloth bags with them for their shopping. So sitting down to *obiad* was always an exercise in realizing the physical hardship it took to get the supplies, to use the ration card allowances, to spend the extra złoty on special expensive items, and to finally cook the meal and serve it to the family.

As beautifully attired and groomed as Joanna appeared, I was well aware of the drudgery of the days spent before and then the many hours on the day to make that meal. I have not sat an *obiad* that did not include a homemade soup to start—*żurek*, a barley soup with sausage and hard-cooked egg; or *barszcz z kołdunami*, Polish handmade macaroni afloat in the traditional beet soup; or *rosół*, a type of Polish chicken soup served over the slenderest of noodles; or a rich but light tomato soup with rice. Joanna had prepared *rosół*, my favorite, and considered particularly special because of the preparation it requires. Her *rosół* was served in china tureens as delicate as butterfly wings. After the soup course, the meat cutlets appeared, and these, too, a sort of miracle, considering that the choices of rationed meat were less than plentiful. *Ziemniaki*, boiled potatoes prepared with fresh dill and butter, a marinated cabbage salad completed the main course. The silverware we used was elegant and old, and Joanna told me it was her grandmother's. Dessert appeared, a Polish *gateau*, Polish honey cake (*piernik* or *ciasto miodowe*) made with toasted hazelnut, brown sugar, honey, eggs and butter, served with whipped cream. All such desserts were made "from scratch" since cake mixes and the like were not available in any case. Cordials followed the coffee (*kawa*) and tea (*herbata*); tea in Polish homes is made with tea leaves in a small pot atop a samovar—I have never tasted a tea richer or more delicious. Tiny silver spoons accompany the tea glass which sits in a filigreed silver holder with a handle to protect hands from the heat. Sugar is available, but a twist of *cytryna* (lemon) is essential.

Meals in Polish homes are distinct from restaurant-produced ones, just as they are in the United States, not just by quality, but by the care in preparation. The dill sprinkled on the potatoes has been picked from the family garden, which in block housing consisted only of pots on a windowsill. The other items would have been procured at the cost of physical exhaustion, not to say mental frustration. I noticed that with each course at Joanna's table, a different wine was served. Good wine was difficult to find in the first place, and when discovered, often prohibitively expensive. But on that day bottle after bottle emerged from the dining room sideboard, and I could see they were old bottles which had been saved for a special occasion.

The feeling of being the recipient of such care and generosity is particularly powerful when one is already the privileged person in the room. It is a kind of embarrassment awash in appreciation, a gratitude difficult to express at the risk of appearing patronizing. There is really nothing to do but to enjoy and thank; I had to hope that my hosts knew that I knew enough to understand the gift of that meal. At Joanna's table, and in Poland at that time, the food which makes the meal becomes a kind of offering, a measure of sacrifice for love of family and friends. A communion, these dinners celebrated what had been wrested from the hostile, outside world. Even a single item of food like a banana, represented triumph over adversity in the name of love—parents standing on line in the hope of purchasing for their children this fruit that might inexplicably appear for a day or two. Milk stood as a category all its own--"Pewex" or "dollar stores" offered homogenized milk, but the line was long and the price dear.

After *obiad* at Joanna's, it was twilight, but time enough for a walk outside around their property. Despite the agricultural fields that belonged to the family and sat adjacent to the yard or garden, the house really was in a forest. Huge and ancient trees covered the yard's large expanse in every direction around the house. The house itself was in decay—it would have required too much money to renovate it then. But it was so obviously a place of former grandeur: a deep front veranda, gabled windows, wood and stone walls—romantic and poignant in its decline. Joanna moved through the garden of her earliest childhood memory, quiet and just looking around, too conscious of what was around her to be conscious of being observed. At one point I saw her touch and then kiss the trunk of one of her trees—that picture astounded me—took my breath away, resonating as it did with all my childhood associations with trees and the woods in which my family had lived, and the heavy history of Poland's forests which now living there, I was particularly aware. There really was no difference between Joanna and her trees, her garden: her green dress and auburn hair, the changing fall light, she was an indigenous plant herself.

Darkness followed quickly and we returned to the house. I was led to the back of the house, up a beautiful wood-planked darkened stairway, as if to an attic, and climbing up, came to a tall hallway, off of which sat three rooms. One of these was to be my bedroom for the night. This was a large wooden room, one wall of which had windows festooned in a simple lace curtain pulled aside and fastened with a faded ribbon, and facing the back garden, then entirely dark. An immaculate bed sat against one of the walls, made with starched white and sun-dried and ironed bedding, alongside which sat a stout chest. On the chest was a vase of dried flowers, and on the floor just next to the bed, for my feet, an intricately woven rug, the design of which showed a proud white rooster in folk art style. The air was cool and fresh in the room; I do not know if I ever slept so well or so deeply. I cannot recall any dreams I may have had as I felt like the entire experience was already a dream, one I must have imagined—from a former time in which I could not have lived, and yet one that felt so strangely familiar … in which I must have lived, the same feeling of *bashert* I had at my grandparents' apartment in Brooklyn.

The next morning I woke to sunlight pouring in the windows and those windows filled with the pageantry of green and gold trees. Down below, I saw Joanna already in her garden, now hanging clothes on a line, the whitest laundry I had ever seen, and white chickens like the kind on my rug, gathering around her as she threw seed to them from the pockets of her pristine apron.

Joanna knew that my father had been born in Poland, that he was Jewish, and that I had come to Poland to see what I could learn of the Jewish past in Poland, the role of Poles towards their Jewish neighbors before and during the war, and now, afterwards, Polish attitudes about the destroyed Jewish community in their country. That afternoon the family had arranged for a lifelong friend of theirs, Dzidzia, a Polish Jewish physician, to come to the house so that she and I could meet. Joanna had laid out a table of delicacies and aperitif glasses on a smaller, more intimate table in the sitting room. We all gathered there, and Dzidzia and I began to converse with the translation help of Antoni. She told me how she had been a hidden child in a Catholic convent during the war—that other members of her family had been annihilated, but that she had managed to survive, to be educated, and that she had married a man of Czech background with whom she had one daughter, Mariola, now in her early twenties. Dzidzia was in her mid-fifties. She had dark hair in a conservative, even old-fashioned style and she wore large glasses, behind which appeared a handsome and intelligent Jewish face. It was her gaze, though, that was most arresting. It was friendly enough, but wary, with a kind of reserve born of feelings I could only guess at. The family's mood was animated and welcoming—it was obvious they all had known each other a long time; there was familiarity, casualness and warmth. She was a kind of family member, I could see that. Yet as I asked my questions of her, and someone would translate when my Polish lacked the capacity to express the nuance I needed, I began to see a difference between Dzidzia and the family. She spoke carefully, with sometimes long silences before responding. As she spoke, the smoke from Dzidzia's cigarette wrapped around her face, and she seemed to be shrouded in a private place, a place that seemed to be distancing itself from the one she had always enjoyed with the family. At last I asked, "Did you make the right decision to stay in Poland?" At this, she smiled, a smile both wistful and ironic, "*Chyba nie*" ("rather not,") a stoical Bartleby, and the family registered surprise and dismay. The father, "But Dzidzia, you don't mean that—why?" She remarked about the recent desecration of a nearby Jewish cemetery, and he responded, "You must know that was orchestrated by the government to discredit Polish nationalists, to make it appear that anyone against the communist left is a rightist anti-Semite." But Dzidzia shook her head slowly, and with that wry and tired smile, looked at him as if he had been duped, saying, "I'm not convinced of that, Włodek." He laughed in response—a laugh to shoo away the boogey man and all bad thoughts, a laugh which said "no, no, things are not like that, come now, let's not be so solemn."

But she turned away from him, dismissing his reaction, and instead looked at me, and asked, "Why have you come here?" the bookend question to the one I had asked her about if she had done the right thing to remain. I was still absorbing the dramatic interchange between these people who though they had known each other for decades, had apparently only now voiced their opposed outlooks. I had no perfect answer to her question, that was for sure. I had, if anything, too many answers, and not one of them captured all I felt.

I looked around me at the gracious Polish family who had arranged for me to meet their Jewish friend, a family devoid of prejudice, innocent of collusion, and the words formed in my mouth before I could embellish or improve on them: "I came to rescue hope." At this, Joanna suddenly caught her breath, a sob in her throat and eyes filling with tears, reached out her hand to mine. I was to meet Dzidzia's daughter later, in very different circumstances, in Israel.

A Wedding Coat

I had been in touch with the family of my Polish friend in California early after my arrival to Silesia. Somehow I felt it important to make contact with them, the family of this Polish friend whose angry denial of Polish anti-Semitism had, unknown to him, been in part responsible for my going to Poland in the first place. I did not want to duplicate the close-mindedness in which I felt he indulged. I contacted his brother, Alexi, whose young wife had died of causes not entirely understood, but the suspicion was that the air quality had killed her. That was not an outrageous theory in the least; since Chernobyl people were unsure if they had been affected, or if the well-known pollution of southern Poland was responsible for the many undiagnosed illnesses people suffered. Alexi had two daughters—Malgorzata and Aneta. He was a highly trained and gifted mathematician, but there were no jobs for him in Poland. So he managed a gas station, and struggled to provide for his children. The younger daughter, Aneta, was 8 years old when I met the family. Alexi told me she had been ill for a long time, and that he could not get a reliable medical diagnosis or much medical help for her. He would not have needed to tell me she was ill. A sweet-faced little girl, her skin was so white as to be translucent, and deep, dark circles ringed her eyes. Alexi tried always to obtain healthy food for her, but that was difficult. Fruit was for the wealthy. Whenever I went to visit, I would take a gift of fresh fruit, along with a toy or doll—the fruit only an American with dollars could readily afford.

Aneta broke my heart: she played with her toys and dolls in the tiny space their flat afforded, laughing with joy at times, and then dissolving into coughing fits. I had brought with me a cache of antibiotics from the United States, and I brought them to Alexi, but we could not be sure if they would be safe for a child, and somehow the opportunity to consult a physician was near impossible without money and connections.

The other daughter, Malgorzata, was 20 years old, a caring older sister. I had known the family for some months when Malgorzata told me she was to be married soon, that she was expecting a baby. A wedding celebration had been planned and I was invited. I remember Alexi shrugging as Malgorzata explained her plans. His own appearance mirrored Aneta's; he was exhausted and discouraged, but committed to doing what he could for his girls.

Some weeks after Malgorzata had told me her plans, I received an uncharacteristic phone call from her—uncharacteristic because the phones were entirely unreliable and a phone call could often be more trouble than it was worth. But she called and asked to come to my flat. This too, was strange, but I agreed. She found her way to me by tram, not an easy or streamlined journey from the family flat. I was mystified and even worried that something unfortunate may have happened. But she arrived, smiling and talkative, and though she did not speak English, we somehow always managed to converse. We sat down to tea, but within moments, she stood, and blurted in Polish, "Kate, you know that white coat that you wear, that white coat? Yes, I need your coat for my wedding. I had a coat but now that I am getting bigger (and here she mimed pulling a coat around her widening waist that would not close), it doesn't fit. I need to use your coat."

The funny thing was the white coat was my only warm, winter coat, and it was not mine. My older sister had lent me the coat before I left for Poland—a generous gesture as it was a good, expensive coat. A Californian for a long while, I no longer had a heavy winter coat, and so my sister had kindly supplied me with hers for the Polish winter. I did not hesitate. Of course, I could lend Malgorzata the coat, and it would be pretty on her for her winter wedding day, white as it was and wool. I handed it to her and tears ran down her face as she hugged me.

The wedding John and I attended was itself small, a provincial, meager affair, and as such, charming. A car bedecked with a wedding doll affixed to its hood, an old Polish wedding tradition, drove the bride and groom to the church where we all waited. The church was not old or elegant, but a product of the 50s, more committee room than temple. The ceremony over, we walked a short distance in the icy cold to a hall rented for the reception. A long table had been set with a glass of cherry vodka at the places of all the female guests,

Malgorzata on her wedding day, and her little sister, Aneta, holding the bride doll from the hood of the car. Courtesy Balgley Family Archive

and the real thing at the men's seats. The table took up most of the space in the room, but people did manage to dance to the music played from a tape recorder. A disco ball had been hung in the center of the room, and as the younger guests gyrated to the sounds, the room became close and hot, akin to a sweaty workout room. As the time wore on, I was about to take my leave, and stepping towards the door, a very drunk group of young people hailed me as the American in attendance, and cried out in the only English they had, "Fuck, yes, America, rock and roll!" Their exclamation rather brilliantly summed up the general Polish attitude toward the United States: the land of the free.

Some weeks had passed where I was overwhelmed with teaching responsibilities; I had not heard from Malgorzata since the wedding. I had not had time to travel to Kraków or Warsaw where I could purchase a winter coat to tide me over, and had managed with layered sweaters under a light jacket. Thinking I could retrieve the white coat at some point, I called Alexi since Malgorzata had no phone in her in-law's flat. Alexi, polite and considerate as always, told me Malgorzata would be in touch to return the coat. More time passed. Weeks went by. By this time, I had gone to Warsaw and purchased a coat, but I was concerned that I would be able eventually to return the borrowed coat to my sister in California.

One day after a long teaching day, climbing the fourteen staircases to my flat, I saw a plastic bag sitting on the floor just outside my door. This was unusual. No one climbed these steps to the top except me, and there were no "deliveries" in Poland. Gingerly, I opened the bag, and at first thought I saw just a rumpled chunk of fabric rolled to fit in the bag. As I took this out of the bag, it unrolled and there I saw that I held a miniature, ruined version of my sister's coat. They had apparently put it in a washing machine, and now it might fit Aneta or even the doll on the hood of the wedding car, but not Malgorzata or me—or my sister. The wool was mummified, congealed to a cement-like texture. It is one thing to lend one's own property, another someone else's, I realized too late. But could I have said no to Malgorzata? Unlikely. Had I imagined the coat was in danger of destruction, I suppose I could have offered to make a gift of a new coat, bought for the wedding. It just had not occurred to me that the coat would be ruined. I did write my Polish friend in California about it, and wondered if he would offer to replace the coat, but he was offended even by my sharing of the story. And in fairness, it had been my decision, one I could not reverse, and maybe would not even if I had known the outcome at the start. No more was ever spoken about the coat with Alexi or Malgorzata. For me this story tells so much: Malgorzata did need the coat, and was grateful I lent it. And I was only too happy to be able to help in this small way. That the coat should be returned ruined was a poignant statement about Malgorzata's bind—she was horrified, but did not know what else to do. Her living circumstances in Poland at that time were so trying that this was the least of her problems. I suppose I was hurt as a friend who had done a good deed, but the more I thought about it, the more I realized how Malgorzata had to keep on with her life's struggles; she did not have the luxury to register this unfortunate event among more pressing priorities.

Cheating?

Like Malgorzata, more than a few of my students at the institute were coping with pregnancies. I had heard numerous stories of miscarriages in Silesia, and some Poles felt that these were the consequences of Chernobyl. I could not doubt that, but even without that disaster, I could believe other environmental issues could have untold outcomes. Filters were not used on the factory smoke stacks, and it was impossible to know what was contained in the yellow, bilious smoke that poured into the sky. These pregnant girls, and I use the term intentionally, as they did not yet seem to be women—early married, living with parents, and still in school—would come to me with special requests. And these requests presented the same sort of ethical dilemma Malgorzata's request had called up. The girls explained to me that they needed to do all their work for a semester-long (or longer) course from home, that they required bed rest and coming to the institute to attend classes put their pregnancies at risk. I was not in a position to disbelieve them. The problem, obviously, was the issue of fairness to all. It would be possible to take a leave from school, and return post-pregnancy to finish. There were other students struggling to finish, and some of those also had children or were pregnant but had not asked to be in absentia from lectures or classes and still get the credit for doing the work. I decided each case ad hoc, as there really was no other way. But in almost every case, I counseled the pregnant students to suspend their studies officially, and return when they could. That was by far anything but an ideal solution and I found myself in an ethical bind a good deal of the time; there was no general solution that would insure fairness across the board.

One pregnant student came to see me with her husband, and both eventually got to the reason for this conference. They asked that I just give Małgosia the credit for the class, even if she did not do the work. There was a certain clarity, even bravery, and chutzpah in this request. I reflected that this couple may have reasoned that after all, I was a privileged American, a visitor to their country, and essentially, from their point of view, free from any of the impossible dilemmas that plagued them: why could I not just be generous, sympathetic, and do this? It was tempting. The problem, obviously, was that if I extended such a luxury to one student, I might end up with a mass exodus from all my courses, and for all sorts of reasons. Again, I had to tell them that she should temporarily withdraw from the institute and come back later when she could. They left my office visibly disappointed, and on further reflection, I found myself sympathetic, and at the same time, amazed at the request itself. It was, in short, a request to cheat, if you like, to get credit for no work, while other students fulfilled the requirements. I was almost one hundred percent sure they would not have asked this of any of the Polish faculty; they would have been laughed at and kicked out of the office. I was vulnerable, a target, but I could not blame them for asking.

Rules change with circumstances, even if unofficially. The entire American notion of cheating was cause for hilarity among my students. The first time I gave an examination to a large class, they began to talk freely to one another during the test. I called time out, "What are you doing?" I stopped the test, and asked for an explanation. It was one of the most interesting unplanned discussions in the course titled "American Culture" because it pointed up more than anything else we had discussed that semester the difference between American and Polish cultures. Or more precisely, the difference between a democratic culture and a communist one. The students felt no compunction about sharing answers on a test; they explained to me, "Everyone in this country cheats, if you want to call it that. Look, the government cheats us every day, and the only sensible thing is to 'cheat' back. A worker steals toilet paper from his factory. Of course, he does. It's only sensible. Same at school."

They were amused by what they saw as my quaint attitude toward cheating—there was not an ounce of embarrassment on their parts. It really was a breakthrough moment in the course. I explained the American attitude toward cheating—at least the advertised American attitude—and then we were able to go on and talk about how in the United States corporations cheat, how white-collar crime goes unpunished, how the American government can cheat its people by withholding information, like during the Viet Nam War, for example. And all this in the face of the Horatio Alger story--that any American can make it if she or he works hard and is honest. In the end we came back to the idea of personal integrity: it is convenient to make excuses and blame circumstance. What is integrity in a system that is itself corrupt? Finally, I told them that since this was a course in American culture, we would run the class according to American practices, even if there was flagrant hypocrisy about these standards in America. So I collected the unfinished tests, and we all laughed about the situation. I explained that tomorrow I would present a different version of the exam, and that our class would become American in practice, not just in theory—a laboratory miming a typical American classroom during a test situation. They came in the next day, and observed the "no talking" rule, and for all the world, that classroom of delightful, intelligent Central European students gave the appearance of an American academic test scenario. What I did not tell them, though, was that there were at least four different versions of the test, and I had taken care to be sure students sitting near to one another had different versions. This, was, after all, a class in the "American experience."

Two of my Polish student essays in response to the question: "What is your position on Polish emigration? Do you see emigrating Poles as heroic, misguided or courageous?" Historic documents at a time of massive world change. Courtesy Balgley Family Archive

Final draft (essay 3)

IV/3

I am going abroad.

Everyday we hear that a known person, an outstanding scientist, or just a bowing acquaintance of ours stayed abroad, asked for political asylum, fled the country. Then there is much talk about this illegal emigration and various opinions are given. Some people will always express envy and applause, others will boil over with rage. To my mind, the problem is too complex to state precisely which attitude is right and which is wrong. Still I think I am in favour of those who leave. And I have some good reason to think so.

1. I do not believe in patriotism and any sacred duties to any particular country and nation. And I do not like any kinds of nationalism. It is true that every nation makes a unique whole, founded on history and culture, but more and more cultural borders are rubbed, and it is said that the world is tending to internationalism, isn't it? We all belong to the same species, homo sapiens, and wherever we go we will never be superior or inferior to anybody. Why should we prefer one nation to another? And the state? It is nothing but a conventional arrangement, a result of policy and bureaucracy, and it is often created regardless of any natural national borders.

And patriotism is only an empty word developed
by clever politics and demagogues; ~~wh~~ they use
? it as tool for <u>hebetating</u> people and making
them cannon-fodder.

2. I do not like hoping against hope,
which means that I do not think the political
and economic situation will ever change for
the better. I am even not going to ~~talk~~ [say] much
about it. I may only tell you that some years
ago I was an optimist, I believed in many ~~things~~
ideals, and I was actively engaged in politics;
I have given it all up. It makes no sense.
And when I look at the pages of Polish history
revealing a long sequence of missed opportunities,
absurd wars, stupid political decissions, and falls,
I lose my heart. We are always looking for
new reforms and making great plans. but
we never carry them into effect, we never
succeed. Poland seems to be doomed to fall over and over again.

[new paragraph] → Why don't I try to find the cause of our
misery and struggle against it?
I have already tried. And my parents, grandparents, and great grandparents also tried.
We all failed.

3. We experience a general decay of
all values in our country and it is sometimes
hard to believe that Poland is still in Europe.
(I think it results mainly from the economic
situation.)
Day by day we are becoming more and
more mean. We are ~~interested~~ [care]

all cultural values are depreciated.
Thievery and alcoholism are becoming our national
vices, and rising prices are our only interest.
Morality, art, knowledge, and education are
more and more often empty words.
We have only few outstanding individuals; the fame
of Polish thinkers and philosophers belongs to the
past. Polish nation is gradually melting
into the indistinct ~~grey mass~~ rabble, devoided of almost
all traces of proud humanity.

4. I want my children to be free, in
the full sense of the word.
I am not able to tell you, what freedom is
but let me tell you a short story.
Some time ago a Polish film director,
J. Hanuszkiewicz, was spending his holidays
in Mazury (a lake district in Poland).
One day he was sailing with his friend when
he noticed a group of men on a distant
coast. They were wearing only swim suits
and they looked like average holiday-makers,
yet, Hanuszkiewicz said they were French.
His friend smiled expressing surprise and
distrust but when they came nearer the group
they found Hanuszkiewicz had been right.
'How did you know it?' asked his friend.
The answer was short: 'They breathed freedom!'
I would like my children to breath as

I have a nice family and good
friends. I love many places and often wonderful
scenes arise in recollection of my past.
I have never been abroad and I am a little
afraid of going anywhere. Yet, I know I cannot
stay here. I should leave.

This is very
beautifully written and
moving.   (5)

WHAT IS <u>YOUR</u> POSITION ON POLISH EMIGRATION. DO YOU SEE EMIGRATING POLES AS HEROIC, MISGUIDED, COWARDLY OR COURAGEOUS?

— 1 —

QUITTING, LEAVING OR JUST MOVING ON

There must be as many reasons for leaving Poland as there are people who rack their brains and wring their hearts before they make that decision. Perhaps those who quit in a huff, with smoke coming out of their ears and nostrils, are spared the worrying. But when they look themselves up and down I doubt if they see themselves as downright heroic or cowardly. When Poles emigrate they can almost invariably congratulate themselves on being SENSIBLE. The only difficulty in formulating a firm stand on this issue is that one can never know what kind of life an immigrant will forge for himself, just as a "loyal" or simply passive Pole cannot tell what the regime will put him through next year or even next week. But since the Polish situation is far less stable and reliable than that abroad, emigration really is the sensible choice. (Fortunately it is not so for all of us).

To say that when leaving one's country one needs to be a hero, ~~courageous~~ or simply misinformed and unwise, implies that on the whole immigration is unsuccessful; that pitfalls, hardships and disillusionment are all that awaits the dreamer. Obviously this is untrue for most, and only partly true for a handful. Poles abroad HAVE done well. Few have become eminent, but proportionately as few would have succeeded back home.

To say that cowardice drives people to the West makes even less sense. Political cowardice, fear of repression and discrimination was understandable seven or eight years ago, but today, I feel, few people would fit into that category. It seems more appropriate to

— 2 —

describe Poles trying to get to the America of their dreams as enterprising and interested in money – not necessarily easy money, but slightly more accessible than our worthless, commonly despised currency. This money for Poles is a means, not an end in itself, not even a way of achieving better status. A room, a fridge, a baby dressed in frills, plump from good baby-food, a decent holiday and security for the future, are some of the DREAMS those dreadful, degenerated materialistic Poles want to pursue.

presumably ironic

Because of a discrepancy between our upbringing and expectations, and reality almost all young people sincerely and deeply long for something better, not really knowing what their longing is, nor whether that feeling is not something to be ashamed of. Dreadful injustice is being done in educating and inspiring a nation, but providing it with a sub-standard present and a vaguely hopeless future.

Idealism feeds a fear, but for the majority the emptiness is frightening. No ties, no obligations, no regrets, noone to be indebted to – or so it would seem – NOTHING to keep us here. Even if we are not angry enough to quit, nor dissatisfied enough to leave, I think our sensibility tells us that it must be time to MOVE ON – to better, bigger, undecayed worlds. Evolution, biologists tell us, is a universal process affecting all forms of life. Has evolution stopped in our little dead-end called Poland?

"Moving on" is the key word for me, because it is so natural. It does not assume the need to break with what is old and familiar. It does not require the burning of bridges. Being ungrateful or disloyal is not an issue here.

— 3 —

But best of all — "moving on" is possible even without becoming a displaced migrant. Those who have matured and mellowed must move on, gently, up or Left or Right but definitely forward. The only way for them to do this may be by finding a new country, where they will at least be able to afford to be honest. I feel, however, that even some SENSIBLE people can hope to make progress in this country.

~~Needless to say~~ The one example I can quote is my own. The decision to leave Poland was not mine, so perhaps the decision to return came more easily to me. In order to make even the most shakey step forward I had to get back my right to claim that this plot of scraggly grass, however unkempt, this cracked communal sidewalk, however ugly, is mine. It is more mine than any foreign, freshly-moved, flower-scented, trim front lawn will ever be. I too tried to be sensible. Choices are very individual moments and most are wrong and right at the same time. Just as sensibility has no unambiguous definition.

And so, though I see nothing heroic or cowardly in Polish emigrants, I understand their decisions as reasonable, if they have weighed up their chances abroad, and realized how much, or how little, they are <u>leaving</u> behind. For myself — moving on is the only option and as long as Poland allows me to do this I will not quit.

Emma Bovary, Polish Style

I had the opportunity to write a course on women's literature and offer it as a small seminar to advanced students. Not surprisingly, only women signed up for the course. But that was fine; I thought it might give female students the chance to share their views more fully or openly.

It was a warm and beautiful day, the sun was shining in a sky that was characteristically gray and polluted. I had often taken my classes in the United States outside on days like this. I suggested it to my women's seminar; they were surprised, amused, and nonplussed, but when I explained that this was typical in an American university, they were game. I did have a moment, however, to wonder what my Polish colleagues would think when they looked out their windows. Chalk it up to the odd American, the Californian, I could not afford to worry about their judgments all the time.

The seminar read *Madame Bovary* that week, and I was anxious to share with them the influence of naturalism on Flaubert, the story of his court case for obscenity, and his famous statement, "I am Madame Bovary," and to get their reactions. I was in for a big surprise. The notion that Emma Bovary was a romantic, even an artist, caught in a prosaic world, infuriated them. For them, Emma Bovary was a spoiled woman who did not know how good she had it. They compared her to their own mothers, "My mother has no servants, she cooks and cleans and has a job and deals with this stupid regime. If anyone should be unhappy, and want to escape, my mother has more claim than this silly protagonist." I played devil's advocate to their quick judgment, "But what about unhappiness that isn't about material comfort? What is it that Emma wants?" The students dismissed this out of hand, "There is no room for this in real life." they rejoined, "But it exists—is it just folly? Why would Flaubert create a character like this? What should we understand?" to which they replied, "It doesn't matter. Emma Bovary does not deserve our attention."

All this made good sense, of course, given the circumstances in which the students lived. Intelligent and discerning as they were about other matters in other texts, they were having no excuses for poor Emma. The same held true when we studied Kate Chopin's *The Awakening*. Edna Pontellier was an elite, a blind and spoiled one, who made herself unhappy for nothing. To move beyond this immediate dismissal, I turned their attention to well-loved Polish Romantic literature of the eighteenth century which featured aristocratic female protagonists. They acquiesced a bit with this point, but maintained that such characters in Polish literature could not really be compared—too many historical and cultural differences. I conceded they had a point. With a history like Poland's, one made such comparisons at risk: perhaps Poland really is an exception among the nations. Still, I maintained that characters can be seen in a light that transcends the boundaries of time and space. They understood that, they assured me, and would have liked to transcend their own time and place to critique these literary characters, but it was not possible, they could not manage that or afford it now, not with the life their history had forced upon them. If that meant intellectual narrowness, for now, then so be it: this was the best they could do.

IV

VISITORS ❀ GREEN AGAIN

A Decision Reversed

During this first fall and winter in Poland, I had been writing to my parents regularly. I shared with them the vicissitudes and victories of living in what felt like another universe, much less a foreign country. So I was shocked when my father who had stated unequivocally when I learned I would be going to Poland on the Fulbright, that he and my mother would meet me in France or Britain, but not Poland—shocked when my father wrote to tell me that he and my mother *would* come to Poland to visit me. He made no mention of why he had changed his mind, but perhaps the stories in my letters had moved him, and moved him to this new decision.

My parents arrived in Warsaw in March of 1988. By then, I knew my way around the country, and my Polish was good enough to manage everyday life and travel. I had the use of *Pani* Zofia's beautiful pre-war flat in Warsaw on *Aleje Ujazdowskie*, so when I met my parents at *Okęcie* Airport in Warsaw, though I was anxious for them to see the isolated and polluted part of the country where I lived, I could bring them there to rest before moving to the rougher existence in Silesia. I also wanted time to show them Warsaw.

That spring was extravagantly glorious. By the time my parents came, the landscape was in full bloom—green and gold—with the brilliant colors of native trees and flowers. After their long and exhausting flight (they were in their 70s when they made the trip from their home in California), I took them by taxi to the apartment on *Ujazdowskie*. The cab took us to this fashionable address, and as we walked through the curved entrance to the open courtyard where a single, giant and beautiful tree stood, my father suddenly stopped, dropped his hand luggage, and looked with amazement at the surroundings. I had never seen him in such a stance. He was literally riveted to the spot where he stood. After a few moments, he said as if in a dream, "This is familiar to me. I remember this now. If not this exact building, then it would be one just like it. When I came to Warsaw from Brest-Litovsk with my mother and siblings, we came to a relative's home that was precisely like this. I had forgotten this for six decades. But this is it."

I had known that such pre-war apartments on *Ujazdowskie* and other parts of Warsaw had been Jewish homes, and the courtyard that had stopped my father was characteristic of these very elegant dwellings. Typically, before the war, a Polish gentile would be the keeper of the courtyard and would safeguard

March 1988, when my father Ely and my mother Margaret visited me in Warsaw and stayed in Pani Zofia's apartment on Al. Ujazdowskie. They were in their 70s at that time. Courtesy Balgley Family Archive

the entrance. At the time, I wondered if the apartment where I had been staying regularly when I visited Warsaw was not the actual home of my father's relatives, my own family? Years later, like finding a needle in a haystack, *bashert* took a hand and led me, and I was to learn exactly the address where my father and his family had been received.

My father's recognition of this place and his willingness to share what he had never spoken of before, set the tone for my parents' entire visit. My father and I had only skirted issues of his Jewish identity up till now, and here we were, in Poland, sunk into the world he had left behind, had actually erased from his memory seemingly by force of will. But he had made the decision to come—so perhaps something in my letters home, combined with a personal transformation in him—made him decide to visit Poland.

We visited the monument at the Warsaw Ghetto. I had known that my father's uncle Benjamin had come to the United States from Brest and Warsaw, and had established a prestigious photographic studio in Manhattan. But then he strangely returned to Poland before World War II and the family never knew exactly why. Some cynically said he had real estate there he wanted to claim, but others said he had a wife and child there. In any case, after he went back to Warsaw, he was never heard from again. That was one casualty I learned about then, but years later, again in very unlikely circumstances, like that needle in the haystack once again, I was to find proof of my other countless family members who were murdered. As we walked the bleak cement blocks which form the pavement of the Warsaw Ghetto, my mother took me aside, and said, "This must be very hard for your father."

My mother had always been more willing to show feelings than my father, and her comment was especially poignant at that moment because it was obvious by his behavior that he was trying to absorb what he was seeing as a necessary education, but at the same time to brace himself against what must have been a huge wave of emotion. Later, again in a taxi, we passed by the lovely park, *Ogród Saski*, across from the Victoria Hotel, where there stood an historical marker which read, *"Auschplatz,"* and I heard my father murmur to himself, "Attack Place, oh, I see." We went to the Jewish State Theatre in Warsaw, the home theatre of the famed Jewish actress, Ida Kaminska, one evening and saw *Night at the Stary Rynek*, a play about religious tolerance, all too relevant to the history we were ourselves re-experiencing.

My father, Ely, with Chopin's piano at Żelazowa Wola 50 km from Warsaw, during my parents' visit to meet me in Poland when I was teaching in Silesia. Courtesy Balgley Family Archive

Green again

By the time we traveled to Kraków, my father had been observing my identification with the Jewish story in Poland, and I think his own feelings, complex as they must have been—ranging from sadness to guilt to awe—were coming to the surface and his reserve was quickly evaporating.

After our visit to Kazimierz, the former Jewish section of Kraków, where I introduced my father to Pan Jakubowicz, the nominal head of the small remaining Jewish community in Kraków whom I had met within my first days in Poland, we walked back slowly to our hotel.

I will never forget that evening. My parents and I were physically exhausted from the days of travel within Poland, and no doubt we were emotionally on edge after what we had been seeing and reliving. Although he is a person capable of great empathy, from my childhood I knew my father could also be stoical under strain. I now realize that stoicism likely came of necessity from the extreme circumstances of his early life. But that stoicism was draining from him rapidly that night, and a very different mood possessed him. He turned to me in the quiet of our hotel room and tears streaming down his face, he said, "I thought Poland was a land of ashes! A dead, winter place! And yet it is a beautiful spring here. The trees bloom! In spite of everything, life is here!" I could only respond with tears running down my own face. It was as if we had to go together to this heart of darkness for him to reach into himself to unveil his own heart. At one point, we both agreed, "And yes, it will be green again and in bloom next spring." I had come all this way around the world initially to see if I could rescue hope in Poland, if I could find my own identity, if I could see that even now, when I had learned that Polish acquaintances in America were in denial about their country's history of anti-Semitism, that the real hope I had come to find was my father's acknowledgement of his Jewish self, of the pain and even the shame he had kept hidden from himself, and with that acknowledgement, clarity for myself about my split or dual identity. It was in that discovery where the flowers would perpetually bloom, in spite of everything. We were silent and cried together for some time. The next morning we boarded a train to my remote part of Poland, to show my parents where I had been teaching.

My parents and John and I made our way by train from Kraków, a showplace city in Poland, to the particularly polluted and unglamorous Silesian part of the country, to Dąbrowa Górnicza, to my lowly residence. As our taxi from the train station in Katowice pulled into the parking area of my block building, the unremitting grayness of the area met my parents' eyes for the first time.

The fact that there was not a word said from either my mother or my father in reaction to what they saw made clear to me that they had together decided they would display no shock at the conditions of my life in Poland. I was proud of them. In their seventies, they climbed the fourteen steep staircases to my flat at the top. Once inside, and for the two-week duration of their stay in my home, they slept on the rickety pull-out bed in the main room of the flat.

I went back to my work at the institute in the following days. Mysteries continued to abound there. I would arrive to teach my seminar or a large lecture class only to learn that the "administration" had cancelled it for that day, for example. No prior notice was given to me in those instances. No reason provided. That was particularly ironic since there always seemed to be an unspoken but expected Polish Old World graciousness to transactions at the institute; we foreigners were supposed to know what was considered polite, and what was otherwise, and we were judged accordingly. Our faux pas, things we could not possibly have known, were met with aghast reactions. And yet the behind-closed-doors decisions that were made concerning we foreigners were, to us, high-handed, inconsiderate, and rude.

It was especially galling during my parents' visit to the institute. I took them to the institute to see where I taught, and to attend a lecture I would be giving. Given the length of their stay in Poland, that would be my parents' only opportunity to attend one of my classes, and I was excited to introduce them to my students and to have them audit the lecture. Within moments of the scheduled start of the lecture, the chair of the department came by the lecture hall with a visiting scholar from the United Kingdom, and explained to me that Dr. So and So would be giving a guest lecture today. "I hope that is okay?" he said. But it wasn't a question; this was a *fait accompli*. I explained to my parents and took up a seat next to them in the large lecture hall. Unfortunately, as things turned out, the British speaker had such poor delivery and enunciation that neither my parents, the students, nor I could understand a single word! Despite that missed opportunity, by the time my parents left Poland to return home, they had seen my life there. And my father had witnessed the depth of my connection to Jewish identity.

"That's all there is to it"

Shortly after their departure, a close friend from graduate school visited me. A feminist who was leftist and cosmopolitan, she had had a Fulbright in Barcelona some years before. She was a veteran traveler, and she wanted to see communist Poland. Deborah and I shared the same politics throughout our friendship; we had, after all been schooled in our graduate school literature department in the Marxist analysis of literature. Despite all we had in common, we found ourselves disagreeing frequently in Poland. I had taken up the attitude of my Polish friends: communism was the bane of Poland. Given what I was experiencing and what I saw the Poles endure, it was impossible to conclude otherwise. My students and friends could not get visas to travel and they were called in by the authorities for questioning about their relationship with me, an American. Food and other necessities were scarce and too expensive for the average Pole, even though those commodities were readily available for the wealthy or those with dollars. But more than all that, an atmosphere of secrecy and punishment pervaded every aspect of society. I had become accustomed to complaining about those issues, and Deborah would stop me and remind me of the aspects of capitalism that were arguably just as bad or worse.

She had a point. I had become indignant about the deprivations, prohibitions and indignities, and I no longer possessed an objective compass. When she brought up subtleties that used to be the center of our conversations, I brushed her aside with "I understand your theory, but none of that works here. In practice, my friends and colleagues are victims of their regime." She would shake her head at me, saying "You've become a reactionary." Maybe I had, I thought, maybe I had lost all subtlety and complexity of understanding, but it could not be otherwise. I was mired in the struggle of the people around me.

On one occasion, our difference of opinion took on another dimension. Deborah knew I had come to Poland to learn what I could of Polish attitudes towards Jews, to learn more about my own Jewish identity, and she was herself Jewish. I had taken her to Kraków to the former Jewish district of Kazimierz, then decrepit and sad, its synagogues in disrepair, a slum for the Poles who then inhabited it. A Jewish beggar approached us. It was impossible to know his age, so beaten down was his appearance. Had he survived the Shoah, I asked myself? He walked painfully, stooped over, and as he crossed the plaza in front of the synagogue, some Polish children shouted anti-Semitic epithets at him. He ignored them, but greeted us with an outstretched hand. He was in rags. That day I had no dollars with me, and they were what would have made sense to give him. I asked Deborah if she had any. No, but she did have some deutschmarks. That would work for the beggar, too; I told her to give the deutschmarks to him, I would pay her back, but we should give him something. She resisted my request—probably because it really was not a request, but a demand I justified with the offer to pay her back. I appreciate her point today. It was hers to decide if she wanted to respond in that way to the beggar. But I had lost my compass there, too. During my time in Poland, I was filled with a sympathy so overwhelming, not only for that Jewish beggar, but for the Poles I was meeting, that I could not see or entertain any other point of view. Was it guilt I was feeling? I had so much and they so little. And this a consequence of fate, and nothing else. Despite the fact that before coming to Poland I was already fully cognizant that I was a white person of privilege in my own country, the disparity there shocked me—it was up close and personal everywhere. Perhaps it was shame I was feeling, and for better or worse, I acted out of that in many situations. Deborah did give the pauper the deutschmarks. When I went to reimburse her, she shrugged me off, annoyed. I cannot say that I blamed her at all. My emotions had directed her, and that was, no matter what, in its own way disrespectful of her autonomy—ironic, as that was what I claimed I hated most about communism in Poland.

Later that week, Deborah and I were invited to a social evening at a student's flat. Actually, the hostess was a former student, a graduate of the institute, but her sister was a current student, and they both had friends among the younger faculty. As was typical on those occasions, people tended to drink too much. At one point in the evening, our inebriated hostess asked Deborah if she had visited Auschwitz. We had not; Deborah had demurred. "Well," Renata, the hostess continued, "you aren't missing anything—except those long lines of people looking ridiculous in their mournfulness. It's become nearly comical—this solemn parade of visitors." Renata perhaps did not know, or maybe care, that Deborah was Jewish, and she certainly did not know my background. She continued, "You know, many German people who lived right here were murdered. My family was German and their homes were taken from them."

The Nazi plan before Germany's defeat had been to remove Jewish and Slavic people from Eastern Europe in order to settle those areas with Germans. I knew she was referring to the expulsion of people of German ancestry in the late stages of and after World War II as part of the geopolitical plan for ethnic reconfiguration. During the period from 1944 to 1948, millions of people, many of them ethnic Germans and German citizens were forcibly moved from Central and Eastern Europe. The number of deaths attributable to these forced moves is disputed, and during the Cold War it was thought the numbers were exaggerated for political propaganda. The Allies' postwar Potsdam Agreement had reconfigured the borders of Europe, so that for instance, Lwów, a Polish city with a large and important Jewish population, became part of the Soviet Union. I looked at Renata. To me she was the person who looked ridiculous with her drunken, smiling face. No one else in the room seemed to take objection or be upset by her comment about Auschwitz. But I was most concerned for my friend, Deborah. What a horrible thing to hear. Yet here again, Deborah and I had separate reactions. I was furious, insulted, disgusted, and wanted to say so. Deborah, instead, gulped, shrugged, remained silent, and told me later,

"Kathy, so many times I have been in situations, sat around dinner tables with otherwise presumably civilized people—in Barcelona on my Fulbright and the many other places I've traveled in the world—and heard this sort of thing. People hate Jews, and that's all there is to it."

Women's Studies/Studies of Women
Dubrovnik, 1988

Later that spring I was invited to present at a conference in Dubrovnik, still then in a place called Yugoslavia, on "Women and Writing." My paper, "*Le Langage de Connaisance*," "The Language of Knowing" looked at the work of Hélène Cixous, to develop and find a new language that would make female expression possible, to break out of a language that by its very structure is patriarchal. The exciting element of that conference was that women had come from over forty countries to participate. There were women scholars from Africa, Asia, Europe and the United States, all of whom had read the same theories, but applied them to texts from their own cultures. There was plenty of time for follow up discussion and informal conversations and it was thrilling to see women in bright turbans mix with their European and American colleagues, though not many Americans were in attendance. It would have been quite a luxury for an American academic institution to cover the expense of sending a delegate to Dubrovnik. The talks were all interesting, some better than others as is always the case, but there was the shared idea that women were second class citizens, no matter from what culture.

I had traveled from Warsaw to Dubrovnik with a Polish lecturer from another university in Poland. That way our institutes could arrange our travel more efficiently. Katarzyna was pale, quiet and younger than me, and we would meet up with participants after talks, but she did not join the conversation among feminists. I wondered why she was there.

When Katarzyna and I had time alone, we talked about the presentations and the informal conversations. I asked what she thought. She told me, "I do not relate to this Western brand of feminism. Look, in Poland, women do not feel this way about their men. We are partners, not adversaries. If a woman wakes in the morning before her lover, she will go stand in the line for some good bread for breakfast while he sleeps because she loves him and wants to do this. Maybe she goes every time and he never goes. What if she does all the domestic work? He goes to his job and brings the money home. This must sound hopelessly unenlightened to you, but in my country, we cannot afford the sort of feminism espoused here. We are, men and women, all victims of our system. We are all oppressed—together. And this creates our solidarity."

Her explanation made sense: oppression makes equals out of men and women in her country. But from my perspective as a "Westerner" living in Poland, this opinion only addressed part of the situation, and I told her, "But Polish women as 'victims-in-solidarity' with men, still have much less personal freedom. They are expected to always put their families first, whether as daughters, mothers, sisters, wives, while it is routinely accepted that men's careers, jobs, and their personal wishes trump all." She nodded, smiling, and responded, "Yes, you are right there, but we have bigger problems in my country, and as I say, this brand of feminism would be an indulgence we cannot now afford."

I met another woman at the conference who had been born in Poland, but had left as a child with her parents in the 1960s. She was now an American citizen, an academic specializing in women's studies. Since her departure from Poland, she had visited Poland a number of times with her mother, and I was curious to know her views as a feminist, particularly about the situation of women's personal freedom in current Polish society, the topic Katarzyna and I had talked about. She had been an expert downhill skier at one time, and it was from this vantage point that she responded to my question. Urszula explained looking back now in the late 1980s, that the 1970s had been the "good old days" for Polish athletes, women athletes in particular, because communist Poland took on the Soviet model of support for their athletes. Athletes, she pointed out, went from so-called "amateur" status to that of professional. She suggested that sport is different for Poles than for westerners, "Sport represents an inner sort of freedom, an individual, personal accomplishment, where for Americans, it is a question of competition with others."

I suggested that musical achievement might be similar—the achievement of excellence offers this same individual inner freedom. "No," she responded, "music is already creative, freedom of expression is constitutional to it, but achievement in sport is circumscribed—it's in one's head, it's a self-liberation within the tight bonds of political and cultural strictures. And women athletes in communist Poland for the first time had that experience of personal freedom."

She went on to explain the irony of this situation. Poland in the 1970s experienced a particularly clamped-down regime, and despite what the decade offered athletes, it was hardly the "good old days" for the Polish people. Urszula had been born in Lwów, a city that experienced the largest displacement of people in history, where post-World War II, as Yalta shifted the national boundaries of Poland, Germany and the USSR, citizens of Lwów (which had been a beautiful Polish city before the war) were displaced to Wrocław in Poland, formerly Breslau in Germany. With regret in her voice, she relayed how sorry she was that when she returned there with her mother for a visit, she could not feel what her mother was feeling. She had been in the United States long enough by then that she was distanced from Poland, so when she visited there she was not "at home" any longer. I suggested that this could be an advantage for a writer like herself, this outsider perspective, if perhaps a personal loss. She agreed, but wistfully added, "Oh, yes, a benefit, yes, certainly, but at a great cost."

I left Dubrovnik with my head full of new subtleties about feminism, Poland, and personal freedom. On my return to Poland, I stopped into the American Consulate in Kraków to pick up my mail. I had a friendly relationship with a Polish woman who worked there. I had been frustrated by the obstacles put in my way at the institute to show American videos to my students. In particular, I wanted to share the then newly-released nine-episode film, *The Struggles for Poland*. In our previous conversations, my friend at the consulate had been refreshingly honest about her disgust with the regime's "trickle down" effect on the institutes throughout the country, as I had many times before confided to her the difficulty I was having arranging to show the videos to my students. She looked at me knowingly, seriously, and kindly said, "Wait, wait for a while … until after the Round Table talks." I had known that in February these talks would be televised in Poland: the government had finally agreed to talks with Solidarity and other opposition groups. "Maybe then. But be careful. I know that some people even here (tipping her head towards the consulate's hallway) look at notices on the board announcing certain events at the institutes, and if these seem 'suspect' to them, they report them," she said. "But to what end?" I asked. "The only repercussion for me and other Americans teaching in Poland would be to revoke our visas and send us home." She went on, "Yes, that's true, that's fine for you, but your institute could be punished. For example, I know that your institute has applied for another building—this could be withheld. Also, questions could be asked, 'What do these films have to do specifically with the curriculum?' Be cautious. Be aware. They are watching."

I thanked her for her advice and wondered about the bounds of my own personal freedom to do what I thought best for my students versus what grief I could unwittingly bring to the institute. A classic Polish dilemma: personal integrity versus the "reality" of consequences. But my situation was different than that of the Polish citizen—I had a way out.

A case of mistaken identity

While in Poland, I had continued my American subscription to the magazine, *Tikkun*, edited by the Jewish American Middle East peace activist,

Michael Lerner, and I regularly collected it in my mail at the American Consulate in Kraków. There had been a heated exchange on the subject of Polish anti-Semitism in one issue, and in a later issue, I found a remarkable letter to the editor:

To the Editor:

Mr. Brumberg analyzes with great subtlety the attitudes of Poles towards Polish anti-Semitism—something that no one has done heretofore, at least not with the same exactitude. Those attitudes oscillate between, at one extreme, failing to recognize anti-Semitism, and at the other, justifying it. As the author correctly notes there are defense mechanisms that make it possible for nations to ignore certain insalubrious chapters in their own history. No doubt each nation is equipped with these mechanisms, and each—for its own reasons— would rather forget such chapters. Prof. Mendelsohn, cited by Mr. Brumberg, asserts that "victims are extremely reluctant to admit that they have victimized others." Perhaps there are exceptions to this rule, but Mendelsohn and Brumberg are certainly right with regard to the Poles. We cannot admit to ourselves the thought that we may have been wrong doers. Numerous generations, including my own, has imbued Poles with a belief in the messianic mission of the Polish nation. The original form of this idea, of course, has not stood the test of time. Incarnated hundreds of times in literature and in the visual arts, the exceptional suffering of the Polish people and its exceptional role in the history of mankind have nevertheless become integral parts of the Polish national myth. The Romantic slogan—"Poland—the Messiah of Nations"—has meant for us the distinctive suffering we as a people chosen by God to bear and suggested our *guiltlessness*. It has also fostered a profound sense of grievance against the rest of the world, which is presumably unaware of the first and does not believe in the second. This firm conviction about our inculpability has engendered a peculiar national immaturity, an attenuated sense of responsibility, and an inability to tolerate criticism.

When Poland, after nearly 150 years, again reclaimed its independence, Poles were wont to see it as the realization of the messianic promise—that is "resurrection." In time Poland turned out to be like any other country; yet the dream of an ideal state endured. The average Pole finds it difficult to fit the scourge of anti-Semitism into this mythical image, the more so since after the Second World War criticism of the past signified not a recognition of historical consciousness but a political declaration, rooted in the present and firmly on the side of communism. As a result, the subject of anti-Semitism became—in times that I, for one, remember—cloaked in silence. As Mr. Brumberg so incisively remarks, this silence had to be broken for the sake of our national consciousness. For national consciousness, so important to the Poles, is inseparable from national conscience.

The most painful problem is that of WWII. Brumberg shows how groundless are the illusions on which Poles are nurtured today— illusions bolstered by their journalists, their writers, as well as, unfortunately, their historians. Among them are illusions about the magnitude of the help extended to Jews during the War and about the number of Jews saved by Poles. Shedding those illusions would mean recalling the indifference, the deliberate refusal to help, and the (let us hope, marginal) co-participation in the crimes by means of blackmail and persecution.

Every war is an assault upon life. In the last war, however, murder was the goal, rather than the means. For this reason it was imperative to defend, above all, the vale against which the war was waged— that of life. Independence, territories, and so on should have been of secondary importance. But we proved to be altogether unprepared to accept that moral challenge. We were misled by the church, which unfortunately had participated before the war in the dissemination of hatred—something that I, as a Catholic, I am bound to acknowledge. To be sure, in time the church provided a haven for a certain number of persecuted Jews, yet countless Poles reaped the fruits of the evil sown in the past. We were led astray, too, by many who were regarded as the teachers of the nation. The War found us weak not only militarily, but also morally. Yes, we were heroic, but this heroism was a legacy of an earlier era, singularly insufficient in the era of gas chambers.

I do not know what the future of the Polish-Jewish dialogue will be. There are opportunities that history offers us but once. The intractability of the dialogue stems not from the fact that Poles are not in the position to understand the "Jewish experience"—as one writer, quoted by Brumberg, observes. It is neither possible nor necessary to enter into the experience of others. The basic condition for such a dialogue is the acceptance of the distinctive nature of that experience and of its sovereignty. Unhappily, the only dialogue that is possible now is the dialogue of historians. It is one that deserves respect, especially in Poland, where the interest in history is greater than even the historians themselves realize. A good historian can weaken the strength of stereotypes and condition his people to accept truths injurious to their national pride. At the same time, the historian who panders to national pride is apt to wreak much harm. Personally, I am grateful to Prof. Norman Davies (to whom Mr. Brumberg alludes in his article and with whom he recently debated in the pages of the *New York Review of Books*) for his enormous sympathy for my people; yet I would rather that he did not retouch the past. The history of Poland is sufficiently great and heroic, and there is no need, therefore, to conceal its faults. Forgive this personal note, but I am moved to make this remark because I find Prof. Davies' impact on many young Polish historians highly disturbing. There is, of course, the danger that if this problem is left entirely to historians, it will lose its moral edge. But this is something we can do nothing about. The common past of Poles and Jews is becoming ever more distant, and all we can hope for is to be able to save some of its remnants.[5]

The letter was signed by a certain Ela Szlufik from the "Research Center for History and Culture of the Jews of Poland, Jagiellonian University, Cracow, Poland." I had kept the letter with me so that I could make contact with the department. I wrote a letter of interest commenting on my admiration of the letter to *Tikkun*, and asking about the work of the Center. I also asked if I could visit at some point. I received a letter in response that, like so much at the institute, left a strange, impossible to interpret, impression. The handwritten letter began with a thank you to me for my "so kind remembering (sic) my letter to '*Tik*' (sic)." The letter to the editor had been fluent and eloquent in English, nothing at all like this current response to me from Ela Szlufik with its errors in English. The second paragraph she wrote added to the mystery: "It is rather difficult to tell anything about the work of my Center. We are just one of the university departments and we work as the others do." The Ela Szlufik who had penned the letter to *Tikkun* had a sophisticated understanding and knowledge of Polish-Jewish history, and of the controversy about Polish anti-Semitism. How could this paragraph be written by the same person? Her letter to me did agree to my visit, and now particularly curious, I wanted to see this "Center" as she called it, and to meet the person who had signed the letter to the editor of *Tikkun* and this letter to me.

The day I traveled to Kraków was a cold, December day. I had the address of the "Center," as Ela had referred to it. The letterhead on which she had written to me in careful cursive indicated a "Department" at Jagiellonian University, so I expected to find the office within the location of the university where I knew it to be. It turned out that, no, the address Ela gave me was in the city proper, but at some distance from the university. The street was tiny and narrow, the area a bit rundown. I followed the numbers until they ran out, and then just at the end of the little road, a small wooden and brick building, bringing to mind a cabin from the previous century in the Polish mountains, appeared bearing a nearly hidden sign which read (in Polish): "Center for Research on the Polish Jewry." This could not be a place where classes were held, certainly, so I could not see how it might be "just one of the university departments and we work as the others do." As I approached the only door to the building—it seemed more like a house than an office—a young woman opened the door before I could knock, addressing me by name and cordially introducing herself as Ela Szfulik. Before me stood a person much, much younger than what I would have expected based on the letter to *Tikkun*, a letter which seemed to speak for the "Research Center for History and Culture of the Jews of Poland, Jagiellonian University." Ela looked to be in her twenties, the age of my undergraduates at the institute. Her stature was so slight and frail, she seemed to be a waif. This impression was added to by her manner of speaking--quietly, deferentially, even timidly. She showed me into the rooms of the place—there were only a few rooms and they had the look of offices for business secretaries. No one was present. She was not comfortable in her English, and I decided not to query too much, but just to observe and listen to see what I could glean about this "Department" or "Center"—I had no idea which or what it was—and to understand how this person could be the same person who composed and sent that important letter to *Tikkun*. The walls were mostly bare, save a Jewish calendar hanging in one room, and a handsome small tapestry featuring the Polish eagle and the Star of David together. All the lights in the place were off. After this minutes-long glimpse of the rooms, Ela suggested we go for a coffee and led me to the door. Together we walked back the same way I had come from the Sukiennice at the center of the city, and found a café. We sat together and she told me that she "works in the archives." As politely as I could, I asked her to explain which archives and to what purpose. She was clearly nervous and uncomfortable. Rather than answer the question she thanked me again for my appreciation of the letter in *Tikkun*. But by now, it was obvious to me, and she likely realized this, that she had not been the writer of that letter.

Feeling as I did when I experienced the invisible machinations at the institute, I left that meeting believing that Ela's name had been used on the letter perhaps to protect someone else, or as a complicated chess move between the key opponents in the argument about Polish anti-Semitism. That someone writing about this subject should need to hide his or her identity was unsettling, but not surprising given what I had seen already in reactions to this subject. I thanked her and said goodbye. As I made my way to the railway station to return home, it occurred to me that it was not impossible that the person whom I had just met was not Ela Szfulik, but a person assigned to meet and dispense with my American and Jewish inquiry. Sounds outlandish, but in that looking glass world, I was learning that believing I could have certainty about anything might be the most outlandish idea of all.

My epiphany with We Three Kings

The outlandish had its delights as well. One late winter afternoon in January, I was working in my flat in Silesia when a knock at the door surprised me. It was a rare occasion that anyone would climb the fourteen staircases to the floor where nothing except my flat was located. True, at times Oskar woke me before dawn with the warm *bułki* he would bring, and another time I was amazed to find two Jehovah's Witnesses who had made the climb up the block's stairways, sliding *The Watchtower* written in Polish from a briefcase and hoping to convert me. If anyone was coming to my place in out-of-the-way Dąbrowa Górnicza, I generally knew about it in advance.

I peered through the peephole, and at first saw no one. Standing on my tiptoes, I looked down into the peephole, and was surprised to see two little, smudge-faced and ragamuffin boys, not more than 7 years old, waiting for my door to open. When we stood face to face, they began to speak rapid fire Polish, quite adamant about their message. I could not understand their purpose and told them so. As they appeared to be neighborhood children, they had likely never met a non-Pole. They were absolutely frustrated by my inability to understand their explanation. Finally, in exasperation, one of the boys pushed past me in the doorway and made his way into my flat. I stood nonplussed. The second boy followed quickly, practically running, and talking all the while to me in Polish I could not follow. They quickly surveyed the small space and made their way to my tiny kitchen, trying to reassure me that they knew what they were doing—they would show me. These miniature intruders opened my cabinets one after another until they found a bowl, and taking it down, they filled it with water, and placed the bowl on a table in my main living area. They gestured reassuringly to me, all four hands indicating I should wait, not to worry, they would be back. I looked at the door slamming behind them, and stood in my narrow hallway, slightly stunned. The transaction had only taken minutes, and I had no idea what I had just experienced. Ten minutes or so passed—when the door was knocked again. And again, I looked through the peephole—I was not entirely comfortable with what might be following that bizarre performance—and looking down again, I saw the same boys, this time garbed in Roman Catholic altar boy vestments, faces still smudged but with their formerly tousled hair now flattened with water in an obviously hurried attempt to look respectable. Each held a lighted candle. I opened the door immediately and in they walked solemnly and ceremoniously while I continued to stand aside to see what was to be done for me or to me. In a moment, an imposing figure appeared rounding the penultimate staircase. Wearing a miter and full flowing Mass vestments, a very tall and large Catholic priest swept dramatically into my flat, wearing wrap-around sunglasses, hardly taking notice of me at all, and following the little boys, brandishing his silver aspergillum, he was guided by his diminutive cohorts quickly to the bowl of water. Here he paused only a second, bending slightly to dip his instrument in the water, and then suddenly straightening up military style, he whirled around spraying water about the living room—the television got most of it, I found later—and then taking giant steps like a pole vaulter, he dashed about the other rooms of my flat shaking his sprinkling wand over my papers, books, and unmade bed.

The entire spectacle lasted less than a minute. Suddenly all three were gone, and I was left understanding a little bit more perhaps, but dumbfounded nonetheless.

I later learned from Polish friends that my house was being blessed for me in recognition of the Epiphany, those days between New Year's Day and 6 January— Three Kings Day in Poland. The Epiphany is the epiphany for Christians that Jesus has been made human by God, his father. So, of course, there were three of them, the two altar boys and the priest, the three kings, and the smudging on the faces of the boys—I had thought both boys looked like they had just come from playing in the dirt—was actually the attempt of one of the boys to traditionally smear his face black to resemble the black wise man, Melchior. While commercial interests would have us think the so-called twelve days of Christmas are the shopping days left from 12 December, the traditional twelve days mark the time from Christmas Day to the Epiphany. The Twelfth Night was in medieval England the day that ended a festival that started on All Hallows Eve, Halloween. The following day, All Hallows Day, the first day of November, Poles go to the graves of their families to clean and decorate and visit with the dead; in other parts of the world, most notably in Mexico, the Day of the Dead is celebrated on that day. Again in medieval and Tudor England, Twelfth Night had been celebrated with drinking, dancing and general carousing. On that day all things in the world were turned upside down or reversed—the peasant a king for example, so there was crowned a "King of Misrule" to lead the festival. By the next day, all was to be returned to normal.

I had noticed fading chalk marks inside blocks outside flats: "K + M + B" so now I understood these to be the initials for Kaspar, Melchior and Balthasar—the marks placed by the priest after visiting my home.

I had received a visit from the Magi, my neighborhood's version of the Three Wise Men. After they left, I looked out my window facing the mural of Lenin's face and pointing finger, to see beyond to the Catholic Church. Twilight had fallen by now and I saw that atypically, the usually darkened church was alight tonight. It was unthinkable to anyone in the neighborhood that someone might not be Roman Catholic. Or if they thought about it, it really did not matter--that night all houses and all people were to be blessed by the Roman Church throughout Poland. I could not say that I did not feel part of a community and momentarily cleansed by the entire experience.

Adam and Majka
A Christmas tree in Warsaw

I had not spent Christmas in Dąbrowa Górnicza, but instead traveled to Warsaw to be with Polish friends whom I visited each time I went to the capital. Majka and Adam were married, but in their small flat, kept separate rooms. I understood that Majka was chronically and seriously ill for years—she had a pulmonary condition, and could not have weighed more than ninety pounds. She was hospitalized from time to time, and when I traveled to West Berlin, I purchased a list of medications she needed but could not get in Poland.

Majka was so small and frail, she was a miniature human being. This made her sonorous voice and her intellectual observations all the more powerful. Her field was American music, the Blues in particular, and she had had a well-known and highly successful radio program on the subject in Warsaw for many years. She was also modest and warm. When I went to their flat, I felt like I was going home.

Adam was a short, compact fellow, barrel-chested, and thick as Majka was thin. His manner was antic and hilarious—think Inspector Clouseau. Having lived in Paris earlier in his life, his accent in English was more French than Polish, and he often unconsciously mixed in French when we spoke in English. He was a discographer and his huge record collection lined all the walls of his room. The collection contained rare recordings in every genre and rivaled any I had ever seen or even heard of. Adam could lay hands on any request in seconds, so organized was his collection. He would pull out an esoteric album, exquisitely maintained, and play it carefully on his turntable. This was all the more impressive since the space was so small and the collection so large. Majka's room was filled, too, but with books on music. It was a library really, for anyone interested in music.

Their flat was on a high floor in a post-war 1950s block on a busy corner in Warsaw. It was much superior to where I lived. There were elevators for one thing, and at the bottom floor buttons to press for response and admittance. There still was, though, the ubiquitous concrete. When I visited we sat in Adam's room, the place fitted with table and chairs where he and Majka had their meals and used as a communal space during the day. The room opened on to a balcony with glass doors. Windows were adjacent to the glass doors, and the exposure was such that glorious warm sunlight often filled the area. Adam and Majka had healthy plants placed nearby, the tendrils of which climbed up the windows in a beautiful filigreed pattern. Though I was in a concrete flat in a cement block building, I felt like I was in a garden sitting at their table. At night, given the flat's high storey, the glassed balcony offered a view of a transformed Warsaw—only light and stars—the concrete erased by dark. Adam always had food ready when I visited, and a particular wine—red, Bulgarian, delicious, and not easy to find in the city. We were never at a loss for subjects to discuss, and many times my tales of an American's life in Silesia overcame all of us with fits of laughter.

Before going to their home, I visited the commissary at the American Embassy not far from their street. Taking an empty suitcase on wheels and leash, I filled it to bursting with all the products they could not get. These included items made

At Adam and Majka's apartment in Warsaw with John left of Adam, and our American friend who visited us in Poland, across the table. Courtesy Balgley Family Archive

in Poland, like excellent ham, preserves and chocolates. The irony was not lost on any of us, and again gave us occasion to laugh wryly. The Poles who worked in the commissary figured I was taking the trove to Polish friends, and they smiled conspiratorially as I handed them my dollars for the lot. One day, for reasons I cannot now recall, I took some cans of Coca-Cola from the commissary shelf and added them to the suitcase. When I unpacked it at their flat, they were reduced to uncontrollable laughter at this addition, "Kasia, now, we really ARE American!"

The Christmas I went there, I discovered that Adam had not done what he planned to do earlier—procure a Christmas tree. It was already Christmas Eve, and Majka was half laughing and half despairing as she shook her head at him. Adam and I determined we would go out, even though twilight was coming on, to find a Christmas tree.

He wanted to take his customary tram, but I knew that would take too long, so I insisted on a taxi that I would pay for. He relented and agreed. We decided to go to the *Pałac Kultury* where he knew Christmas trees had been on sale. The scene was rather dismal when we arrived. It was not completely dark and most of the lights strung around the lot were not working. A few customers milled about, but there were no trees left, only twigs on the ground. Adam looked at me and made one of his caricatured sad clown faces. Then he shrugged, and somehow both of us got the idea to start picking up the larger twigs, almost branches—what constitutes a "tree" anyway? By the time we had finished, we had a bouquet of branches vaguely resembling a tree, and we were laughing like lunatics. Hurrying back to the flat by taxi, we were met by Majka at the flat's door. Holding the branches together entirely obscuring his face and chest, Adam presented the bouquet to Majka with a stylized bow. I thought she might be disappointed, but instead she burst into laughter. This is Poland, she seemed to say, no Christmas trees left! We tied the branches together with a ribbon Majka had, placed them in a floor vase, and decorated with the few ornaments they had set aside for the purpose. The lights turned down, candles lit, the lights of Warsaw outside their window, this became the most beautiful tree I can remember. We added some tinsel to our heads as laurels and toasted with the Bulgarian wine. It remains for me an unforgettable Christmas Eve.

When I did not stay at Pani Zofia's flat, I sometimes stayed at the Hotel Victoria when I was in Warsaw. Adam insisted on escorting me back to the hotel that night, and I asked the taxi to stay when he walked me to the hotel's entrance so that he could take it back home. It seemed he had not even thought about

that, and I am not sure the trams were even still running at that late hour on Christmas Eve. The hotel was usually brightly lit, almost garishly in what was thought an imitation of luxury hotels in the West. But that night all the lights were dimmed, all was quiet: Christmastime in Poland is experienced as a quiet time, a holy time, Christmas Eve termed *"Wigilia,"* the vigil to wait for the birth. American-style office Christmas cocktail parties were not the Polish way. I found it comforting, the dimness, the quietness. All was hushed at the commercial hotel so much so that it felt church-like in its own way.

The next day, Adam and Majka had invited me for Christmas dinner at the time *obiad* is traditionally served—2 p.m. Adam was a considerable chef, and he had made for us a lamb dinner replete with a special French sauce. I had told them that regrettably I had to catch a train later that day—I had work to do at home—so we enjoyed the day before it was time for me to go.

That time, both Majka and Adam wanted to go with me to *Warszawa Centralna,*

Sharing a joke with Adam on Christmas Eve (1987) when he entertained me with his amusing wit and light-hearted attitude, despite the difficult circumstances under which people like Adam and his wife Majka had to live at that time in communist Poland. Courtesy Balgley Family Archive

the main train depot, to see me off. Adam always asked what I ate in Dąbrowa Gornicza, and regularly disapproved of what I reported. He began to wrap up portions of the lamb for me to take with me. I demurred, but he proceeded.

And the three of us, Adam bearing the packet of lamb, made our way to the train station. We said our goodbyes at the platform, and I took a seat on the train on the side where they were standing so I could see them as we pulled out. I had only a moment to wave when the train started moving; Adam, waving and smiling, suddenly realized he had forgotten to hand the lamb to me, and eyes popping in comical fashion, he began running after the train, lamb held in his outstretched arm, crying, "Kate! Kasia! Your lam-B! Your lam-B" But it was too late.

Letters from Uncle Morris

Spring began with the dark sky lightening a bit, despite the pollution. And even with the poison air, buds on trees and water dripping from remaining snow reminded me of the springs I had known in my childhood before I moved across the country to California, where until I adjusted, it seemed always to be spring. I had written from Poland to my father's eldest brother, Morris, in Forest Hills, New York, to learn more about their family's experience in Poland. Morris was the oldest brother when the family left Poland, so I thought his memory might be fuller than my father's. I had no idea whether or not Uncle Morris would write back to me. It had been his wife, after all, who had been most vocal in condemning my parents' engagement; it was she who had said to my father at his family gathering where he had brought my mother to announce their plans, "You are bowing to Jesus Christ!" she exclaimed. My father had told me this story, and he added that his response was "Go to hell, all of you! You are hypocrites!" after which he and my mother abruptly departed the dinner. He told me, "It was a put-up job—they had already planned what they were going to say."

To my knowledge, I had never met my Uncle Morris, though my older brother and sister had received gifts from him in their childhood, in particular, a child-sized beautiful wooden table and chairs, which we all had used, and had become one of those iconic objects around which family sentiment accrues. We still have it in the family. It had never been adequately explained to me, not withstanding the "put-up job," how it was that my father was estranged from his family for their sins, and yet gestures like that had been made. I often found myself wondering if it was not my father's choice to never forgive any of his family, even the innocent ones—to purposefully cut communication with them all, to enforce an estrangement.

But Uncle Morris did write back, and generously. He was in his eighties, and I could see that the letters he wrote had taken his full attention. Carefully printed, well-written, his letters provided stories and information about their life before leaving for America. He was complimentary to me, remarking how impressed he was that a niece of his should be a "Fulbright Professor." There was no trace of bitterness or resentment or prejudice. I had to wonder again where responsibility for the estrangement lay. I believe that there were details to the story I would never know—long-ago arguments, insults, hurt feelings. I trust that my father had his reasons for disconnecting with his family, though at that time, I could not accept his disconnection from his Jewish identity. Looking at the warm letters, I felt a sadness. I had never known this man who seemed to want to know me, to be interested in my work and my life. It was, after all, Uncle Morris who told me the story of his mother's whipping for alledgedly stealing a horse blanket. He explained that in the short time of his life in *Brześć*—he was 11 years old when the family left, my father was 8—their city had been governed by three different countries, such was the upheaval at that time: Germany, Poland and Russia. He wrote, "And to tell you the truth, ironic as it is, the Germans were the best ones. My brother David and I used to water their horses for them, and they paid us. The German government built Jewish schools." I confirmed with him what I knew about the family ancestry, and he filled in as I asked questions.

This last letter shown here is from Uncle Morris to my father. It is warm and inviting, so again I have to wonder where the responsibility for the estrangement lay. But Morris's letter here indicates it is a response to a letter to him from my father. So my father reached out to him, not vice versa, and this correspondence began after I had contacted Uncle Morris from Poland.

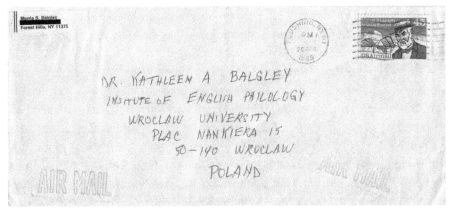

Letter addressed to me in Wrocław in March, 1989 from Uncle Morris, my father's elder brother then living in Forest Hills, New York. Morris had been estranged from my father many years previously for reasons I knew nothing about, but he still corresponded warmly with me while I was living in Poland. Courtesy Balgley Family Archive

Letters to me in Poland from Uncle Morris.
Courtesy Balgley Family Archive

DEAR KATHLEEN

MARCH 4, 1989

Morris S. Balgley
Forest Hills, NY 11375

I WAS PLEASANLY SURPRISED AND HAPPY TO HEAR FROM A NIECE WITH A PhD AFTER HER NAME – COMPOUNDED BY A FULBRIGHT FELLOWSHIP.

I WILL ATTEMPT TO ANSWER YOUR QUESTIONS CHRONOLOGICALLY.

MY GRANDFATHER ON MY FATHER'S SIDE LIVED IN BREST LITOVSK AND HIS FAMILY CONSISTED OF 7 BOYS AND LATELY ONE GIRL. AFTER WORLD WAR II 5 MEMBERS OF THIS FAMILY CAME TO THE U.S. ONE OF MY UNCLES BENAN WAS AN EXPERT PHOTO GRAPHER – IN RETOUCHING NEGATIVES. HE MADE A GOOD SALARY AND ACCUMULATED A LOT OF MONEY AND ALAS RETURNED TO POLAND A RICH MAN. HE PURCHASED THE BEST PHOTOGRAPHIC EQUIPMENT IN GERMANY AND OPENED THE FAMOUS STUDIO IN WARSAW. THE HOLOCAUST PUT AN END TO HIM AND HIS FAMILY.

TWO OF MY UNCLES – LOUIS AND MAX HAVE SAME DIED. ONE UNCLE NAMED MORRIS – THE SAME AS MY NAME, AND MY AUNT ARE BOTH LIVING IN BROOKLYN. MY AUNT NAME IS BEATRICE MIRANKER, WHO IS LIVING IN A GOV'T SUBSIDIZED HOME VERY COMFORTABLY.

MY FATHER LEFT POLAND JUST PRIOR TO THE OUTBREAK OF WORLD WAR I, BECAUSE OF ECONOMIC REASONS. IT WAS VERY DIFFICULT TO MAKE A LIVING IN POLAND.

FOR SEVEN YEARS MY MOTHER STRUGGLED WITH 4 CHILDREN. HER FATHER THOUGH WELL OFF DID NOT HELP.

– 2 –

SHORTLY AFTER MY FATHER LEFT FOR THE US. WORLD WAR I
BROKE OUT AS BREST LITOVK WAS A FORTIFIED CITY ON THE
BORDER WITH RUSSIA. THE RUSSIANS TOOK THIS CITY AFTER
A BATTLE, MY MOTHER + FAMILY WERE RELOCATED TO A
SMALL HAMLET CALLED KOBRIN. AS THIS LITTLE TOWN WAS
DESERTED WE TOOK POSSESION OF A SMALL FARM HOUSE
AND A SMALL TRACT OF LAND THAT WE CULTIVATED
AND FARMED FOR FOOD. THE FARM HOUSE HAD AN OVEN
CALLED A "PRIPICHOK" WHICH SERVED FOR COOKING, BAKING
HEATING.

ON THE PLOT OF LAND WE FARMED FOOD ON A
ROTATING BASIS. ONE YEAR POTATOS FILLING THE CELLAR TO
THE CEILING, ANOTHER YEAR BEANS – ALL SIZES & COLORS, A THIRD
YEAR CABBAGE WHICH MY MOTHER CONVERTED TO SAUERKRAUT
AS WE HAD NO MONEY WE BARTERED THE CROP FOR
WHEAT ETC. MY MOTHER BAKED BREAD TO LAST FOR
TWO WEEKS AND SUSPENDED OR HANGED THIS FROM THE
CEILING TO PROTECT IT FROM MICE.

SHORTLY AFTER THE RUSSIANS LEFT THE GERMANS TOOK OVER.
STRANGE AS IT SEEMS CONDITIONS UNDER THE GERMANS WAS MUCH
BETTER THAN UNDER THE POLES. THEY OPENED SCHOOLS WHERE I
LEARNED TO READ & WRITE YIDDISH.

ONE COLD WINTER MY MOTER STOLE A HORSE BLANKET TO
MAKE WARM CLOTHING FOR US. IT WAS FOUND OUT + MY MOTHER
WAS HORSE WHIPPED FOR THIS.

OUR DIET CONSISTED OF BREAD AT TIMES HARD AS A
ROCK- TO WHICH WE SOFTENED IT WITH THE JUICE OF A
HERRING. WE COULAN'COULD NOT AFFORD TO BUY THE HERRING.
POTATOS & BEANS WAS OUR STAPLE. BECAUSE OF A VITAMIN
DEFICIENCY IN OUR FOOD WE DEVELOPED RICKETS, THAT IS
WHY ELY AND I ARE BOW-LEGGED.

—3—

AND SO WE STRUGGLED FOR SEVEN YEARS UNTIL THE WAR ENDED. WE RECEIVED A LETTER FROM MY FATHER, AND SHORTY THEREAFTER FOOD PACKAGES AND MONEY, AND LASTLY TICKETS FOR PASSAGE TO THE U.S.

THE TRIP TO THE U.S. IS ANOTHER STORY. BY HORSE & WAGON WE TRAVELED OVER NIGHT TO WARSAW. THERE WE LIVED FOR A SHORT TIME WITH ONE OF MY UNCLES. WE WERE CALLED THE HOMELESS PEOPLE AND WERE HELPED BY HIAS – HEBREW IMMIGRANT AID SOCIETY. FROM WARSAW TO PARIS MY MEMORY FAILS ME. WE REMAINED IN PARIS FOR SEVERAL DAYS. THERE MY MOTHER SHOPPED AND BOUGHT A FUR SCARF AND SOME CLOTHES FOR THE CHILDREN. WITH THE AID OF HIAS WE TRAVELED FROM PARIS TO ANTWERP WHERE WE EMBARKED ON THE FRENCH LINER LA LORANNE.

AS MY FATHER BECOME A U.S. CITIZEN – HIS FAMILY, WIFE & CHILDREN WERE AUTOMATICALLY CITIZENS. THIS LAW HAS SINCE CHANGED. AS U.S. CITIZENS WE WERE TREATED GOOD, AND WE TRAVELED SECOND CLASS ON THE BOAT.

ON THIS BOAT TRAVELED A FRENCH PUGILIST NAMED GEORGES CARPENTIER – WHO LATER LOST A FIGHT WITH JACK DEMPSEY. ALSO ABOARD WAS A CARTOONIST WHO DREW A CARTOON OF THREE CHILDREN – DAVE MORRIS & ELY AND LABELED IT THE THREE COMMUNISTS & POSTED IT ON THE BULETIN BOARD. ONE DAY AT DINNER WE WERE SERVED LOBSTERS. NONE OF US EVER SAW A LOBSTER BEFORE. WE GLARED AT IT AND DID NOT TOUCH IT. AS WE DID NOT SPEAK FRENCH. THE WAITER TOOK IT AWAY AND SERVED US ANOTHER DISH.

— 4 —

THE FIRST DAY ON SHIP ALMOST EVERYONE ABOARD GOT SEA SICK. AFTER THAT IT WAS SMOOTH SAILING. WE SAW PORPOISES JUMPING IN & OUT OF THE WATER & FOLLOWED OUR SHIP AS SCAVENGERS.

FINALLY WE GOT TO ELLIS ISLAND AND SAW THE FAMOUS LADY OF THE ISLE — THE STATUE OF LIBERTY. ALL WERE EXCITED & HAPPY. ALSO IT WAS THE FIRST TIME WE SAW A COLORED MAN. AS CITIZENS WE HAD NO PROBLEM CLEARING IMMIGRATION OFFICIALS. MY FATHER EMBRACED US ALL WITH TEARS OF HAPPINES.

I WAS 10 YRS OLD AND ELY ABOUT NINE WHEN WE LANDED IN 1920.

I COULD GO ON WRITING — BUT I FEAR TO BORE YOU WITH DETAILS.

YES — MY MOTHERS MAIDEN NAME WAS SLOMIANSKI AND SHE & MY FATHER BOTH SPOKE POLISH & RUSSIAN. NOT VERY GRAMATICALLY — BUT ENOUGH TO GET BY. MY MOTHER'S BROTHER IS NOW LIVING IN SOUTH AMERICA.

BOTH RACHEL & SHANDE SPEAK VERY LITTLE ENGLISH, BUT IT IS VERY EASY TO GET A TRANSLATER IN ISRAEL. BESIDES HEBREW — ENGLISH IS THE SECOND LANGUAGE.

I HOPE YOU WILL FIND MY PECULIAR SCRIPT EASY ENOUGH TO DECIPHER.

WITH AWE, AFFECTION AND RESPECT

YOUR UNCLE

Morris Balgley

— OVER —

LIFE WITHOUT A FATHER WAS NOT VERY PLEASANT.
WE HAD TO STRUGGE FOR FOOD. IN BREST LITOVSK THERE
LITTLE ANTI JEWISH FEELING AT THAT TIME — 1920.
THE ONLY LANGUAGE I SPOKE WAS YIDDISH.
THE TRIP COMING TO AMERICA WAS A HAPPY
EVENT IN MY LIFE.

THE NAMES OF MY UNCLES WHO HAVE SINCE PASSED
AWAY IN ISRAEL ARE CHAIM AN NAUCHAM.

LASTLY I AM ANXIOUS TO MEET YOU.
AS YOU ARE A BALGLEY. BLOOD IS THICKER THAN
WATER.

WHEN YOU GET BACK TO THE U.S.A.
WE COULD ARRANGE A RENNEW RENDEZOUS.
EVEN WHEN SAN DIEGO IS THOUSAND OF
MILES FROM N.Y.

PLEASE FORGIVE THE GRAMMAR d
SPELING — AS I DID NOT EDIT THIS SCRIPT.

(1) MARCH 25, 1989

Morris S. Balgley
Forest Hills, NY 11375

MY DEAR NIECE,

IN REPLY TO YOUR LAST LETTER I CONSULTED MY
MY LAST SURVIVING UNCLE MORRIS BALGLEY (MY NAME IS MORRIS S BALGLEY)
IN ORDER TO ANSWER ALL THE QUESTIONS ACCURATELY.

MY GRANDFATHER'S NAME WAS ZEV WOLF (WILLIAM IN ENGLISH.)
HE HAD 7 SONS AND 1 DAUGHTER.
① ISRAEL (MY FATHER) THE OLDEST ② HERSHEL ③ CHAIM
④ BARUCH ⑤ LOUIS ⑥ MENACHEM (MAX) ⑦ MORRIS. THE GIRLS
NAME IS BEATRICE.

THE 2 BOYS WHO DIED IN ISRAEL WERE SONS OF MY
UNCLES. NAHUM SON OF HERSHEL, ABBA SON OF CHAIM.
THEY MIGRATED TO ISRAEL IN THE 1920's. ONE OF THEM
JOINED THE HAGANA WHO BATTLED THE BRITISH BEFORE
ISRAEL BECAME AN INDEPENDENT STATE. THEY ARE BOTH
DECEASED NOW. THEIR SURVIVING WIVES ARE LIVING IN ISRAEL.
MY UNCLES WHO CAME TO THE US CAME IN 1925 (ABOUT)
MY UNCLE BENNY (BARUCH) THE PHOTOGRAPHER WORKED IN THE
U.S. FOR FIVE YEARS — MADE A BUNDLE (MONEY) AND WENT
BACK TO WARSAW. HE LEFT US. ABOUT 1930

JACOB BALGLEY IS A GRANDSON OF MY GRANDFATHER'S
BROTHER.

THE MAN WITH THE RED BEARD WHO POSSESED A FRUIT
OR ORCHARD WAS MY GRANDFATHER FROM MY MOTHERS SIDE.

WE WER RELOCATED FROM BREST LITOVSK TO KOBRIN
BEFORE THE BATTLE WHEN THE RUSSIANS TOOK OVER. AFTER
WORLD WAR I POLAND WAS PARTITIONED AND BREST LITOVSK
WAS AGAIN POLISH.

THE RESIDENTS OF KOBRIN FLED TO AVOID THE HAZARDS
OF WAR. WHEN WE WERE RELOCATED TO KOBRIN THAT
HAMLET WAS DESERTED.

(2)

MY KNOWLEDGE OF HISTORY IS VERY HAZY - REMEMBER
I WAS ONLY 10 YEARS OLD WHEN I CAME TO THE U.S.
THE CHRONOLOGY OF THE BATTLE FOR BREST LITOVSK
THE RUSSIAN - THE POLES - THE GERMANS - THE EXACT
FACTS I CANNOT TELL YOU. IT WAS AN EXPERIENCE
I WOULD NOT WANT TO EXPERIENCE AGAIN.

MY UNCLE MORRIS DOES NOT KNOW THE NAME OF MY
UNCLES STUDIO IN WARSAW. ALSO THE SPELLING OF THE
NAME BALGLEY IS APPROXIMATELY THE SAME AS IN POLISH.

MY MOTHER AND HER FAMILY COME FROM KOBRIN. THE
REASON MY RED BEARDED GRANDFATHER DID NOT HELP HIS
DAUGHTER (MY MOTHER) WAS BECAUSE OF A FAMILY FEUD.

THE PRODUCE OF OUR FARMING WAS TRADED MOSTLY WITH
JEWISH PEOPLE AND A LITTLE WITH THE POLISH ALSO.

THE SCHOOL I WENT TO WAS MOSTLY JEWISH
BUT I SUSPECT IT WAS SUBSIDIZED BY THE GERMANS.

YOU ASK MANY QUESTIONS THAT I CANNOT ANSWER.
I KNOW NOTHING OF A RELATIVE PHYSICIAN WHO WAS HUNG.
YOU ASK ME WHAT THE DOMINANT CULTURE WAS AT THAT
TIME & PLACE. REMEMBER WE ALWAYS LIVED IN A JEWISH
COMMUNITY AND I AS A CHILD HAD LITTLE CONTACT
WITH NON-JEWS. BUT I DID HEAR OF HATRED AND
DISCRIMINATION AND VIOLENCE AGAINST JEWS.

(3)

FOR MORE PERSONAL INFORMATION. I CAN TELL YOU MY SON IN-LAW WILLIAM GROSKY HAS A PhD IN COMPUTER SCIENCE AND IS NOW A PROFESSOR IN THAT FIELD IN WAYNE STATE UNIVERSITY. DETROIT SEVERAL YEARS AGO THE UNITED NATIONS SENT HIM TO VENEZUELA TO TEACH COMPUTER SCIENCE. TWO MONTHS AGO THE U.N. AGAIN SENT HIM TO

BEIJING CHINA FOR A MONTH TO SET UP A PROGRAM FOR THAT GOVERNMENT.

MY DAUGHTER ROSLY BALGLEY GROSKY IS NOW AN ART INSTRUCTOR IN A JUNIOR COLLEGE. MY GRANDDAUGHTER IS NOW ATTENDING UNIVERSITY OF MICHIGAN WITH A MAJOR IN ENGLISH.

IT IS HOPED YOU DO NOT HAVE TOO MUCH TROUBLE READING MY SCRIPT.

WITH RESPECT AND ADMIRATION

YOUR UNCLE

Abin S. Balgley

Morris S. Balgley
Forest Hills, NY 11375

JAN. 30, 1990

MY DEAR NIECE KATHLEEN,

MY CHILDREN MADE ME A BIRTHDAY PARTY ON JAN. 26. WHEN I TURNED FOUR SCORE - So Now I QUALIFY AS AN OCTOGENARIAN. YOUR FATHER, ELY, IS NOT FAR IN AGE TO MAKE A PARTY WHEN HE TURNS 80. THIS IS A MILE STONE IN A PERSONS AGE.

MY WIFE IS ABOUT TO UNDERGO SURGERY ON HER EYE, CATARACT SURGERY. SO OUR TRIP TO SAN DIEGO WILL OCCUR IN LATE SPRING OR EARLY SUMMER. I REALLY AM LOOKING FORWARD TO OUR RENDEZVOUS.

ENCLOSED YOU WILL FIND PHOTOS OF YOUR FATHER AND YOUR GRANDPARENTS. THOSE OF THE THREE MUSKETEERS OR COMMUNISTS AS WE WERE CALLED ABOARD SHIP. SAILING TO THE U.S. 1920 WERE TAKEN ABOUT 1929 WHEN YOUR UNCLE DAVID AND I WERE WORKING AS BELL HOPS AT A SUMMER RESORT IN THE "JEWISH ALP" THE CATSKILLS. WE MANAGED TO HAVE ELY WITH US FOR SEVERAL WEEKS AT A SPECIAL RATE.

I AM CONTEMPLATING TO TAKEN A COURSE
22 A

IN COMPUTER SCIENCE AND THEN TO PURCHASE
A COMPUTER. MY CHILDREN WANT TO
PAY FOR THIS. QUEENS COLLEGE IS GIVING
COURSES IN COMPUTER SCIENCE. MY SON-IN-LAW
WHO TEACHES THIS SUBJECT ADVISED ME IT
IS NOT PRACTICAL FOR HIM OR ME TO LEARN THIS
MATERIAL VIA MAIL.
          I HOPE HOPE YOU WILL FIND THE
PHOTOS INTERESTING. AND WHEN YOU
HAVE CHILDREN YOU MAY BE SURPRISED
TO RESEMBLE THEM.
                    SINCERELY YOUR UNCLE
                              Morris

OCT. 4, 1988

Morris S. Balgley
Forest Hills, NY 11375

DEAR ELY,

I WAS VERY HAPPY TO HEAR FROM YOU.
ESPECIALLY SO ON ~~HEAD~~ LEARNING OF YOUR
DAUGHTER'S FULLBRIGHT SCHOLARSHIP.

YOU HAVE 5 GRANDCHILDREN, MAY
YOUR TRIBE INCREASE!

I HAVE 4 GRANDCHILDREN — 2 BOYS
AND 2 GIRLS. THE OLDEST A GIRL IS NOW
IN HER 2ND YEAR IN COLLEGE — WAYNE
STATE UNIVERSITY — IN DETROIT. WHERE HER
FATHER IS A PROFESSOR IN COMPUTER
SCIENCE. HE RECEIVED HIS PhD FROM
YALE UNIVERSITY ON A SCHOLARSHIP.

IT IS A VERY GOOD IDEA FOR KATHLEEN
TO VISIT ISRAEL. THE NAMES & ADDRESSES
OF OUR RELATIVES ARE :—

suburb of Tel Aviv {
RACHEL BALGLEY
41 GOLOMB St
GIVATAYIM. ISRAEL
}
Morroccan; speaks some English → children too; live nearby.

"Yaffo" born in Poland, left at 19; no English speaks Polish and Hebrew {
SHANDEL BALGLEY
KIRYAT MOTZKIN
SHIKM ROSTO 24
HAIFA ISRAEL
}
Shikun Rosko

THESE 2 LADIES ARE WIDOWS AS
OUR UNCLES PASSED AWAY.
— OVER —

IT WOULD BE A VERY GOOD IDEA
FOR THE BALGLEY CLAN TO HAVE
A GATHERING- REUNION- IN ISRAEL.
WRITE TO DAVID- IN FLORIDA-
MIAMI AND HEAR WHAT HE
THINKS OF THE IDEA.

TIME MARCHES ON AND BEFORE
YOU KNOW IT MIGHT BE TOO
LATE.

I AM SURE YOU WILL ENJOY
THIS TRIP.

WRITE ME AND TEL ME WHAT
YOU THINK OF THIS IDEA.

WITH LOVE

YOUR BROTHER

Morris

Apparently, in his letter to his brother my father had written about his children and grandchildren. To me, this was an overture for reconnection, and Morris's letter in response suggests a family reunion. That never happened, but at least there was a warm exchange between the two.

I had known about relatives we had living in Israel, but I did not know their names until Uncle Morris provided them. Through a colleague at UCLA interested in my desire to reach out to my Jewish family, I had been put in contact with an American journalist living in Israel. Marc and I corresponded between Poland and Tel Aviv where he lived, and he generously looked up my surname in Tel Aviv and Haifa phone books, and wrote back that, yes, he had found Balgleys listed. He had gone to the trouble to phone them, explain who he was and who I was, and asked if they would be amenable to a visit from me. Again, I had no idea of how they would respond; I suspected they knew the story of my father's intermarriage, and if they therefore would not welcome me, I surely wanted to know that now, before I traveled to meet them. Marc wrote back that they were anxious to meet me, and that in fact, one family had explained there was other Balgley family nearby who would also be very happy to meet me.

V

Tel Aviv 🌳 An Unattainable Identity

First post-war flight from Warsaw to Tel Aviv
Tel Aviv, 1988

I was on one of the first, if not the very first, flight from Warsaw to Tel Aviv since before World War II on LOT, Polish national airlines. That I should be there for that occasion was an accident of history and a bracing experience. But I was also thinking about the strange *bashert* I had already experienced in Poland.

I lined up to board with an admixture of passengers. Hasids in full wool coats and hats though it was summer. I never found out whether they were from Poland flying from Poland to Israel or vice versa. In any case, it felt momentous—a half century or more later, we were traveling the route fortunate Polish Jews had taken in just enough time before 1939, and even just twenty years after 1968, when political machinations created another Jewish exile from Poland to Israel and elsewhere.

Now, in 1988, twenty years after that exodus from Poland, I arrived in Tel Aviv in June. Living in the polluted part of Poland, and California by now a faded memory of another planet in a different century, the hot sun came as a surprise. The airport with its armed soldiers, the modernity of the place, the westernness of the scene, bustling and hurried, also surprised me: I registered that I had been in communist Poland for a long time. I have never spent so long in passport control, cordial enough, but more intense than even the communists in Poland, "Why have you come to Israel? You are an American—why do you fly from Poland? Please show your return itinerary. Has anyone given you anything to bring with you to Israel?"

And so on. This was, of course, before September 11, 2001 (9/11), but since the Six-Day War in 1967, security in Israel had become more stringent. Israel had already endured the March 7, 1988, "Mothers Bus Attack" where a squad of three Palestinian Arab militants, members of the Fatah organization, infiltrated Israel from Egypt. The militants hijacked a bus full of women returning from work at the Negev Nuclear Research Center near Dimona and threatened to kill the passengers one by one if Israel would not release Palestinian prisoners from Israeli prisons. After the militants executed one of the passengers, members of the elite civilian counter-terrorism unit, Yamam, broke into the bus, killing all three hijackers, but not managing to prevent another two Israeli passengers from being killed. Just two months later, on May 11, 1988, a car bomb near the Israeli Embassy in Nicosia, Cyprus, had killed three and injured fifteen. A caller claimed that the Abu Nidal organization had carried out the attack.

When I retrieved my bag from the carousel, it was festooned with more tags and labels than I had ever seen before. I had the address of a hotel I had booked, and lugging my too-heavy bag (I had brought family records with me, just in case they would be needed), made my way into the now sweltering heat to the stop where I had been told I could catch a shuttle into the city. From the darkened air-conditioned cool of the bus I watched as Israel went by. That's how it felt—like a movie reel or a dream. My arrival to Israel was so emotionally momentous for me that I think I was a bit numb. The feeling stopped abruptly when the driver shouted to me that we had arrived at my stop. I was awakened from my dream by the reality of the situation— my bag was much too heavy for me to manage without misery, and the heat had stepped up a notch. I stood on the baking sidewalk with my albatross suitcase, and soon realized that my hotel was located several long city blocks away. Now the dream-like quality returned, but it was a new version—dizzying heat and discomfort made it hard for me to even see where I was going. But I trudged up the street—it was an incline—and soon to my right I saw the sea. Now that I had passed the building that had blocked its appearance, I was suddenly wrapped in the soft, cooling air that wafted off the beach. I got my bearings then, and putting down the burden, I stood for a bit just looking out at the sea, and emerged out of the dream to the realization that I was actually in Israel.

I found my hotel directly across from the beach, small like I had wanted, and in walking distance from the water and central for bus stops. The lobby had the feel of a Californian beach hotel—the breeze coming through, the light. I was so relieved and glad to be there that maybe my greeting to the woman at the desk was a little too enthusiastic. A taciturn expression on her middle-aged face, she did not return my smile, but nodded and got down to the business of checking me in, without further greeting or conversation. She did, however, say that I was in time for breakfast, and gestured to a buffet behind me.

This buffet was a thing of beauty. I had not seen fresh fruit like that in months, and the spread was a cornucopia of watermelon, honeydew, banana, blood oranges, grapefruit and grapes. There was also excellent hummus, good bread and good coffee. I sat at a small glass-topped table in the lobby, and enjoyed the feast unselfconsciously, despite the concierge's glances at me.

I found my room afterwards—perfect—a desk, a bed, a shower with the smell of salt and soap. My journey had wearied me, but I felt a new energy in its place. I put on a swimsuit, took a towel, and walked to the beach. It was late morning, but people had already gathered there, but not too many. I found a place near the water, dropped my belongings, and went into the Mediterranean sea. The temperature was perfect. I swam out toward the horizon and saw the military guard boats far beyond. A paradise, but one that required vigilance for survival. I floated on my back for a while and contemplated this paradox—if it was a paradox. Maybe all hard-won treasures had to be guarded. I felt a surge of compassion and gratitude for the country: I could float here in this luxury and be unafraid because of its work.

I stayed too long at the beach that day, and being olive-skinned, I never had been sunburned before. I acquired my first one that day. I was unconcerned. I returned to my room, showered, and fell deeply asleep. At twilight, I woke, and dressed to go out to dinner. Stepping out of the lobby, I found the street transformed at night: the air no longer hot, but just balmy, lights from restaurants and clubs, voices and laughter from outdoor cafés and bars, music. I walked a short distance and found a place to have a drink. The restaurant opened onto a patio and I took a seat outside to view the water. The sky had darkened to a rich deep royal blue, and the sea was just one shade lighter. I looked around me at the other customers. Seated not too far from my table were three of the most physically beautiful people I have ever seen—two young men and a young woman. She made me think of the queen in the Rudyard Kipling story from my childhood, *The Butterfly that Stamped*, the beautiful and wise, Balkis, wife of The Most Sovereign Suleiman-bin-Daoud—Solomon, the Son of David. Dark-haired like her companions, her shining long hair had glints of gold from the sun. All three had eyes that appeared light in contrast to their darkened skins with black eyebrows that arched naturally yet exotically to the edges of their faces. I looked at them and all three smiled back at me. Before I knew it, she was at my table, and smiling again, explained that she saw I was alone, would I like to join her and her brothers at their table? So they were siblings. They looked like royalty from a story book, and acted like it in the best ways. The brothers stood immediately as their sister and I approached their table, warmly shaking my hand, and bowing inconspicuously. They politely asked where I was from, and when it was their turn, they explained that they were Iranian Jews, that they visited Israel often. I was not too far off then in my initial impression: they were sultans in their own way.

We found it easy to converse, as they told me about their parents and grandparents, how these elders, though they like Israel, would never leave their beloved home in Tehran, and so the three of them only visited Israel, but returned always to the family home. Their family had been in Iran for centuries and had remained in the Middle East in ancient times. I amused myself for a moment with the reflection: would we all look like this if we had not dispersed? They were so welcoming, and our conversation enjoyable, that when they asked me to have dinner with them, I readily agreed. They took me to another shining spot where we ate fish. I admitted it was my birthday, and they insisted on toasting me with champagne. As the night grew late, I thanked them, and told them how pleasant they had made my first trip to Israel. We embraced and I found my way back the short distance to my hotel, walking slowly and savoring the night sea air—my first night in this contentious Promised Land.

Israel Family

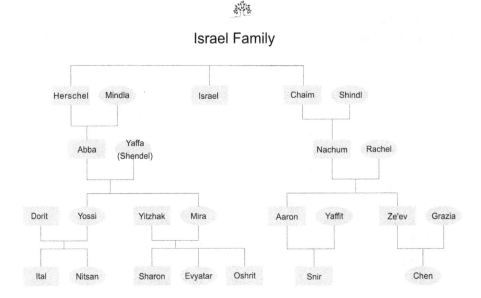

The next day it was time to find members of my family in Israel. The American journalist had set up the date and time. I had an address scrawled on a piece of paper, and I had intended to find my way there by bus or taxi, depending on the distance. But that morning there was a message at the hotel desk from my "cousins." They insisted on collecting me from my hotel. I had wanted to avoid putting any of these still-to-be-met family members to any trouble. I would arrive at their homes with flowers, just as I had regularly done in Poland. But their call confounded all that. I waited in the lobby again under the watchful eye of the lady concierge. She had taken to greeting me in the morning because I would present myself for breakfast and before going to the buffet table, I made it a point to go to the desk where she worked and greet her. She had no choice but to return my "Good morning, how are you?"

A handsome dark-haired man in his early 30s, dressed in khakis and a sports shirt walked through the lobby door and I stood with a questioning smile on my face. He smiled back, a warm smile, and we knew we had found one another. It is always a bit awkward at first meeting a family member whom you have never met—or even heard of, for decades. But I have found it is best to dispense with self-consciousness or worry about how the other will feel. We started with a handshake, but then moved to embrace each other. After that, everything was easier.

Aaron Balgaly (I knew from our letters that that part of the family added one letter to our surname) led me to his car, and we headed off to his mother's house on Golumb Street in Givataim.

The trip took nearly an hour. Tel Aviv is like a smaller Los Angeles, and how I ever thought I would find my way there now makes me smile. Maybe a $100 cab ride? It would have been worth it, but the intricate path Aaron made as he turned onto tiny ancient streets—well, I was not convinced that even a good Tel Aviv cabbie could have found the address.

The place was a modest and pristine apartment, and Aaron's mother, Rachel, was waiting with the rest of the family. I knew that Rachel was the widow of my father's cousin, Nachum, and that Nachum was the son of Chaim, my grandfather's brother. Like my grandfather and father, Chaim was born in Brest, but his fate was unknown to the family, as they did not know if Chaim had remained in Poland or had come to Israel. I was not able to learn where Nachum was born, whether in Israel or Poland, or how he came to be in Israel. But Aaron explained that his father, Nachum, had died in 1975 at 59 years of age, having served from 1944 to 1949 in the PALMACH (an acronym for *Plugot Mahatz* in Hebrew, translated as "strike forces"), the elite fighting force of the Haganah, the Jewish paramilitary organization during the British Mandate of Palestine from 1921 to 1948, fighting to drive the British out.

Aaron introduced me to his mother, Rachel, who had no English. She was a trim, black-haired woman, dark-skinned, with lively light brown eyes. She embraced me immediately and made me feel welcome. Aaron would have to do the translating for us, as I was again regretting my lack of Hebrew. But we managed. I asked Aaron if he and his family knew that I was a product of intermarriage. The story had reached them and he said, "We don't care about those things, Kate; we are just very glad you came to meet us." Then smiling, he added, "Besides, my mother and father 'intermarried' too—my mother is Sephardic." I paused for a second, looking into his face to get a clue on how I should respond, and seeing him shake his head and chuckle, we both laughed aloud.

I then met Aaron's brother, Ze'ev, who presented a very different impression from his clean-cut older brother. Dressed in a tight black t-shirt with "Pink Floyd" emblazoned on the front, and blue jeans, Ze'ev's massive head of black curls fell down his back and to the sides of his face. His skin was dark, his eyes black, his manner playful. During the conversation, he told me that his van had taken a beating recently when for his work he had to drive to the desert. Palestinians pelted his vehicle with rocks, and in a jocular manner, told me he had to get out of there fast. He shrugged as if to say he did not blame them necessarily, but gee, his van would not last long under those conditions.

Aaron introduced his hugely pregnant wife, Yaffit, chestnut-haired and tanned, but very uncomfortable in the heat as their baby was due any day. Her English was very good, and I told her I had been reading David Grossman's *Yellow Wind*, the journalist's first of many books to come later critical of Israeli policy. I wanted to know what she thought. She shook her head, saying, "He will be our undoing." I nodded respectfully and said nothing. I was interested in what they thought, not to bring my views to them.

Ze'ev introduced his very young wife, Grazia, from Italy, but conversant also in Hebrew. She carried with her a robust baby boy, with her deep blue eyes and Ze'ev's black hair. Setting him on the floor, the entire family group enjoyed his early attempts at crawling. Grazia was as hip as her husband in her casual style—and she would have been a good-looking "hippie girl" in the United States.

I noticed a large collection of photographs on a wall and asked about them. Aaron stood next to me and pointed to his father, Nahum. "Yes, he was in the PALMACH, but later did other work for the government." At that moment, I recognized in one photograph the image of David Ben-Gurion sitting at a table with Nachum, and the table was the one around which we were presently seated, not a government office desk in a government building. I pointed in amazement, and turned to Aaron. "Yes, he did important work for the government for many years after the PALMACH." His tone was light, but it was clear he had told me all I was to know.

Nachum Balgaley's records in service to Israel.
Courtesy Balgley Family Archive

*Rachel Balgaly, the widow of my father's cousin Nachum,
pictured with her husband in Tel Aviv, where he worked
with the PALMACH (an acronym for Plugot Mahatz in
Hebrew, translated as "strike forces"), and later for the
Israeli Intelligence Agency, known as the Mossad.
Courtesy Balgley Family Archive*

Years later, I learned from another relative that Nachum Balgaly had been a member of the *Mossad*, the Israeli Intelligence Agency. I did not learn that night the cause of his early death, but it was enough for one evening. That family spelled our surname "Balgaly," with an additional "a" after the "g," and left out the "e" after the last "l." I had long been in search of the meaning and origin of Balgley, and noted how remarkable it was that in my genealogical searches, the spelling had remained mostly intact among my American relatives, despite the typical mangling done to names as immigrants came through Ellis Island. Indeed, I had years of difficulty finding my grandfather's entry documents because the surname had been so badly bungled.

I had researched and traveled far and wide to find a possible meaning of the surname; ironically, I found the surname years later when I was studying Judaism at a local Jewish Community Center in La Jolla, California, a couple of exits down the freeway from my home in San Diego. In the library of that Jewish Community Center were two impossibly thick volumes written by Alexander Beider, the titles: *A Dictionary of Jewish Surnames from the Kingdom of Poland* and *A Dictionary of Jewish Surnames in the Russian Empire*. In both volumes I readily found "Balgley," indicating that Brest and Vitebsk were the cities where the name was found, but then more precious

My grandfather's documents: one an "oath of allegiance to the United States" signed June 1919, just before his family arrives in September, 1920. Document signed by my grandfather on July 15, 1913. He signs that he "renounces forever all allegiance to any foreign prince...particularly to Nicholas II, emperor of all of the (sic) Russia." Further: "I am not an anarchist or a polygamist...." Courtesy Balgley Family Archive

Baldoszewski (Suwałki, Kalwaria) T: see Bondziszkowski().
Baldyga (Ostrołęka, Pułtusk) N: bałdyga [Polish] duffer, lubber, lout {*Baldygier (Beldygier)*}.
Baldygier (Pułtusk) N: see Bałdyga < ~er> (Yiddishized form).
Balewski (Łódź) T: from the village of Bale (Siedlce d., Radzymin d.).
Balfan (Łomża, Ostrołęka) A: see Helfand.
Balfand (Ostrołęka) A: see Helfand.
Balglej (Warsaw) N: from 'baɛal-gleybn' [Northeastern Yiddish, the first part is from the Hebrew component] faithful person, religious person(?). This surname originated in Belorussia (see the entry Balglej in DJSRE).
Balgman (Mazowieck) O: Balg [German] pelt, skin {*Balk*}.
Balicki (Kielce, Pińczów, Będzin) T: from the village of Balice (Stopnica d.; Kraków d. of Galicia).
Balin (Warsaw) T: from the townlet of Balin (Kamenets d. of Podolia) or the estate Balnie (Tel'shi d. of Kovno gub.) (see the entry Balin in DJSRE) or the village Balin (Turek d., Rypin d.).
Baliński (Sejny, Warsaw) T: from the village of Balinka (Augustów d.).
Balk (Krasnystaw) O: see Balgman.
Balkiem (Warsaw) A: see Balkien.
Balkien (Konin) O: Balken [German] beam (timber); prop

Band (Władys..., Jędrzejów, Olkusz, ... ribbon, string, band
Bendel (Bendzel), Be Bendler}.
Banda (Sokołów, Rad ... into a knot; gang {*I*
Bandalik (Radzyń) O
Bandalin (Mariamp 'mandoline' [Yiddis
Bandas (Węgrów) O
Bande (Radzyń, Łód
Bander (Gostynin, W bandera [Polish] (
Bandman (Puławy,
Bando (Łęczyca, Łó
Bandos (Łęczyca) {*Bandas*}.
Bandrymer (Ostro saddler.
Bandt (Łowicz, Łó
Bandurek (Rypin

From The Dictionary of Jewish Surnames in the Kingdom of Poland, in which my family name was included, indicating that the first syllable is from the Hebrew.

Balof, Balji.
Balevich (Minsk, Vitebsk) T: see Belevich.
Bal'f (Kovel') N: see Balev.
Bal'fer (Odessa) O: see Begel'fer.
Balgarskij (Chernigov) T: see Bolgar.
Balgelej N: see Balglej.
Balglej (common in Brest; Kobrin, Vitebsk) N: from 'bal-gleybn' [NEY; the first word is from Hebrew בַּעַל] faithful person, religious person(?) {*Balgelej, Baglej, Balklej, Bolgaleev*}.
Baliban (Kremenets, Starokonstantinov) SZN:, SZA:, SN:, SA: see Balaban.
Balibar (Mogilev-Pod.) SO: see Barber.
Baliber (Rovno) O: see Barber.
Baligula (Vladimir) O: see Balagula.
Balik (Rovno, Vinnitsa) A:, T: see Balyk.
... Shavli, Ponevezh, Orsha, Ostrog,

An entry in The Dictionary of Jewish Surnames in the Empire of Russia which indicates that the second syllable may be from the Yiddish meaning "faithful person"; confirming that the first syllable from the Hebrew translates to "master of"; and showing that people with this surname lived in Brest and Kobrin, as my own family had, but adding "Vitebsk," also Chagall's home, which I had not known. The translation, then, "Baal" from the Hebrew translated as "Master of" or "Owner of," followed by the Yiddish "gleybn" translated as "faith," may indicate that perhaps centuries before my ancestors were rabbis.

this: "Bal" is from the Hebrew "Baal" meaning "owner of" or "master of";
the "gley" is from the Yiddish, "glebyn" meaning "faith." Could it be that
my earliest ancestors were rabbis who had been given this name or somehow
taken it on? So far, I have never learned the answer to this question.[6]

The food served at the Balgaly home that night was a Sephardic spread
of *sambusak*, a beautiful half circle of crusty dough filled with spices and
hummus; *pestelas*, pastry filled with meat, onion and pignola nuts; *chamin*,
a delicious stew which I learned was the Sephardic version of the Ashkenazy
cholent my father once described from his childhood. They had gone to trouble
to make this occasion a pleasure, and their efforts and warmth made me feel
that, yes, I was among family. Late at night, back at my hotel, I reflected that
this was only my second day in Israel. I read another chapter in *Yellow Wind*
and fell deeply asleep, the same sort of unconscious sleep I had experienced
the night before.

The next morning I planned to visit the Diaspora Museum and I had noticed
a pamphlet on it behind the concierge's desk. I greeted the concierge as usual
and asked her for a copy. As I looked over it standing at her desk, I felt her
looking me over, really looking at me at all for the first time. When I glanced up
to thank her, she did not move her attention away from me this time, but instead
queried, "Where are you from in America?" I told her and added that currently
I was living in Poland—that I had come to Israel to meet family I had never
met before. She asked why I was in Poland, and I told her about the teaching
Fulbright and that my father had been born there. "In what city do you live?"
she asked. I explained that I lived in the southern part of the country, that I spent
a good deal of time in Warsaw. At the mention of that city, her face took on an
entirely new expression—soft in a way I had never seen, attentive yet far away.
For once, she was not distracted or busy or abrupt. She gazed at me and through
me, and I saw that she was quite beautiful and elegant with her elbows now
set on the desk before her. "*Stara kochana Warszawa*," she murmured, "Dear
old Warsaw." I smile a gentle smile at her, "You know it, then?" "Oh yes, my
family was from there, and I remember it from my childhood. It was such a
beautiful place." It was not possible to ask further questions of her—her answer
had already told much—except whether the entire family had made it to Israel or
just her—whether she had escaped before the Shoah or survived it. All there was
to do now was to nod to show my respect for and understanding of what she had
not told me. A second later, she quickly recovered from her reverie and told me
to keep the pamphlet, they had more somewhere. But after that encounter, she
always smiled a sweet smile when she saw me in the lobby.

I took a bus to the Diaspora Museum. On board were several older women who I needed to get around to find my seat. Without thinking, I automatically said, *"Przepraszam,"* Polish for "excuse me." Startled, they looked at me, not unkindly, but with confusion. They had ceased their animated conversation in Hebrew, and one of them asked, "Are you Jewish?" She was obviously wondering how someone my age could be a living Polish Jew. The question brought me up short. I could not say yes because that would have been untrue. But neither could I say no because that would also have been untrue. In Polish, I said simply *"Pół"*—"half"—a very unsatisfactory answer, I felt, but I was unable to think what other way to reply. They asked no further, and I felt what I had often felt—split, double, displaced.

The Diaspora Museum was a wonder. For the 1980s, the technology there was impressive: computer programs where a visitor could look up a surname or a city and get a printout with a respectable account of information. I looked up both my grandmother's maiden name and my surname and Brześć, and the very first lessons I learned about my family's history began there.

But most astonishing for me was the entire section of the museum devoted to obviously miniature model recreations of synagogues destroyed by the Nazis. The exhibition rooms were dimly lit in order that the lighted models looked more dramatic, and where it was thus possible to see inside the windows at the interiors which had also been recreated. In museums where an artificial world is created in any case, we often forget the outside world, and seeing these village names known to me made that dislocation even more pronounced because I had just recently passed through those villages on a train. Just as my spoken Polish had been an historical oddity for the women on the bus, those village names, currently existing and familiar to me, contributed to my sense of time collapsed, so that there was no time and no space. The models were so beautiful, so real, so specific in their dates and places, that it made it even more difficult to imagine them gone—and more disturbing than ever to know they had been destroyed. It was strangely difficult to remember where I was—in Tel Aviv in a museum, looking at models of Polish synagogues now gone but looking very alive at the moment, and in towns I had recently passed through. Boxes within boxes—which is the real thing, which the recreation? At one point I turned a corner in the exhibition rooms that themselves felt like villages of synagogues, and saw a model of the famous, block-long, Warsaw synagogue on Tłomackie Street, known as The Great Synagogue and built between 1875 and 1878 in a section of the city where Jews were given permission to settle by the Russian Imperial administration. At the time of its opening, it was the

A564

BREST-LITOVSK (BRISK, UNTIL 1921 BREST-LITOVSK; FROM 1921
UNTIL 1945 BRZEC NAD BUGIEM; AFTER 1945 BREST), CAPITAL OF
BREST OBLAST, BELORUSSIAN S.S.R.; IN THE MEDIEVAL GRAND
DUCHY OF LITHUANIA, FROM THE 14TH TO THE 17TH CENTURIES, IN
PARTICULAR AFTER THE UNION OF POLAND AND LITHUANIAN JEWRY.
ITS SITUATION ON THE RIVER BUG, AT THE JUNCTION OF
COMMERCIAL ROUTES AND NEAR THE BORDERS OF THE TWO
COUNTRIES, MADE BREST-LITOVSK AN IMPORTANT COMMUNICATIONS
AND COMMERCIAL CENTER. JEWISH MERCHANTS FROM BREST-LITOVSK
ARE MENTIONED IN 1423-33 IN THE MUNICIPAL RECORDS OF DANZIG
(GDANSK) WHERE THEY BOUGHT TEXTILES, FURS, AND OTHER GOODS.
BREST-LITOVSK BECAME IMPORTANT ORGANIZATIONALLY AS CONTACTS
WITH POLAND STEADILY EXPANDED. THE JEWS OF BREST-LITOVSK
ENGAGED IN COMMERCE, CRAFTS, AND AGRICULTURE. SOME
CONDUCTED EXTENSIVE FINANCIAL OPERATIONS, FARMING THE
CUSTOMS DUES, TAXES, AND OTHER GOVERNMENT IMPOSTS. THEIR
BUSINESS CONNECTIONS EXTENDED THROUGHOUT AND BEYOND THE
DUCHY. BY 1483 JEWS IN BREST-LITOVSK HAD ESTABLISHED
COMMERCIAL TIES WITH VENICE.
IN 1495 ALL JEWS WHO REFUSED TO ACCEPT CHRISTIANITY WERE
EXPELLED FROM LITHUANIA. ONLY ONE CONVERT, OF THE
JOSEFOWICZ FAMILY, REMAINED BEHIND IN BREST-LITOVSK. THE
JEWS WERE PERMITTED TO RETURN IN 1503, AND THE COMMUNITY
REGAINED ITS FORMER EMINENCE. THE INFLUENTIAL SAUL WAHL OF

PADUA, WHO LIVED IN BREST-LITOVSK, ESTABLISHED A SYNAGOGUE
AND YESHIVAH IN THE TOWN.
THE SATISFACTORY RELATIONSHIP BETWEEN THE JEWS AND THE
TOWNSPEOPLE IN THE 16TH CENTURY SUBSEQUENTLY DETERIORATED.
IN 1636 CHRISTIAN STUDENTS MADE A SAVAGE RAID ON THE JEWS.
JEWISH STORES WERE LOOTED AND BURNED IN 1637 BY THE
TOWNSPEOPLE, BUT THE POLISH AUTHORITIES COMPELLED THE
MUNICIPALITY TO RESTORE THE STOLEN MERCHANDISE TO ITS
JEWISH OWNERS AND PUNISH THE RIOTERS. A MIXED JEWISH-
CHRISTIAN WATCH WAS INSTITUTED TO GUARD THE STORES. DURING
THE CHMIELNICKI UPRISING OF 1648-49, MANY JEWS WHO HAD THE
MEANS ESCAPED FROM BREST-LITOVSK TO GREAT POLAND AND
DANZIG; HUNDREDS OF THOSE WHO REMAINED WERE MASSACRED
(ACCORDING TO ONE SOURCE, 2,000). THE WARS WITH RUSSIA,
SWEDEN, AND TURKEY CAUSED MUCH HARDSHIP AMONG THE JEWS, AND
MANY WERE MASSACRED BY THE RUSSIAN ARMY IN 1660. IN 1661,
IN ORDER TO RELIEVE THEIR DISTRESS, THE KING EXEMPTED THE
JEWS FROM THE OBLIGATION TO BILLET TROOPS, AND ALL OTHER
TAXES FOR FOUR YEARS; JEWISH DEBTORS WERE GRANTED A THREE-
YEAR MORATORIUM. IN 1669 KING MICHAEL WISNIOWIECKI
CONFIRMED THE PRIVILEGES GRANTED IN FORMER CHARTERS, AND
PERMITTED THE JEWS TO RETAIN THE LAND AND BUILDINGS THEY
HAD OWNED BEFORE THE WARS, INCLUDING SYNAGOGUES,
COURTHOUSES, PUBLIC BATHS, CEMETERIES, AND STORES. JEWS

WERE PERMITTED TO ENGAGE IN EVERY SPHERE OF COMMERCE AND
CRAFTS, AND REQUIRED TO PAY ONLY THE SAME TAXES AS
CHRISTIANS. THE MUNICIPALITY AND NON-JEWISH CITIZENS WERE
ORDERED TO COOPERATE IN SUPPRESSING ANTI-JEWISH AGITATION.
THE PRIVILEGES WERE RATIFIED IN 1676 AND IN 1720. BY 1676,
THERE WERE 525 JEWS (EXCLUDING CHILDREN UNDER 11) LIVING IN
BREST-LITOVSK. THE NUMBER GREW DURING THE 18TH CENTURY. THE
1766 CENSUS RECORDED 3,353 JEWS IN THE TOWN AND ITS
ENVIRONS. FOR MANY GENERATIONS, THE BREST-LITOVSK COMMUNITY
ASSUMED THE LEAD IN COMMUNAL AFFAIRS AND CULTURAL
ACTIVITIES OF LITHUANIA. IT WAS ONE OF THE THREE FOUNDING
COMMUNITIES OF THE COUNCIL OF LITHUANIA (1623-31).
BREST-LITOVSK WAS A STRONGHOLD OF THE MITNAGGEDIM IN
OPPOSITION TO CHASIDISM. SOME OF THE EARLY DISPUTATIONS
BETWEEN THE LEADERS OF THE TWO GROUPS TOOK PLACE THERE.
DISTINGUISHED RABBIS OFFICIATING IN BREST INCLUDE JEHIEL B.
AARON LURIA, THE GRANDFATHER OF SOLOMON LURIA (MID-15TH
CENTURY); MOSES RASKOWITZ; MENAHEM MENDEL FRANK; KALONYMUS,
THE FATHER-IN-LAW OF SOLOMON LURIA (16TH CENTURY); EPHRAIM
ZALMAN SCHOR; JOEL B. SAMUEL SIRKES; DAVID OPPENHEIM (17TH
CENTURY); ARYEH JUDAH LEIB; AARON B. MEIR, AUTHOR OF
MINCHAT AHARON (18TH CENTURY); B. MORDECAI ORENSTEIN; MOSES
JOSHUA LEIB DISKIN; JOSEPH BAER SOLOVEICHIK, AND
DESCENDANTS.

AFTER ITS INCORPORATION INTO RUSSIA IN 1793 THE ECONOMIC
IMPORTANCE OF BREST-LITOVSK DIMINISHED. MANY HISTORIC
EDIFICES OF THE JEWISH QUARTER, INCLUDING THE OLD SYNAGOGUE
AND CEMETERY, WERE DEMOLISHED TO GIVE WAY TO THE BUILDING
OF A FORTRESS IN 1832. THE ECONOMIC POSITION AGAIN IMPROVED
AFTER THE COMPLETION OF THE DNIEPER-BUG CANAL IN 1841, AND
THE JEWISH COMMUNITY, WHICH HANDLED MOST OF THE COMMERCE
AND INDUSTRY IN THE CITY, BEGAN TO GROW APPRECIABLY. A
TOBACCO FACTORY AND TWO LARGE MILLS WERE ESTABLISHED BY
JEWS IN 1845, A HOSPITAL WAS ERECTED IN 1838, A NEW
SYNAGOGUE IN 1851-61, AND A HOME FOR WIDOWS IN 1866.
THE JEWISH POPULATION NUMBERED 30,608 IN 1897 (OUT OF
46,568); 3,506 OF THEM WERE ARTISANS, AND MANY OF THEM WERE
SHOEMAKERS AND TAILORS. THE CITY WAS ALMOST COMPLETELY
DESTROYED BY FIRE IN 1895 AND AGAIN IN 1901. IN THE POGROMS
IN THE WAKE OF THE 1905 REVOLUTION, SEVERAL JEWS IN BREST-
LITOVSK WERE WOUNDED OR KILLED. A NUMBER OF JEWS THERE WERE
ACTIVE IN THE UNDERGROUND REVOLUTIONARY GROUPS. HOWEVER, AS
ELSEWHERE IN RUSSIA, THEIR ACTIVITIES SUBSIDED WITH THE
FAILURE OF THE REVOLUTION. ALTHOUGH THE JEWS COMPRISED 70%
OF THE POPULATION BEFORE WORLD WAR I, THEY HAD ONLY THREE
REPRESENTATIVES ON THE MUNICIPAL COUNCIL, WHILE THERE WERE
20 NON-JEWISH MEMBERS.
THE JEWS WERE DRIVEN OUT OF BREST-LITOVSK ON AUG. 1, 1915,

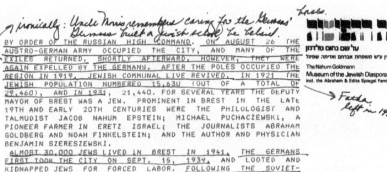

ironically: Uncle Morris remembers caring for the Germans' German built a Jewish school he believed.

Loses.

→ Father left in 1922

BY ORDER OF THE RUSSIAN HIGH COMMAND. ON AUGUST 26 THE AUSTRO-GERMAN ARMY OCCUPIED THE CITY, AND MANY OF THE EXILES RETURNED. SHORTLY AFTERWARD, HOWEVER, THEY WERE AGAIN EXPELLED BY THE GERMANS. AFTER THE POLES OCCUPIED THE REGION IN 1919, JEWISH COMMUNAL LIVE REVIVED. IN 1921 THE JEWISH POPULATION NUMBERED 15,630 (OUT OF A TOTAL OF 29,460), AND IN 1931, 21,440. FOR SEVERAL YEARS THE DEPUTY MAYOR OF BREST WAS A JEW. PROMINENT IN BREST IN THE LATE 19TH AND EARLY 20TH CENTURIES WERE THE PHILOLOGIST AND TALMUDIST JACOB NAHUM EPSTEIN; MICHAEL PUCHACZEWSKI, A PIONEER FARMER IN ERETZ ISRAEL; THE JOURNALISTS ABRAHAM GOLDBERG AND NOAH FINKELSTEIN; AND THE AUTHOR AND PHYSICIAN BENJAMIN SZERESZEWSKI.

ALMOST 30,000 JEWS LIVED IN BREST IN 1941. THE GERMANS FIRST TOOK THE CITY ON SEPT. 15, 1939, AND LOOTED AND KIDNAPPED JEWS FOR FORCED LABOR. FOLLOWING THE SOVIET-GERMAN AGREEMENT ON THE DIVISION OF POLAND, HOWEVER, THE CITY CAME UNDER SOVIET RULE (SEPT. 22, 1939). THE SOVIET AUTHORITIES DISBANDED THE COMMUNAL BODIES, REPRESSED INDEPENDENT POLITICAL ACTIVITY, AND ARRESTED JEWISH LEADERS. AMONG THOSE EXILED TO THE SOVIET UNION WAS ISRAEL TENENBAUM, THE LOCAL "BUND" LEADER. ON JUNE 28-29, 1941, THE GERMANS KIDNAPPED 5,000 JEWISH MEN SUPPOSEDLY FOR FORCED LABOR, BUT THE MEN WERE TAKEN OUTSIDE THE CITY

LIMITS AND MURDERED. IN THE AUTUMN OF 1941 THE JEWS WERE SEGREGATED INTO A GHETTO, AND ONLY A FEW PHYSICIANS AND THEIR FAMILIES WERE ALLOWED TO REMAIN ON THE "ARYAN" SIDE. A JUDENRAT WAS IMPOSED, HEADED BY ZVI HIRSCH ROSENBERG AND HIS DEPUTY, NORMAN LANDAU. WITHIN THE GHETTO, AID WAS ORGANIZED FOR THE NEEDY, AND VARIOUS WORKSHOPS WERE CREATED TO PROVIDE THE JEWS WITH PRODUCTIVE WORK FOR THE GERMANS IN AN ATTEMPT TO PREVENT THEIR DEPORTATION TO DEATH CAMPS. AT THE END OF JUNE, 1942, A GROUP OF 900 SKILLED ARTISANS WAS TAKEN AWAY FOR FORCED LABOR IN THE EAST. ONLY 12 OF THEM CAME BACK TO THE GHETTO SEVERAL WEEKS LATER. IN MID-1942 AN UNDERGROUND RESISTANCE MOVEMENT, LED BY ARIEH SCHEINMAN, CAME INTO BEING IN THE GHETTO. ITS MEMBERS RAISED FUNDS TO BUY ARMS TO PROVISION FIGHTING TROOPS WHO WOULD SET THEMSELVES UP IN THE FORESTS. ON OCT. 15, 1942, THE GERMANS BEGAN TO LIQUIDATE THE GHETTO. FOLLOWING THE AKTION THE GERMANS CONTINUED A MANHUNT FOR THOSE HIDING IN BUNKERS. THE JEWS WHO HAD MANAGED TO FLEE THE GERMANS JOINED THE PARTISAN UNITS OPERATING IN THE FORESTS. A NUMBER OF BREST'S JEWS BELONGED TO THE "KOTOWSKI" SOVIET PARTISAN UNIT, AND HAVA GINZBERG OF BREST WAS REGARDED AS AN OUTSTANDING PARTISAN. WHEN BREST WAS LIBERATED IN JULY 1944, THERE WERE LESS THAN TEN JEWS TO BE FOUND IN THE CITY. THE JEWISH POPULATION OF THE TOWN WAS ESTIMATED AT

2,000 IN 1970. IT HAD NO SYNAGOGUE, THE LAST ONE HAVING
BEEN CONVERTED INTO A MOVIE HOUSE IN 1954.

and in 1997 ?

The Nahum Goldmann
Museum of the Jewish Diaspora
incl. the Abraham & Edita Spiegel Family Bldg

June 1988

I was amazed by the detail and quantity of the information about my heritage that I was provided at the Diaspora Museum in Tel Aviv on my visit there in June 1988. Courtesy Balgley Family Archive

largest synagogue in the world, and although built in the nineteenth century, its design by architect Leandro Marconi, was neo-classical.

I had just stood at the spot of its location days before in Warsaw, and wanting to be certain I was in the right place where the synagogue had been, I asked an old peasant woman who happened to be standing near. Pointing to the construction site of a tall building which looked as if it were being built —a building now known as the Blue Skyscraper— at that time it appeared abandoned and old with broken windows and rusted iron, she was eager to explain. Eyes widened and face intense, she indicated that yes, this was where the synagogue had stood, she remembered it. But now, she explained, workers kept falling to their deaths from the scaffolding. She exclaimed, shaking her hands in front of her, "They cannot build there." It was impossible to know the source of her scolding: consistent with the Polish folklore of the evil mysteries of Jewish rituals, was it malevolent Jewish ghosts who kept throwing innocent workers from the heights? Or was it sacrilege that Poles were building on the site of the synagogue? In Poland, it could have been both at once.

The sense of unreality I experienced at the model synagogue exhibition did not abate until I was out of the museum. The Tel Aviv blinding sun and the noise of the traffic brought me back to my senses and to the current place and time.

The following day I was to meet the other Balgley family whom the American journalist had contacted for me. They were in Haifa, and again those family members also insisted on picking me up at my hotel. It was a long round trip drive, but they were clear in the concierge's message to me. They would find me at my hotel.

Early the next morning, I waited in the lobby, and met Yitzhak Szpilman, the husband of Mira Balgley. Her grandfather, Herschel, and mine, Israel, were brothers. Herschel had never gone to the United States or Israel. He had remained in Poland, but at some point unknown to us, he had relocated from Brześć to Warsaw, and established a successful furrier business there. I was to learn years later Herschel's precise address and that Herschel was my grandfather's brother, uncle to my father. When my father came with his mother and his three siblings from Brześć to Warsaw, it was to Herschel's home that they went. Thus it was Herschel's home that my father was remembering when I took him and my mother from Warsaw Airport to *Pani* Zofia's flat on *Aleje Ujazdowskie*. It was Herschel's beautiful courtyard in 1920 that looked just like *Pani* Zofia's in 1988 which had stunned my father and brought back the memory of his childhood arrival to Warsaw.

Herschel's son, Abba, was Mira's father. The story of how the family came to Israel was testament to the accidents that allow survival. An 18-year-old in Warsaw, Abba had been forcibly drafted into the Polish army at the start of World War II. He became part of the well-known Anders' Army, the name given to the Polish Armed Forces in the east of Poland because of its commander, Władysław Anders. Though the Soviets had invaded Poland in September 1939 (sixteen days after the Nazis had invaded), British pressure on the Soviets eventually created a British-Soviet-Polish pact where the Soviet Union reversed territorial agreements it had made with the Nazis and released the many thousands of Polish citizens it had deported to the Soviet Union in 1940 and 1941. In August 1941, a Polish-Soviet pact allowed the creation of a Polish army in the Soviet Union: Anders' Army was that force.

From the start, the Soviets had wanted to recruit only citizens of the Second Polish Republic (the interwar period from 1918 to 1939) who were ethnic Poles, excluding Jews, Belarusians and Ukrainians. Nonetheless, there were significant numbers of Jewish Poles in the Anders' Army—numbering 4,000 soldiers. Abba and his battalion remained in Russia until March of 1942 when Anders' Army, then under British command, was evacuated from the Soviet Union and sent through Iran and Iraq to Palestine. As Anders' Army departed the Soviet Union headed to the Middle East, Jewish war orphans, and other Jews devastated by the war, followed the Jewish soldiers. By the time Anders' Army reached Palestine, 3,000 of the 4,000 Jewish troops had left the army.

*Here circled, Abba Balgley, a member of the formidable 'Anders'Army',
stationed in Eastern Poland, photographed with his Polish army comrades
during World War II. Abba was the father of Mira Balgley, and Yossi
Balgley (BenGal). I was to meet Yossi in Michigan years after my trip to
Israel when I met his mother, Yaffa, and his sister, Mira at her home in
Haifa. Herschel, Abba's father, and Mira and Yossi's grandfather, was a
brother of my own grandfather. Courtesy Balgley Family Archive*

Believing they could do more for their people annihilated by the Shoah by
staying in Palestine and helping to build a Jewish state, these Jewish soldiers
became part of the existing settlements in Palestine. This was how Abba had
come to Israel.

Yitzhak brought his elder son, Sharon, to meet me. Sharon was the age of
my university students, an age group for which I had a special affinity, and he
and I quickly struck up a friendship. On the drive to Haifa I learned from Sharon
that he had been a solder in the Israeli army, and as he quietly relayed some of
his experiences, I could see that he had been already traumatized by what he had
seen and participated in. I thought of his grandfather's experience in the Anders'
Army, the journey out of the Soviet Union to Palestine, and had a moment to
reflect briefly on how for that part of my family, soldiering never ceased.

Yitzhak first brought us to his mother-in-law's home. She was Yaffa,
her Hebrew name, which had been changed from Shaindel when she went to
Palestine. She had come from the town of Ratne in Ukraine to Palestine under
the auspices of *HeHalutz*, "The Pioneer," a group of Zionists who sought to
prepare Jewish Youth to live in Israel. Shaindel/Yaffa arrived in Palestine with

this group in 1930 and started kibbutz *Eyelet Hashachar* in northern Galilee. Soon after that kibbutz began, Yaffa was sent to the top agricultural school in the country in Nalhallal, the original home of former Israeli Defense Minister, Moshe Dayan. Yaffa's parents were brought to the kibbutz, but her father Joseph later went back to Ratne in Poland to sell property; when World War II broke out, he was never heard from again. That was the same story with my great uncle Benjamin—the family never knew his motivation for his return to Poland. Some reported he had property there, while others believed he went to find his wife and son. Whatever the reason, he was lost.

Like Rachel, Yaffa's husband had died before I visited Israel. After he left Anders' Army in Palestine in 1945, Abba, like Nachum, became a member of the Haganah. When Israel achieved statehood in 1948, the Haganah became the core of the Israeli Defense Force (IDF). Abba served in the IDF's medical corps during the War of Independence and began work in civil life after the end of the war. And like all

Early photo of Yaffa (formerly Shaindel) and her husband, Abba. Courtesy Balgley Family Archive

Israelis, he continued serving in the reserves—thirty days a year on average— until age 50, the mandatory age for retirement in Israel. I learned that Abba had never spoken of the Shoah, and had strenuously avoided viewing photos or films depicting it. From his 20s and throughout his life, he had never seen images of the Holocaust. On Holocaust Memorial Day in Israel, at the age of 56, Abba decided it was time to watch a televised documentary: he died of a heart attack in his chair in front of the television.

His widow Yaffa's home was sparkling clean and neat, as was her person. An elderly woman, she was spry and energetic and welcomed me with a hug. Her daughter, and my direct "blood relative" was Mira. She was younger than me by some years, was beautiful and exotic looking—central casting for a film featuring a young Hebrew woman in ancient Palestine. Her hair had been highlighted with blonde, and her light green eyes stood out from her olive skin. She, too, received me warmly. And again, it was obvious that careful plans had been made for my arrival. Yaffa offered food, though I learned soon that I would later be the houseguest of Mira and Yitzhak.

Before I left Poland for Israel, I had communicated with Antoni's family in Poland, and with Dzidzia, the Jewish Polish friend of his family's whom they had arranged for me to meet, as I knew Dizidzia's daughter, Mariola would have been newly-arrived from Poland to live in Haifa just as I was visiting. Before my departure from Poland, I had checked with my American translator in Tel Aviv that it would be fine for Mariola to meet me at my new-found relatives' home.

Mariola arrived an hour or so after my arrival. Mira had been translating for her mother and me, but it was interesting to find that her Israeli mother could follow my Polish a bit, though she explained she had not spoken Polish in over a half century. A native speaker of Polish, Mariola's English was good and allowed her to participate in the conversation, with Mira translating for Yaffa. It was Mariola's wish, however, to become fluent in Hebrew, and she had been studying the language before she arrived to Israel, so she understood some of what Yaffa was saying. Such a Tower of Babel this was with Hebrew, a language spoken by the Jewish people in ancient times recovered for use in this new land, and Polish, a language once spoken by the largest Jewish community in the world, now silenced by cataclysm. Again, I had that feeling of the collapse of space and time.

It was odd to meet Mariola in that new setting. Her paleness and apparel made her suddenly seem like a character out of an antique portrait from a place no longer in existence and from a time past. Jewish like my Israeli relatives in the room, she seemed a faded photograph of what they would have looked like in the Old World before the war. It was poignant to see young Mariola there; her struggle to start a new life was a later version of what Polish Jews would have faced coming to Palestine before and after World War II.

Polish-Jewish culture is not Israeli culture, and nothing could fully prepare these Central Europeans for the shock of the desert and the sea and the language. Like those earlier newcomers, Mariola wanted

Yaffa, mother of Mira and Yossi, formerly called Shaindel, who settled in Israel from Ukraine. She was the widow of Abba, whose father Herschel was a brother of my own grandfather. She is photographed here at home in Haifa with her grandson Evya Szpilman. The art behind is by her daughter, Mira Balgley. Courtesy Balgley Family Archive

to feel at home here, like this was where she belonged, but it had to be difficult to achieve that feeling. At least now, with Israel's statehood, she was not stopped and detained in Cyprus. Mariola, Yaffa, Yitzhak, Mira, Sharon and I chatted for a while, with Mariola having the opportunity to get answers to questions about living in Haifa. After Mariola departed, Mira suggested we then drive to her house so I could unpack and settle in.

Yitzhak was a saavy, experienced urban driver, and we reached their home quickly. It was an inviting bright apartment, one wall covered in Mira's artwork—accomplished

Yaffa's older grandson Sharon, who had served in the Israeli army before my visit there in 1988. Courtesy Balgley Family Archive

drawings and paintings of Israeli faces and streets. Another wall was shuttered from top to bottom, but could be opened and closed as the sun necessitated— so it felt like an apartment in an Italian city.

I met Sharon's younger brother, Evya—only 5 years old, and the delight of all the family. Mira also introduced her beautiful pre-teen adopted daughter, Oshrit. Sharon showed me his room: rock and

Mira Balgley's family in Haifa, from left: Evya, Oshrit and Sharon. Courtesy Balgley Family Archive

roll posters and emblems of other youthful enthusiasm covered the walls so that his gun leaning again a wall surprised, despite the stories he had told me. He lifted the gun carefully but with familiarity and confidence, and showed me how he was trained to handle it. Of course, he looked too young to be a warrior, as did all the charming uniformed young women and men I would see walking on the streets. They were just like my freshmen university students, except instead of book bags they carried rifles.

Sharon suggested the two of us walk together and get an ice cream. As we walked the bright Haifa streets, he pointed out his neighborhood haunts, and it was difficult then to think he was the soldier who had shown me his fighting stances.

They had told me to bring my suitcase—I could stay with them in Haifa— so I did, but I knew I would have to return to Tel Aviv for my flight back to Warsaw, and so I booked my hotel for my final days there. I asked the concierge if it were possible to have the same room when I returned. I had felt at home there. Friendly now, she said she would see to it. I still had places I wanted to visit before I left the country.

Despite their busy work schedules and parenting duties, Mira and Yitzhak made it seem that they had all the time in the world for me. We drove together to Safed, a famed city in Galilee. Known as Israel's art capital, the city is also a center for a sizeable Kabbalistic community. Tiny synagogues dot the leafy streets with hand painted ceilings featuring folk art from various historical periods. The city has an ancient and complex history.

It was my father's birthday, and I had in any case wanted to phone him when I was in Israel. It felt important to me, even necessary, that I speak to him from there. Mira immediately insisted I use their phone and not be concerned about the long distance cost. My father and I spoke briefly, but it was clear from the excitement in his voice that he understood the significance of my being in Israel among family of his whom he had never met, and my phoning from there on his birthday.

And what was the significance, I asked myself then and wonder now? At that time, it was a feeling of joy, of celebration, but I could hardly name exactly why. In some way, it was a gift to my father—a healing of sorts after wounding—a recompense for alienation, disconnection, loss, regret, the unspoken ambivalence he must have felt in his decision to separate from his family and his former self, I wanted to say, "It's alright now—you don't need to blame yourself, or grieve, or apologize." It made me think of that moment in the hotel in Kraków where he tearfully told me he was surprised to find there could ever be a spring again in Poland, that trees could ever bloom there again, and we had agreed in a kind of awe that spring would come there again and again, despite everything. And it is also true that I was trying to convince myself that hope could be rescued, that the reasons my father had kept his background hidden from himself and from me could now be brought into the light. And this: that maybe I could forgive him, even if that unveiling never happened.

Mira got me safely back to my hotel in Tel Aviv, and the concierge had indeed saved my room for me. The time with Mira and Yitzhak, Yaffa, Sharon, Evyatar, and Oshrit had exceeded any expectation of hospitality that I could have had--I really was welcomed as a family member.

Back in Tel Aviv, I only had two days left in Israel before my return to Poland, and I had planned from before I left Warsaw that I would visit Yad Vashem, The World Holocaust Remembrance Center in Jerusalem. The trip there from Tel Aviv was an easy bus ride. I did visit the Western Wall and walk around the city streets for a time, but I was anxious to get to Yad Vashem.

The area where Yad Vashem has been built is beautiful--in the Har Hazikaron region of the city on the southern slopes of Mount Herzl. Stately trees cover grassy hills and it is quiet there, as you might expect. That day the only sound I remember hearing as I approached the entry was the sound of the wind. I toured the exhibit of the Righteous Gentiles and saw the largest number listed for Poland—an honor, yet one had to remember that Poland's population included the highest percentage of Jews in all of Europe at the time of the Shoah. On exhibit also was one of the small Danish boats that carried Jews to safety in Denmark.

At one point, I took an elevator that opened directly onto an open-air plaza. There stood a life-sized replica of the current Warsaw Ghetto Monument and platz in Warsaw. Having just come from Warsaw, and having stood on that platz many times, it was surreal to see it here. The desert summer sun made the figures shine and shimmer—so different from the antique, gray look at the actual Ghetto Monument in Warsaw. The sculpture looked more like a gleaming trophy than a somber memorial to the dead. Its appearance and its presence there suggested survival, continuity, even defiance. I stood for a long time looking at the memorial, even though I knew its detail well from Warsaw. But there I stood to absorb a separate feeling, the sun all around me, and a sense of hope. As I departed this section of the exhibit, I saw a sign in lights that resembled burning flames: *"Zakhor"*— ("Remember").

I walked to a special building reserved for the remembrance of the Jewish children murdered by the Nazis. I approached with trepidation, my stomach jumping. The sun was high and bright, so much so that on first entering the structure, I could see nothing, so black was the interior. I stood inside for some minutes and waited for my eyes to adjust, hoping maybe to recover myself, my emotions, but the fear only increased. But this is how it is supposed to be, I told myself. You should be afraid of what you will see and how you will feel. I realized in a moment that the interior was entirely dark, except for tiny holes of light in the ceiling, like stars, and dim lights just above the floor pointing downward to prevent visitors from losing their way. There was a handrail and I held tightly to it with my left hand as I began to move. Gradually I made out lit photographic portraits of children appearing in the dark, seemingly suspended in space, floating. And then I heard a voice, a recording, quietly and simply stating the names of the murdered children. I was walking, but felt as if I were on a moving sidewalk: the slow revelation of the photographs at all different levels in space—eye level, above me, below me, all around me—and the sound of the names being read out—created the illusion of space and time moving past me rather than my making progress on my own volition. Like the faces of the children, I was floating in space, too; I was joined to them. The effect is nearly indescribable. The closest I could say is that a wall of grief and sorrow welled up inside of me—and outside of me: I was enveloped. Flashes of fury, outrage, revulsion broke over me, too. Though I had the sensation of floating, my body had become rigid and tensed, every muscle knotted, every organ convulsed. I cannot say how long I was in the building; in the same way that space was suspended in the exhibition, so was time. The finish of the path was one door. I leaned on it, not fully cognizant that this was an exit. The open door releases the visitor abruptly—that has to be part of the design—into the searing sunlight. I staggered out. A tiny slab of cement surrounded by a knee-high wall sits at the exit. I lost my balance for a moment. And then standing in the sun on the gray cement patch, I sobbed. I reached for the handrail that had been inside, but there was none here. In a moment, I had to move aside because another visitor had come through the flung open door: she staggered, too, looked for the absent handrail, and then I heard her cry out as I had done.

An Unattainable Identity

Before I left Israel, it was important for me to meet Marc, the American journalist who had been so generous in contacting my family members in Israel for me. He really had invested a good deal of time, gone out of his way—and for someone he had never even met or knew, made phone calls to relatives who had never met me or known of me, to explain who I was, and make arrangements with them for me. I wanted to thank him in person, take him to dinner, if he was free.

Marc was available and we met near my hotel the evening before I was to depart Israel. It was an especially beautiful night, a cool breeze coming off the sea, the clouds pink-hued, the water turquoise. Only slightly older than me, Marc, though American, had the looks of particularly handsome Israeli men—bearded, tanned, athletic, a cool customer. Yet his Americanness came through immediately when we started to talk—not only his lack of an Israeli accent, obviously, but also the sense that though he lived here, he was an outsider. He would not have thought of himself that way, I believed, as he was a journalist there, and planned to stay. But there was a lack of humor, an absence of lightheartedness about him, a solitariness. As we talked, it became clear that he was seriously affected by Israel's precarious political situation, as well he might be as a journalist who followed disturbing events closely. It might just have been his personality, not his work, but he remained remote during the evening. I told him my story briefly, and in a taciturn manner, he told me I would continue to be lost, given my mixed identity. He shook his head as he told me my search for identity would be ill-fated—would be impossible—I would never find myself. It was unfortunate, he said, but I would have to make up my mind to either become Jewish, if that were even possible or allowable, or remain unpleasantly adrift all my life. After the warmhearted reception by my family members who would have had more reason to be prejudiced against me, Marc's sternness was a surprise. The fact of our shared generation, our similar outlook on American politics and culture, our identification with Jewishness, all of this notwithstanding, there was a barrier between us.

We spoke of Poland a bit, and he told me that when Menachem Begin, who was born a year after my father in the same Polish city, Brześć, would bow and kiss the hands of women in the tradition of the Polish aristocracy, he was disliked by Israelis for what they saw as a connection to an Old World that had persecuted and murdered them. I had found the custom charming, but I took the point. And as we said goodnight and goodbye, that small observation about hand kissing became a metaphor for the barrier between Marc and me; he had dispensed with any romantic ideas about the world, if he ever had any, and I still held on to the hope that human gestures, no matter how fraught they were with the ills of history, still possessed an authenticity that trumped evil. As I prepared for bed on my last night in Israel, I realized that Marc's views reminded me of my father's: this world has no innocence in it.

Tel Aviv

February 12, 1989

Dear Kathleen,

I'd be happy to help you in any way I can. I'm sure this country is a
wealth of information on Polish Jewry and from the academic aspect alone it
would be worth your while visiting this country.

As to your two great aunts. Both are alive and well and seem to be very
nice women (I contacted them by phone). Rachel is of Morxoccan background
but speaks a little English. Her children also speak English and they live
nearby. Her telephone number is   ,. Shendel nox longer calls herself
Shendel but Yaffa. She was born in Poland and emigrated to Israel at the age
of nineteen. Polish is the only common language between you. Note the spelling
of her street in Kiryat Motzkin: Shikun Rosko 24. Her telephone number is

As I mentioned, both seem to be warm pleasant women. They'll receive you
with 'open arms' (that's a quote) and both expressed the willingness/desire
to put you up. The practise of putting people up is common in this country
so you shouldn't consider it an imposition. Neither woman has received a
letter from you yet. Givatayim is a suburb of Tel Aviv. Haifa is an hour's
drive north of Tel Aviv. I suggest on landing in Israel you spend your first
night in Tel Aviv. A hotel I redommend to my relatives (it's clean, by the
sea, about $25 a night) is Hotel Maxime, 86 HaYarkon St., tel. #   .
A bus from the airport takes you more or less to it.

If you have any more questions you can write or call me (   ). Your
letter took about two weeks to reach me.

                              Regards,

*A letter I received from American journalist, Marc, based in Tel Aviv,
indicating his willingness to trace my Jewish relatives in Israel and
offering me advice prior to my visit there in 1989. Courtesy Balgley Family
Archive*

"I don't remember"
Zakhor ("Remember" in Hebrew)/Nie pamiętam ("I don't remember" in Polish)

I flew from Tel Aviv to Warsaw early the next morning, Marc's comments about the hopelessness of my search in my head, mixed with the images of Yad Vashem, the photographs of the children, and the full-sized replica of the Warsaw Ghetto Monument there. Despite the sunlight all around me on the way to the airport, my heart was solemn. Maybe Marc was right. Maybe everything I had been absorbing in Poland, and now in Israel, perhaps all I had been learning, could not finally erase the profound fear that lay behind my search: my father's *crie de coeur* after Munich: "This world is not worth living in!"

Arriving back in Warsaw, I experienced what I had predicted I would feel—a trip back in time, not just because communist Poland was stunted, but a trip back to the daily reminders of what had been and all that was lost. I took a taxi from the airport into the city, found my hotel, and though tired from the travel, I had a sudden and irresistible urge to visit the actual Warsaw Ghetto Monument.

I knew it was near the hotel where I was staying, and in a sort of frantic frame of mind, I set out walking. Normally, I would take a taxi to a destination if I was not positive about how to get to it, but I was not thinking logically and instead I was driven by a strange instinct I could not and still do not now entirely understand: *I had to be there.*

It was early evening and the light was gradually fading. I was always aware of the Jewish ghosts of Poland, but this evening was different. Even the cobblestones beneath my feet sent up messages: who, exactly, had walked here? I became disoriented in streets that I knew. I felt dizzy and slightly nauseous. Why had I not planned out my route as I always did? I continued to walk rapidly but knew I was lost. I saw a woman walking towards me and I stopped her and said *"Gdzie jest getto?"* ("Where is the ghetto?"). She stared at me for a second, and then coldly replied, *"Nie pamiętam."* ("I don't remember"), Not "I don't know," but instead "I don't remember." Which struck me as much worse. Suddenly as unspeakably cruel. I knew I had to get a hold of myself, to right my route, to stabilize my mood. But all I could see in my mind's eye were the lighted flames at the close of the Yad Vashem Memorial: *"Zakhor"*— ("Remember"), and hear reverberating in my head the Polish woman's "I don't remember." I sat down on a street bench and wept. I never made it to the Memorial that night, and it took some time for me to finally find my hotel.

VI

Wrocław ❄ Snow Falling on Radiators

"No fly"

Every American Fulbrighter whom I met had been issued a multiple exit visa from her or his *milicja* (government police) office. That meant they were not required to appear at the police office to obtain a stamp in their passports giving them permission to travel internationally each time they wanted to leave and to re-enter Poland. I learned soon enough that because I had been assigned to Silesia, that part of Poland that Poles called "red," particularly cooperative with the communist regime, I, like other American Fulbrighters to that region before me, had been instead issued a *jednokrotnego przekroczenia granicy* visa, which meant that every time I left Poland I would have to appear at the *milicja* office for an exit stamp, and every time I returned to Poland, I was required to go back to the office for an entry stamp.

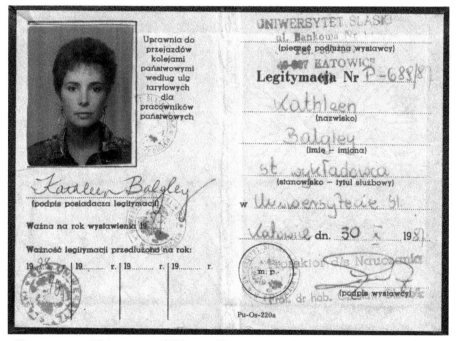

First year at University of Silesia "Legitymacja" proves I was a professor in Poland. Courtesy Balgley Family Archive

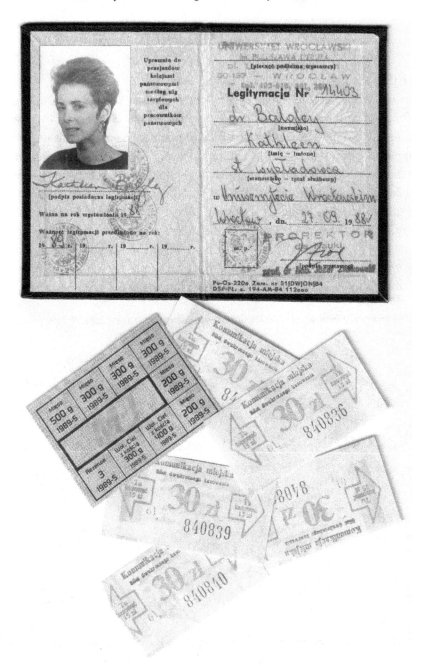

Second year at University of Wrocław
These documents were important for many reasons, in particular to allow
purchase of airline tickets and hotel stays as a Polish citizen would pay.
The green card was my meat ration card; the others are tram tickets.
Courtesy Balgley Family Archive

UNIVERSITY OF SILESIA
Institute of English
and General Linguistics
Bando 10
41-205 Sosnowiec

26th August, 1987

Ms. Kathleen Anne Balgley

Venice, California 90291
USA

Dear Ms. Balgley,

We hereby confirm that the Ministry of Higher Education
and Science in Poland has approved of your application to
be employed at University of Silesia, Institute of English
and General Linguistics, at the post of lecturer in American
literature from 1st October, 1987 until 30th September, 1988.

You are advised to arrive in Poland at the end of September,
1987.

This letter should be presented at a Polish Consulate to
obtain visa allowing you to enter Poland on work permit visa
basis.

Please inform us about the date of your arrival in Poland—
you will be accomodated at Hotel Asystencki 2, ul. Paderewskiego
32, Katowice, Poland.

We are looking forward to meeting you in Poland.

Yours Sincerely,

Prorektor d/s Nauki

Prof. dr heb. Maksymilian Pazdan

*Official letter of
acceptance to teach at
University of Silesia,
19987-1988, my first
year Fulbright. Courtesy
Balgley Family Archive*

UNIWERSYTET SLĄSKI
ul. Bankowa Nr.12
Tel. 51-72-81 nagłówkowa zakładu pracy)
40-007 KATOWICE

Katowice,dnia 1987-1o-23
(miejscowość i data)

UMOWA O PRACĘ

1987-1o-23

zawarta w dniu _____
(data zawarcia umowy)

pomiędzy ____ Uniwersytetem Slaskim w Katowicach

(nazwa i siedziba zakładu pracy)

zwanego dalej zakładem pracy, reprezentowanym przez

Obywatela(kę) prof.dra hab.Sędzimira M.Klimaszewskiego - Rektora USl.
(imię i nazwisko, stanowisko)

a Obywatelem(ką) p.Kathleen BALGLEY - Obywatelką USA
(imię i nazwisko, adres)

Zakład pracy zatrudnia Obywatela(kę) w Instytucie Filologii Angielskiej
(w miarę potrzeby podać nazwę komórki organizacyjnej)

na Wydziale Filologicznym

na czas określony tj.od 1.X.1987 do 3o.IX.1988 r.
(okres próbny, wstępny, czas nieokreślony, czas określony, czas wykonania określonej pracy — podać jakiej. W przypadku zastrzeżenia wypowiedzenia umowy o pracę zawartej na czas określony dłuższy niż 6 miesięcy — należy to zaznaczyć)

w wymiarze pełnego etatu
(w przypadku niepełnego wymiaru czasu pracy — podać ten wymiar)

i powierzam obowiązki starszego wykładowcy
(stanowisko wg taryfikatora kwalifikacyjnego — tabeli płac)

Obywatel(ka) obowiązany(a) jest zgłosić się do pracy w dniu 1.X.1987

W czasie trwania umowy o pracę Obywatel(ka) będzie otrzymywał(a) wynagrodzenie płatne w sposób i na

warunkach przewidzianych w Rozp.RM z 2.VIII.1982 wraz z późn.zmian./Dz.U.Nr 19
(przepisy o wynagrodzeniu — układ zbiorowy pracy)
1987/

a mianowicie:

1) stawka płacy zasadniczej — wynagrodzenie uposażenie

_____

(podać kategorię zaszeregowania grupę wynagrodzenie uposażenia)

37.500,-zł (słownie zł) trzydzieścisiedemtysięcypięćset zł m-cznie

2) grupa i stawka dodatku funkcyjnego specjalnego

w wysokości _____ zł (słownie zł) _____

3) premie i dodatki na zasadach i warunkach określonych w przepisach o wynagrodzeniu, układzie zbio-

rowym pracy _____
(podać odpowiedni akt prawny, układ zbiorowy pracy, a jeżeli dodatek ma charakter stały podać kwotę dodatku)

Prof. ____ podpis kierownika zakładu pracy
lub upoważnionego pracownika

Oświadczam, że egzemplarz niniejszej umowy otrzymałem(am) i po zapoznaniu się z jej treścią zaproponowane mi warunki pracy i wynagrodzenia przyjmuję. Równocześnie przyjmuję do wiadomości treść obowiązującego w zakładzie regulaminu pracy i oświadczam, że zobowiązuję się do przestrzegania porządku i dyscypliny pracy. Ponadto oświadczam, że znane mi są przepisy dotyczące naruszenia tajemnicy państwowej i służbowej zawarte w art. 260—264, w związku z art. 120 § 15 i 16 ustawy z dnia 19 kwietnia 1969 r. Kodeks karny (Dz. U. Nr 13. poz. 94).

Kathleen Balgley
data i podpis pracownika

podpis przyjmującego oświadczenia

DUS. 13ćzieo n 10000

*My contract with the University of Silesia, signed October 23, 1987,
indicating my post as Professor. Courtesy Balgley Family Archive*

This meant that each time I wanted to travel out of Poland, and each time I returned to Poland, I was required to go to the Katowice *Milicja* to receive a stamp. There was no reason for this requirement other than harassment and punishment, and it was regarded at the American Embassy as an insult to the Fulbright program. But there was nothing to be done to remedy the situation—the Embassy needed to get along with the local authorities. This single entry/exit visa was onerous: if I only took a train trip to Prague, for instance, before I departed I needed to get to the *milicja* station, a good distance from where I lived, and stand in a line for hours to procure my stamp. When I returned to Poland I was required to repeat the ritual, otherwise I was not legally present in Poland.

When the school term ended for the year in summer of 1988, I had planned to go to Spain to meet John. Naturally, I would fly from Warsaw. On my return to Warsaw from Spain, I was due to travel to the States, my first trip back in nearly a year. A once-a-month charter flight from Warsaw to Chicago was most convenient and economical, but to catch that flight on my return to Warsaw from Spain, I would not have time to travel by train from Warsaw to Katowice to get that "re-entry" stamp to Poland. I explained this as best I could to the severe matron at the Katowice *Milicja* when, after hours in line, I reached her desk for the exit stamp to Spain. I asked, "Since I leave immediately from Warsaw to Chicago once I return from Spain, is it necessary to come here for another entry stamp and a new exit stamp?" She shook her head and said "Nie." I was relieved I had gotten my point across and would be able to leave from Warsaw without the long train ride to Katowice before departing for the United States.

I had accepted a second year Fulbright assignment but in another Polish city, so I was leaving Silesia for good. I had packed up all my belongings and vacated the flat in Dąbrowa Gornicza. Antoni's family had kindly offered to store my books, with the plan that I would retrieve them in the fall when I returned to take up my teaching position. Still, since I was going back to the United States for three months, my load of luggage was much larger than it would normally have been when I travelled inside Europe.

I made my way to Warsaw from Katowice by train like I had done many times in the past. That time it was tougher because of the bags. But that was not the first time I would have struggled with luggage and would not be the last.

After the brief vacation in Spain, I returned to Warsaw with the plan to catch the charter flight to Chicago. I arrived in Warsaw from Spain, and loading my luggage off the carousel onto a cart and through customs and passport control, I moved quickly to get to the charter flight, which was departing in two hours.

I was lucky—the airport was not as crowded and chaotic as usual. Moving into the outbound line for passport control, I began for the first time to think about what a return to the United States would feel like after nine months in Poland. I had mixed feelings; in an odd way, I had grown accustomed to the difficulties there, and had habituated myself to them. And those difficulties were far outweighed by the friends I had made and the things I was able to learn and experience. I was glad I was returning to Poland for a second year—and from what I had been told—to a city, Wrocław, where life would be less arduous and less isolated than it had been in Silesia.

It was my turn to slip my passport through the barely large enough chute for inspection. In Poland, you did not see your inspector; the booth was opaque. You communicated through that tiny chute, if you communicated at all. I had done this so many times it felt routine. There was an unusual pause before the passport was returned, and this time there came a shock. The passport flew into the tiny tunnel as if hurled from the other side. The faceless voice behind the booth declared, "No fly!" I was stunned. For some seconds, I failed to equate the refusal with the lack of the additional entry/exit stamp from Katowice. Briefly, I tried to explain I had been given permission. But of course, that was only verbal—no one was impressed there by that. The imperative was restated, "No fly!" My mind sped over all the meetings the Embassy and the Council for the International Exchange of Scholars had required Fulbrighters to attend—those meetings were meant to troubleshoot such events as this. But none of that information made sense just then. I might have been able to find a way to phone the American Embassy, but time was short, and I seriously doubted if they could do much to intervene.

I was being pushed from behind by the next person in line, and suddenly I heard voices from the carousel where my luggage had been placed. The voices, I realized, were shouting at me, and the men working at the carousel were hurling my suitcases off the carousel. I was escorted to a small room where an official told me that I needed to return to Katowice to get the proper exit stamp. I explained I would miss the once-a-month charter flight to Chicago. The official told me I could try my luck at the Warsaw *Milijca* in the *Praga* district of the city, but he could guarantee nothing. As I got up to go and gather my scattered bags, he told me I had twelve hours to depart the country. Second shock.

As I left the airport I saw the Chicago-bound flight take off. I ran to find a taxi, stopped at the closest hotel to the airport to store my luggage—this involved renting a room as they did not store luggage for non-guests, even though I offered to pay—and continuing on across the city to the Praga district to find the *Milijca* station where I hoped to get an exit stamp. I had no guarantee that they would provide it; I would have to wait to learn my fate.

The taxi brought me to an abandoned looking municipal pre-war building, the *Praga Milijca*. From the outside, it seemed non-functional, but this was the address. I could not keep the taxi waiting as I had no idea what would transpire or how long it would take. I kept flashing on what I would do if I could not get the stamp and my twelve-hour visa expired. I had no idea.

I deciphered the directory in the dusty lobby, and found my way to the office that issued visas. I was not at all certain if this was the right office for my purposes, but I climbed the many staircases, and came to a taciturn woman sitting at what appeared to be a sort of reception desk. I explained what I needed, and she sullenly pointed to a stiff wooden chair and indicated I should sit. I sat. And sat. At intervals I saw the door behind the receptionist open just a bit, the receptionist going in and out, but no sign of other people or any progress for my case. The receptionist studiously ignored me, made no eye contact and offered no explanations or hope. I knew better than to push. Warsaw might not have been as "red" as Poles liked to call Katowice, but an American with a visa problem was not likely something about which they would have much sympathy even in Warsaw. I had no reading material, so there was nothing to look at. I sat in the uncomfortable chair not four feet in front of the desk of the stoical receptionist. Every so often I surreptitiously stole a glance at my watch. Just before I had left the airport, I saw that there was a LOT Polish Airlines flight to New York at 10 p.m.—the last one of the day. If I missed that, I was out of luck. The twelve-hour amnesty had begun at 2 p.m. when I was refused departure, so the 2 a.m. deadline would be moot if I missed that flight.

It was now 5:30 p.m. I had waited over two hours. Offices in Poland had a maddening way of suddenly closing with no warning, and I worried that the receptionist would start packing up, and remembering me, would inform me that the office was now closed, and that I would have to come back another time. I knew that the Lot Airlines office at the Forum Hotel was open until 9 p.m., but not if there would be a seat on that New York flight. Again, I could have tried to call the American Embassy, but I had no thought about how they might help or if they would, and I could not afford the time.

At approximately 6:15 p.m. the receptionist glanced up at me as if I had just suddenly appeared and told me I could now enter the sanctum sanctorum. I found an elderly white-haired woman sitting in an oversized chair which looked to be immoveable; the two—the woman and the chair—seemed to be all of a piece, a kind of sculpture in the Soviet realist style. The woman did not greet me, but held out her hand for my passport. She did not invite me to sit, though two chairs sat across from her desk. She rifled through my passport, occasionally looking up at me after viewing a page, and then continuing her survey of my travel. I was not asked to explain what mistake I had made—she could read the story in my passport: I had failed to return to Katowice to get the exit stamp; it was marked in my passport that I had only the "*jednokrotnego przekroczenia granicy*" (one time entry visa) requiring a fresh stamp whenever I left or entered the country, and further, that only my local *milicja* could issue that. I stood as if on trial. There was nothing to say, though she could see that I had dutifully returned to the Katowice *milicja* for all the trips I had taken outside Poland up to this point. But again, I was not tempted to make a case for myself. It seemed that she was actually trying to be dramatic. The entire tableau was the stuff of American movies about Russia —the evil empire. She paused, looked at me again, and then very slowly, removed a stamper from a drawer below my eye level, and hovering over my passport, slammed the instrument down, freeing me to leave communist Poland … if I could manage that in the time remaining. I flew down the stairs, the smell of ancient dust all around me, found a taxi stand, and raced to the Forum Hotel. Twilight was upon the city.

As always, there was a line at the LOT Airlines office, but I had no choice: I stood in it not knowing if I could even get a ticket. Often I had stood in a line in that office, and because I possessed a *zaświadczenie* and a *legitymacja* proving I was a teacher in Poland, it allowed me to pay the price of airline tickets which Poles paid, but it also meant that the clerks there could deal with me at their whim. Maybe, they would claim, the *legitymacja* was not so clear, even though it had been acceptable the time before.

Within a half-an-hour it was my turn. Here was luck: I had sometime before dealt with a very lovely blonde Polish LOT agent in that office who spoke beautiful unaccented English. I had forgotten all about her and about the time when I had complimented her English, and how she had blushed with pride. But she remembered me, and smiled warmly. There was a ticket for the 10 p.m. flight, and she sold it to me without difficulty or intrigue.

I now had to collect my luggage at the hotel room and get to the airport. It was 8:45 p.m. and I was aware I might not make it. I ran from the LOT office to get a taxi—they were not always plentiful, but I found one. I indicated my urgency, and like some cab drivers in Poland, he seemed to enjoy the need to speed. First to the hotel near the airport to get my luggage. The clerks there were slow in adding up the bill, but I was able to get back to the taxi (he waited) with my luggage. It was now 9:10 p.m. and I should have been at the airport by then for an international flight. Rain had begun to fall and I wondered if we would make it in the dark and wet and the traffic. He sped so carelessly that I wondered if I would even survive the cab ride. But he got me there and helped me with my luggage to the entrance to the airport. There were no suitcases on wheels at that time. I got into the passport line, and again, when it was my turn, I could not see the person who reviewed my (new) credentials to depart. There was no conversation. My passport was simply returned to me by the faceless officer when shoved into the little chute barely large enough to accommodate it. I was free to proceed to the plane waiting in the wet night on the tarmac to take me to the free world.

English as/is a foreign language
Wrocław, September, 1988

I had decided that one year in Poland was not enough. I felt I had just begun to scratch the surface of Polish society, of Polish attitudes towards its former Jewish community, of the meaning of my own connection to what I was absorbing. I requested and was awarded an additional Fulbright year, this time in Wrocław, in the western part of Poland, formerly Breslau, Germany. After the war, the territorial changes in Poland were dramatic. With decisions made by the Allies at the Potsdam Conference of 1945 at the insistence of Stalin, many eastern Polish territories were permanently annexed to the USSR, and most of their Polish inhabitants expelled. Post-war Poland, in turn, received Danzig (Gdańsk) and the former territory of Nazi Germany east of the Oder-Neisse line. The German population was forcibly expelled from these areas and repopulated with Poles who themselves had been expelled from eastern and central regions of Poland. Thus, German Breslau became Polish Wrocław. What was most important for me as a new resident of Wrocław was the fact that almost all the Poles who then inhabited that city had been or had families who had been inhabitants of the beautiful and famed Polish city of Lwów. A mere mention of Lwów in Wrocław would consistently bring tears to the eyes of people I came to know in Wrocław. They felt they lived in exile from a former paradise. Lwów was their lost city, their lost home.

But Lwów was also a famed Jewish city. Lwów, Lviv, Lvov, Lemberg—the city variously named depending on the nationality of the regime over the centuries, was a leading center of Jewish education and culture in Poland. At the time of the Nazi invasion of Poland, Lwów had 340,000 inhabitants of whom 110,000 were Jews. The tragic fate of that Jewish community is a key chapter in Shoah history. Jewish life in Lwów has become a subject all of its own in the Spielberg Jewish Film Archive, dedicated to the preservation and research of Jewish documentary films. The archive is jointly administered by the Abraham Harman Institute of Contemporary Jewry at the Hebrew University of Jerusalem and the Central Zionist Archives of the World Zionist Organization.

Today Lviv, as it is now named, is the largest city in western Ukraine, situated less than 40 miles from the eastern Polish border. So Polish Wrocław, just over 150 miles from Berlin, became my new home, and I began my work as a professor of American literature in that city's Institute of English Philology.

Because Wrocław is a larger and more cosmopolitan city than the Silesian community I had lived in the year before, my students were themselves more sophisticated and experienced than the students I taught at Sosnowiec. Also, I was now assigned to direct students who were to write their Masters' theses on subjects in American literature, rather than to teach standard survey courses.

The Institute of English Philology of Wrocław University was housed in a building of former grandeur. From the outside the stone walls and tall windows presented a façade suggesting previous glory, and inside, too, the parquet floors, wide staircases, old world-style crème moulding, and wood fittings contrasted so dramatically with the Soviet-style block dwellings where most students (and faculty) lived, that immediately upon entering the foyer, one felt the significance of the place and one's own enterprise there. That feeling had its irony: the popular phrase among the students was "no future" so despite the setting's grandeur, the work students came to do there held no promise for a future fuller life. Since the waiting list for a flat was absurdly long (a decade or more), students expected to live with their parents into their adulthood. Married students in my classes typically converted the childhood bedroom into conjugal space and shared all meals with the entire family—the mother doing all the shopping and cooking and caring for grandchildren, if there were any. This arrangement created a feeling of extended adolescence in these students, one they accepted but resented, placing the blame unequivocally on their form of government. While it was widely felt that some faculty spied on other faculty for the Party, and that students and teachers alike were subject to the politically-motivated, unprincipled whims of a university rector who could hold up careers and advancements based on "reports" he may have received, the irony was that when students came to the institute, there was nonetheless a sense of temporary escape from the domestic space imposed by forces beyond their control to the counter world universities have at least theoretically provided throughout history. Students entertained no illusions about getting a job they cared about, so in some contradictory, remarkable way our work on literary texts truly was "art for art's sake."

It was only when I arrived at the Institute in Wrocław that I learned I would head the Masters' (*Magister*) seminar for students who had completed survey courses and all other requirements to advance to candidacy for the Masters' Degree in English Philology. In American universities, faculty could expect to know their teaching assignment well in advance of the start of classes. But I was the American Fulbright, and expected to be flexible, to be ready for all exigencies, and of course, it was Poland.

I discovered to my surprise that unlike American students in the same position, Polish Masters' students did not have the liberty to select the topic for their theses. Instead, it was traditional there that professors present what they would offer as a specific course of study, and students would have to choose from those topics for their specializations. How undemocratic, I thought: students are limited to the set of topics determined by professors, rather than the standard American practice of the students first figuring out what their area of interest would be, and then finding the appropriate faculty advisor to oversee their work. I did not believe the Polish practice was a consequence of the communist regime, though it might have become more rigid during that time. I had instead the sense that Polish university studies in general followed much older European models, and there would be no trifling about what students might "prefer."

So I was informed that I would be one of three professors who would present the topic of my choice to all students who were ready to proceed with the research for and writing of their *praca magisterka*—the two year-long study comprised of a four-hour weekly seminar. Like so many other revelations during my experience in Poland, I was given to understand in an indirect way, without much explanation, that I would be one of the three presenters—and that the presentations would happen in two days' time. I was at once thrilled and anxious. On the one hand, here was an opportunity to select what I would like to teach—every teacher's dream, but on the other, I had no sense of the genre of such presentations. Was it to be long, short, formal, conversational? Should it be a brief overview of the plan of study, or should it be a fuller explanation of the "why" of the course—why such a topic is worthy, important, what of the history and philosophy of the topic—why the topic mattered and why they should dedicate themselves for a year to such a study, and further, to then be earmarked for their teaching future with their particular specialization?

The only requirement I was given was that the topic be "American literature," and when I inquired further of my colleagues, I quickly perceived that any more questions about the presentations put them on the spot. They themselves seemed to lack a clear explanation of the model presentation. Like past queries about invisible transactions or rituals in Poland, from changing money to proper party etiquette, I got the message: "just do it."

Under pressure for time, I spent the next day-and-a-half thinking about what those Polish students at that stage in their studies would likely not have been exposed to, and what they would even *want* to study. I knew from the previous year in Sosnowiec what survey courses undergraduates were required to take, but I was unconvinced that the program there in Wrocław was the same as in Sosnowiec. It was one of those times where I would just have to "jump," like Van Halen's lyric: "Just jump—jump in." What would I want to study in their place; I had brought with me works I cared about: collections of fiction, poetry and essays by so-called "ethnic" American writers, *The Norton Anthology of Literature by Women*, among others. I reasoned that my own passion for those subjects might translate to the students. I could only hope. Jump, just jump.

The day the presentations were to be given was as willy-nilly as the assignment itself had been. I knew the time of day, but despite my having asked, had yet to be given the room number in the institute. Looking back, I realize no one yet knew, and everyone was accustomed to such last minute arrangements. Somehow I found out where I was to be—and just in time, as it turned out, because the room was in a part of the building where I had never (and would never) have reason to go—the Linguistics Department. I had dressed thoughtfully for the day—formal enough, but not off-putting or austere: after all, was I not making a sales pitch of a sort? Writers and speakers are advised always to consider the "rhetorical situation"—who is the audience, what is the purpose? The information I had about my audience was whatever I had managed to learn when I taught the year before in Sosnowiec, but this was a different part of the county, a more urban locale, and the students were older and having to make a crucial choice. The purpose was quite obvious: sign up for my course!

The room was large and high-ceilinged with a wall of windows which on that fall day filled the space with sparkling sunlight. That vitality was contrasted by the two other faculty members who were to give their presentations--solemn, humorless, formal and remote, both were aged professors who perhaps rightly lacked enthusiasm for that ritual. After all, from what I had seen in a year, the life of an academic in Poland was not enviable: poorly paid, overworked, and harassed by university politics along with the daily difficulty of living in communist Poland. It was unfair to expect those two colleagues to be bubbling over with excitement.

But then I was in for a surprise. Despite the fact that this was the Institute of English Philology where students were expected to speak the language of their study, the entire proceedings were conducted in Polish! I was at an immediate loss. My Polish was serviceable for the street and the home, but not for the specialized vocabulary of literary history and theory. I had been in Poland a bit over a year, and I had learned to simply *wait*, wait to see what will happen. And so I sat through two presentations describing literature topics delivered entirely in Polish, read from a prepared speech without as much of a glance at the gathered student body. For all I knew, though, the contents may have been brilliant, high-level, inviting. There was really no way to know.

I gathered it was my turn, and took the podium to deliver my presentation in English. I had "handouts" for students describing the course and listing works to be read. That way, I had reckoned, I would not need to spend time on the nuts and bolts of the course, but instead focus on why the course was important in American literature, why it might be worth their time. I made a case for the study of so-called "multicultural literature" or "ethnic literature" as it was then tagged. We could discover a parallel but different American history from the perspective of writers whose voices had not been heard in the traditional canon of American literature. I spoke "American," I was from California, I was, at least on the face of it, offering something novel, and so not surprisingly, mine was the longest line of students who queued up at the table and signed on for the year. I was relieved and hopeful. They had assumed a risk and "jumped" in their own way.

Snow falling on radiators
(with apologies to David Guterson)

Although the interior staircase of the institute was a grand swirl of lush crème marble wide enough for two vehicles to pass with room to spare, the state of the halls and classrooms of the building boggled the Western mind: rusted pipes littered a fine centuries-old black and white parquet floor; begun but abandoned repairs loomed like sculptures in corners beneath high curved meticulously-crafted mouldings on walls and ceilings, paint peeling, huge gashes in plaster. And dimness—light mostly through windows, many cracked or broken. And cold: marble and parquet and high ceilings do not afford much warmth to begin with, and there was no heat.

We were well into the semester, and it was winter by the time I took my familiar route down the marble staircase, the steps so broad, I found that I always stayed to one side and held onto the heavy wooden banister like a rudder. The hall below was dark as usual, but the classroom for the Masters in American literature which I taught, sat at the end of the hallway with one of its walls featuring huge windows facing the morning sun, so unlike the halls, our room was bright. The contrast between the building's dispiriting surroundings and the faces of my students never ceased to strike me. There we were confronted at every turn with the signs of a decaying society, yet the vitality in those students lit the room like nothing else could. When I turned the corner of the hall and walked into the room that vitality was palpable. They were alive, they were ready for all exigencies, intellectual and otherwise. The world they operated in made them savvy and mature in ways my graduate students in California could not be. Although most of those students had not traveled out of their own country, they were worldly and prematurely wise. Their sense of the irony of their situation in communist Poland gave them a sophisticated sense of humor and a heightened perception which they profitably brought to bear in their analyses of ethnic American literature, our subject.

But no amount of vitality could warm the freezing room. We all kept on our coats for much of the four-hour seminar, or we stripped down to our layered sweaters, all of us with wool scarves around our necks. We always got down to business quickly. But over the weeks students had smilingly reminded me that we should break at least once during the four hours—they needed to have a cigarette. I had to laugh at my own obtuseness—in my enthusiasm for their work, I often lost track of the hours going by.

One particular day the light was gray, and a fine snow was falling steadily outside the seminar room windows. We took the break and relaxed for a few minutes; a pleasant quietness filled the room as we all turned our gaze to the falling snow outside. All at once, the room erupted into laughter: outside the windows on the frozen ground lay a stack of radiators torn from the classrooms, gathering layers of the quickly falling snow.

That darkly humorous picture of discarded radiators ripped from their moorings once inside now gathering snow outside while we shivered inside without heat, distilled in one image all of Polish life under communism: everything in a constant state of *"remont"* (ubiquitous signs indicating "renovation"), buildings growing old before they were finished. All the wrong-headedness of life there represented by these mistaken starts, uncompleted beginnings, unwisely chosen sequence of work, running out of materials—a metaphor for the entire broken system, an external manifestation of the existential plight of my Polish students. That they could laugh at the image was the heart of their charm.

A perfect day for bananas
(with apologies to J.D. Salinger)

I had noticed during those breaks in the seminar (which students at last had trained me to remember) that students brought sweet pastries typically covered in rather toxic-looking crème or icing. During my years of teaching at home I often offered some food to students during class to make them feel considered and to establish community among us. One morning as I walked along the Oder from my flat at *Plac Grunwaldzki* to the institute, I wondered what I might take to those students—what would be welcomed, what would be culturally appropriate? The ages-old *Targowa* Market Hall was close by, and I was early enough before class to stop in. The hall was huge and filled with all variety of items—from household wares like pots and pans to a display of produce. I quickly scanned the offerings and felt that nothing would suffice when I happened to notice a wooden box filled with a modest number of bunches of bananas. My first reaction, judging from the sugary pastries they had brought, was that bananas might be the wrong choice.

Class began as usual with students prepared, game and ready to work. I remembered that time to break after an hour or so, and students had begun to take out their smokes when I recalled the bananas in my briefcase. I had forgotten all about them in the day's busy agenda for the seminar. Again, I wondered if such an offering would be ridiculous or even insulting. I presented the fruit with an apology, saying, "I'm not sure if you will like what I brought us, but here you are ..." The students looked surprised, and then faint smiles appeared on their faces. I distributed a banana to each student as they sat at their desks and took one for myself as I relaxed back at my own desk. I was thinking that as usual their always courteous behavior was at work here: they accepted the fruit, but would not have told me that this was a silly gift. As we each peeled our banana, I casually asked, "I mean, do you even like bananas?" At that moment, all the students looked at me and one of them said, "We believe we do, Kate, but we haven't tasted one in so long, we can't remember." I understood in an instant what I should have realized before: the price of bananas made them an unaffordable luxury for most people in Poland—they were a gourmet treat. I nodded and indicated how once again I learned from them. Then the thirteen of us sat quietly gazing out the windows at the snow and slowly savoring our bananas until break was over.

But despite smoke breaks and bananas, the room was uncomfortable because it was freezing cold. After I had gotten to know each of the students personally, I had an idea--why not ask them if they would rather meet at my (heated) flat for the weekly seminar? I stopped myself there as initially with the bananas: could this be a cultural faux pas? Would such

Some of my Masters' students in Wrocław during our seminar class at my apartment, after I suggested that it would be more pleasant venue than holding the class in the freezing classroom at the institute.
Courtesy Balgley Family Archive

LIST OF STUDENTS IN AMERICAN LITERATURE M.A. THESIS SEMINAR
                         (topics for thesis indicated)

Anna   --------the work of Kate Chopin (see her enclosed list)

Renata   ----------comparative study of the work of Zora Neale Hurston and
                         Alice Walker

Dominika   --------Asian-American literature (see her enclosed list)

Kinga   --------the work of Willa Cather (see her enclosed list)

Agnieszka   ----the relationship between blues music and select Black
                         American writers (one sheet include herrrequests)

Elzbieta   --------The work of Toni Morrison   (see herreaalosed list)

Anetta   ---------the work of Zora Neale Hurston (see her list)

Krystyna   ----------the question of how gender influences a writer's work
                                    (see her list)

Anna   --------------legend and folktale in contemporary Native American Indian
                              poetry (list included)

Tomasz   ----------select novels by contemporary Native American Indian writers:
                         Momaday, James Welch, Leslie Marmon Silko

Eugenia (Mousia)   ----------Jewish-American literature: Abraham Cahan,
                         Henry Roth, Saul Bellow, Phillip Roth (list included)
                         (This student has asked me to convey to you that she may
                         leave for Canada in November, and return to Wroclaw in
                         February or March).

Piotr   ----------recurring motifs in the fiction of Native American India
                              writers (he has all the texts, primary and secondary
                              he needs)

*Top: My list of Masters' students and their chosen topics for our seminar
studies in American literature. Courtesy Balgley Family Archive*

*Below: a student demonstration with banners hung on the Classical-style
facade of the university building at Wrocław. Courtesy Balgley Family
Archive*

The residential block in Wrocław where I lived when I was teaching there. Shown here is a makeshift election poster invoking the memory of Solidarity for the first free election in Poland (1989). Karol Modzelewski was one of the most revered Solidarity activists; he served as a senator from 1989 to 1991. Duda was Professor Roman Duda, a mathematician and former rector of the Technical University in Wrocław, not to be confused with Andrzej Duda, current right-wing president of Poland since 2015. Courtesy Balgley Family Archive

an offer embarrass a student who might not easily be able to find transit to my place? What if they had work or classes just before or after that would make the extra time or expense involved an additional difficulty? Maybe for some students it would be simple, but for others a burden they would not want to admit to, since it would prevent the plan for all? I decided to ask each one privately and casually, and underscoring the notion that this was just a possibility, no pressure, no problem if not convenient for them. We were lucky. My flat was not at a great distance from the institute and all the students seemed very glad to meet there.

At school in my flat

At my flat I made tea and coffee, offered food, more comfortable chairs and a decent-sized couch. The casualness did not undercut the seriousness of our purpose; if anything, it seemed to me that the offer of my home to the students made them feel uncharacteristically respected by an "authority," so accustomed were they to bureaucracy in every aspect of their lives, including, it has to be admitted, at the institute. Because my colleagues were humane people, I was struck by their attitudes and behavior toward students; ironically, this classless society imposed so many obstacles on individuals, that a caste system developed where people were tempted, maybe unconsciously even, to take advantage of what little power they had.

The kitchen in my apartment in Wrocław in 1988. Courtesy Balgley Family Archive

The route I walked along the River Oder to work at the University of Wrocław. Courtesy Balgley Family Archive

Students often confided to me that their professors at the institute treated them like peons, and I had observed during office hours the change that would come over a professor when she or he would turn from a conversation with me, for example, to one with a student looking for help. There was no doubt that a student visit was seen as an annoyance, and no attempt was made to hide this. So though students never gushed their gratitude (I was grateful myself for that), there was just a sense of mutual respect, and growing friendship among us.

View from my flat in Wrocław. Courtesy Balgley Family Archive

Before the seminar moved to my flat, I had returned briefly to the United States for interviews for tenure-track professorships there. By that time in the semester, students in the seminar had determined with me what specific areas of ethnic American literature they would specialize in and about which they would write their Master's theses. Books on such subjects were non-existent in Poland at that time; they would have been banned anyway even if people in that country were able to procure them from western publishing houses. One of the greatest pleasures in my life to date was going to an American university bookstore after one of my job interviews, trailing a large empty suitcase on wheels, dragging the behemoth up and down the aisles marked "Ethnic Literature" or "Multicultural Literature" (as that literature was then called), loading up at least five key sources on each of the twelve students' chosen topics, and being able to afford to pay for the purchases since living in Poland and being paid in dollars by the American Institute of Foreign Study provided me with the disposable income. What an indulgence! Thankfully, most of the texts were in paperback, so the weight of the suitcase did not exceed airline restrictions. When I returned to Poland after the two-week series of interviews, that suitcase made its bumpy way along my cobblestoned route from my flat to the institute, down the marble stairs to our seminar room, and there with the aid of the students, it was upended on my desk, unzipped and opened. I had tied together with ribbon the texts meant for each student and handed the packets over. The bananas paled by comparison: here was a treasure trove making possible the research each student needed to do to complete the Masters. What struck me as with so many instances before, was how easy the gesture had been for me, and how maddening it was in this case that access to such materials was so difficult, not to say, impossible for such bright and game students. As it was, no questions about the books were asked at the airport police desk when I returned to Poland.

For the rest of the year then, equipped with needed texts, and meeting in a heated place with refreshment (and privacy), our sense of shared purpose, of community, of friendship grew automatically. The course plan included shared weekly reading and writing assignments, along with continual reading and writing in each student's chosen topic. This way students had a shared text which they could discuss collectively, and thus regularly practice their analytic skills in a group; I had the opportunity to guide this close reading, as well as to provide historical and social background to the ethnic American experience. We looked at the Native American experience, including the genocide and the current status of "Indian Reservations," the African-American experience of slavery, Jim Crow, lynching, the murders of those who went to the South to attempt voter registration; Executive Order #9066 and the Japanese internment camps; the exploitation of the Chinese railroad worker and the harshness of Chinese immigration laws; the Hispanic American story, starting from the earliest periods of the Spanish conquest of the Indians through the Zoot Suit Wars and the contemporary *barrio*.

I had learned that the American Embassy in Warsaw had lent a television and VCR to the institute. I inquired regularly about this at the institute's literature office, but was always given a vague answer—"not sure where it is," "have to get authorization for use." And so on. One day, I approached a custodian with whom I regularly exchanged friendly words and asked him if he had a notion about that equipment. He led me to a locked closet, produced a key from a huge collection he had on a ring, opened the door, and leading me behind all manner of unused furniture and equipment, showed me the television and VCR on a typical American rolling cart. It was obvious that this had never been used, and as with other unnecessary bureaucratic obstacles or needless power play, I, and probably others, had been denied its use. It was clear that I would not be able to regularly open this closet on my own. I asked the custodian to help me take the equipment up the stairs to the main entrance of the institute, and it was unspoken but obvious that this help would go unreported so that the custodian's job would not be endangered. The two of us on either end of the cart held the television and the VCR in place as we slowly and laboriously rolled the cart up two staircases. We rested at one landing and then continued on. As he stood guard with the equipment, I went to the taxi stand, and procuring one, got into the cab and asked to be driven around to the doorway where the custodian waited. Before we piled the equipment into the trunk and back seat, I asked the driver, "I need to get this out and up an elevator at *Plac Grunwaldzki*. Can you help me at that destination—for extra payment?" He nodded and shrugged, indicating that this was no big deal—he had had tougher assignments before. So off we went the short distance to my block building, and driving his taxi right up on the sidewalk (this was standard in Poland—as a pedestrian one had to watch for automobiles in unexpected places), lifted out the equipment, rolled it to the elevator up and into my flat. We found a place for it in a corner, I paid him dollars, and we were both very pleased.

Since the American cultural attaché at the Warsaw Embassy had told me before my move to Wrocław that a television and VCR were at my disposal at the institute, I had a stack of good American films stowed in my bookcase in my flat. Now, finally with the equipment I had been promised in my home (and feeling that justice had been served when I smuggled it out), I began hosting "film festivals" on weekends for my Masters' students. It was interesting that Woody Allen's Jewish humor, for example, transcended cultural experience--students burst into laughter at all the right places. But I detected also, a vestigial sense somehow retained in the Polish psyche of the bittersweet Jewish experience in Poland. Poles seemed to understand Jewish humor more immediately and fully than, say, Americans in the Midwest. On one occasion, I went to the American Consulate in Kraków to hear the American-based, Polish-Jewish writer, Jerzy Kosinski speak. The thrust of his talk was how Poles and Jews have everything in common due to their experience of victimhood, and for the nearly ten centuries they spent living in proximity to one another. Maybe. Polish defensiveness about the claims of their anti-Semitism and Jewish animosity towards Poland made Kosinski's message both inspiring and controversial. I can say this: my Polish students who would never have met a Jew had a sort of natural simpatico response to Jewish humor. Of course, a Pole's daily life under communism could be summed up with a "damned if you do, damned if you don't" reality, so perhaps this accounted for the students' connection.

We were set to see *Sophie's Choice* on a Sunday, June 4 in 1989, and from my windows high above *Plac Grunwaldzki*, I watched as a number of my students filed off the tram that stopped in front of my building. All of them wore black armbands. I had not seen or heard the news yet that morning, but my students had: the massacre at Tiananmen Square had occurred, and those students felt they had everything in common with the 271 people murdered by their government. They came into the flat quietly that morning; we discussed what they had learned thus far. I remember among the American films I had selected out at the American Embassy, I had also chosen some foreign films; one of those was *Yellow Earth*, an important Chinese film apropos on that day, so *Sophie's Choice* would wait till another day.

A community had been established among us; we were friends, and the topics we delved into through texts, films, and the students' writing and talking about these lent to our group a sense of the importance of our work together. They were not just academic subjects to be gotten through for a grade, but instead were matters that affected people's lives—even people's survival.

The conversation that must be had

After four months of American ethnic literature, of study of the history of prejudice and persecution in my country, I felt it was time, it was now fair to ask them to address the subject of their own country's former "ethnic minorities." I did this casually, not wanting to put anyone on the spot or on the defensive. Surely, I reasoned, I had been candid about my country's atrocities, we had surely established enough trust for them to speak openly about their own country's past. I mildly queried, "What are your thoughts about the former Jewish community so significant in Polish history?" I was in for a shock. The atmosphere immediately changed from its characteristic comfortable openness to a dead silence. I was transported back to the undergraduate classroom in Sosnowiec the year before where the innocent young girl had embarrassed her fellow students in the large lecture class when she stated matter-of-factly that; "Polish writers from Poland and Jewish writers from Poland come from completely different traditions." This, remember, notwithstanding the fact that Poland's vaunted list of her great poets counted an overwhelming percentage of Jews. This time, though, we were among friends, and in my home, so the feeling was even more intense. The veil had come down—again. Heads were lowered, faces blushed red. Yet one of my best students, Tadeusz, rising to his feet and gathering his papers and books into his satchel, stood and angrily announced, "I am sick and tired of hearing this charge of Polish anti-Semitism! I have only met one Jew in my life and I didn't like him!"

Tadeusz made his way to the hallway of my flat and exiting, slammed the door behind him. I said not a word during his outburst. At his dramatic departure, we were all left looking at each other. Again, this was one of these moments in Poland (and in teaching, generally, I have found) where it is best to allow silence. Wait. Moments passed. I could not read the emotions of the other students, and I suspected that each may have likely been feeling different things. More moments passed. Then another particularly bright (and typically soft-spoken) female student, looked directly at me, her face afire, and said simply, "Kate, you have exposed us and we are ashamed." The other students looked at her—some seeming to be in agreement, others nonplussed, and still others drawing back. The last thing I wanted to do was to alienate. The point always in our discussion was to open up possibility and allow for people to figure out what they thought by being free to voice tentative ideas. Another student sighed and looked at me sympathetically and began to clear the dishes from our regular repast. At some point I remember saying, "Your country's history has been more than sufficiently courageous that you do not need to apologize; still, as we have seen in our study of ethnic American literature and the history it reveals, it's incumbent upon us to acknowledge those parts of our national pasts of which we are anything but proud. In acknowledging, we honor the best in our country." Another student spoke briefly only to say, "All we know, Kate, is that we were victims ourselves."

The time left in that day's seminar was about over, and that juncture in the seminar's history, I judged it was better now to let students leave with their own thoughts with the hope that we might in the future discuss this obviously loaded subject. Everyone left a bit shaken, but as always with polite and friendly thanks. For my part, after they left, I sat stunned and immobile for hours in my "seminar seat" alone in my flat and felt very, very vulnerable in this suddenly-seeming alien and even unsafe place.

Days later at a social evening at the home of a Polish university colleague who had become a good friend, I told Olga and her husband, Cezary, a computer scientist who taught at the Wrocław Polytechnic University, about the incident. Without any ambivalence, shaking their heads in disapproval, they both agreed, "Those students know very well what they are not speaking about."

Even after this, though, I could not believe that these humane students would simply deny a truth they knew to be accurate and I harkened back to the argument I had had in California three years before with my well-educated Polish friend, who had angrily stated there was no anti-Semitism in Poland. I remember his sentence exactly, "The only anti-Semite I knew in Poland was my father-in-law, and he was an ignorant peasant!" This felt like the bookend statement to Tadeusz's, "I only met one Jew and I didn't like him!" Was this akin to the American cliché: "I'm not prejudiced; some of my best friends are……." (fill in the blank—Black, Jewish, gay, what have you)?

And there was a discussion on that topic with another faculty member, Agata, who had not yet completed her doctorate, so was still at a "lecturer" status, and I noticed, not taken as seriously by students as those of us with full professor status—another example of the ironic caste system in that communist society.

Agata and I met one rainy night in the city center for dinner. She was always uncomfortable at the institute, lowering her voice to a whisper when we talked in our offices, her eyes flitting about nervously, so I thought she would be more comfortable at a rendezvous away from the school. I had earlier noticed she relaxed when she visited me at my flat. At first, our discussion of the topic of Polish anti-Semitism was rather generic; she agreed with Olga and Cezary essentially that the students were not owning up to a truth they knew, but her voice was quiet and her reaction subdued. Agata was often quite vocal about her condemnation of the politics of the institute and the regime—of course, only in private and not at the institute—so it felt uncharacteristic that she be so temperate about this subject. We finished our meal and walked out arm-in-arm (a charming habit among women one would regularly see on Polish streets). Although the rain had stopped, the broken sidewalks and streets were wet and shiny black, the smell of diesel was in the air, and the air itself very cold. I had thought Agata had an angelic look from the time I first met her, but this night that appearance was even more so. A slight person wrapped in an oversized black wool overcoat on the dark street haloed with her mane of black curly hair, the only part of her that shone out was the luminescent oval disk of her lovely pale face with its characteristic sad expression. As we walked the dark street, she turned her blue-eyed gaze to me and said in a low voice, "Kate, actually, I am half-Jewish like you; my father is Jewish, and he left for Israel in 1968 in the Polish purge of Jews. I don't tell anyone that I have Jewish parentage. It's too dangerous for my career." And she asked me not to tell anyone. I wanted to hug her at that moment, protect her, tell her it was okay somehow, but maybe it was not okay in the least. So much for reaching consensus on Polish anti-Semitism.

A postscript: At the close of the *Magister* seminar year in my flat, the students presented me with a beautiful book of drawings and writings by the Polish-Jewish writer, Bruno Schulz, who had been murdered by the Nazis, shot by a single officer as he was walking on the street of his village, Drohobych, where he had been born and lived all his short life.[7] Each student had signed the book with notes of thanks and friendship, including Tadeusz, who wrote, "Kate— thank you for everything! Please come back to us someday!"

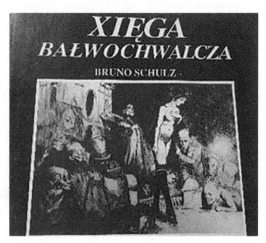

The book of drawings and writings by the Polish-Jewish writer, Bruno Schulz (who had been murdered by the Nazis), presented to me by my students on completion of their 'Magister' seminar year in Wrocław. Courtesy Balgley Family Archive

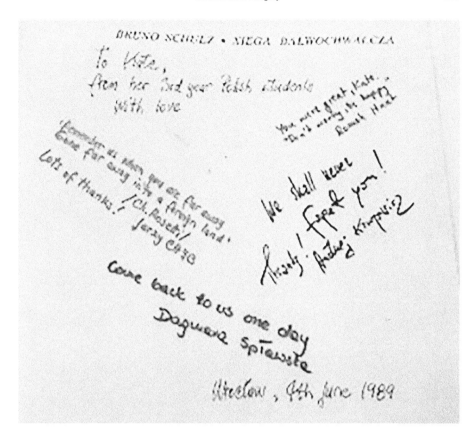

As it happened, on one of my trips to Poland eighteen years after the seminar, I met with some of the seminar students. At least two of them had gone on from the Magister degree to complete the PhD in the United States on American ethnic literature. Tadeusz sat next to me at a dinner table in Kraków, and as I was wondering if he thought back to his outburst on the day he angrily left my apartment, but he leaned in closely and said to me, "You know, Kate, I was a stupid boy who just hated communism—I didn't know anything, certainly not about Polish Jewry—I was absolutely ignorant." Later, I Googled Tadeusz and saw that he had published articles on Polish Jewish writers. About Agata: I see that she is now a full professor of American literature in Canada and has written widely on the topic of Polish anti-Semitism.

VII

New York 🌲 California

Reverse culture shock
California, 1989

I had accepted a position as a tenure-track assistant professor in the English Department at California Polytechnic University in San Luis Obispo, California. A whole new set of challenges lay before me. What I had not predicted was how I would feel by being abruptly jettisoned into another culture—my own— but one the experience of which had faded from memory. I had learned so much in Poland. I had tied that learning to my family history and made contact with relatives I never would have known. Yes, obviously the time in Poland had been a profound displacement for me, for any American. But perhaps for me it was at last a "placement": situated in the heart of darkness, I was finally in a position to follow the questions that had been so long in my own heart. Always looking to understand, I saw each day in Poland as part of a journey I had chosen. The stakes were high. The time was limited. I had to attend to every detail so I could learn as quickly as possible, take everything in, try to fit my understanding to what I had learned. The intensity was exhausting, but it held meaning at every turn. Nothing was dispensable. Everything was to be heeded. Not only had I become accustomed to life there in an everyday, pedestrian sense, but every moment was weighty, shot through with significance—historical, political, personal — even psychological. Living in Poland I was at the core of what I believed had always been the central tropes of my entire life. How does one leave such experience behind?

One could call it reverse culture shock. Maybe because the outer world was so shut down in communist Poland, when people gathered for social evenings, there really was little superficial talk. Everyone was suffering some kind of injustice or hardship, and everyone had opinions, especially when it was possible to lay those out with a westerner like myself. The conversation was always alive; there was a sense of urgency on those social occasions. They were times to discuss important controversial matters, as where else was one free to do that? Politeness was observed, but intimacy came quickly. In the midst of struggle, people wanted, needed to talk.

So when I arrived at my post in San Luis Obispo, as a new faculty member, I was invited to "official" new faculty cocktail parties, and there I found myself standing holding a drink for hours exchanging pleasantries with nice people who certainly had opinions and ideas, but would have felt it untoward and prematurely intimate to have conversations about those. Thus,

I suffered a reverse culture shock. I wanted to connect at first meetings, to move past politeness to something true and real about the person with whom I was speaking. In fairness, there are Americans having important exchanges in social situations from New York salon society to San Francisco activist centers, and many places in between. But that was the first time I was in the role of newly-hired tenure-track faculty, and because that meant I was a candidate for a lifelong place in the department there, it involved a specific social initiation all its own. Even the friendliest of those people seemed to be holding back, sizing up the situation, strategic in their choice of topics, distant.

In retrospect, all that seems predictable. I was a new hire in a university where personal politics, and by "politics" here I mean making (or not making) alliances that could make or break people's careers, not politics as that would be understood in Poland. But while I am making this distinction, it is only fair to add that in Poland a personal misstep (which could be one's political leanings—or just a private affront) in a workplace could result in a colleague's "report" to government authorities. In Poland, even if I offended, my hire was not potentially permanent, and I was an outsider in any case. But in this new position in San Luis Obispo, people were naturally sizing me up, keeping their counsel, strategically holding their private opinions to themselves. It only made sense to do so. And the town itself was small, tidy, mostly affluent, picturesque, pleased with itself. It was just that I was coming off two years of heightened experience, "moments big as years," as Alfred Kazin wrote borrowing from T.S. Eliot, and by comparison, this new world lacked weight and gravitas. The "hunger for the world" that had taken me to Poland was here undernourished.

Father Jimmy redux

At one point the two worlds, the "old" one from Poland, and the one I came from but now a stranger to, met in what can only be described as a surreal experience. I was not looking, but the past found me.

One night I was visiting San Diego from San Luis Obispo—dining at an outdoor café in late spring at twilight, a lovely atmosphere. Our waiter approached the table. As he greeted us, he bent over our candlelit table, the glow illuminated his profile, and I was seized by the realization that I knew this man. But not in this world. Dressed as he was in white, and leaning over the white tablecloth to place silverware, his face took on a beatific look: here was a priest at our table, an altar of sorts, the altar in Kraków, Poland. It was Jimmy, my friend from the Fulbright dormitory, whom I had last seen when he served Mass in Kraków. I was stunned. The linens of the table, the linens of the altar. I had watched him serve Mass in Kraków in a black cassock.

Now in black slacks and a pristine white shirt, he asked us if we would like a drink before dinner. My first reaction was amazement and then incredulity in my own recognition. But I knew this was my "brother," as people had often taken us for siblings, both of us half-Jewish, half-Catholic, from the Midwest, and he with a sister who reminded him of me. I remembered how he was the heartthrob for all the women in our Kraków Fulbright group, and at the same time, how he seemed asexual or effeminate or androgynous. He was above gender; he seemed holy. Once I knew this truly was Jimmy, the American priest from Poland now impossibly working as a waiter, my waiter in San Diego, I thought it was possible he would not want to be recognized. After all, whatever had led him from where he we had met in the first place had to be a complicated, and very likely, personal, private story. But he looked at me and I quietly said, "Jimmy?" He answered immediately, and with warmth, "Kathleen." Whatever embarrassment there might have been evaporated in our genuine pleasure in seeing each other again—no matter the circumstances. I took the lead, "If you have the opportunity, please call me."

Within days, he did call. I learned that he was soon to leave for Ukraine to work as a teacher. He was then living with an elderly, disabled man, for whom he worked as a caregiver. At nights, he worked at the restaurant where we had met, to supplement his income. But what had happened to his vocation?

When we met again later at my home he told me he had stayed in Poland and continued to serve as a priest in Kraków. He told me that the Polish priesthood was rife with anti-Semitism. Aside from that, he was becoming more and more generally disillusioned every day. Finally, he had had a complete mental breakdown, and had been sent by the Church to a psychiatric hospital for priests. He paused at that point and looked me in the eye without a trace of melodrama, matter-of-factly stating, "I had lost my mind. I thought that I had died, and the hospital was hell."

As I think on this story now, I have to wonder if those events were not related to the Church's sexual abuse scandals later revealed; the reports show that priests involved in one way or another in sexual abuse were sent to such hospitals before they were moved to another parish. I do not know if this was any part of Jimmy's story. As we talked further, he did not detail how he had been released from the hospital, left the priesthood, and came back to the United States, but somehow he had managed to survive, to regain his sanity. Now he stood before me and explained that he was shortly to leave for Kharkov, Ukraine where he would teach American literature and sociology. He then asked me if I had any materials he could use. Together we culled through my library and files, and found texts and syllabi that could help him. No matter that he was not a priest any longer, he had retained his calm presence, that wordless sense of empathy and knowingness that emanated from him—that "holiness" from when we had first met.

I could not escape the feeling that such an intersection of our lives for a second time was supposed to teach me something. From the day we had first met in the Kraków dorms when everyone thought we were related, something about looking into his face felt like looking into a mirror. He was at once familiar and yet a sort of phantom—then and now. I recalled how in Kraków he disappeared at strange times when all of us were supposed to be together. He had waited a long time to tell any of us he was a priest, and there had been murmurings amongst the group that he was a member of the American Central Intelligence Agency (CIA).

He loaded the books I gave him into a borrowed pickup, and as we hugged goodbye, he promised to write. Six weeks later, I received a postcard from Kharkov with word that he was organized in his teaching position. That was the last time I ever heard from him. He had vanished again. I could look for him, I tell myself, now with the internet, I might discover him. Yet something holds me back. Even though our second meeting felt destined, sensible people would say it was only an uncanny accident, and maybe he would rather not be found. But I feel like I lost a second self, a version of myself that suffered because of his (our) mixed identity, while I went free. As it is, I pray for him—in both Catholic and Jewish prayers.

Meeting Uncle Morris
Forest Hills, New York, 1992

John and I had married and now had a baby daughter, Emily. While she would ultimately travel with us on our regular trips to Europe, this trip to meet Uncle Morris, my father's brother who had written so generously to me in Poland, would be a fast trip, possibly sleeping on couches of newly-met relatives, so I knew it would be best to go on my own. I was determined to meet Uncle Morris in person. His first wife had died (the person who had been so vocal in condemning my parents' engagement at that dinner my father called a "put-up job"). My uncle had remarried, and now lived in Forest Hills, New York.

My mind's eye conjured his letters to me in Poland, written as they were in a shaky hand,

In Spain with husband John and daughter Emily, who was born in June 1991. Courtesy Balgley Family Archive

but with intelligence, humor and honesty. It was he who wrote me that my grandmother had been accused of stealing a horse blanket and was whipped as punishment. He never made clear whether she had committed that "crime" or not, but he did say she had wanted to make warm clothes for her children. It was he who told me that the family of five tied their bread to the ceiling of their quarters in Brześć so that mice would not eat it.

His letters had been full of praise and pride in me. I was not accustomed to that kind of talk; my parents loved me, but they never raved about my accomplishments, nor those of my siblings, which were considerable: good work was expected of us, that was all. There was no trace in Uncle Morris's letters to me of any past anger or prejudice. If he once cared greatly that his very talented and successful little brother was marrying a non-Jewish girl, he did not visit upon me his anger or judgment that because my mother was non-Jewish, according to some Jews, I was not Jewish at all. I found myself wishing that Uncle Morris could write a loving letter to my father even now, late in life, to show he had changed his views. For all I knew, maybe he had. And perhaps it was my father who kept his family at arm's length—more than that—at such a distance from his children that I barely knew them at all.

Uncle Morris and I could not remember ever meeting—I believe we never had. I did know and was fond of my father's second elder brother, David, and his wife, Irene. They visited us from time to time, and I felt the affection between them and my parents. Dave and Irene never had children of their own, and so I think they were especially happy to be with us. But Uncle Dave had died by the time I was in Poland.

There had been a sister, too, the eldest of the four children, Rose, they called her, Rivka, the name I discovered for her in my genealogical searches, also indicated as "Rachel," elsewhere. She had been in her early teens when the

A photograph of my father's Jewish family taken in a New York photographic studio. Back row, from left: My grandfather Israel, Uncle David and Uncle Morris, Front row from left: My grandmother Sarah, Aunt Rose and to her left my father Ely... Photo circa 1924. My father would be 12 years old. Courtesy Balgley Family Archive

family left Brześć for Brooklyn, and my father had always remarked that she did badly in school, unlike himself, perhaps because she was too old to adapt to the challenges of a new language and culture by the time they came to America. I knew I had never met her, but I had seen photographs—early portraits of the family finally together in the United States, with her three younger brothers looking dapper and adjusted, and she looking thin and uncomfortable, her eyes averted sideways from the camera, as if she might be frightened by something unexpected. I do recall, though, that her hairstyle was in the manner of a flapper (it was the 1920s, after all), and so she or her mother must have cared to make her fit in somehow. Later photographs showed a heavyset woman who had sad eyes and dyed red hair. I had heard the story that her first husband with whom she had a son, had simply left the apartment one day, and disappeared forever. As an adult, the son never managed to assume responsibility for his own life, and instead lived with his mother till her death. She did, however, marry a second time, and my mother remarked on the irony of the fact that Rose, who had been so vocal in her disapproval of my father's marriage outside the Jewish faith, had taken as her second husband an Italian-American. So much for consistency, not to mention, hypocrisy. So Uncle Morris was the only one of my father's siblings still living, and he seemed very willing and anxious to meet me at his home on an agreed date.

That visit would come later in my trip as on my arrival to New York, I was met by Shirley Balgley Tainowitz, my father's cousin, daughter of Moishe (Morris), my grandfather's youngest brother.

Shirley was a decade-and-a-half older than I since my grandfather's siblings covered a wide span of years. Again, this was a first meeting, and like the Israeli relatives, Shirley took me into her home, gave me a bed in my own room, and made the time to drive me to meet her father, Uncle Moishe, as well as Moishe's sister, the only girl among my grandfather's siblings, and the youngest of the eight children. My grandfather's parents had died in Poland when she was just a child, and she, along with her brother, Moishe, only a teenager himself, travelled alone to America with tickets purchased by my grandfather after he had arrived to the United States. This was whom they called "Aunt Beatty" for Beatrice, but again I found documents in my genealogical work which named her "Bobel." But first was the visit to my own Uncle Morris my father's brother, the letter writer.

The day was hot and clear when Shirley and her twenty-something charmingly enthusiastic daughter, Randi, drove me to my Uncle Morris's home. The sky got larger and bluer as we left Shirley's dense neighborhood and headed to the affluent suburbs where my uncle lived. As we drove into Uncle

Family of Shirley Balgley Tainowitz

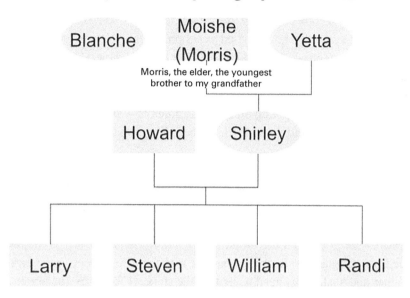

Blanche   Moishe (Morris)   Yetta

Morris, the elder, the youngest
brother to my grandfather

Howard   Shirley

Larry   Steven   William   Randi

Morris's neighborhood, Shirley began to comment in an impressed voice on the area. When we arrived at his large white house, she could barely contain herself. I wanted somehow for her to be above this sort of class admiration, but there was nothing to be done about it.

Uncle Morris greeted us and came toward us in his wheelchair. Silver-haired and with a mustache to match, I remembered photos of him in his youth where his hair hung appealingly over his forehead. It still did. Dressed in a maroon cashmere cardigan, oxford cloth blue shirt, grey trousers, and well-groomed, Morris projected a dignified, even stately impression—and he looked very much like my father. His speech underscored the impression—articulate, even eloquent—again, like my father's. Shirley had confided in me that my Uncle Morris was renowned in the family for resembling the film star,

My father's brother, my Uncle Morris, with whom I corresponded when I lived in Poland. I went to meet him at his home in Forest Hills, New York, in 1992. Courtesy Balgley Family Archive

Omar Sharif (he did, even on meeting him that day). His son David stood protectively by his father's wheelchair. Twelve years my senior, as I later learned, David, whom I realized from photographs I had seen years before, resembled his mother, who had died years previously. He was slow to smile, quiet and a bit remote, but kind and certainly polite. Uncle Morris asked after my daughter, Emily, and I learned that he had misunderstood and thought she would be coming, too. He explained that thinking Emily would accompany me, his second wife had put up all the breakables of which there were many—fine decorative china and crystal. He seemed disappointed and I found myself wishing she were with us.

Two memories about Uncle Morris suddenly jumped into my head at the mention of my daughter, both concerning children. The first was the story about his gift of the beautiful child-sized wooden table and chairs that my siblings and I had all loved as children. The second memory was about how despite the fact that Morris the boy loved the violin and practiced diligently, my grandparents stopped his lessons after a trained auditor told them he had no special talent. My father had shaken his head as he told the story, "I felt sorry for my brother when my parents took away the violin. He really loved to play." For his part, my father explained that he never questioned the number of hours he had to practice the piano. "After all," he said "my parents had bought the piano and my music—I had to practice to make the expenditure worthwhile." This mercantile view of musical accomplishment took me by surprise at the time when my father told me the story, but on reflection, it fitted with everything I knew about my grandparents. How could they be any different, having come from an Eastern European shtetl? All things were weighed by their worth in terms of economic survival. Even the geographical and cultural transplantation, and their relative financial security, had not changed their views.

While Shirley continued to admire the house and its furnishings, David, my cousin, warmed a bit—he seemed the sort of person who did not produce bubbly enthusiasm on call, striking me as genuine, truly himself on all occasions. I had found this to be a trait of extremely bright people with whom I had studied and later taught at the university. They were not socially adept, but when they did say something, it was worthy of attention. This was David. I liked him.

Artist Jacob Balgley: thrice found

The conversation with Uncle Morris centered on my experiences in Poland, how I had come to go there and my interest in our family history. At one point, David excused himself and briefly returned with some papers, he explained, he had brought along to show me. Here was a cache of letters from a Rachel Blanc-Balgley; she had written to David seven years before, her stationery indicating her home address in Paris. Apparently, at the time of the writing, she was in Manhattan visiting, and had found his name and address in the phonebook.

Her letters in charmingly imprecise English had a plaintive, touching quality to them. She wrote modestly, "My father was a painter."

Rachel BLANC-BALGLEY
Place Louis Barthou
94290 VILLENEUVE-LE-ROI

November 8th

Dear Sir,

During Holidays this Summer in N.Y on friends living in Manhattan I find your name in the PhoneBook.

My name is the same that yours, Rachel Balgley. My father died in 1934. I have in this time Uncles, consins in America, Varsovie and Israil. After the war I lost all news of my family.

It is important for me to know if I have some family and if you are relative for me. My father was a painter.

Please it would be kind to answer me about this problem.

Thanks and sincerely.

Rachel Blanc Balgley

Rachel BLANC-BALGLEY
5, Place Louis Barthou
94290 VILLENEUVE-LE-ROI

21/8/1983

Dear Mr David Balgley
Since my last letter many problems
and I have no time to write you
again about my father.
To day I send you a little book
about my father.
In this book you will look
pictures of my father, grand father
and grand mother, so with these
pictures it is the best manner to know
if we are relatives because I suppose
in your family there is also
photographies.
Thank you answer me about that.
Yours truly.

Rachel Blanc Balgley

David Balgley
█████████████
New York, New York 10025
December 2, 1982

Rachel Blanc-Balgley
5, Place Louis-Barthou
94290 Villeneuve-le-Roi
France

Dear Ms. Blanc-Balgley,

The letter you sent me was a surprise. It is
highly probable that we are related. The name BALGLEY
is not common. (See genealogy chart)

My great grandfather (William), grandfather (Israel),
and father (Morris) are from BREST LITOVSK (at that time
Poland - now Russia).

My grandfather, Israel, came to the USA in 1912.
My father, Morris, came to the USA with his mother,
sister and brothers in 1920. Louis, Max and Morris
(my father's uncles) came to the USA about 1922.
Benjamin came to the USA in 1922, he was a photographer,
and he returned to Europe - Warsaw where he had a studio.
He had one daughter ____?____. He was not heard from
after the Germans entered Warsaw during WW II, nor was
his daughter heard from.

Aba and Nacham went to Israel before WW II, when
it was called Palestine. They died a few years ago I
believe. Aba had two children a son __?__ and a
daughter __?__ in Tel-Aviv? Nacham had two sons __?__
and __?__ in Haifa? If you are interested I may be able
to get their names and addresses in Israel for you from
my father.

I hope this information can assist you in some way.
If indeed we are related (I think we are) it is good to
know about. Please let me know what you know about the
BALGLEYS and your family and relatives, their origin and
current whereabouts. Thank you.

Yours truly,

David Balgley

Rachel Blanc-Balgley
5 Place Louis Barthou
94290-VILLENEUVE LE ROI

                              to   David Balgley

                        ███████████████████

                        New York 10025

December 20 1982

Dear Mr David Balgley,
I am sorry I cannot answere you before to day, forgive me.
Your letter was a great pleasure for me.
I suppose your grand-father Israël who came in U.S.A. in 1912
was an elder brother from my father. My father came in Paris
in 1913.
It seems I remember my father have one brother in U.S.A. a
this time and one in Haïffa. (I have not any papers or letters
from this time). An other brother stayd in Varsaw during the
war. He was a chemist I think and he had two children Assinka
and Mechinka. We helpd them at this time during the war and after
we never heard about them. If they live, these children are now
about 60 years old.
My father had also a sister Eva Horzhorn in Varsaw. After the war
we don't hear also about her.
My father Jacob BALGLEY born the 8 Marz 1891 in Brest Litovsk
(exactly as you say Poland and no Russia) from father
Moïse Iosselovitch and mother Khasha Meilanovna. His father
was a barrister rabbin. That is all I know in the present.
I found some papers in hebraic and russian. I asked some friend
to translate and after the new year it is possible for me
to write you again.
Sure I am interested to get the addresses of Aba and Nacham and
from your father .
Thank you again for your nice letter with the genealogy.
                              Sincerely yours.

                    Rachel Blanc Bry

Then David produced a book, entitled, *BALGLEY* by a woman called Jeanine Warnod, written in French, about the life and work of painter "Jacques" or "Jacob" Balgley. He had been born in Brześć, like my father and his family, and had departed as a young man to Paris along with Marc Chagall (1887–1985) and others. In his short life (1881–1934), he produced a body of brilliant work—some of which was reproduced in the book. The cover was a painting of a father and child in a forest, used as the cover illustration of this book. The first page showed the painter's signature. David explained that he had written back to Rachel immediately, and more than once, but he never heard from her again.

The signature of artist and relative Jacob Balgley. Like my father and all of the Balgley family, he was born in Brześć., He departed as a young man to live in Paris, moving in the same circles as artist Marc Chagall.
Courtesy Balgley Family Archive

La femme au chien huile 1918

La femme au chien (Woman with a dog) — oil on canvas painting by Jacob Balgley, painted in Paris in 1918. Courtesy Balgley Family Archive

My relative, artist Jacob Balgley, in his studio at Impasse de'Lenfant Jésus, Paris, in 1917. Courtesy Balgley Family Archive

Autoportrait (Self-portrait)— another painting in oil by Jacob Balgley from 1920. Courtesy Balgley Family Archive

Album de famille

*Top: Jacob Balgley's family
My and his family trees
were finally connected to
show specific relationship.
Courtesy Balgley
Family Archive*

*Right: Balgley à
l'Université. Courtesy
Balgley Family Archive*

After the visit to Uncle Morris. I wrote to the French address myself, but with no luck. A friend living in Paris at the time, went to the address to see what he could learn of Rachel. He did find the address, but no one knew of Rachel. David put the book and the letters in my hand; I promised I would make copies and return the originals to him.

I had known about a painter called Jacob/Jacques Balgley. Before I departed on the Fulbright to Poland, I had created a course at UCLA, *Writing about the Fine Arts*. It was a welcome opportunity for me to teach a topic that had long been of interest to me from my early days as an undergraduate—the

Les alliés au bord de la Seine - huile - 1918 (Beside the Seine in Paris in 1918). Another painting by artist Jacob Balgley. Courtesy Balgley Family Archive

relationship between visual art and writing. When I wrote an essay suggesting that Joyce's short story, *Araby* in *Dubliners* had been a cartoon for the fresco that was later to become *Portrait of the Artist as a Young Man*, arguing that just as the light in Renaissance paintings by Catholic artists seem to emanate from an unearthly source, the light in genre paintings by Protestant artists is a natural light, Joyce's writing was marked by a Catholic sensibility, in contrast to for instance, D.H. Lawrence. And a poem, among others I had written based on works of art, this one on Cezanne's *Suicide House at Auvers* had won notice from my undergraduate professor, an "established" poet. Offering this course was a chance to return to this earlier interest.

When I contacted the Grunwald Center for the Graphic Arts on the UCLA campus to ask for a class visit, I got the distinct impression that rarely, if ever, was the gallery called upon to host a class of student visitors, at least not *en masse*, and not outside the visual arts. But the director agreed and we had a look. A few days after the class had visited the Grunwald, a student in my seminar approached me to say she had found paintings at the gallery by somebody who was likely a relative of mine. My first reaction was to say she had probably misspelled my surname, or mistaken his for mine. But no, she insisted, and explained that the artworks were scenes in Poland and (the then) Palestine. I then knew she must be right. Contacting the Grunwald, I learned that Jacob/ Jacques Balgley's work was now collected at the Armand Hammer Museum in Los Angeles, just blocks away from UCLA. I read that Jacob had been born in 1891 in Brześć, my father's birthplace, that he had left the town for Paris, along with other painters from that region, most notably Marc Chagall, from Vitebsk. It was indisputable that he was a relative—our surname and the

Rue à Jérusalem - eau forte 1931, a work by Jacob Balgley. Courtesy Balgley Family Archive

town were no coincidence. Serendipity—that feeling of *bashert* again—like the childhood experience in my grandparents' apartment in Brooklyn: I could not have known that my interest in visual art would fuel a future search for family history, unknown, not sought by my father. I decided the best way to view those works was to invite my father to go along with me.

What I remember most about that spring day my father and I went to the Armand Hammer together was my excitement to show him something refined, something grand from his origins, which he had disdained. I wanted him to see that someone from his birthplace, someone from his family, a speaker of Yiddish, a language he once referred to as a "non-language," was an accomplished person.

Together we climbed the steps to the museum where we were greeted and our appointment acknowledged. Guided then to a small anteroom where comfortable chairs were provided for us at a pristine table, we were given white gloves to don in order to handle the work which would be brought to us. The portfolios were placed on the table, and together we turned the pages— scenes from country life in France, the shtetl and later, street scenes from Palestine. They were beautifully executed prints and lithographs. I had learned that Jacob/Jacques had died young—in 1934 at 43 years of age, reportedly of a heart ailment. At least he had escaped the horror that would have engulfed him only a few years later.

My father delighted in the works along with me. We took our time and marveled. For once, he seemed relaxed and open about the place he had come from.

We finished our perusal and went to the museum dining room for lunch. For the first time, he seemed willing to talk about his origins, his memories. The dining room was filled with light from an open atrium near where we sat, and it was as if we had entered a new dimension, a place of light, where matters formerly shrouded could be brought into fresh air and sunlight. I was ecstatic. At one point as we discussed Jacob/Jacques and the obstacles he would have had to overcome as a Jew in that region at that time to become a virtuoso artist, I remembered a phrase I had heard—and I could not then remember where I had learned it, nor can I now recall, but intuitively I felt it fit our conversation. "There's nothing so whole as a broken Jewish heart." We had been talking about Jacob, about his difficulties and his premature death, but I realized as I said it, that I was really saying this to and for my father. His face lit up with understanding—he smiled at me and at the irony of the sentence—and the love embedded in it. He understood my connection and I his, without saying a word. Little did I know at that time that I would meet the name of Jacob/Jacques Balgley again and in circumstances I could never have predicted.

It was time to leave Uncle Morris and cousin David. The look on Morris's face from his wheelchair made it clear to me that he knew we would not be seeing each other again, because he was infirm, and this would be our first and last meeting. Everyone in the room sensed this—Shirley and her daughter, certainly David, who while he had begun to smile more than at the start of our visit, wore an expression that conveyed that now he, too, understood this was a final farewell. I gathered up the book on "Jacques" from David, along with copies of the letters from Rachel Blanc Balgley, Jacob's daughter, and said my goodbyes to Uncle Morris and David. I felt a mix of sadness and happiness: why could we not have met decades ago? And yet, though this was the first and last meeting, I was grateful that I had met him at all.

A necklace
That evening back at Shirley's house, sparked by the visit to Uncle Morris, Shirley began recalling memories from her childhood. She recounted a story from very early childhood, shortly after her mother had died, one she had

forgotten over time. Shirley's spontaneously remembered story took its power from the fact that she was motherless as a very small child. One Sunday, Shirley explained, she and her father came to visit my parents in their Brooklyn apartment. Unannounced visits were conventional in those days— people, relatives mostly, dropped in. Shirley's face lit up with the memory, "I remember your mother. She was so beautiful— so young—and so kind to me. Remember, I was only a little girl, and had no mother of my own. I remember that your mother came towards me with a warm smile and embraced me. I couldn't believe the feeling of having a woman hug me. She was so

My mother Margaret and her son, my brother Michael, pictured in Brooklyn, New York in 1945. Courtesy Balgley Family Archive

kind and loving to me." I pictured my mother—if Shirley had been a child of 5 or so, then this would have been 1945, and my mother would have been 29. She would have one baby of her own, my brother, 4 years old, and my older sister would have been on the way. Shirley's eyes squinted as if she were peering into the past to survey the scene, as if she were once again there and discovering details. "I remember she was wearing a tiny gold cross around her neck." Shirley smiled, "That was fine, that was no problem. She was so, so warm to me."

This image of my mother bending low to hug the motherless Jewish child, this cousin of my father's, relatively unknown to my parents, the emblem of her own faith around her young neck summed up my mother entirely. My mother was intelligent, insightful and intuitive, but her genius was her heart: a Roman Catholic who married a Jew in 1940, she had no agenda, just a purity of spirit that had no space for bigotry. That sort of narrowness just was not in her DNA—or her family's, for that matter. Her family had embraced my father entirely. With them, there were no politics, theory or guile involved. Shirley's face continued to glow at the memory of the embrace.

It was some years later that I discovered in my genealogical research that Shirley's mother had been employed in a millinery factory. "Mad as a hatter" was no figure of speech. It found its origins in the neurological disorder caused by mercury poisoning in hat factories, leaving the victim delirious, afflicted with personality change, physical deterioration and pain. This was the explanation that the family never had for Shirley's mother "going insane," in the vernacular of the time. Shirley had not known her mother worked as a milliner and never realized her mother's demise was not the result of any personal weakness or psychological malady, but the result of the work she did. When I explained this to Shirley, tears ran down her face. When I was back in California, I wanted to relay to my mother the story of Shirley's fond memory of that hug; I imagined she would find it touching and complimentary to her. I certainly did. But in characteristically modest fashion, my mother at the turn in the story where I explain she was wearing her cross necklace, suddenly and instinctively raised her hand to her throat and apologetically exclaimed, "Oh! I didn't know they were coming!"

Uncle Morris, the Elder, youngest brother to my grandfather, Israel

Shirley was a dedicated hostess. The day after meeting my Uncle Morris, she took me to meet her father, Morris the elder, my grandfather's brother. The old man who sat on his front porch wearing a khaki-colored baseball hat, rose from his chair to greet me, and in his face I saw a distinct version of my father's: unwrinkled, olive-skinned, his eyes had the same intense intelligence and alertness, but unlike my father's brown eyes, Morris the elder's eyes were an intense green like my brother's and mine. They glittered out of his tanned face, and seemed almost too bright for his complexion. The second to the youngest of my grandfather's siblings, his age was not far from my father's, 80-something, but he was much more aged than my father. Slow to move, not steady on his feet, he spoke slowly and had trouble hearing. Still he fully realized who I was, and haltingly but vividly told me his recollections of the old country, of coming to America with his younger sister, the only girl in the family, and the youngest of the seven siblings.

What stood out in these tellings was my grandfather's obvious persistence in getting all his family out of Poland and to America. Having himself been the first of the immediate family to arrive to New York in 1913, my grandfather continued to work from America to bring out the others. Morris the elder, my grandfather's youngest brother was one of these, along with Rivka, the little sister now known as Beatty or Beatrice, for some reason I never knew, though I learned recently a female infant sister had died, and this name change was very likely the traditional Jewish attempt to hide the child from the "evil eye" by giving a new name. Morris and Beatty were orphans in Brest; by the time my grandfather arranged for their exit, both my great-grandfather, Ze'ev (or "Wolf," "Velvel," "William"), and my great grandmother, Bluma Auerbach Balgley, had died. Though years later I was able to find the tomb of Ze'ev, Morris did not explain the circumstances of his father's death. Perhaps they were unknown to him, having been quite young at the time. But Morris did remember his mother's death—and powerfully.

It was a hot summer, she was ill, and the children gathered round her in what would have been a dirt-floored dwelling like the one my father was born into. Wanting to make her as comfortable as possible, the children lifted her sickbed to the outdoors where it was cooler, where there was a breeze. And he explained that it was there in the shadow of a tree that she died. He told me this matter-of-factly, but his eyes filled with tears.

I know that some of my grandfather's siblings who were older than Morris and Beatty, had ended up in Warsaw, but I do not know when they left Brest. I know that some of the siblings remained there, and are now assumed to have been annihilated in the Shoah. But it seemed the case that when Morris the elder and Beatty boarded the ship that would bring them to New York—he a teenager, and she about 11 years old—there were no older family members to see them off. I did, however, find a photograph of my great grandmother's, Bluma's, tomb. Gathered around the grave and looking somberly into the camera, figures stand, one of whom is a little girl I can definitely identify as Beatty, another is Morris, a young man in his late teens. But the others seem much older, mustachioed men in overcoats and homburgs. I take these to be the older brothers, so perhaps some of them saw their youngest brother and little sister off to America. Morris explained that on first arriving to New York, he and his sister lived for a time with my grandfather and grandmother, but Morris explained that my grandmother complained of their presence, and other lodgings had to be found.

Morris had eventually remarried after the death of Shirley's mother, and Blanche, this second wife, took very good care of him. Aged as she was, she cooked Shabbat dinner while I was there, and all of Shirley's children and her husband, Howard, joined in. Again their warm welcome of me brought me back to the fact of my father's "divorce" from his family, and the question of whether he departed because of their narrowness, or his need to shed his Jewish identity.

*My great grandmother's grave, Bluma Auerbach Balgley, on right in Brest
with children.
Inscription: "Daughter of Baruch and wife of Ze'ev Balgley.
She died on the 20th of Tammuz, 5660 [July 17th, 1900] in the 56th year of
her life."
Far Left: My grandfather's youngest brother, Morris.
On the bottom right is Rivka (Beatrice/"Bobel"), whom I met years later at
Brighton Beach, New York.
Others unknown. (Grave on left, Miriam, no relation). Courtesy Balgley
Family Archive*

Aunt Beatty, my grandfather's only sister
Brighton Beach, New York, "Little Odessa," 1992

After the visit to Morris the elder, Shirley took me to Aunt Beatty, the little girl in the photo taken in the graveyard in Brest all those years ago, the youngest sibling of my grandfather's, and the only girl among six brothers. She lived in a nursing home in Brighton Beach. The building in which Beatty lived was old, several storeys tall with a brick facade. Standing just across a street from the shore, it seemed out of place, a relic from another era, where beachgoers would have been wearing bathing costumes from the 1920s. The sun was setting just as we approached the building, and the structure glowed amber in the fading light. The entire scene had the look of a postcard from a former time, a tintype. This was a Jewish home for the aged, and the arched brick eyebrows over the windows and doors created the look of an old, burnished synagogue. I knew that Brighton Beach was sometimes called "Little Odessa" for the number of residents who settled there from that city, and that it has also been a place where an influx of Jewish immigrants had come from the 1930s to the 1950s, many of them Holocaust survivors. Still another Jewish immigration occurred in the 1970s when the Soviet Union eased its emigration policies. So as I entered the building to take the elevator to Aunt Beatty's apartment, I heard voices speaking in Russian and Yiddish, and it seemed that in some odd way Beatty was finishing her days in a community not so different, except for the material comforts, from where she had been born.

Carefully dressed and coiffed and sitting in a wheelchair, Aunt Beatty smiled at me warmly as Shirley, Randi and I entered her apartment. Once again, I had not known how she would receive me, being Ely's daughter, he who had fled the family and Jewishness. But again, all that seemed like ancient history—what these relatives seemed to pay attention to was the fact that I had journeyed to meet them.

Beatty's apartment was quite large and well appointed. This was a home, not a hospital room. As with Morris the elder, it was Beatty's eyes I noticed right away: surprisingly bright green and alert in a face so old. Both Beatty's and Morris's eyes brought my father's to mind—not the color—but the quickness with which they followed conversation, an awareness, a sharp intelligence, a mind always at the ready.

The walls of Beatty's home were covered in art. As she explained, these were the works of her son, Willard, a professor of mathematics. The works were high quality. Framed photographs appeared among the paintings. She pointed to one photograph and explained that these were her parents, Ze'ev and Bluma, my great grandparents, and that the baby seated between them on a kind of podium in a formal style I recognized from other photographs of Jewish families during that period, was their youngest—Beatty, herself. Further along the wall I saw a painting of the photograph, one of Willard's.

We talked of her experience in Europe, her trip to America, and her brothers, in particular, Benjamin, whom my father over the years had referred to as "Uncle Benny," he who had come to America and was a successful photographer in Manhattan, but then decided to return to Poland and was never heard from again. I asked if he had had an American passport, and she raised her hand from her lap, and nodding her head, said, "That was just it. He hadn't yet become a citizen. He was trapped." I asked why he had gone back. "I believe he had some property there he wanted to claim." I told her some other family members had suggested he returned for a wife and child there. She gazed at me for a moment, "It's possible."

It was time for Aunt Beatty's dinner to be served, and in the same courtly way of both the Morrises, she invited us to stay. But her dinner was brought in by a nurse, and it was clear that we should go. I bent to kiss her goodbye and to thank her for the memories she had shared with me. She took both my hands in hers and said, "Ely was a good boy. He was a brilliant boy. Thank you for coming to see me."

It was dark outside when we left Brighton Beach. The waves moved quietly toward the shore, glimmering slightly from the lit windows of the Jewish home for the aged.

The time in New York had been well spent. I had had the chance to meet the remaining relatives before they died and the opportunity to know those of the younger generations. I had traveled from Poland to Israel and met those family members I had never known. The two-year Fulbright in Poland, fraught as it was with challenges of every variety, and full as it was with private experience of Polish attitudes towards the former Jews of Poland, was now over.

*Painting by Professor Willard Miranker, son of (Bobel/Beatty) Balgley
Miranker — a painting from the photo. Gifted to me by Bobel's grandson,
Andrew Miranker, Willard's son. The photo showed my great grandparents
Bluma and Ze'ev with daughter Rivka (Bobel/Beatty, aka "Beatrice").
Courtesy Balgley Family Archive*

The original photograph on which the above painting was based — my great grandparents Bluma and Ze'ev with daughter Rivka (Beatrice/ Bobel). Courtesy Balgley Family Archive

Middles, Halves, Splits
Michigan, 2005

I had traveled to distant Israel and sought out my relatives there, but ironically I had somehow never made it to Michigan, an easy trip, to meet Yossi, the son of Yaffa and brother of Mira whom I had met in Israel. Yossi's and Mira's grandfather, Herschel, was a brother to my grandfather, Israel. Yossi had been sending me holiday greetings ever since I had met his family in Israel, but we had never met. When the invitation to his son's wedding in Michigan arrived, I decided it was time, past time, to meet Yossi and his wife, Dorit.

Once in Michigan, in the middle of the country, I perceived that everything about the wedding had to do with middles, with halves coming together (or remaining split), with an equipoise of opposites: the wedding took place on a boat moving down the Detroit River, along a border, the city on one side, Canada on the other. Yossi's Israeli son took as his bride, a German gentile; the *chuppa* was held in place against the strong wind coming off the river by four young friends—two were Israeli, one German, and another African-American, all in their wedding party tuxedos. The bride's parents had come from their small city in Germany. They spoke neither English nor Hebrew, the two languages used there at the party. I was told the bride would convert. I was also told in hushed tones that her parents were not asked to sign the wedding contract, the *ketuba*, and it was suggested they would not sign in any case. But there they were. The bride's mother, father and elderly grandmother, all sat in the first row of the gathered party on the top deck of this luxury yacht on the opposite side of the groom's Israeli family, the ceremonial aisle cutting a middle between the two groups. The boat made its way while the American Midwestern sun set on the Detroit River, the wind ripping at the *chuppa*, threatening to overturn it. The German family sat tight, and they nodded and smiled, understanding very little, if anything at all. No one was speaking German at the party. No one spoke German to them. They looked shy and eager to please. They looked respectful of what transpired in front of them. Under the *chuppa* for the groom stood his parents and his sister, but who for the bride? A woman who the night before had introduced herself to the out-of-town guests as the person who had brought the bride to the United States to be an au pair for her daughter in New York City explained that the family then moved to Michigan where the bride began attending the university in Ann Arbor, and that was where she met her Israeli groom. The rest was history, she said, and the group of guests smiled at her and the couple. The au pair mother added that she herself was a Jewish convert, and felt she could take some pleasure, and laughingly, some credit, that it was her Jewish home the bride came to from Germany which helped her find her Jewish husband. So it was the au pair mother and her young daughter (the little girl for whom the bride was au pair) who stood under the *chuppa* for the bride in the place of honor as her parent. The German parents looked on. It was not possible to know their feelings. Did they approve, disapprove, were merely confused, felt out of place, felt guilty, sought redemption for their country's past? I could only see that they had taken care with their dress and wore kindly expressions on their faces.

There the middle divided rather than cohered. Despite this unification of halves in the middle of the country, the river, the couple, the boat skimming down the border, I learned that there were guests present who spoke German, certainly some who spoke Yiddish, but no one spoke to them in their language, and the boat that rode the border could not connect the boundary between the two groups she carried. I thought of my time in Tel Aviv with Marc the young American journalist who told me I would never heal the split in me, that I would always be compromised in my quest for identity, that as he put it bluntly, I would always be "lost."

At Home in the Tense Middle

But one day I was listening to NPR's *This American Life* and heard a talk by Roald Hoffmann, a Nobel Prizewinner in Chemistry, and a Holocaust survivor. His talk was titled "The Tense Middle," and I leaned into listen closely: "I believe in the middle. Extremes make a good story, but the middle satisfies me. Why? Perhaps because I'm a chemist." Now I was particularly interested since my father was a talented chemist—he had a passion for its symmetry. Hoffmann continued:

> Chemistry is substances, molecules and their transformations. And molecules fight categorization—they are poised along several polarities. Chemistry, like life, is deeply and fundamentally about change. It's about substances—say A and B—transforming, becoming a different substance—C and D—and coming back again. At equilibrium—the middle—all the substances are present. But we're not stuck there. We can change the middle; we can disturb the equilibrium. Perhaps I like the middle, the *tense* middle, because of my background. I was born in 1937 in southeast Poland, now Ukraine. Our Jewish family was trapped in the destructive machinery of Nazi anti-Semitism. Most of us perished: my father, three of four grandparents, and so on. My mother and I survived, hidden for the last 15 months of the war in a schoolhouse attic by a Ukrainian teacher, Mikola Dyuk. I couldn't formulate it then, as a child, but I knew from our experience that

people were not simply good or evil. They made choices. You could hide a Jewish family or you could choose not to…. Being a chemist has helped me see plainly that things—politics, attitudes, molecules— in the middle can be changed, and we have a choice.

I was riveted by the analogy, but it got better:

The middle is not static…my psychological middle as well as the chemical equilibrium. I like that. Yes, of course I also want stability. But I believe that extreme positions—the things you start out with in a chemical reaction, the things you finish with (all people A, bad, all people B, good; no taxes at all, taxed to death)—all of these are impractical, unnatural, boring: the refuge of people who never want to change…I like the tense middle and I am grateful for a life that offers me the potential for change.[8]

My own dual identity was a mixed molecular formulation and it was tense—an intensity that could cause anxiety, but also tense as in alive, vital, built for change and for choices. I thought of E.M. Forster's novel *Howards End*, where the narrator corrects the Schlegel sisters' Aunt Juley, "No; truth being alive, was not halfway between anything. It was only to be found by continuous excursions into either realm, and though proportion is the final secret, to espouse it at the outset is to insure sterility." Forster of the "rainbow bridge that should connect the prose in us with the passion." Marc was wrong about me. His view was static. I was in a dynamic position. A split self can feel thwarted, like the journalist argued, but I realized that this doubleness of mine had necessitated "constant excursions into either realm," had created in me from as early as I could remember a kind of psychological shuttling from side to side, had fueled the movement across the continuum Roald Hoffman analogizes from chemistry, had propelled me on literal journeys to actual "realms" I had not known—Poland and Israel—and to meet relatives I had never known. Like Hoffmann, I too, desired stability. As in Forster, "proportion" was the "final secret." But I had not, perhaps could not, settle for equipoise, "espouse it at the outset" since "sterility" lie that way. Instead, my "splitedness" had been the source of my curiosity, my sense of doubleness had since childhood ignited in me a momentum that was so much a part of my person I was hardly conscious of it as a force separate from myself. Whatever moved me on this journey felt built in, hardwired, and as such, irresistible.

Not surprisingly, the tense middle had its painful moments. After my return to the United States from Poland, I had been invited by a local attorney and his wife to address their Havurah group. This attorney had found me through a civil rights attorney friend of mine, so I made assumptions about the attitudes of the Havurah group—they would be open to a complex report on the history of and current status of the relationship between Poles and Jewish Poles, and my own experience with the issue living and teaching in Poland for two years.

I was welcomed warmly to the affluent home, dined with the group, all of whom were youngish, for the most part, in their 30s and 40s, originally from South America and well-heeled. They were a jovial group at dinner, clearly well-known to one another, and ready for a social and entertaining evening. My host had billed my talk as "A Daughter Returns to the Shtetl," a title I thought was fine if not absolutely accurate. But looking back, it was misleading. The group was not prepared for what they were to hear. As I recall, I had selected a poem by the Polish poet, Antoni Słonimski, to recite as an entrée to my talk. Known for his commitment to social justice, Słonimski (1895–1976) had been president of the Union of Polish Writers in 1956–1959, during the "Polish October," known also as the "Polish Thaw" or "Gomułka's Thaw" or the "Polish October Revolution" when the Stalinist influence on the regime significantly weakened and Polish citizens experienced liberalization of their government. It was not as dramatic as the same "revolution" in Hungary, and it was temporary, as it turned out. In any case, though, Stalinization had ended. Słonimski was the grandson of Rabbi Hayyim Selig Słonimski, founder of the first Hebrew weekly, *ha-Tsefirah*, in Poland. His father had converted to Christianity when he married a Catholic, and Słonimski had been baptized and brought up as a Christian. He had spent the war years in exile in France and England, and returned to Poland in 1951.

Despite his formal identity as a Christian, his Jewish heritage was noted by his readers and the public at large. Because of his dual background, and his devotion to Jewish subjects in his writing, his work seemed particularly relevant to the topic of my talk. I excerpted a portion of his poem, *Elegy for the Jewish Villages* to begin my talk:

Gone now are those little towns where the shoemaker was a poet,
The watchmaker a philosopher, the barber a troubadour.
Gone now are those little towns were the wind joined
Biblical songs with Polish tunes and Slavic rue,
Where old Jews in orchards in the shade of cherry trees
Lamented for the holy walls of Jerusalem.
Gone now are those little towns, though the poetic mists,

The moons, winds, ponds, and stars above them
Have recorded in the blood of centuries the tragic tales,
The histories of the two saddest nations on earth.[9]

I felt it was important to be immediately candid about my own background, that I had been raised Catholic, that my father was Jewish but never acknowledged it, that I had gone to Poland to learn what I could about the history of Polish-Jewish relations, about the charge of Polish anti-Semitism and wartime collaboration, about current Polish anti-Semitism, and also—look for my own identity as a Jew. Thinking back, I remember one of the goals of the talk was to open up and reconsider the standard stereotype of the Pole, particularly for American Jews. I also knew that this required a careful, deft approach. I tried, and I had some success. Some in the audience were willing to complicate their monolithic view of the Poles, but I only learned this after the talk when members of the audience approached me and quietly, even whispering, confided that they understood and appreciated what I had offered. But they did not want to say so in front of the entire group. During the talk when I took questions from the whole group, an indignant and angry woman stood up and from the back of the room, demanded, "So what are you then? Catholic or Jewish? What's your point?" Her tone was rude, but I recognized that from her perspective, it was a fair question, given her experience, an honorable question. I tried answering honestly, "I am reporting only my experience in those two years. I found during that time in Poland that the debate over Polish anti-Semitism is much more complicated than many have realized. As to my private journey, right now I am neither and both, depending on your point of view. But having this double identity did send me on the journey in the first place, and I would argue provided me a lens that was particularly effective through which to view the so-called 'Polish-Jewish question'." She grimaced. Later a more conciliatory fellow, who had winced during my talk whenever I provided evidence of Polish philo-Semitism, confided to me: "Your talk is like an Almóvador film—it's live flesh—we can't hear that there's any middle ground on this subject."

There could be no tense middle there. As Roald Hoffman had warned, such thinking always led to a sterile, static conclusion: it was clear that Poles equaled bad people, and there was no more to be said about it.

I gave a similar talk at a Jewish Community Center a month later. I was still committed to trying to address this controversial interpretation of Polish-Jewish history. In this audience were several survivors. Again, I identified myself candidly, and added that I stood in respectful deference to their experience, that I was providing a report of my recent two-year experience, and that I was aware that what I was about to present was controversial.

Talk about live flesh—if anyone could rightly object to a middle ground on this subject, surely it was this audience who had seen and suffered so much. It was therefore an astonishing moment when I realized during and after my talk, that this group was willing to entertain the complexities of the issue. Many of them had grown up in Poland, and they recognized my description of a place and time in history where Jews and Poles were not consistently enemies. At one point, a man rose to his feet with difficulty, and leaning heavily on a walker, made his way to the front of the room where I stood at a podium. Reaching the front of the room, he stood next to me, and facing the audience, declared, "I grew up in Poland and I know what she is describing. I survived Auschwitz. But my life in Poland up to the time of the Nazi invasion was not one of misery—there was joy in my life in Poland. She is a bridge. We should walk over." There was a sudden and complete silence in the room. From where I stood, the audience was now a sea of upturned faces wearing concentrated expressions. He who had suffered the most, was willing to take Forster's "excursion…into another realm," he who could justify psychological sterility and stagnation, was able to occupy Hoffmann's "tense middle." It was extraordinary. The young Havurah members likely had grandparents who had had an experience like this man's, but they themselves had not lived through what their forebears had survived. Yet they could not "disturb the equilibrium" Hoffmann described. The man had used the word "bridge"—I had not invoked that term in my talk; it was his entirely. I thought then immediately of Forster's "only connect the rainbow bridge." The discussion concluded, this man took my hand in his, we both bowed slightly to the audience, and turning to each other, so humbled was I by his greatness, I lifted his hand to my cheek.

Adoption

The decision to formally convert to Judaism involved an entirely different set of emotions from the affiliation I felt in my childhood. It was one thing to feel as a child the inexplicable but definite shock and pull of *bashert* when I met my grandparents; to then have been so marked by the experience; to live with my family's secretiveness about my father's identity, and thus I felt, my own Jewish heritage; to have journeyed to communist Poland to live and teach there for two years as an adult to expose myself firsthand to Polish attitudes towards their former Jewish neighbors and to the question of Polish collaboration; and then finally to travel to Israel to meet my relatives. But it was quite another to embrace a religion, a god. I was equivocal about my readiness to move on to what some preferred to call "adoption," rather than "conversion." I liked the first term better. I felt I was not "converting" to anything—I felt instead that I was returning to what I had always been. So "adopting" was closer.

While converting, or even adopting, seems the opposite of the "equipoise" I had accepted finally during my stay in Israel, I had already found in my study of Judaism a philosophy that encourages those "constant excursions into either realm," as E.M. Forster had named them, in which I had been immersed. I had once been stabilized in Catholicism; that stability eroded and ultimately disappeared as I learned the Church's history and its contemporary positions. Now I needed to find this other part of myself, long veiled, that part that came alive in my grandparents' Brooklyn apartment, that revealed itself in the moments with my father in the Kraków hotel when we both acknowledged a loss and tears followed, that time at the Armand Hammer Museum looking at the Jacob Balgley folio when he knowingly nodded and smiled at my "There is nothing so whole as a broken Jewish heart."

I now believed I was always being led here by a sense of destiny or *bashert*, call it what you will. I needed to follow where I felt I was always being led. This powerful urge became even more dramatic as another literal journey, this time to my father's birthplace in Brest, Belarus, formerly Brest-Litovsk, Poland would soon show me. But first I needed to grapple with the decision to "adopt" or be "adopted."

A struggle

The day I had made an appointment with Rabbi Shai whose writings and talks had impressed me, I was unsure what I wanted from such a meeting. I knew that the accumulated experiences I had had up to that point, the "tense middle" I inhabited, had given me insights for which I was grateful, and had also thrown into relief a need in me to tell my story whole and ask someone outside looking in to give me another perspective.

I was nervous. I recalled the woman in the first Havura audience fairly shouting at me, "So what are you then!" The only other time I had confided my personal feelings about my mixed identity was to Jimmy, my priest friend, and he had made it easy because of his forgiving, consoling manner, not to say, his own experience of a mixed heritage. Here I was about to confide to another "priest," a conservative rabbi, and I could not know how he would respond. I had heard him teach, and in all those presentations, I consistently detected those "excursions into either realm," no matter the subject, not only a willingness, but a marked habit of "fighting categorization" like the molecules in Hoffmann's chemistry analogy. His observations never settled for the "stable and sterile" pat conclusion. Still, despite the presentations and writing I had done on the subject, I had not opened the door fully to what drove the whole enterprise to begin with. That was a very personal matter.

Rabbi Shai and I met in his modest school office. His manner was open and friendly, and he signaled that he was there to listen. It was difficult to know where to begin, and I cannot say that I can even remember now how my narrative began. But I recounted the travel, finding the relatives, the Fulbright experience in Poland, the time in Israel, my father's denial, as briefly as I could, because I knew that what had brought me to his office was behind and beyond those experiences: I could not escape the feeling from the earliest memory that all of this had been destined not by me but for me, that I had followed a path that had already been laid for me, that somehow I was meant to be on this journey, that maybe my heart was from the start a Jewish heart yearning to fulfill its purpose.

Rabbi Shai listened without a word. I kept expecting a question, an interruption, but no, he gestured for me to continue my story. When I had finished, he took a sheet of paper and wrote the word for "Israel" in Hebrew: "Yisra-El," one struggles with God (El), the name given to Jacob by the angel after Jacob's nocturnal struggle. He turned the paper so I could see the writing in Hebrew— the very word in Hebrew visually presented "struggle" graphically, the letters

$$\text{יִשְׂרָאֵל}$$

themselves a tableau of struggle (literally translated, "Israel"). He said, "The entire enterprise of understanding and learning is struggle—in Judaism one is constantly alert to the need to readjust, to look more deeply, to consider all arguments." Here was Hoffmann's "disturbing the equilibrium," Forster's "constant excursions." I was in the right place.

Among the subjects I learned about during the months of my study with Rabbi Shai, I was introduced to medieval Jewish mysticism, the Kabbalah, a vocabulary of dynamic symbols that many Jewish medieval mystics used to describe their understanding of God and God's relationship to the world. Maimonides held that God is unknowable; Kabbalists believed that there is a way to access and understand God through the "Ten Sefirot," a system of symbols resembling a ladder, a dialectic that allows the mystic to "climb back up the ladder" and access God. Taken together, the symbols show how the relationship between God and the world is in a constant state of flux, depending on human actions. A constant state of flux, a tense middle, excursions into either realm, Jacob's struggle. And I learned further that

Torah study itself consists of this shuttling back and forth, like the exegesis I learned as a literary scholar.

When it came time for my *Beit Din*, the meeting with three rabbis to formalize my adoption, I had the opportunity to tie this learning to my personal tense middle. Drawing from the Kabbalistic symbolic vocabulary, I presented a prepared statement to my three interlocutors. An excerpt:

> Within the inaccessible God, the EYN SOF, there can be a flash of consciousness—KETER (nothingness)—which can lead to HOKHMAH (a beginning, some wisdom), and thus to BINAH (understanding). With an understanding that is constantly refreshed and continually renewed, not static, or monolithic, I see my adoption … as an ongoing dialectic, an ongoing reconciliation of seeming fragments from the self and the world.

Judaism had created a new space for me, a rich ground on which I could move up and down Hoffmann's molecular spectrum, back and forth in Forster's "constant excursions," a home for the "tense middle."

Opposite: Getting to know God in the Jewish faith through the Ten Sefirot in the Kabbalah — a vocabulary of dynamic symbols that many Jewish medieval mystics used to describe their understanding of God, as well as God's relationship to the world. Kabbalists believed that there is a way to access and understand God through this system of symbols, resembling a ladder, allowing the mystic to "climb back up the ladder" and access God.

Ten Sefirot

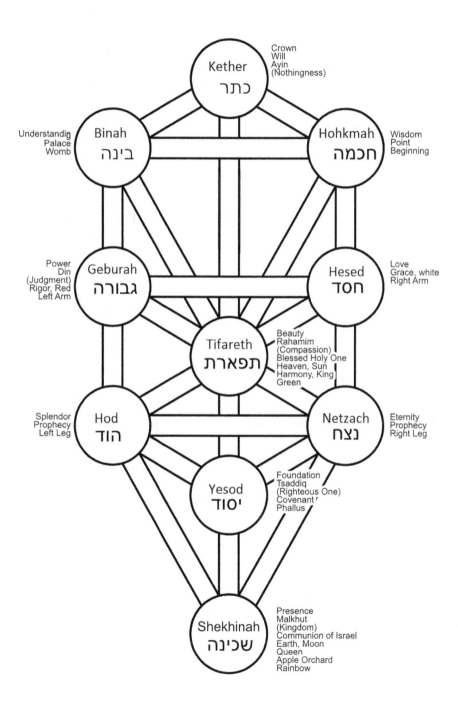

Mikvehs, Masada and Los Angeles, 2012

When I was in Israel, I had taken a bus in the breath-stopping heat of summer from Tel Aviv into the Judean desert to see the ruins of Masada, the famous fortress where 1,000 Jewish Sicarii committed suicide in 73 CE rather than be taken prisoner by the encroaching Romans. Even by Israeli standards, that day was spectacularly hot. The group I traveled with was international, primarily European, and as we were led by a guide up the steep winding cliff, a teenaged girl from Poland accompanied by her mother, fainted dead away on the path. We went to move her out of the sun, though there was not much shade to be found. Others on the trail were much older than she or me, and seeing them sweating profusely, I worried we could have even a fatality en route. But we continued on, the Polish girl now weak but conscious and ambulatory. At a designated spot, the guide brought us to a stop. This was the Masada mikveh, 2,000 years old, and discovered only in the last four decades by the Israeli archaeologist, Yigal Yadin. A mikveh is essentially a small, deep pool, but that description does not really render up its impact on first sight. Seven still intact steps led down to a jacuzzi-sized tub. A ritual bath traditionally used by women for cleansing after menstruation (*niddah*) to ready the womb for procreation, and by others wishing to sanctify an occasion, the mikveh can only be filled with water from a natural source—rainwater from a cistern, the sea or lake, river or spring. The water may not be carried to the mikveh in vessels. Ancient Jews in the desert of Israel had no access to a flowing stream all year to purify themselves, so the mikveh, I thought, acted as a spiritual substitute for a flowing stream.

I looked down the seven steps into the arid, stone space and imagined the clear, blue water glimmering there in the Masada desert plateau 2,000 years before. At the moment, the sun was so blinding that the surroundings took on a blurred appearance. Walls shimmered and lost their clear outlines. Mirages appeared. We visitors peered into the astoundingly well-preserved steep tub, sweat running down our faces, and I thought that like me, the others were wishing the mikveh was filled for us to enter its cooling waters that day.

The water kiss

That was the first time I had ever seen a mikveh. I had not imagined then that I would experience the ritual itself. But after the *Beit Din*, it was arranged as part of my adoption. I met Rabbi Shai at the Rabbinical Assembly of the American Jewish University in Los Angeles. I had invited two friends in addition to my husband John—one, Sherry, was Jewish, the other, Kay, a student of Eastern religion. And I invited my father. By then, at 100 years old, he could only easily travel by wheelchair. I picked up my friends at the airport, and John brought my father.

On an August day in inland Los Angeles, the heat brought back the memory of the mikveh at Masada. We were met by the mikveh supervisor, a welcoming, energetic woman, who provided us all with an introduction to the mikveh, and then led me to where I would prepare for immersion. This was a bathroom off the larger room which housed the mikveh. It was a standard, modern bathroom where I was to cleanse myself before entering the mikveh, as Jewish law prescribes. There was shampoo, soap, dental floss and nail polish remover. Everything had to be removed—clothing, jewelry, band-aids, nail polish—so the mikveh's water could reach every part of the body.

Showered with wet hair combed back, I donned a robe and met the mikveh supervisor at the door which led to the mikveh

Attending my Mikveh in Los Angeles on 6 August, 2012, from left: my friend Kay, my husband John, myself and Rabbi Shai. My father Ely, aged 100, sits in front in his wheelchair. Photographer: Friend Sherry who also attended Mikveh

itself. There I was about to experience *Tevilah*—complete body immersion. This room was quite large, tiled blue and white, with water reflected off the sides of the room which gave the entire space an underwater or subterranean aspect. It was extraordinarily quiet. There was a space behind a curtain where Rabbi Shai, my father, my husband, and my two women friends sat during the ritual. I shed my robe, and guided by the mikveh supervisor, slowly descended the seven steps to the floor of the bath, each step representing a day of creation, with a blessing for each of the seven steps. The ancient Hebrew unit measurement for liquid is a *seah*; five *seah* to a gallon times forty, the forty

RECORD OF
MIKVEH IMMERSION

This is to certify that

Kathleen Balgley

English Name

נעמי רויה בת אבא'

Hebrew Name

has undergone immersion in the Mikveh on

August 6, 2012   corresponding to   18 AV 5772

Judith Golden

Mikveh Supervisor

Rabbi Chai Levy

Witness

Judith Golden

Witness

Henry Morrow

Witness

RABBINICAL ASSEMBLY · PACIFIC SOUTHWEST REGION

My certificate of Mikveh immersion in Los Angeles on August 6, 2012. My father attended at the age of 100. Courtesy Balgley Family Archive

תעודת השלמת גירות למבוגרת

*T*his is to certify that on the ___sixth___ day of
___August___, in the
year ___2012___, corresponding to the ___18th___ day of ___Av___ ___5772___ in the
___city___ of ___Los Angeles___, in the ___State___ of
___California___, ___Kathleen Balgley___ came before
the undersigned duly constituted Bet Din and stated that she has long since cast her lot with the Jewish people,
but without the benefit of immersion.

Whereas she now wishes to complete her course and affirm her place among the people Israel, accepting the *brit*
and *mitzvot* which God gave to Israel, in accordance with the full requirements of *halakhah*, we have supervised
___Kathleen Balgley's___ immersion in a proper mikveh, as prescribed by *halakhah*.

We therefore declare her to be a true and full member of the Jewish faith and Jewish
people and bestow upon her the name ___Margalit Rut___, daughter of
___Eli___

May the God of our ancestors Abraham and Sarah bless her and grant her the strength and courage to abide
faithfully and loyally by the precepts and observances of our holy Torah, so that she may be a worthy member of
the House of Israel, called upon to bear testimony to God's unity and righteousness.

Signed in the ___city___ of ___Los Angeles___ in the ___State___ of
___California___, on this ___sixth___ day of
___August___, in the
year ___2012___, corresponding to the ___18th___ day of ___Av___, ___5772___

Witness 1 ___Rabbi Shai C___   הרב ישראל 'ע ג'ר'
Witness 2 ___Amy Mott___
Witness 3 ___Judith Molden___

© Rabbinical Assembly 2009 כנסת הרבנים תשׁ"ע
www.rabbinicalassembly.org 212.280.6000

My certificate declaring me to be 'a true and full member of the Jewish
faith'. Courtesy Balgley Family Archive

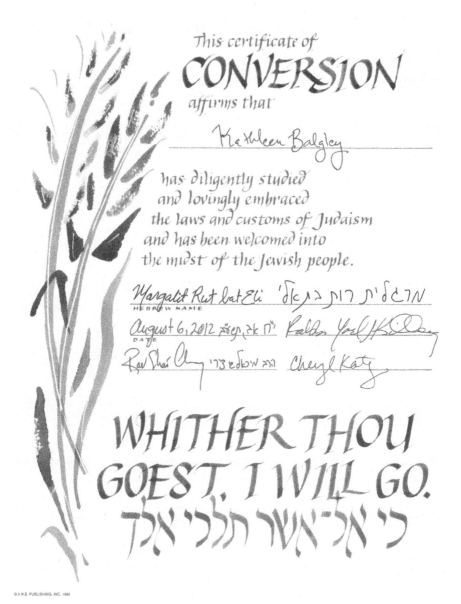

Certificate announces my Hebrew name, "Margalit" (Hebrew for my mother's name, Margaret); "Rut" (for Ruth, ancient and first convert to Judaism); "bat Eli," daughter of Ely. Courtesy Balgley Family Archive

taken from the forty years in the desert, makes for a minimum of two hundred gallons of water in the mikveh. The mikveh pool is connected underground to a tap water source that mixes with the fresh, flowing water of the immersion mikveh when a plug or valve is removed for each ritual immersion. The two waters meet in what is known as the "water kiss," a conjoining of the two waters. Again, how was this achieved in ancient Israel, a desert, where there was no flowing stream? Rainwater was captured in a treasury and would then be drawn into a large tub. When the rainwater and the drawn water would meet, would "kiss," the whole was spiritually transformed into a flowing stream. The mikveh I stepped into had brought ice from a freshwater source, transported according to a specific set of rules.

One of the most memorable, but still to be documented, stories about the mikveh I heard was from a lovely elderly woman in one of my Judaic classes with Rabbi Shai in California. When she learned I had lived in Poland and had traveled to the famed former Jewish center of Vilna, Lithuania, she told me about the Vilnia River which runs along the Lithuanian-Belarusian border for about 80 kilometers and flows into the Neris River at Vilna. From the Neris River, the waters drain into the Neman River, which finally flow into the Baltic Sea. The confluence with the Neris is in Vilnius, the city that got its name from the river's name, Vilnia, meaning 'ripple' in Lithuanian. In any case, this woman told me about a legend, which I have researched and for which I have been unable to find documentation, that below the earth under the Neris River there flows a mythical river, known to the Jews of the region, a river that offered the supreme, universal "water kiss" of a naturally occurring or god-made mikveh. An enchanting and enchanted story—one that I would claim as true.

Although there was no outside source of sunlight as at Masada, the pool sparkled. It seemed to have a life of its own—with tiny ripples catching light from an unknown source. Once immersed, I realized the water felt like no water I had ever felt before: it was soft to the point of feeling creamy, but the opposite of oily—light, so light, as to have no weight of its own at all. Indeed, the feeling of water on my body disappeared for me; I felt suspended in space, in a non-element. For a moment, I thought of the unborn child in the womb's amniotic fluid—perhaps the sensation was akin to that. The mikveh supervisor led me in reciting blessings in Hebrew as I submerged my head in the mikveh waters. Meanwhile, Rabbi Shai had my father, husband and friends recite blessings from behind the curtain. But in large part I had forgotten about them--a sharp sense of solitariness had engulfed me in the mikveh. The womb-like feel was like birth in its aloneness. Or like a kind of death—an end to a former self. After the ceremony when I rejoined the group and certificates were signed, I checked in on my father's state of mind. He was quiet, though part of that had to do with the conversation among the rest of us—difficult for him to hear, and too fast for him to enter. Later I learned what he had been thinking. I took for my Hebrew name, "Margalit," in honor of my mother, Margaret, she who from the first had modeled for me open-mindedness and open-heartedness.

Unfounded: birther charge and Found: my father's file
Seal Beach, California, 2011

My father's apartment in "Assisted Living" in California contained pieces of the life he shared with my mother for sixty-six years: his old desk, her special chair with the curved right arm for writing and reading with a drawer under the seat for her playing cards, their Ethan Allen couch, his Boston rocker, the bookcases he has had since his undergraduate days at Brooklyn College. But she had died, and despite the effort to make the place feel like home, these transplanted objects only made his singleness more melancholy— at least for me. Having no space to accommodate it, my father had shipped off his Steinway grand piano to my brother on the east coast, but not before he corresponded with The Juilliard School to arrange selling it to them. Like other times in his life, his strange lack of sentimentality about the piano, which was like a member of our family, struck my siblings and me as unacceptable, business-like with no regard to feeling. He was all too willing to dispose of it. My sisters and I had no room for the piano in our homes, so my brother, who felt that the piano was part of our father, at his own expense generously offered to ship the piano across the country, no small feat, and explained that he would be the piano's "custodian" until such time any of our descendants might become serious pianists and would also have room for the grand. When my father was still able to travel to visit my brother, he would greet his piano as "my old friend," and sit and play for hours. So much for the "business decisions" he had earlier favored.

My siblings and I had replaced the grand with a small studio piano, but that substitution only emphasized what was missing: my mother, his piano, their home, their former life. He had recently fallen and damaged his right shoulder so that one of his hands was now impaired, and though by anyone else's lights, he played like the virtuoso he was since childhood, he grimaced and shook his head at his playing.

Years before, at his 75th birthday, my siblings and I had arranged a professional recording studio to make sure we had a record of his playing. The studio was in Los Angeles, and the technicians, young pony-tailed men in black rock and roll T-shirts, told us that Michael Jackson had recently recorded there. I was quite certain my father did not know Michael Jackson, but no matter; we were glad we had chosen an apparently desirable studio.

My father carried a leather satchel that held all the music he planned to play for the recording session. When he opened it, the technicians were astonished. "You mean you're just going to play and we take it down?" they asked. My father looked puzzled, and replied, "How else?" "Wow," they rejoined, "We haven't heard of anyone doing that since Sinatra. We always splice and mix." "Well, I'm just planning to play, if that works," my father said.

And he did. Marvelously. For hours. First, the classical pieces he cared most about. And then what he called "popular music," which meant songs like *Begin the Beguine* and *Fascination*, all songs he had played in orchestras as a young man in the New York nights of the 1930s—songs from my parents' courtship days, and later in that restaurant in the Berkshires to supplement the family income after he was married and had children.

We made CDs of the session. The classical portion showed a formal photographic portrait of my father as a young man seated at the piano, probably made not so many years after he finished at The Juilliard School. His gaze was away from the camera, a concentrated, even dreamy facial expression, white handkerchief in suit pocket in the fashion of the day, and elegant hands placed lightly on the keyboard. The popular song portion we titled "On the Sunnyside," featuring a black and white photograph of my parents in their 20s, good-looking, smiling, walking hand in hand; the photograph though posed, seemed candid, an incidental still of their lives in motion. For the next two decades we would put on the CD for his and our pleasure, but finally at one point, he said he no longer wanted to hear it, "This reminds me of what I used to be able to do, and what I've lost."

One day sitting with my father on the Ethan Allen couch, he brought up the subject of the attack on President Obama's citizenship. Conspiracy theories had been circulating claiming that according to Article Two of the United States Constitution, Obama was not a natural-born citizen of the United States, and was thus ineligible to be President of the United States. The theorists, dubbed "birthers," alleged that Obama's birth certificate was a forgery, that his actual birthplace was Kenya, not Hawaii. Others had asserted that Obama became a citizen of Indonesia in childhood, and thus would have lost his American citizenship in the United Kingdom and the United States. The birthers had sought court rulings declaring Obama ineligible to take office. That John McCain had been born in Panama, Ted Kennedy in England—these facts were ignored in this smear campaign—a disturbing racist reaction to the fact that America had elected its first African-American president.

The specially-designed covers of the two CDs (both classical and popular) our family had made of my father's piano playing. The music was recorded at a studio session in Los Angeles when my father was 75 years old. Courtesy Balgley Family Archive

My father's politics had always been informed; he was a longtime "man of the people." His days coming of age as a well-informed teenager and later as a university student in the politically-charged period of the Depression in the leftist circles of Brooklyn and Manhattan, had confirmed in him a deep sense of the importance of social justice. But perhaps even more than those influences, though he never mentioned it, was that he and his parents and siblings had been Jewish immigrants from eastern Poland. Surely that had exposed him to the hardships and prejudices of life in America? However, when he spoke of anti-Semitism, he spoke of it in its generic sense, as a plague on society, not as a personal experience, though it would have been impossible for him to have escaped its reach. "I've kept a file over the years—a file on my citizenship." He said that during this discussion of Obama, and gestured to where his desk sat against a wall. "Go ahead, go get it, if you're interested."

I was nonplussed. Citizenship? I had understood he had derivative citizenship from his father who had arrived to the United States seven years before he, his mother, and three other siblings followed. I had never heard of any problem or question related to my father's citizenship. "The folder is in the file drawer of my desk." I had known that drawer since I could remember—it was the repository for the dark army green-colored files that since childhood were not to be touched by me. I can remember looking at the drawer of files as a kid and seeing a label, "TAXES," along with other files, including one with my own name written on it. "Under what title will I find that file?" I asked from the other room where he sat. "Citizenship."

I saw the fountain-penned faded tab bearing the label under the "C"— my father had always been meticulously organized. It was quite thick, and apparently had not been moved in a long while, as I had to give it a tug to remove it from its tight quarters. I returned to the room, held it up to him, and for a moment he looked intently at the folder in my hand, and stated, "No one has ever seen this before except me."

There was in the room an atmosphere of a privacy finally shared, of a decision to at last surrender or come to terms with something kept secret, something hidden, even from my mother all these years. And I had a moment to think about all the unspoken and unspeakable in my father's relationship to me—about all that had lain hidden away, what he avoided saying to me and I to him.

I felt a sudden protectiveness towards him. Whatever secret of shame he had hidden, I had at that moment, for a moment, already forgiven him, and I wanted to be a gentle confessor, if that was what I was to be. I sat beside him on the couch he and my mother had shared for decades, wanting to look at the contents together, so that he would feel the director of ceremonies, in control of this revelation. But he handed the folder over to me, and it became obvious that he knew the file by heart. He needed no reminding about what it held.

I opened the folder to find wisps of thinnest onion skin pages of correspondence dating from 1937, his own carbon copy letters and the responses to those letters all in careful chronological order. At first, I could not take it all in, because it was too astounding. This personal correspondence was fit for a museum. One letter, an onion skin carbon copy of his own letter, impeccably typed and after seventy-five years, in perfect condition, like it had just been completed the day before, but at the same time feeling like ancient parchment painstakingly preserved, was written to the American Embassy in Warsaw, Poland. Then there was a response from Brześć, Poland, my father's birthplace, dated 1937 regarding "Jewish Records." Unbelievable. I held a piece of paper that had come from pre-Holocaust Poland, from a place that would soon become a world of ashes and death, from a small office in a town came this artifact that— so innocently, so humanly and humanely—explained the facts of this person's life. As if it mattered, one individual's story. A civilized dispatch before the end of civilization. A marriage, a birth, a circumcision, like family photographs or treasured family documents—a diploma, a marriage license, a baby picture. Then to think that all of this, the records and the persons, were annihilated, erased—the tiny and intimate human moments here recorded, they and millions like them, savagely destroyed, murdered. As I held the paper, so fragile, precious, I felt as if I held a child's hand in mine or maybe a very elderly person's hand, a missive from a place and time that could not have known what catastrophe would befall it. Sent by a clerk, who had typed and signed his name, doing his workaday task before his world went insane. For a second a surreal thought slipped through my head: can we turn back time, undo the past?

The letterhead indicated *"Starost,"* a centuries-old Slavic term for "official" from the Polish root, *"star"* for "old." With a record number. And again signed by a person with his name. Then there followed a letter from my father dated 1953 (the unimaginable has happened between these two pieces of paper). He is upset, it is "entirely regrettable," I read, that "my files were not returned to me, but were disposed of." Other letters show that his inquiry had been sent on to Moscow after the war, since now Brześć had become Brest and part of the Soviet Union. It appears no one was taking responsibility for the "disposed" records. But would it not be the case that such records were destroyed along with the people whose lives they chronicled? And would my father not have automatically known this? In that sixteen-year span, everything had happened in my father's former home; and in his new world—he had been married and had three children.

The letter he wrote in 1953 was sent just months after my birth. There was also some correspondence missing—there was no letter to say the files were lost or disposed of. From whom did that letter come? The same "starost"? But there would be no office, no clerk, no such place called Brześć in Poland by the year 1953. The letter would have had to come from the post-Shoah, the Soviet bureaucracy. And there was a letter that told my father his request has been sent to Moscow as Brześć was then Brest and no longer in Poland, but in the Soviet Union. As if a person would not know the excruciating backstory to that fact. And another letter told my father that his request would go from Moscow to another office in the Soviet Union. Then a perfectly preserved, "homemade" document on quaint desk pad paper from a certain "Sarah Goldberg" of the Bronx, testifying as cousin to my grandmother, Sora Feyge Slomyansky Balgley, that she, Sarah Goldberg, was present at the wedding of my grandparents in Brest-Litovsk in 1907. So Brześć had also been Brest-Litovsk earlier (Brest "of Lithuania"). What else would Sarah Goldberg have known? I learned that my father's date of birth was actually July 8, 1912, in accordance with the Jewish law of waiting one week exactly from the date of birth before a male infant's *bris*.

Below is the extensive correspondence my father had to wade through in establishing his citizenship of the United States and the evidence and supporting documentation he was required to present to prove his case. Despite several setbacks he persevered until he obtained his Certificate of Citizenship in 1954.

U. S. DEPARTMENT OF LABOR
Immigration and Naturalization Service
Washington

File Number

2270

December 17, 1937.

C-1263437
NC

Mr. Ely Balgley,

██████

Brooklyn, N. Y.

Dear Sir:

Reference is made to your letter of recent date, wherein you request that you be furnished with a copy of the naturalization papers issued to your father.

In accordance with the naturalization laws and regulations copies of naturalization records may be furnished only to the person naturalized. However, this office has a record which may relate, and it is to-day being forwarded to the representative of this Service referred to below. If you will call upon him and advise of the particular purpose for which a copy of the naturalization record is desired, he will be pleased to give you appropriate advice and assistance. You should present this letter when you call.

Assistant District Director of Immigration and Naturalization, 641 Washington St., New York, N. Y.

Cordially yours,

By direction of the Commissioner,

J. H. Wagner

H. Wagner, Assistant.

Correspondence dating from 1937 from the US Department of Labor advising my father, then living in Brooklyn, about how to obtain proof of his American naturalization. Courtesy Balgley Family Archive

Translation

County Starost's Office   Stamp fee in the amount
       in Brzesc   of 3 zloty cancelled on
                                                petition
     Nr. IV-2-e.

Brzesc on Bug, January 11, 1937

E X C E R P T

from records of the Jewish Community
in Brzesc o/B
pertaining to Jews born in the year of
one thousand nine hundred and twelve (1912)

Consecutive number: 184; Who performed the ceremony of circumcision: person authorized by the rabbi; Date of birth: christian - July 8th; Date of circumcision: christian - July 15th; Jewish date: ./.; Place of birth: Brzesc o/B; Surname and names of father and mother: BALGLEJ, Srul and Sore-Fejge daughter of Aron; Who was born and what name was given him or her: son "ELA".

I certify that the above excerpt conforms with the entry in records and with the law.

                                                For the County

            Seal   /-/ J. Paluszkiewicz
    of the County Starost   Under Referendary
      in Brzesc on Bug.

My father's correspondence, also dating from 1937, providing proof of his Jewish birth in Brześć on Bug in Poland. Having sent this to the American authorities in support his application for citizenship, he was subsequently informed that it was 'no longer in existence'. Courtesy Balgley Family Archive

Fair Lawn, N. J.
Oct. 30, 1952

Immigration & Naturalization Service
70 Columbus Ave.
New York, N. Y.

Att: Mrs. A. E. Werth
Re: File 2 A - 6880

Gentlemen:

In connection with my pending application for a certificate of derivative citizenship, I request that my case be reopened.

Please advise if you can locate File 2 A - 6880 and particularly, if my birth certificate is present therein.

Thank you for your cooperation.

Very truly yours,

E. Balgley

My father's correspondence addressed to the Immigration and Naturalization Service in New York in 1952 to obtain proof of his American citizenship and requesting if his Polish birth certificate was on file. Courtesy Balgley Family Archive

Fair Lawn, New Jersey
                                    May 4, 1953

United States Department of Justice
Immigration and Naturalization Service
1060 Broad Street
Newark, New Jersey

                        Re: File # 0300-429825

Gentlemen:

        It is entirely regrettable that file 2A-6880
which, among other papers, contained my birth certificate is no longer in existence.

        I went to considerable expense and trouble to
procure this birth certificate from Brest Litovsk,
Poland. It seems to me the Service could have returned
the file to me rather than disposing of it otherwise.

        Please advise the details of the records re-
tirement program to which you referred in your letter
so that proper action may be taken to recover the document.

        As you requested, a new application is en-
closed, duly executed. Thank you for your assistance
and cooperation.

                        Very truly yours,

                        Ely Balgley

My father's 1953 letter to the Department of Justice, stating that it was "entirely regrettable" that his original naturalization papers, including his birth certificate, no longer existed. Courtesy Balgley Family Archive

Fair Lawn, New Jersey
May 13, 1953

American Embassy
Consular Division   Via Air Mail
Warsaw, Poland

Gentlemen:

      I was referred to you by the Polish Consulate
in New York in connection with procuring a birth certificate.

      I was born in Brest-Litovsk, Poland, about
June 27, 1912. I am a United States citizen and have
resided in the States since 1920. My father's name is
Israel Balgley, mother's name, Sarah Balgley.

      It would be most appreciated if you arrange
to procure my birth certificate and forward it to me.
May I please have your advice at an early date?
Thank you for your cooperation.

      Very truly yours,

      Ely Balgley

cc Immigration & Naturalization Service
    1060 Broad Street
    Newark, N. J.

EB ✓

*A 1953 letter from my father to the American Embassy in Warsaw,
requesting a copy of his Polish birth certificate. A carefully-made
carbon copy of the letter was also sent by him to the Immigration and
Naturalization office in New Jersey. Courtesy Balgley Family Archive*

Form N-14-
(Rev. 12-24-52)   File No._____

U. S. DEPARTMENT OF JUSTICE
IMMIGRATION AND NATURALIZATION SERVICE

May 6, 1953

Mr. Ely Balgley
███████████████

Fairlawn, N. J.

Your application Form No. N-600 has been received and is returned herewith. Please follow
the instructions only in the items below which are checked (✓) in red.

☐ 1. Answer or complete the lines checked (✓) in the enclosed application, and mail or bring
   it to this office with this letter.

☐ 2. Please follow the instructions checked (✓) in the enclosed application, and mail or
   bring it to this office with this letter.

XXX 3. Mail or bring, with this letter:

   XXX Marriage Certificate of _your parents._
   XXX Birth or baptismal certificate of _yourself._
   ☐ Divorce papers of _____
   ☐ Death Certificate of _____
   ☐ Naturalization Certificate of _____
   ☐ Evidence that you lived in the United States before _____
   ☐ (This evidence may be a marriage or birth certificate; school, church, employment,
      police or census records; insurance policies, bank books, leases, deeds, licenses,
      receipts, or letters; or photostatic or photographic copies of such papers).
   ☐ _____ photographs of yourself, exactly alike. These must be 2 X 2 inches, printed
      on thin paper, have a light background, and should show a front view without hat.
   ☐ Sign full name on front of all photographs. Sign in the margin and not across face
      or clothing.
   ☐ The attached Form No._____, after it has been filled in.
   ☐ Marriage certificate, divorce decree or other court order showing change of name.
   ☐ The mutilated or other document for which you request a replacement.
   ☐ Your visitor's permit issued at the time of admission (Form I-94 or 257A).
   ☐ Your passport.
   ☐ Certificate from your attending physician.
   ☐ Documentary evidence to show your continuous residence in the United States from
      shortly before July 1, 1924 to date (If you wish any of these documents to be return-
      ed to you, copies must be enclosed).

☐ 4. Have application Form No._____ sworn to before a Notary Public, with seal, or
   an officer of this Service.

☐ 5. Please complete the following blanks concerning your arrival into the United States:
   Place _____ Date _____ Steamship _____
   Exact name under which you arrived _____.

☐ 6. Show your Alien Registration number, if known, in the space provided.

(Over)

7. You did not enclose a check or money order in the amount of $_____, as required by the instructions on the application form.

8. Your check or money order cannot be accepted because it must be for $_____ and payable to the "Treasurer of the United States".

9. If you are married to a citizen of the United States, give name, date and place of marriage at the bottom of this letter and mail or bring it to this office.

X☒ 10. In the event you are unable to obtain your birth certificate and parents' marriage certificate, you are required to submit the following secondary evidence
(a) Copy of the Federal Census Record for 1930. Application attached hereto.
(b) Letter from the first school you attended in the United States, showing the date of your birth and the names of your parents, as appears in the school records.

XXX 11. It is noted you refer to File No. 0300-429825 and File No. 2A-6880. Please furnish additional information concerning same, especially as to whether you ever filed application for a Certificate of Citizenship.

SEND ALONG PHOTOSTATIC COPIES OF ANY DOCUMENTS YOU WISH RETURNED.

Very truly yours,

R. G. HOFFELLER
Officer in Charge

GPO 83-45570

The reply from the US Department of Justice, dated May 1953, requesting exhaustive further information to support the granting of citizenship to my father. Courtesy Balgley Family Archive

Registered Mail   Fair Lawn, New Jersey
                                                     May 19, 1953

U. S. Dept. of Justice
Immigration & Naturalization Service
1060 Broad Street
Newark 2, N. J.

Gentlemen:

        Thank you for your form letter of May 6, 1953. As
you requested the following documents are enclosed:

        1. Original & photostat of earliest school record
in the United States.

        2. Original & photostat of receipt File No.
2A - 6880.

        3. Your letter of Jan. 16, 1953 explaining File
Reference 0300-429825.

        4. Application Form No. 600 duly executed, check
and photos.

        5. Extract from matricula for year 1912. Original
& photostat.

        6. Original & photostat of letter from U. S. Civil
Service Comm. dated 3/30/37.

        7. Notarized statement dated Feb. 11, 1937 as to
my citizenship. (2 originals).

        8. Original & photostat of letter from Brooklyn
College dated Oct. 11, 1937 certifying birth day.

        9. Copy of my letter to American Embassy, Warsaw,
dated May 13, 1953 requesting copy of birth certificate.

        10. My letter of May 4, 1953, transmitting Form
N-600.

        Application was made to the Census Bureau for a
copy of the 1930 records. The data will be forwarded to
your office as soon as received.

(2)

         I would appreciate your early advice as to the next step. Thank you for your cooperation.

         Please return the originals of the enclosed documents after they have served your purpose.

                 Very truly yours,

                 Ely Balgley

My father's painstaking compliant letter of May 1953, satisfying every request from the U.S. Department of Justice in support of his citizenship application. Courtesy Balgley Family Archive

233.1 Balgley, Ely
JP/nd

THE FOREIGN SERVICE
OF THE
UNITED STATES OF AMERICA

American Embassy,
Warsaw, Poland,
June 5, 1953.

Mr. Ely Balgley,
███████████
Fair Lawn, New Jersey.

Sir:

The receipt today is acknowledged of your letter
of May 13, 1953 requesting assistance in the matter
of procuring a copy of your birth certificate.

In view of the fact that Brest-Litovsk now forms
a part of the territory of the USSR, your letter is
being referred to the American Embassy at Moscow for
its appropriate action and direct reply to you.

Very truly yours,

Josephine Pasquini
American Vice Consul

*Another setback for my father in relation to his application for American
citizenship. Having already engaged in detailed correspondence, the
American Embassy in Warsaw tells him in June 1953 that his application
for a new birth certificate will have to be referred to the American Embassy
in Moscow. Courtesy Balgley Family Archive*

All my father's frustrating and patient efforts of the previous year come to fruition in March 1954 when he at last received his Certificate of Citizenship. He had been in the United States for thirty-six years with derivative citizenship from his father, the documents proving this having been earlier misplaced. Courtesy Balgley Family Archive

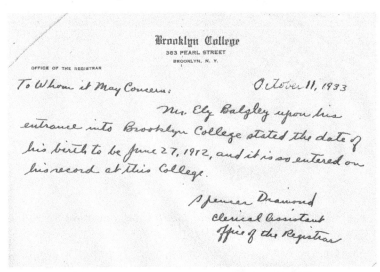

A 1933 letter, signed by Mr. Spenser Diamond of Brooklyn College, advising "Whom it may concern" that my father's date of birth is June 27, 1912. This date, as we learned from official documents, was incorrect. Courtesy Balgley Family Archive

NEW YORK, January 28th, 1937.

IN ANSWERING REFER TO NO. 5962

EXTRACT FROM MATRICULA for the year 1912.

Eli Balgley was born July 8/15.

Dated Brzesa, November 1st, 1937.

Seal   Signature

A true translation.

A letter from the Legal Aid Bureau in New York in 1937, stating that July 8th is the correct date of my father's birth, but the year is incorrect, his actual birth year being, in fact, 1912. Courtesy Balgley Family Archive

-433
ev. 7/19/49

UNITED STATES DEPARTMENT OF JUSTICE
Immigration and Naturalization Service
1060 Broad Street
Newark, 2, N. J.

NSTRUCTIONS TO APPLICANTS FOR CERTIFICATES OF CITIZENSHIP UNDER THE PROVISIONS
OF SECTION 341 of the Immigration and Nationality Act.

Before executing your application read this sheet carefully; also read
he detailed instructions on the application Form M-600. Every question in
he application form must be fully answered to the best of your knowledge.

This application, photographs, and remittance for the sum of $5.00 as
pecified in the application, and documents to support the application, should
e mailed to the IMMIGRATION AND NATURALIZATION SERVICE, 1060 Broad Street,
ewark, 2, New Jersey, or brought to the Information Section of this office
t the above address.

DOCUMENTS REQUIRED

In general, a person who acquired citizenship at birth through the citizen-
hip of a parent, or parents, or who derived citizenship through the naturaliza-
ion of a parent, or parents, should submit the following documents;

1. Birth or baptismal certificate of the applicant.
2. Civil marriage certificate of the applicant's parents (if claiming
    through the naturalization or citizenship of ather, or the citizen-
    ship of both parents).
3. If parents were married prior to their marriage to one another,
    documentary evidence of the termination of any previous marriage of
    either parent.
4. If the applicant is a married woman, applicant's civil marriage
    certificate.
5. Birth certificate of father or mother if born in the United States.
6. Death certificate of person through whom you claimed to have acquired
    citizenship, if person is deceased.
7. Immigrant identification card, if in possession of one.

WHERE CITIZENSHIP IS CLAIMED BY A WOMAN THROUGH
HER HUSBAND'S NATURALIZATION OR CITIZENSHIP.

1. Official civil record of marriage to husband through whom citizenship
    is claimed.
2. Official civil records of any subsequent marriages of applicant.
3. Official civil record of termination of any previous marriage (s) of
    either the applicant or the husband through whom citizenship is claimed.
4. If marriage to the husband through whom citizenship is claimed has
    been terminated, official civil record of the termination.
5. Official civil record of the birth of the husband through whom citizen-
    ship is claimed, if he was born in the United States.

If you are not in possession of any of the required documents, it will
e necessary to communicate with the appropriate officials in charge of the
ecords where the events occurred.

If the required official records are not available, you must submit
ith your application a statement setting forth specifically which documents
ou are unable to obtain and why such records cannot be procured.

NJ-260)   (over)

Evidence required to prove citizenship. Courtesy Balgley Family Archive

-2-

A photostatic, photographic, or other acceptable copy of each document,
except naturalization papers, must be furnished if you desire the original
documents returned to you. If photostatic, photographic, or other acceptable
copies of documents are not received here at the same time with the original
documents, it will be taken for granted that you agree to have the original
copies become a permanent part of the records of this Service and they
will not be returned to you. Submit both the original documents and the
copies with the application and the originals will be returned to you when
they are no longer required. Do not submit with your application the certificates of naturalization through which citizenship is claimed. Do not make any
copy of a naturalization or a citizenship certificate inasmuch as the making
of such copies is unlawful.

Evidence required to prove citizenship. Courtesy Balgley Family Archive

BOARD OF EDUCATION·

OFFICE OF THE PRINCIPAL OF PUBLIC SCHOOL NO. ____71____

BOROUGH OF __Brooklyn__

____March 7,1940____ 19__

The following is a transcipt of the records as found
in P.S.71 Brooklyn

Name- Eli Balgley

Date of birth----1-12

Father's name-------Israel

Entered P.S.71 Brooklyn- 10-6-20

Transferred from P.S.71 Brooklyn 11-10-21

Very truly yours,

L.B. Cogin

L.B.Cogin
Principal

Evidence required to prove citizenship. Courtesy Balgley Family Archive

Documentary proof of my father's American citizenship from an attorney in New York, thereby proving his derivative citizenship. Courtesy Balgley Family Archive

Form AdS-367
(Rev. 3-10-53)

DEPARTMENT OF COMMERCE
BUREAU OF THE CENSUS
WASHINGTON 25

May 29, 1953

Re:

Ely Balgley

Fair Lawn, N. J.

The following information, including spelling of name, relationship, age, etc., is an EXACT COPY of the census record as reported by the census taker on the original schedule.

Census of __1930__, taken as of _____April 1_____

_____101 Rodney Street, Brooklyn_____

County _____Kings_____   State _____New York_____

Name	Relationship	Age	Place of birth	Citizenship
Bagley, Israel	Head		Poland	*Naturalized
- Sarah	Wife			
- Ely	Son	17	Poland	**Naturalized

*Year of immigration 1913
**Year of immigration 1920

Robert W. Burgess
Director
Bureau of the Census

The above information is furnished upon application with the understanding that in no case shall the information furnished be used to the detriment of the person or persons to whom the information relates, in accordance with Section 18 of the Act of June 18, 1929 (46 Stat. 25; 13 U.S.C. 218).

dg

The Bureau of the Census does not issue birth certificates, but this record is often accepted in place of one.

U. S. GOVERNMENT PRINTING OFFICE : 1953—O—243200

Evidence required to prove citizenship. Courtesy Balgley Family Archive

117—Blank Affidavit.   6 K. 8 H D   JULIUS BLUMBERG, INC., LAW BLANK PUBLISHERS
71 BROADWAY AND 1 RECTOR ST., NEW YORK

State of New York,
County of...........*Bronx*...........} ss.

.........*Mrs. Sarah Goldberg*.........being duly sworn, says that

a) *She resides at 964 Tiffany St. Bronx, Apt. 8*

b) *Kobryn (Poland) is her birthplace and
she was born on Jan. 21, 1890.*

c) *She arrived in the United States in 1913*

d) *She is a cousin of Sarah Balgley and
a second cousin of Ely Balgley.*

e) *She was present at the wedding of
Israel Balgley and Sarah Feye Slomiansky
which took place in 1907 in Kobryn
(Poland).*

Sara Goldberg

Sworn to before me, this.........................day }
of.........................193 }

*Proof of Ely's parents' marriage in 1907 in Kobrin: verbal testimony
of my father's relative Sarah Goldberg, in support of his request for
certification of citizenship. Courtesy Balgley Family Archive*

The misplaced proof of my grandfather Israel's citizenship. If my father had been in possession of these documents, he would have been spared much worry and his longtime search for proof of his own citizenship between 1937 and 1953. Courtesy Balgley Family Archive

There are actual file numbers on these documents. All I can think is: can I pick up the trail from here? The 1953 letter from the Soviet Union which says my father's documents have been "disposed of," I do not trust. I lived in communist Poland long enough to know that responses like these were regularly provided just to get rid of people.

I paused, though, because we had always celebrated my father's birthday on June 27, so I asked him about the July 8 date. He shrugged and laughed a little, explaining that he had asked his father the date of his birthday, and his father had told him to count back seven days from the date of the *bris*, the date on which is recorded. But it then seemed the *bris* and birthdates were reversed, confused or misremembered, so my father had done his best to designate the day of his birth. And then the poignancy of it struck me: what age is a child when he asks his father the date of his birth? Suddenly a recollection flashed through my mind: my father commenting that once as a little boy when his family was living in Brooklyn, he and his older brothers went across the street to the empty house of neighbors who had just moved. The neighbors had left behind some items that made the boys curious, as they had never seen anything like them before. My father concludes his brief tale, "We at last realized that these must be toys." The child who does not know his birthday, who cannot recognize toys—these described my father. With my father's permission, when my older sister arrived at his apartment, I tried to summarize what I have seen and learned. She turned to him and said: "So Dad, your birthday isn't really June 27th?" I had to smile. My sister had always been the planner of all family celebrations, and she needed to adjust to the fact that for all those years we had been celebrating on the wrong day. But I was thinking that somehow he felt embarrassed by all this—maybe it was uncomfortable, even painful to remember why he would not have known his true birthdate. My question was of a different kind, "Why did you desire proof of your citizenship in 1937 when you were 25 years old?" He told me his father had misplaced his own naturalization papers and that because his mother and he and his three siblings all had derivative citizenship, there was really, in my father's mind at least, no proof of his. This is the reason he gave me. It is plausible. But what forces made him feel he needed proof, I wanted to ask, but in the end I did not ask him. It had been enough for one day. I asked if I could borrow the file to make photocopies. He paused for a moment, then agreed, but stated emphatically, "This original file returns here and stays with me!" Still secret.

My father did get his proof: the last document in the file is a photograph of him in his 40s stapled to a certificate of sorts which calligraphically states that he is, indeed, a citizen of the United States of America. And I think of the biography written recently on the occasion of his 100th birthday for his residence's newsletter, wherein he reports that his birthplace was "Brooklyn, New York." When I remarked on it, my sister held with her old opinion, "He wanted to protect us, his family." Fair enough. But why did he continue the untruth at that stage of his life? Perhaps he got so accustomed to his story that this version was automatic. Maybe. But it was also undeniable that he disdained his origins. It was unseemly for me to keep blaming him for passing—he was too old, too fragile. Yet he remembered that file, and he remembered, too, that it had been for his eyes only, and insisted that proof remained within his ready reach.

Even if it provided information my family had never known, the file raised questions that for me were at the heart of the secrecy with which I had been raised: what had incited him at the age of 25 to have written proof of his citizenship? It was 1937 and I recalled that American anti-Semitism had increased in the 1930s. Father Charles Coughlin, the Catholic priest and radio preacher, regularly condemned the Jews in his broadcasts; Henry Ford reprinted *The Protocols of the Elders of Zion* in his newspaper; right-wing American groups connected the Depression, the New Deal, President Roosevelt, and the possibility of war in Europe with their invented Jewish international conspiracy. The New Deal became the "Jew Deal" based on the belief that Jews controlled Roosevelt's administration. An opinion poll taken in the mid-1930s indicated that more than half of the American population believed that Jews held too much power in the United States, that they were dishonest and greedy; a poll in 1939 showed that 53 percent of Americans believed that "Jews are different and should be restricted." Some 10 percent were in favor of deporting Jews from America. I wondered how much my father had suffered as a consequence of that thinking. But more: given that our family regularly discussed prejudice and oppression, what prevented him later in life from referring to his own experience? What kept him telling anyone who asked even then that his birthplace was in the United States? It seemed to me that in those answers lay the reasons that throughout my life had contributed to an atmosphere of anxiety, omnipresent but not to be acknowledged.

I knew, though, those answers would not come easily, if they ever would come at all. Maybe it is true, as a friend of mine likes to say, "the truth will not set you free." Still: there was this astonishing artifact in my hands, something actual, concrete evidence of the past my father had kept from me. It might not be possible to mend the anxiety I had inherited, but there was a gift, a chance to get at least the facts of a repressed story straight. The quaint office of the "Starost" in Poland would be no more, but maybe the records were saved. The letters that had informed my father that the Brześć of Poland had become the Brest-Litovsk of the Soviet Union was by now the Brest of Belarus. I needed to go there in search of the records that might still exist.

VIII

Brest and Grodno 🌳 The Trees

Behind curtains
Cork City, Ireland, en route to Brest, Belarus, 2012

It was the fall. I had been in West Cork, Ireland, for some weeks, and now the time had arrived for my departure to Belarus. It happened that the day I was departing Ireland first to Poland and then on to Belarus was the time changed throughout the world—well, almost throughout the world. I learned that Lukashenko, Belarus's president and the last dictator in Europe, had decided not to change the clock in his country in solidarity, it was presumed, with Russia and Mr. Putin. There was always a one-hour difference in time between Ireland and Poland, but I was wondering if the departure and arrival times on my plane ticket purchased months before represented the old time or the new time changes. With a few phone calls, I ascertained that the departure time of my flight from Cork city, Ireland to Warsaw, Poland reflected the new time change, so I planned accordingly to make my trek from Bantry Bay in the southwest of Ireland to Warsaw, where I would spend one night and then catch the very, very early train east to Brest, Belarus, my father's birthplace. Months earlier, I had obtained my visa to Belarus by paying per day of visit and demonstrating in advance that I had booked a hotel for each day. This used to be the way one visited Poland in the communist days, so I knew what I could expect in Belarus, though now a "free" republic, to be less free than advertised. For the first time in my travels, the visa was a metallic chip in my passport, rather than the now outmoded stamp. The chip was shiny and heavy, and gave heft to my passport, a reminder to me of the novelty of my destination. The train tickets were inscrutable enough as it was, but with the time change, I was still wondering if I would make my connections.

Bus Eireann left from the front of a pub in the small County Cork town of Bantry at 3:30 p.m., but if you were unfamiliar with that place of departure, that was your bad luck. I knew, so I was among the Irish headed for Cork city—a two-hour bus ride. Because my mother and her family had the surname O'Hara, I had always identified with their Irish origins. I grew up with a reverence for Ireland, particularly Roman Catholic Ireland with its history of oppression and martyrdom. Long before I ever visited Ireland, it was an emotional touch point for me, and the years I have spent visiting there have never disappointed that connection with the Irish people, though the Roman Catholic allegiance has been destroyed. The revelation of the Irish Church's collusion with the

British to keep the Irish poor and powerless, the world Church's historical anti-Semitism, and the recent uncovering of long hidden child sexual abuse had cured me of any romantic notions I once had about the Church's moral responsibility to her Irish adherents. But the lyricism I had associated with the people—first through the Irish literature I studied as an undergraduate, and then later in person during my long stays in Ireland—this had never changed. That national personality was matched by, at least in my mind, the physical landscape of West Cork—yes, "the terrible beauty," if clichéd, was always spot-on for me.

As I waited for the bus outside the pub on that fall afternoon, I could see Bantry Bay, just a few hundred feet away from where I stood. The days had grown short and the sky over the bay darkened with oversized slate clouds threatening rain but also an early nightfall. The clouds nearly touched the gray white-tipped waves on the bay, and a wind presaging winter blew over the group of us huddled in the shelter of the pub's awning. The bus ride from Bantry to Cork City always afforded spectacular views of the countryside, but those were brief that day, and soon we made our way in complete darkness.

Our arrival at the Cork city bus station reminded me immediately of that other side of the Irish physical scene: gray, gritty, dusty, worn out and worn down—both the place and the people—the cityscapes of Ireland. I had only a half hour to wait before I caught the next bus leaving Cork city bus station to deliver me to Cork Airport. All memory of the pastoral landscape of rural Ireland had dissipated then and felt like a dream or a figment of the imagination even. My head was already fixed on Warsaw, which though only two-and-half hours by plane from Cork, might as well be in another solar system in a time warp.

The flight from Cork to Warsaw left at 8:55 p.m. I was in the boarding lounge at the gate when a 30-something fellow struck up a conversation with me. Well, not really a conversation, as I saw quickly that he was beyond drunk and wondered if the airline would allow him to board. He was Polish and pretty much out of control. He did have a companion, another Pole of the sort who really is a type in Poland, one that I came to know when I lived there-- pale, bespectacled, nervous, dressed in a fashion from twenty years ago, out of his depth in this foreign place. He seemed not to be intoxicated, and that was good as he might have been able to assist his friend in getting onto the plane. Unfortunately, the drunken Pole, also a stereotype of the loutish peasant sort with a bull neck and loud voice, wanted to continue his "conversation" with me. I could escape this until we boarded the plane and found that he was seated next to me. The airline, "WizzAir," was anything but whiz-like in its efficiency, but I did manage to get a pretty, though flustered, Polish flight attendant to move me to another seat. The drunken Pole was not happy with this change, and bellowed his complaint in Polish for all on board to hear.

I was seated safely at a distance, though, and all I could think of was how that spectacle made me remember the sad alcoholic men I used to see from my high apartment window on Plac Grunwaldzki in Wrocław. They would stand in a line early before a shabby unmarked shop in the freezing snow to get their vodka early in the morning in the event that it would sell out. And I also thought of those who stood in parks and on streets bearing wounds on their faces because they had literally fallen on their faces drunk even in the early morning when I would make my way to teach at the university. There were many scenes that illustrated the hopelessness of Poland in those days, but drunken, lost men with their vacant stares seemed to me a universal mark of a culture that was broken; like the men in Black ghettoes in cities I knew in the United States, humiliated and emasculated fathers and sons signaled a society that had deprived its people of dignity and purpose.

Who knew that fellow's story—he hailed from the "New Poland," but despite the fact he could apparently afford a plane ticket, and unlike my Polish students in the 1980s, he was able to travel outside his country, but he was lost nonetheless. The flight was filled with crying babies and tired children, and those sounds too for me bridged Catholic Ireland to Catholic Poland, where families with young children were always a feature of travel.

I had updated my wristwatch since I knew Poland was always an hour ahead of Ireland, but then I thought I should back it up again because of the time change. Clocks report varying times. I thought how fitting the time confusion was as I returned to Poland, where everything the two years I lived there was the reverse, the opposite, the upside-down of American expectations. As we landed at Warsaw, I was able to ask the same pretty Polish flight attendant the correct time and she smiled at the question, and checking her watch, assured me it was just before midnight there in Poland—time change figured in.

Before I always arrived in Warsaw at Okęcie Airport—the only airport for years in Warsaw. My arrivals were always noisy and complicated, passport lines inexplicably slow, my luggage often lost. But this was a new airport, Modlin Airport, formerly a Russian air force base, which though at some distance outside central Warsaw, had offered me a better and quicker flight from Ireland. I stepped off the plane and felt some sort of welcome home— the smell, particularly—was that diesel? But already it looked like a different Poland from the one I had lived in; that shiny glass airport would have been as alien as a spaceship in Poland of the 1980s. We passengers were sleepy as we filed silently off the plane down the portable ladder. Deep in late fall, the air was crisp, but not cold, the sky black, a windless night. The only sound was the clicking of heels and wheels of luggage on the pavement. We were at some distance from the bright lights of the terminal entrance, so it was in relative darkness that we trudged, lugging our carry-ons. I noticed that we cast shadows, and looking up, I could see that the moon was full. Call it superstition, but that was for me another sign—not of welcome, but of warning: often in my solitary nights in the remote area of Poland where I spent my first year, when I would return to my apartment in its bleak block house after an evening with the new Poles I was meeting, I would stand at my window and hear again in my head the comments made in the discussion that night about the former Jews of Poland—some defensive, some cynically indifferent, some cold. It seemed the moon was always full on those nights, and I remember looking out to the illuminated woods beyond my window and thinking about who might have been hidden there. During those sleepless nights, the "banality of evil" presented itself and I realized it was fear I was feeling. I glanced down at my watch and saw that since I had set it to the time of destination as is always advised, it read midnight—the symmetry of the full moon matching the even hour on the circle of my wrist.

Passport control and baggage were then a cinch, and I had a pleasant exchange with the young Poles at the Modlin Airport transfer office—they reminded me of my former Polish students—who tried but could not find my paid reservation on the bus into Warsaw proper. The fellow in charge spoke unaccented English, and I commented on its precision to which he smilingly responded, "I cheated; I am Polish, but I'm from Canada." He charged me thirty złoty, about ten dollars—a reasonable amount for the ride into the city, though I momentarily recalled that ten dollars was approximately a week's salary for a Polish professor at the university when I lived in Poland. The bus, the "Modlin transfer," was visible from where I stood, and remembering the old Poland where plans always went awry, I worried that it would depart while they looked for my reservation. These young Poles reassured me, "No, no, not to worry, the driver has your name on his roster and will wait for you." A roster? A bus driver has my name? This is a new Poland. I also had had no opportunity to change my euro from Ireland or dollars from home to Polish złoty, so when I inquired, the Canadian Pole directed one of his colleagues to exchange my sixty American dollars for złoty. A service provided with a smile. I was amazed. Changing money in the former Poland was involved, and back then only a greenhorn would make the exchange official, since everyone relied on the black market.

I have not mentioned that I brought along a suitcase nearly as big as I was, and it was red. I normally pack light, but I had documents and notebooks and some books that I might need for the archive in Belarus, and so I had this huge and heavy, but necessary encumbrance. The young Poles saw this monster, and scooped up "big red" as I had come to refer to this annoying albatross, and carried it out to the bus and placed it in the luggage compartment. So pleasant! Don't misunderstand: Poland was one of the most courteous places I ever knew, but only in personal exchanges. I never had to schlepp my suitcase very far in Poland back in the 1980s before a man would tip his cap and pick it up for me. Or two women would help me. But those were personal gestures; when it came to institutions, they would actually enjoy causing you difficulty. These young Poles ask me when I lived in Poland. "Oh, 1987 to 1989." And they responded, "That was before I was born so I don't remember the 'bad old days'." History had overtaken me.

As I boarded the Modlin transfer bus, I had another surprise: the driver made his announcements in English as well as in Polish. I learned that the ride will take sixty minutes. Again, my timeframe was entirely confused. I thought it would be about fifteen minutes to the center of the city.

But the after-midnight ride had magic in it for me: by night from an enclosed comfortable space I saw the "new Poland"—lighted businesses, large modern factories, contemporary signs. I knew that capitalism had wreaked its own version of harm on Poland, but I could not fail to be inspired by the sheer brightness and largesse of the places I was seeing. Life in the last two years of the 1980s in Poland had made for a deadened landscape devoid of human activity. "No hope, no future," my students used to say. Now everything bespoke hope.

We had one stop before *Warszawa Centralna*, the main train station where *Pani* Zofia had years before stuffed me in the compartment. By then, it was 2 a.m. and the Modlin transfer bus had reached its destination. It felt like old Poland as the stopping place was inexplicably in a parking lot across from *Warszawa Centralna*, rather than at the station itself. But everyone seemed to understand and expected that as taxis were waiting. The taxi I took was so slick and the driver so well-groomed that again I had the culture shock of the new Poland. Thirty złoty from downtown Warsaw to my nearby hotel, Hotel DeSilva. I learned there were two Hotel de Silvas—a very Polish quagmire for the foreigner—but to my surprise I suddenly recalled that mine is on ul. Krakowska and off we went.

The driver had zero curiosity in his foreign passenger, another change from the old Poland. We rode through central Warsaw, the night was frosty, the same full moon I noticed on arrival, lighting the way. A clear night, huge silvered buildings, outsized I felt, like a modern St. Petersburg in proportions, but impressive nonetheless. I finally checked in at 2:20 a.m., and wearily remembering I left Bantry, Ireland at 3:30 p.m., I left a wake-up call for 5:30 a.m. I set the alarm on my iPhone, too, quite worried that I might miss the early morning train east to Belarus, but then I noticed that it had not adjusted to Polish time, so I became skeptical—of both the wakeup call and my own alarm. I did manage to hook up an adaptor that downsized the voltage (I did not know at that time that the phone would adjust to any voltage), along with the Polish electrical plug (not the same as Ireland's), so that I could charge my phone. The resulting image was a bit comical: plugs into plugs into plugs extending out from the wall like a series of miniature train cars. I slept immediately, but in that sort of sleep that knows wakefulness is soon to follow. So by the time my wakeup call came, and my phone had sung out, I was already showered, dressed and packed. That was a salutary thing as I thus had forty-five minutes before I would have to catch a taxi to the train station, so I would then have time for breakfast at the hotel.

Polish breakfast deserves a chapter (or more) of its own, but I will just say that I have never found one better in all the countries I have visited. A beautifully set buffet on linen offered radishes, several types of pickles and mushrooms, kielbasa cut on the bias, all variety of ham and sausage, salmon, herring, hardboiled eggs, freshly baked breads, some with caraway seed, my own favorite, fresh dill, light flaky pastries, homemade jams and excellent coffee—or freshly-brewed tea using tea leaves rather than a teabag. If none of that pleased, for no extra charge, scrambled eggs could be made to order. Even in the old Poland, despite shortages, breakfasts were almost always that good. I ate "for the day," not knowing when or if I would have the opportunity to eat again that day. When I had arrived, the hotel clerks had been grumpy in the way of service workers in the old Poland, but I then realized it was just a result of working the graveyard shift. After breakfast the friendly staff saw me off to my taxi.

A faint snow fell as I took the taxi to *Warszawa Centralna*. I was glad to learn that that ride was again thirty złoty, so I knew I was not being taken advantage of the night before. From the outside the train station looked mostly like it had when I lived in Poland, but when I entered I found a new world: bookstores, restaurants, coffee houses, music stores, even a Starbucks. I remembered an extinguished past, and it was a bit disorienting. Although I had purchased my train ticket before I left the United States, it was only with the help of a Polish friend in California that we together were able to decipher its instructions. This friend had said that not many Poles would ever be interested in traveling east. It was not difficult to understand this historically, but I was soon to experience why more directly.

Despite having my ticket in hand, I went to one of the station's many crowded counters to confirm its accuracy and to ask from which platform I would board this eastbound train from Warsaw. I was told this would be *peron* (platform) number 5. I found number 5, but only to learn at the last moment that the *peron* for my train was number 7. Some things had not changed from the old Poland.

The train I boarded resembled modern trains I had taken in Italy, for example, and was nothing like the trains I took for two years when I lived there. Very quietly it pulled into the station, a silent silver snake, featuring large glass windows and easy to negotiate steps from the platform to the train car. There did not seem to be compartments like the ones I used to know—dark, curtained cubicles behind windowed doors off the train's corridors. Instead, there were large, airy spaces, with clean and comfortable blue reclining seats. Even the air seemed blue as I sat there; the light streaming in from the nearly all-glass sides of the train, washed the interior so that it felt like we were sitting outside under the sky.

I took a seat by the window and noticed that the sun had come out. The snow that fell the night before was then lit by this sunshine and along the route the frozen branches and tall grasses appeared crystalline as the light hit them. A cloud appeared like a huge white Rohrschach snowflake in the sky. The first sign for me of "the East" was a stop called "*Minsk Mazowiecki.*"

Minsk Mazowiecki, the first stop on my train journey east from Warsaw. Courtesy Balgley Family Archive

I checked my train schedule. We were to be at that stop at 8:05 a.m.—it was then 8:20 a.m.—we are just slightly late.

I visited the WC and discovered that it was one holdover from the old Polish trains—dirty and odorous—and it brought to mind a train experience I had had in the old Poland. My first trip out of communist Poland during my Fulbright was to West Berlin. Even at that early stage (I had been living in Poland for four months), I had already grown accustomed to the deprivation and brokenness in Poland, so the glittering storefronts, merchandise and produce, the smooth roadways and high-end restaurants were a culture shock. I had with me a lengthy list of medicines needed by Polish friends unavailable in

Poland and easily purchased in West Berlin. I was traveling with an American colleague, also a Fulbright in Poland. She and I planned to visit the huge commissary at the American Army base in Berlin, and I wanted to purchase a portable Olympic electric typewriter, a luxury item in that pre-computer era. At the army base, my friend and I noticed a Burger King restaurant, and thought it would be a kick to have this all-American meal. After our repast, we departed the army base to take in other parts of West Berlin, and finally went to our hotel to sleep—we were catching an early Sunday morning train the next day back to Poland since we had to teach at our respective universities on Monday morning.

I woke in the night as ill as I had ever been (and as ill as I have ever been since). Sweating and freezing, the room was spinning for me in the darkness. Not wanting to wake my friend who was sound asleep in an adjacent bed, I managed to rise from my bed, hold on to the room's walls, to make my way to the bathroom. I spent the rest of the night on the bathroom floor. In the morning, my friend told me I had food poisoning, and I knew she was right. She was also right in realizing that the poisoning had come from the Burger King adventure, ironic since we Fulbrighters had been warned over and over about how food in Poland could make us ill—citing Chernobyl, among other causes. But in my experience the food in Poland was excellent and never made me ill in the least.

Weak and sick, I could hardly stand up straight, but I had to pack and get on the train. I was expected to be in my classroom in Poland within twenty-four hours, and besides, who knew when the next train east was scheduled? My friend helped me carry my bag, now extra heavy with medicines and the typewriter. All I can remember about the train trip back to Katowice was the WC on the train where I spent most of the entire trip—essentially a hole in the floor, splattered and reeking. I tried to brace myself against a wall as the rusted old train moved over the uneven tracks. Somehow I made it off the train, got a taxi (my friend had continued on to Poznan where she lived and taught), and climbed the fourteen flights of stairs to my flat with my heavy bag. I did make it to class the next morning, but I have not forgotten that train's WC. And despite the elegant appointment of the train on which I was now traveling, the WC was reminiscent.

As I looked out at the late October snow, I reminded myself that I was traveling the reverse route my father, his siblings and mother traveled as they made their way from Brest to Warsaw in a horse-drawn wagon during the month of September some ninety years previously. As I looked at the snow,

I wondered was their departure month planned because decent weather was expected? And how cold they must have been, snow or not, traveling in the open air for days and nights on end, making their way to the capital.

But cold was commonplace for them. I called to mind my father's description of their shtetl dwelling—slatted wood with no insulation—only a large pot over a fire that sat between his family's quarters and those

Snow-covered tracks on my train journey from Warsaw to Brest in 2012. Courtesy Balgley Family Archive

of the other family, who entered from the same front door. That was their heat. I recalled my Uncle Morris telling me that shoes were difficult to come by. Did they have warm shoes for the trip west? And then a recollection from my own adolescence: my father had always been temperamental about the heat in the houses I grew up in. I guess his explanation was avoiding wasted energy and expense and safety, and now I think perhaps he was ahead of his time, ecologically speaking. He kept the temperature low, and I often complained that I was freezing, to which he would respond, "Put on a sweater," or "Young girls have poor circulation." He insisted that no one but himself should ever touch the thermostat in the house. One night, I wore heavy socks and mittens to bed, but I never touched the thermostat.

I surveyed the frozen landscape between Siedlce and Łuków. The light was lessened and the pale shadow of the sun seemed itself almost frozen still in the wan sky, the opposite to the hard, clear, cold, full moon of the previous night.

The evergreen trees made me think of a painting by Jacob Balgley, the Paris-based artist I had learned about from my student at UCLA and then again from my cousin David in New York. In that painting a father stands protectively behind his small child, and the two are surrounded by a forest of evergreens.[10] The trees outside my window and the ones in the painting were symmetrical and stood in groups, like families themselves. No wonder my father was so connected to trees. They were his companions here. I think of his boyhood exit from Brest surrounded by those trees. And I think of the Jewish families and the Jewish partisans who hid in the forests.

We passed a sign with a logo of a stylized bison, but too swiftly for me to see what it announced. We could not have been far from the famous Białowieża forest, only 43 miles north of my father's birthplace—the remainder of the huge primeval forest that once covered the European plain. The European bison, or wisent, had lived in the forest for centuries, surviving hunters and poachers, sometimes protected by czars. The forest had been ravaged in World War I when for three years the German army hunted the animals. In 1939 the forest's local inhabitants of Polish ethnicity were deported to the far reaches of the Soviet Union, and by 1941 the forest was occupied by the Nazis. Göring had planned to make the forest into the largest hunting ground in the world. During the war, it was a base for Jewish, Polish and Soviet partisans, as well as for Jewish families in hiding. The Gestapo held mass executions in the forest, and some graves are still visible. When the Soviet Union broke apart in 1991, the forest was divided between Poland and Belarus, and is now protected by UNESCO. I think of the woods of my childhood—how my father always chose houses surrounded by forest, and how the trees offered me companionship and refuge.

I returned from those recollections to the dense woods on either side of the train track. Suddenly, a stunningly beautiful clearing revealed itself—a crystallized meadow of ice and sunlight. The perimeter of the meadow was studded with large stately evergreens weighted down with snow, appealingly shaggy. We passed some dwellings with newish-looking tin roofs, wine and green-colored. We pass through Biała Podlaska, the train station formerly white and elegant, now in bad shape—worn down and worn out.

At last we were nearing Terespol, the Polish city on the border with Belarus. That was where I had to change trains to go to Brest. I remembered the name Terespol, but why? And then I realized it was the town in I. B. Singer's *The Family Moskat* where the young Jewish protagonist came from to study in Warsaw.

My first glimpse of Terespol from the train window was the sight of police in military dress on the platform. The place looked like a corny movie featuring Russian commandants, but it really looks like that. Our fancy train looked out of place in that nineteenth-century setting. On arrival the passengers rushed off the train, unnecessarily it seemed, racing to the one small open door. Everyone pushed. I see a sign, "*Bilety,*" tickets, and although I already had mine, I figured that way I would learn what platform I had to get to. Instead of a line at the ticket booth, there was a mob of people pushing, several people at a glass window all at once. I saw a pretty, fashionably blue-jeaned young woman who reminded me of my daughter and asked for her help. She smiled warmly, took the handle of my suitcase, told me (in Polish) that she was from Brest. I was struck by her contemporary appearance. I suppose without being conscious of it, I foolishly pictured going to Brest as time travel back to my father's days there. She spoke to the ticket booth lady for me, and the ticket booth lady glanced up quickly at me (she was being supplicated from several people at once), and giving me a friendly nod when she heard me speak Polish to my new young guide, said to me, "*Zaraz*," "soon." It is odd how one falls into tribalism so quickly; because she was Polish and saw that I could speak it, I trusted that she would take care of me, not letting me miss my train. The ticket I showed was stamped—what for, I did not know and the lovely young girl insisted on continuing to help me with my suitcase. But it soon became clear she was not going to Brest on that trip so she took me from the ticket booth up more stairs to where I needed to be and took her leave of me, wishing me a good stay in her town.

I saw what appeared to be an information desk of sorts. A female officer of some unclear sort sat at a table that resembled an oversized child's school desk. She was yelling at passengers who queued in a line to speak with her. I did not know what they needed from her. I paused for a moment just to inquire from her if I was proceeding in the right direction. She gestured incomprehensibly to some high arched doorways, but I was not sure which one was right. I hesitated for a moment and then she screamed at me in Russian (or maybe Belarusian, I do not know) in what I took to mean, "There it is! Go! Get out of here!" I took my chances and chose one of the arched doorways. A weary looking middle-aged man was in this corridor, so I asked simply, "Brest?" and pointed down the hall. He nodded. He and I appeared to be the only people in that huge hallway, and as we walked along, me with my huge red suitcase mercifully on wheels, it seemed we were two insects or perhaps rodents, dwarfed as we were by the massive dirty tunnel.

And the tunnel was maze-like, subterranean, freezing. Again, pointless steep concrete steps up and then down again appear at intervals, irrationally overbuilt and difficult to negotiate. We were walking for at least fifteen minutes and it was exhausting pulling the suitcase up and then down these gratuitous steps. It must have been that the place had been built over and over again as cheaply as possible, so the steps may have been installed to make the "renovation" more quickly and cheaply. I wondered where and when that tunnel would end, when at last I saw some light from an outside source streaming wanly from a doorway above me, and a long, steep set of broken concrete steps up to what my fellow walker nodded was for the train to Brest. Pulling the suitcase up the steps was a trial, but with a rest in the middle, I struggled up to the icy, gray platform. Again, a movie set: two identical train officers in military uniform, clichéd caricatures of Soviet officers from western films. These were female officers who appeared military-like, but they worked for the railway. Perhaps they worked for the government? The fact that it was ambiguous added to their intimidation capacity. What power did they have, if any, one wondered? Looking like those corpulent nesting Russian dolls, those women were dotted all along the platform. Heavyset, thick-necked, uniformed with severe short matching haircuts, they ignored me until I took a photo of the sign "Terespol," Uh, Uh, UH! I was told. *"Przepraszam, rozumiem,"* ("Sorry, I understand"), I responded, but realized the second I had said it, that speaking Polish might alienate them further from me. Wagging her finger at me, the guard repeated, *"Granitsa"* (Russian for "border") several times in explanation as to why I should not have photographed the sign. I had already done so. Then she demanded, *"Bilet."* This I had, and wondered for a moment why I had to go through passport control on arrival to Terespol—it was, after all, still in Poland. Should the passport control have been at Brest where I would enter Belarus?

Boarding the train at Terespol: the gap between platform and steep steps onto the train could not really be minded, as it was more of an abyss. A running start might have helped to get one over the barrier, but of course, no one can have done that with a suitcase, and "big red" was heavy, loaded with books and papers and notebooks. I finally needed to squat, get underneath the suitcase from one end, push that end to a resting place on the threshold of the train, forming a sort of suitcase bridge, and then pushed with my back, using legs and shoulders to slide the suitcase up the steps, so I could myself step onto the train stairs. That was achieved in a humiliatingly awkward fashion (though likely comical—think the Laurel and Hardy moving the piano movie). The Russian dolls tilted slightly in my direction just for a moment to glance at my hardship, and seemed to snigger, or did I only imagine that? In any case, their

The forbidden border photograph. Courtesy Balgley Family Archive

authority seemed to have been confirmed by that scene, and I was allowed to get on my train without further comment from them.

On the train: my first impression was that it was not a train but rather the interior of some old office building. Wooden benches, the type you might see in a railway station or even outdoors in a public space, were bolted to the steel floor. The windows were cut in half horizontally by dirty, pink curtains, the sort that you might associate with American bathrooms of the 1950s—ruffled and ugly. Why the curtains, I wonder? To block out the view? To block out vision of any kind? To keep behavior "under control" in this steel cubicle? Or just the opposite: to insulate the inhabitants from the intrusive,

Train from Terespol to Brest with the curtains that block an outside view. Courtesy Balgley Family Archive

cold world of a dictatorship? Curtains, pink or iron, close off for sure. I parted them slightly, gingerly, because they looked not to have been washed in decades—just to have a bit of the outside world to see, to orient by, to think on. But I realized that I had a flash of fear that I would be punished somehow for doing so. Everyone looked miserable, solemn. I thought of the man in the tunnel with me, head down, trudging to this platform. I suddenly recalled that he had replied, "Da" to my query; yes, this was another country. My ticket was checked by a Russian doll on board now for the fifth time as we sat on the train.

Everyone sat mutely on the train. I was now truly worried that I had not understood the time change and that my guide awaiting in Brest would tire of waiting and leave. We sat for longer. There was no obvious reason why— except that no one would question the authority of the Russian dolls or other uniformed "officials." Then finally after an hour or more of going nowhere, the train lurched, and I thought at least we would be underway. It lurched a moment, then stopped; everyone around me was gathering parcels—we had arrived. Brest is just minutes from Terespol. So the wait had no meaning in terms of distance. Instead, since Brest links the European Union and the Commonwealth of Independent States, a break-of-railtrack gauge occurred, where the Russian broad gauge met the European standard gauge. Thus it was necessary for all passenger trains coming from Poland (or elsewhere in Europe) to replace the wheels of their undercarriages (what the British call "bogies") to cross the border from Terespol to Brest. I had experienced this once before when I was on the Fulbright in Poland, and traveled with my students from Katowice to Vilna, but I had forgotten about the railroad track change. So the wait here in Terespol included the time it took to move all freight out of train cars of one gauge to cars of another gauge. I later heard that parts of the Brest railyards had been contaminated by radioactive materials during the Soviet period.

Top image: "Official" photograph of Brest train station.

Below: Under construction when I visited. Courtesy Balgley Family Archive

Julija, Maxim, Alexei
Brest, Belarus, 2012

We arrived at the Brest train station. An imposing, white marble structure, the station stood in contrast to the shabby train, though it was clear that the building had suffered losses since the days of its former majesty. The building was being repaired and appeared to have been scaffolded for a long time. That reminded me of "remont," the term I saw regularly and everywhere displayed in communist Poland, indicating "renovation"—a renovation that was never finished. It will be the same, I thought, here in totalitarian Belarus. I found myself wondering if my father as a boy knew that place. I noticed ugly, out-of-place black statues that had been added onto the delicate white marble façade—emblems of the Soviet period there. As I moved to exit the train, through a window I saw on the outdoor platform a huge fur hat on a young woman in uniform, yet another kind of uniform, so many "officials," whose functions remained unclear to everyone, I think, not just me, the foreigner. There was then the scramble and scraping of the crowd trying to disembark from the train. For such a large structure, the train station had only two small entrances, what might have been sufficient 100 years ago when the place was built. But just then the crowd was a huddled mass of people burdened with parcels, all pushing to get past the next person to reach the entrance first. No one made eye contact with anyone else in the crowd. I had seen this before in communist Poland: people who would have displayed the utmost manners in their homes, for example, metamorphosed into bullies in a crowd. Somehow that mass had to become linear to fit through the door, and everyone fought for position. I saw one young man carrying three baby strollers, shrink-wrapped but still massive, in addition to his other luggage and packages. Another woman pulled a wire mesh tote of sorts filled with what appeared to be packages of dripping raw meat. I tried to glide by with big red, but there was plenty of pushing and bumping. Again, I grew accustomed to that in the old Poland, so I managed.

Through the entrance at last, I had the chance to look at the stunning elegance of the place—marble floors and walls, bronzed clocks—so at odds with the masses filling the place. Down now through a squeezed corridor—ah—yes, passport control into Belarus. I was prepared, having paid for each day of my stay months in advance through the Belarusian Consulate in Washington, D.C.

It was now my turn to approach the glass box to have my visa and passport inspected. For a moment I thought this would be easier, more efficient than in the pre-microchip days, since the chips would be scanned and the traveler's entrance already vetted. A blond woman, quite young, but looking older than her years with dark circles under her eyes, hair pulled back in a tight ponytail, and wearing the ubiquitous uniform, as well as a bored and annoyed expression, took my passport through the small hole. She inspected each page, looking up at me poker-faced at intervals. She presented me with a document smaller than an index card and asked me to sign in three places. I had no idea what that was for, and I also knew I would not find out. Once I had signed, she stared at my signatures, and holding up one finger indicating I should wait, departed her cubicle. I reminded myself to remain calm and to fix my face in what I imagined was a neutral expression. I did notice that she had gone around a corner and was showing my passport and the index card documents to older men in uniform. I turned my head just to my right slightly and saw them looking at me. I heard the word "*podpis*" which in Polish means "signature" and maybe also in Russian, so I theorized that the young passport clerk was questioning whether my recent signatures really matched the one in my passport: in short, was I pretending to be who I was not? The older uniforms shook their heads in the negative to her, and she returned to the cubicle and allowed me to pass.

The crowd was very thick again and I saw that suitcases and packages had to be x-rayed before passengers were allowed through the next set of tiny doors which led out into what then felt like a reprieve or freedom. Suddenly a tall uniformed man came towards me and asked, "*Amerikanets?*" He actually smiled. "Da," I replied. He took big red, moved past the queue, turned back to beckon me to follow, which I did, until the suitcase was whisked through x-ray and I was delivered to the friendly, intelligent face of a stout blonde woman about my age holding a sign on which my name was typewritten in a very large font. She had positioned herself at the front of a crowd of people mashed together awaiting the arriving passengers. And she smiled—at me, and at the officer who had led me to her—it seemed quite clear she had "arranged" that he find me and pull me from the masses to bring me to her.

How can I describe Julija? She was so many things at once. The first impression I had was of an extremely energetic, capable, in-charge, reliable sort of individual. This might suggest an uptight or rigid person. But that was not Julija in the least. Her face was soft, her smile genuinely warm, her manner calm yet canny—she was a veteran of managing her difficult society, that seemed clear. Still there was no visible frustration or bitterness—she just did what had to be done—like getting to the head of the crowd waiting for arriving passengers—without letting it ruffle her. It really was possible to gather this just on first sight. She was about my age, 60-ish, her hair colored a fashionable platinum, wearing a warm beige double-breasted coat about the same color as her hair. She had the wide florid face and clear blue eyes one would associate with the Belarussian look. Stout, yet spry, she took my hand in both of hers and introduced herself, as she moved me out of the doorway, away from the pressing crowd into a place of relative clearing. I then noticed a sort of shadow presence behind her—I was not sure if that person accompanied her or just happened to be there. A tall man of indeterminate age in blue jeans with a five o'clock shadow and a cigarette in his hand, he stood back deferentially from Julija and me. His stance and dress—the blue jeans, a black windbreaker and tennis shoes—gave him a youthful look. Yet there was something about him that seemed prematurely old. The slight beard was matched by his thinning hair so that there appeared to be a circle of unbroken gray around his face and head.

The eyes were a pale blue and seemed to suggest a former bygone brightness. Once in the clearing, Julija introduced Alexei, who she explained, would be our driver. He quickly emitted a puff of smoke over his shoulder as if to keep it from us, and all at once at attention, his body rearranged itself from its casual attitude to a formal one, he nodded and smiled—actually he bowed slightly. With Alexei's sudden movement, I was reminded of the traditional way Polish men greet women: Alexei did not kiss my hand, but his bearing recalled the chivalric tradition of the aristocratic men of Poland. Later, I learned much more about Alexei and none of it could have been guessed at first meeting.

As Alexei lead us to his late model vehicle, Julija was already making plans with me to do the work I came for and for which she was hired. I was impressed at her eagerness. She explained that if we went directly now to the Brest State Archive, we would have at least a half day start on the research, since it was open until late afternoon. She took my arm as we walked quickly towards the car. Alexei was as cool behind the wheel as he was in his general bearing—an excellent, effortless driver in the busy and narrow streets of Brest, he had us at the State Archive in minutes. Things were moving so rapidly that I hardly had a chance to take in the surroundings. We passed a large sports stadium which Julija told me was the former site of the Jewish cemetery in Brest. Although she stated this matter-of-factly, her facial expression conveyed distaste at what had happened to the cemetery, and I think, a hint of resignation.

Alexei dropped us off at the main entrance to the State Archive, a building that, unlike the train station, had no personality whatsoever. Plain beige brick and steel, its architecture late 1940s Stalinist. We were first met by two female clerks at desks stationed in the foyer of the building. They eyed us skeptically if not suspiciously, and again like the too many uniformed workers at Terespol and Brest train stations, I was struck by the redundancy of their presence. I was also reminded of a trip during my Fulbright to the (then) Leningrad with my students from Poland: on every floor of the outsized hotel, a uniformed woman (and it was always a woman) sat at a desk, a desk that looked like a slightly oversized child's school desk, with nothing on top save a clunky, black telephone visibly connected by a thick metal cord to the wall. As a hotel resident, one was supposed to check in and out with her, dropping off and picking up keys. Beyond that, there was no ostensible reason for her to sit there, but that round-the-clock presence undermined any feeling of privacy a guest might have, and gave the intimidating feeling that your comings and goings were being monitored. A stern matron who held you to a curfew. Those two in the lobby of the State Archive gave the same impression. An oft-repeated joke in communist Poland suggested that every office needed one worker to do the job and another to stir the tea. In other words, since communism promised full employment, the state would camouflage the truth by assigning two people (or more) to one job.

One of the State Archive women who stood just to the side of her schoolroom desk actually was stirring tea in a glass. At our appearance, she rather leaned into her colleague sitting at the other desk, and lifting her gaze to us, murmured something to her co-worker inaudible to us. Julija made no sign of noticing any of this, and instead moved with alacrity to the counter behind which the desks stood and (in Russian, so I do not know the words she used) explained that we had an appointment in the archive and were expected. I did not know if she chose her words carefully, but I noticed the tone, a tone that would become characteristic of all Julija's dealings on my behalf with bureaucracy: her face was poker, not cold, but not friendly; the volume of her voice was quiet and moderately polite, but it suggested an authority and a knowingness that even a clerk looking to be an obstacle would be foolish to challenge. I stood silently in the background behind her, also neither smiling nor frowning. She impressed me no end. Within minutes we were allowed to pass through the foyer and up many flights of stairs. Julija was accustomed to such climbs; she moved ahead at full speed.

We entered a door on the sixth floor. Somehow I expected something grander, at least something larger. The room looked like an old-fashioned schoolroom and made me think of school classrooms from my childhood. There was room only for four tables, and each of those about the size of an American elementary school teacher's desk. There was florescent lighting overhead, and with a gesture to what grand libraries or archives would have, small lamps on each table. The lamps proved unnecessary as they did not add any needed light and took up too much space on the table once we got started. The walls were a sickly green, and I noticed curtains—curtains again as on the train—kitchen-like curtains that were out of place over office windows in this administrative place. But then I noticed lush and lovely climbing plants about the room, sitting on filing cabinets and running up the walls to the bit of light coming in where the curtains failed to entirely close. The plants were a surprise, and felt out of place in a different way than the curtains, something living among the dusty dead archives.

The clerks there were positioned behind a deep counter and greeted us with unsmiling faces. With a slight but polite nod to the clerks, Julija maintained her neutral expression, and quickly explained in Russian why we were there. The youngest of the clerks, who was in her 20s and had long dark luxurious hair to her waist, would have been pretty if she had smiled. On hearing Julija's explanation, she slowly rose from her desk and with a nearly visible stretch of ennui, she nodded her understanding and doled out dozens of sheets of the same form. I glanced at the form (written in Russian), and immediately realized that even requesting the records I wanted would be a complex operation. The only way I could describe the form was that it was requesting a bibliography of bibliographies. We had to provide lengthy lists of long serial numbers to even begin to find the place where my family's documents might be on the shelves behind the high off-limits counter. Records, I learned, were not stored by surname or alphabetized. And years did not help either. Fortunately, just before my departure, I had perused a website, "Routes to Roots," a corny name you might say, but it proved to be the most important source I could have consulted. An American, Miriam Weiner, created the site, and I only realized once I was into the depths of the research how exhaustive (and exhausting) her research was. Ms. Weiner had created the most important research tool for people looking for their Jewish ancestry—she was a heroine.

The starting place at the Brest Archive was the "fond" number—a numbered folder-like organizational system. Thinking it non-essential at the time before I left for Belarus, I had printed pages from Ms. Weiner's website which referred to the years I was researching. Little did I know then, that without Miriam Weiner's "fond numbers," I would not have even been able to start the research I had travelled so far to do. I had marked in yellow highlighter the fond numbers I guessed were pertinent, and Julija began the tedious process of handwriting a long list of serial numbers of these fonds. We knew that we would be requesting some, if not all, dead ends, but we had to start somewhere with the years and the type and hope for good luck. So for example, I ideally wanted to find my father's birth record in 1912 in Brest. Right away a blow: the Brest Archive only held records dating from 1920 on. My father left with his mother and siblings in 1920 so his birth record, or "metrics," as I learn it is referred to here, could not be in that archive. This was something I should have learned before I came, but no source I had seen told me that. Julija stopped working and for a moment gazed at my disappointed expression. She had a way from the start of showing her concern for my feelings, of registering her empathy, but then moving to the next best thing. Her reaction was contagious; we both know there had to be many Balgleys in Brest, and their records from 1920 on should be here. The clerks told Julija and she then told me that I would have to travel to the Grodno Archive to find records predating 1920. I readjusted quickly and forgot my disappointment. I could only worry about getting to Grodno, some 150 miles north of here, later on. For then, it was time to get to work and find what we could of my family in Brest from 1920 on.

Using the fond numbers, Julija completed the request form expeditiously, but it still took nearly two hours just to copy in the numbers for the clerks behind the counter. Given how much labor had gone into creating that request (and not just Julija's copying, but the months of my pre-departure research and the years before gathering what information I could from my father and my Uncle Morris), it was stunning how rapidly the clerks produced the fonds. It was a strange, surreal feeling to realize that the records of nearly a century of my family's life and annihilation in Brest could be stored behind that little counter, contained in that small anteroom, within easy reach of the very young, pretty and taciturn clerk.

The fonds looked like oversized heavy brown paper, folded in half vertically. They were handed over the counter to Julija and me—they were several and they were heavy. We plunked them down on a table. There were no other researchers in the room on that day, so I suggested we spread out to two tables. Julija vetoed this politely, and by now, I understood why. Don't overstep or even appear to overstep; things may not go well for you if you seem presumptuous. The two of us

I was stunned that so much information was still available in that Brest Archive in 2012, dating from 1920 and shedding light on my father's Jewish past. Courtesy Balgley Family Archive

huddled over the fonds on the one table and decided to quickly divide the piles—Julija could readily spot my surname written in Cyrillic Russian, and since I could not do that, I looked at the records written in Polish.

With only minutes, we are both finding records in our assigned stacks for "Balgley"—sometimes spelled as "Balglej" or "Balglei, as the English letter "y" becomes "j" in Polish. It was a bit overwhelming, and it took Julija to calm me down a bit. It became clear that she entirely comprehended why this was emotional for me, and she became as focused on this project as I was and as determined to get results. We had only known each other a few hours, but we were already full partners in our project. We were friends, in fact. But there was something more there: I murmured something about déjà vu to Julija. Her eyes widened at my remark, and for a second she grasped my arm and looked a bit—what to call it?—taken aback, awed, even scared, somehow. She said to me in her accented but otherwise perfect English, "I have been thinking the same and have shivers now."

I think immediately of that moment at my grandparents' Brooklyn apartment when as a child I felt that same inexplicable shiver. Destiny. Kismet. *Bashert.* We were always meant to meet there. And I was always meant to be there.

Samples of the documents Julija and I found follow here. There were applications for identity cards with testimony from another person to verify that the information provided was correct. Whether that was a foreboding prelude to the Brest Ghetto Passports was not yet clear. But what struck me as remarkable and poignant was the workaday quality of the transactions, of the everyday "normal" life those documents recorded: along with the architectural plans, there was an application for permission to demolish a fence in order to build a house; also an official document based on a hearing or an interrogation—most to do with a residence on "3-go Maja," "the Third of May Street, that being the date which commemorated the declaration of Poland's Constitution of May 3, 1791 (a holiday later delisted during the communist period in Poland). The dates on the documents indicated that those transactions were occurring right up to the time of their signers' annihilation. That the documents should survive in such pristine, retrievable form, while the people whose future plans they represented would have been murdered en masse, underscored the surreal quality of the very enterprise of that research-- people brutally wiped out in the very moment of improving their gardens and homes.

*In the Brest archive: original architectural drawings for the proposed
construction of a new home for a member of the Balgley family.
Courtesy Balgley Family Archive*

Members of the Balgley family (Chaim and Szejna) registered to confirm a change of address in 1936. Courtesy Balgley Family Archive

There was no time to ponder that further just then. Time was a precious commodity, since we both knew the archive hours were not long, and my visa did not allow me many days in Julija's country.

The first documents with my surname which we examined bore the title "Ghetto Passport." There was one document per person; astonishingly, there were literally dozens upon dozens bearing the name "Balgley," again variously spelt with a final "i" or "j." That stack of my relatives' files, I realized in a moment, could have been simply named the "Holocaust File." I had been standing over the table with the documents and I suddenly sat down hard. I felt my heart pounding and noticed my hands shaking. I registered that I felt nauseous. I had come a long way from the file marked "Citizenship" in my father's apartment to these files. I was about to unbury the murdered, and I was afraid. Julija looked over at me with her knowing and patient expression, with the characteristic readiness in her posture that suggested, "Yes, this is hard, and let's go at it." She was right; that was not the time to become faint-hearted: those people deserved to be remembered, and it was my place to record their bravery. I had no right to weakness then.

Each "Ghetto Passport" showed a photograph of a face. "Ghetto Passport"—what a euphemism—passport to hell. All have the Balgley surname; indicating many ages, from 6 to 96. The photographs—did the Nazis make them? Birthplace was listed along with parents' names. Also a street address. Julija commented briefly that she knew someone who was then researching the former addresses and houses of Jewish residents of Brest.[11]

Rec No	Name	Parents	Born	Passport Issued	Signature Info
55	BALGLEJ, Anna	Berels i Estera	1900	11 Nov 1941	Latin
76	BALGLEJ, Sura	Mordla i Fiejdla	1896	13 Nov 1941	Latin
501	BALGLEJ, Ewgenia	Chaim i Szejna	1917	12 Nov 1941	Latin
801	BALGLEJ, Szejna	Pinchos i iPesza	1888	11 Nov 1941	Latin
1309	BALGLEJ, Mariam	Ruwin i Gela	1924	17 Nov 1941	Latin
1894	BALGLEJ, Bejla	Berko i Pesza?	1882	16 Nov 1941	niepismienna
1909	BALKLEJ, Etla	Dawid i Rywa	1869	13 Nov 1941	niepismienna
1910	BALKLEJ, Jankiel	Ajzak i Chaja	1884	16 Nov 1941	Latin
1975	BALGLEJ, Rywka	Jankiel i Etla	1907	14 Nov 1941	Latin
3302	BALGLEJ, Szepsel	Josel i Gitla	1876	19 Nov 1941	Latin
3329	BALGLEJ, Sara	Bimszel? i Ruchla	1913	19 Nov 1941	Latin
3943	BALGLEJ, Estera	Josel i Cypa	1918	23 Nov 1941	Latin
4133	BALGLEJ, Josel	Izrael i bejla	1884	23 Nov 1941	Latin
4461	BALGLEJ, Cypa	Abram i Chaja-?	1888	24 Nov 1941	Cyrillic
5448	BALGLEJ, Pesia	Moszko i Basia	1901	17 Nov 1941	Cyrillic
7646	BALGLEJ, Basia	Jankiel i Pesza	1924	24 Nov 1941	Latin
7885	BALGLEJ, Motel	Josel i Sara	1927	25 Nov 1941	Latin
8042	BALGLEJ, Gita	Berko i Mirjam?	1898	13 Nov 1941	niepismienna
8059	BALGLEJ, Chaja	Szepsel i Bejla	1918	16 Nov 1941	Latin
9064	BALGLEJ, Rubin	Jankiel i Etla	1892	25 Nov 1941	Cyrillic
9091	BALGLEJ, Mojzesz	Rubin i Gela	1927	25 Nov 1941	niepismienna
9211	BALGLEJ?, Chaja	Szymon i Chisza	1912	26 Nov 1941	Latin
9474	BALGLEJ, Abram	Tewia i Chaja-Sura	1912	25 Nov 1941	Latin
10105	BALGLEJ, Dawid	Szymon i Ita	1927	27 Nov 1941	Latin
10203	BALGLEJ, Chana	Srul i Jenta	1922	1 Dec 1941	Latin
10235	BALGLEJ, Szimon	Abram i Ninda	1861	27 Nov 1941	niepismienna
10238	BALGLEJ, Sara	Josel i Cypa	1925	28 Nov 1941	Latin
10578	BALGLEJ, Leja	Berko i Mindla	1913	28 Nov 1941	Latin
11448	BALGLEJ, Liba	Jankiel i Pesia	1927	5 Dec 1941	Latin

My family members, Motel 14, Sara 16, among all my other family members, which I found listed in the Brest Ghetto Passport archive and pictured in the Protokols below. Document kindly provided by JewishGen.

14 year-old Motel Balgley applied for an identity card in 1941, the preliminary step to receiving a Ghetto Passport. Courtesy Balgley Family Archive

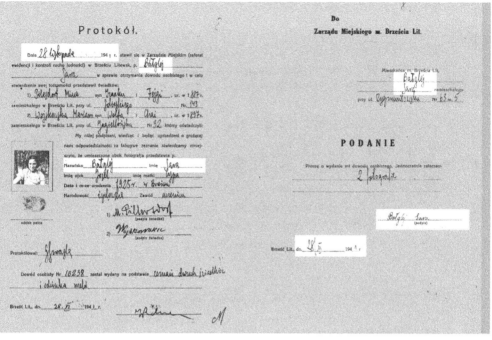

16-year-old Sara Balgley's application (as Motel's above). Courtesy Balgley Family Archive

Sprawdzenie danych, zawartych w projekcie budowy, albo przytoczo-
nych przez ubiegającego się o pozwolenie.

(art. 343 rozporządzenia z dn. 16 lutego 1928 r.)

Protokół

oględzin nieruchomości w Brześciu n.-B. przy ulicy _3go Maja_

pod Nr. _45_ , dokonanych dnia _20/VII_ 19 30 r. wskutek prośby _Jankiela_

Bałgleja o pozwolenie na budowę

Dnia _20/VII_ 1930 r. wskutek prośby _Jankiela Bałgleja_

z dn _14/VII_ 19 30 r. o pozwolenie na wykonanie _drewnianego partero-_
wego frontowego domu i drewnianych komórek

na nieruchomości, znajdującej się w Brześciu n.-B. przy ulicy _3go Maja_

pod Nr. _45_ , przy współudziale

rzeczoznawcy budowlanego _Arch. miejsk. Inż. A. Klearkiewskiego_

i w obecności _Etli Bałglej_

dokonał oględzin wspomnianej nieruchomości, w celu ustalenia, czy:

złożony przez _Jankiela i Etlę mał. Bałglej_ projekt odpowiada

rzeczywistemu stanowi rzeczy na gruncie

zawarte w podaniu _Jankiela i Etli mał. Bałglej_ dane odpowiadają rzeczywistemu stanowi rzeczy na gruncie

Przy oględzinach ustalono, że:

Obecny przy oględzinach _Etla Bałglej_ złożył następujące

oświadczenie: _że zastosuje się do zatwierdzonego planu._

Za niepiśmienną Etla Bałglej
podpisała Etla Bałglej

_A memorandum by a building inspector who visited the property of
Etli Bałgley on July 20, 1930 at her request and in her presence, to see
whether the project to expand the house at 3-Maja Street is viable and the
site conforms to the technical drawing in the documentation. A poignant
emblem of everyday lived life which was to come to a devastating end soon._
Courtesy Balgley Family Archive

An application for a passport in July 1930 by a Balgley. The writing here is not clear enough to retrieve a first name. Again, the value of these documents is that they show life caught in the heat of living, unaware of the catastrophe to come. Courtesy Balgley Family Archive

More documentation concerning the property on 3-Maja Street in Brest, this time involving a Jankel Balgley. Note that the spelling of the surname is various: Bałgłey (first and only time I see the first "L" barred in addition to the second "L," yet signed "Balgley" with no barred "L's." The barred "L" indicates a "W" sound in Polish. Also, "Jankel" probably a misspelling of "Jankiel." Courtesy Balgley Family Archive

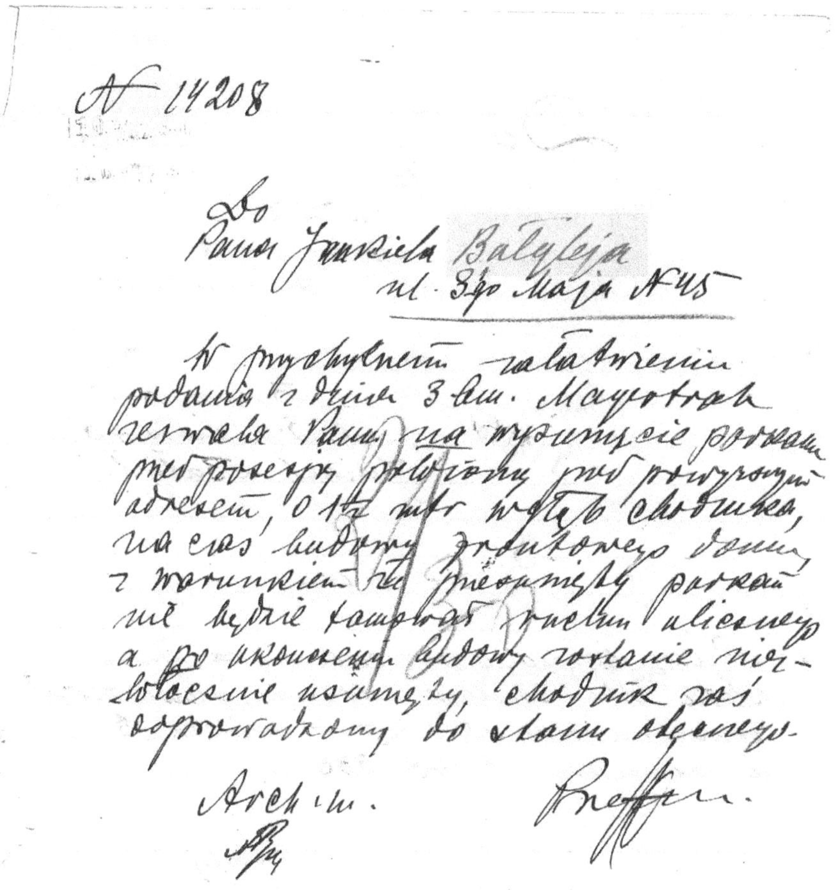

№ 14208

Do
Pana Jankiela Bałgleja
ul. 3go Maja № 45

W przychylnem załatwieniu podania z dnia 3 b.m. Magistrat zezwala Panu na wysunięcie parkanu przed posesją położoną pod powyższym adresem, o 1½ mtr. wgłąb chodnika, na czas budowy gruntowego domu, z warunkiem że wysunięty parkan nie będzie tamował ruchu ulicznego a po ukończeniu budowy zostanie niezwłocznie usunięty, chodnik zaś doprowadzony do stanu obecnego.

Arch. m.

More information about the the 3-Maja Street property in Brest. Note "Jankiel" is now spelled properly, the added "a" shows possession, like "'s" in English. This grammatical rule is shown also in the surname, "Bałgleja." Here the "y" is replaced with the phonetically appropriate Polish "j." Courtesy Balgley Family Archive

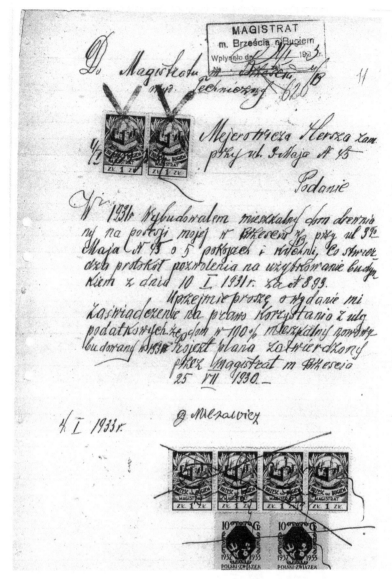

An application to a municipal office in Brest which states, "In 1931, I built a wooden house on my lot at 3-go Maja which has five rooms and a kitchen, as stated in the official permit to occupy the building. Please issue a certificate that will enable me to apply for a tax deduction because the house qualifies as 100% living space." The house for which I found the early architectural plans then seems to have been completed and all necessary certificates issued by 1933. Again, the story of this house struck me as a life caught in the act of living unaware of the catastrophe to come.
Courtesy Balgley Family Archive

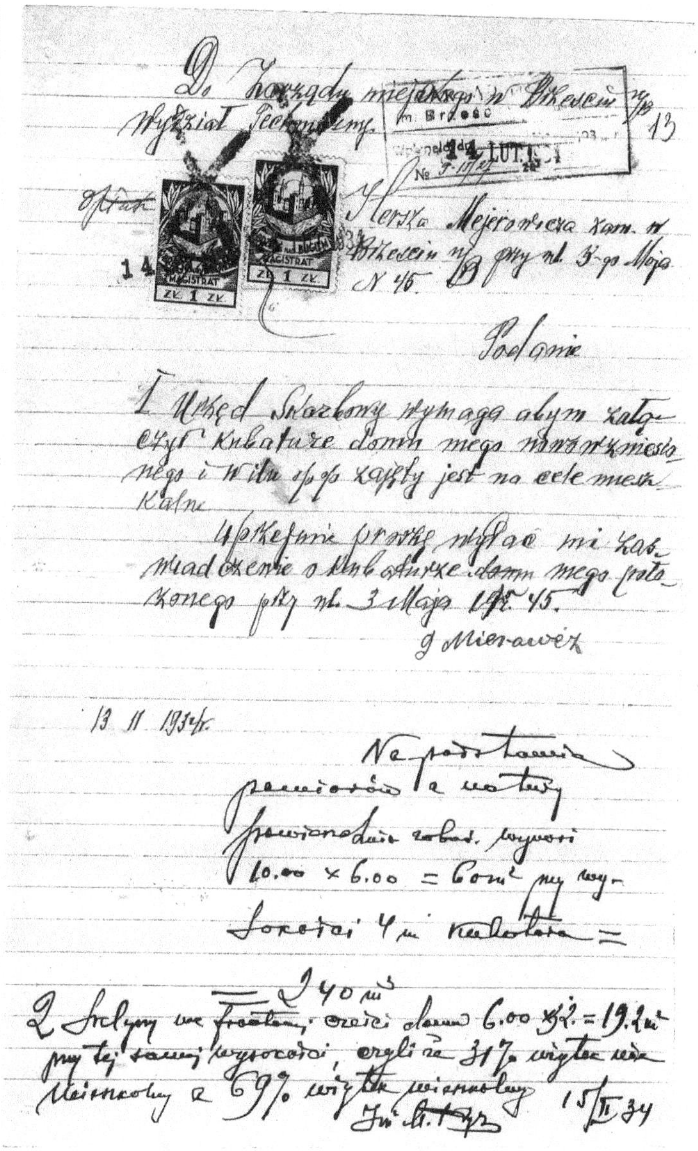
Do Zarządu miejskiego w Brześciu n/B
Wydział Techniczny

m. Brześć
14 LUT 1934
№ 9-19/24

Herszla Mejerowicza zam. w Brześciu n/B przy ul. 3-go Maja N 45.

Podanie

Urząd Skarbowy wymaga abym załączył kubaturę domu mego murowanego i wilu ... który jest na cele mieszkalne.

Uprzejmie proszę wydać mi zaświadczenie o kubaturze domu mego położonego przy ul. 3 Maja Nr. 45.

J Mierowicz

13 II 1934 r.

10.00 × 6.00 = 60 m² ... 4 m ... = 240 m³

2 ... 6.00 × 3.2 = 19.2 m² ... 31% ... 69% ...

15/II 34

More documents about the property at 3-go Maja in Brest. Courtesy
Balgley Family Archive

Protokuł Nr. _____

15

Dnia _15/II_ 193_4_ r., delegowany z ramienia Wydziału Technicznego Magistratu miasta Brześcia n-Bugiem *Inż. Bud.* (imię i nazwisko): *Jn. Mich. Kryursac* , na zasadzie art. 378 rozporządzenia Prezydenta Rzeczypospolitej z dnia 16 lutego 1928 r. o prawie budowlanem i zabudowaniu osiedli (Dz. U. R. P. № 23 ex 1928, poz 202), przy dokonywaniu w mieście inspekcji budowlanej stwierdził, że (imię i nazwisko): *Herz Majorowicz* na posesji swej, położonej w Brześciu n-B. przy ul. _3 Maja_ pod № _45_

Nie zastosował szkło za twierdzonego projektem z dn. II /n 950 r. № 11146/356 i nie polerdował wstępu po orzerdrza na placie posesji, przyczem stary ustęp istniejący nie odpowiada warunkom przepisów praw Budowlanego (dla dobrego wienienia wiem) ustępu, ściany i dno błota własowy nie cięzporona brak wentylacji, brak należnego zaszycia dołu bez odpowiedniego otworu do czynienia

Powyższe stanowi przekroczenie przepisów art. _252, 255, 256_ . rozporządzenia o prawie budowlanem.

Niniejszy protokuł spisano, celem ~~pociągnięcia~~ *uerwania włości do* ~~pobud. ustęp soy za~~ twierdzonego planu do ~~odpowiedzialności karnej z art. 399 powołanego na wstępie rozporządzenia o prawie budowlanem.~~

Inż. Buch Jm. M. Kryz
Technik budowlany

w związku z poyiżyym protokółem zaindenomaum oświadczyło że usterki uyuieuione w protołóle będą usunięte, do wykonania którychel proszę o dłuższ terenia. — J Mierowicz

---

More documents about the property at 3-go Maja in Brest. Courtesy Balgley Family Archive

16

Zarządzenie doprowadzenia budynków do należytego stauu.

(art. art. 378 i 380 p. a. rozporządzenia z dnia 16.II-1928 roku)

MAGISTRAT
miasta Brześcia n. Bugiem
Wydział Techniczno - Gospodarczy

dnia_____ 193____ r.

L. dz._____

Do Pana *Herma Mejerowa*

w Brześciu nad Bugiem

ul. *3 Maja* 45

W drodze oględzin, dokonanych w dniu *15/II*

193 *4* r. przez *Inż. Budanowicza* przy współ-

udziale rzeczoznawcy budowlanego_____

zostało ustalone, że znajdujące się na *pozycji* Nr. hip.

położonej w Brześciu n.B. przy ul. *3 Maja* pod Nr. *45*

i stanowiącej własność *pana*

budynki posiadają wady, a mianowicie:

1) Budynek *dom mieszkalny nie posiada*

posiada następujące wady *nityn zabrigit nządo-*

nego jego kalużnjonego w dn. 25/VI 1930 plan.

wady te powstały wskutek *nieratlojenia oły do*

wazmnia poprawknia za Bezdan dom

frontowego _____ *Hwarzy a-*

wspomniane wady — mogą oddziaływać szkodliwie ponieważ *zlytyni-*
szpecą ulicę (plac)

tecru — waremi otonkawm

2) Budynek_____

posiada następujące wady_____

_____

wady te powstały wskutek_____

_____

wspomniane wady — mogą oddziaływać szkodliwie ponieważ
szpecą ulicę (plac)

3) Budynek_____

*More documents about the property at 3-go Maja in Brest. Courtesy
Balgley Family Archive*

posiada następujące wady

wady te powstały wskutek

wspomniane wady — mogą oddziaływać szkodliwie
szpecą ulicę (plac) ponieważ

4) Budynek

posiada następujące wady

wady te powstały wskutek

wspomniane wady — mogą oddziaływać szkodliwie
szpecą ulicę (plac) ponieważ

Wobec powyższego na podstawie art. 386 p. 6 rozporządzenia Prezydenta Rzeczypospolitej o prawie budowlanem i zabudowaniu osiedli z dnia 16 lutego 1928 roku (Dz. U. R. P. Nr. 23, poz. 202) Magistrat m. Brześcia n.Bug. wzywa Pana do dokonania następujących robót budowlanych mających na celu doprowadzenie budynków do stanu należytego:

w terminie

2) W budynku

w terminie

3) W budynku

w terminie

4) W budynku

w terminie

W razie niewykonania przez Pana wymienionych robót w terminach wyżej podanych, roboty te zostaną wykonane przez Magistrat m. Brześcia n.B. na koszt Pański.

Od niniejszego orzeczenia przysługuje Panu prawo odwołania do Pana Wojewody Poleskiego. Odwołanie wnieść należy za pośrednictwem Magistratu m. Brześcia n B. w terminie dni 14 od daty doręczenia orzeczenia.

Prezydent m. Brześcia n.B.

Architekt Miejski

Although the handwriting is not decipherable, this document concerns a house construction. The ring drawn around the printed word "szkodliwe" means that the project has flaws that may be "harmful" in some way.
Courtesy Balgley Family Archive

The archive was readying to close for the day. We were required to return the fonds, but it was allowable for the clerks to keep them aside for us when we returned to continue our work. I learned that the archive was actually closed the following day—another detail I should have found out before planning my trip—but even Julija was surprised; it seemed some "repair work" needed to be done somewhere in the building, and so they closed the whole place down. Again, that was typical in communist Poland—administrative offices could shut down with no notice at all and it was just tough luck for those who needed a stamp or some important document that day. Julija understood that I needed photocopies of all those documents, but naturally we were not allowed to remove them from the archive. The clerks would make them, but I needed to go to a special window at a special bank to pay ahead of time for that service. That procedure would be seen to later when the archive reopened.

That night I felt a combination of exhaustion and exhilaration. I had uncovered so much so quickly that I was nearly numb. Since the Brest Archive would be closed, Julija and I agreed that the following day Alexei would drive us to Kobrin, the town just under thirty miles to the east of Brest where my grandmother was born and the place where she and the family were displaced from Brześć. My father had sometimes said he was from Brest, but other times he indicated Kobrin. I later learned that during those years Imperialist Russia had displaced Jewish populations from one nearby town to another, and so he and his family moved between the two.

I went to my hotel. It was my first night in Brest, but it felt like I had been there much longer with all the information I had unearthed. I had arranged before I left to stay at a hotel called "The Hermitage," which looked fine online and was reasonably priced. So I was

The dining room at the Hotel Hermitage where I stayed while I was carrying out my research into my father's family history. I was surprised at the comparative luxury of the place, considering that all I had heard about Brest when my father lived there in the early twentieth was associated with poverty and deprivation. Courtesy Balgley Family Archive

surprised to find it so elegant and comfortable. The Hermitage building was old. I tried but could not find out the year the hotel was built. It felt odd to be in such a well-appointed place when exactly 100 years ago my father was born there in a dirt-floored dwelling. I realized my reaction was akin to my father's when my parents came to visit me in Poland. I had associated Brest with death, just as he had thought of Poland as a land of ashes, so it was strange to find civilization in those places.

The outdoor patio at the Hotel Hermitage in Brest. Courtesy Balgley Family Archive

My room was high-ceilinged with period sculpted crown moulding of the sort rarely seen in modern rooms. The furniture was antique, the bathtub an old-fashioned, well-preserved type. A tall window filled a large portion of one of the walls. As I looked out, I saw huge lush trees, the branches of which hung over the amber-colored roofs of the old brick houses that sat behind the hotel. The leaves had turned, and gold and red covered all. Julija had pointed out what she called "Jewish houses" as we passed by in Alexei's car and explained that the brickwork was referred to as the "bricks of Jerusalem," curved windows and doorways—the former homes of Jewish families, she explained. I could not see well enough to know if those houses I peered

An example of distinctive Jewish brickwork on a façade in Brest. Courtesy Balgley Family Archive

down on from my hotel window had these "bricks of Jerusalem." The air was fresh. I felt the strangeness again of being in a place my family lived so long ago—my father's birth year exactly 100 years before. And then the faces of my relatives on the "Ghetto Passports" loomed up—and I think, too, this is where my family was annihilated. Marveling at the beauty there seemed an affront to their memory. I thought back to what I had said to my father in Kraków when he said he was stunned by the spring loveliness in Poland when he visualized

The view out of my hotel bedroom window in Brest, Belarus, during my time doing research at the local historic archive in 2012. Courtesy Balgley Family Archive

ashes. It was not wrong of me to enjoy that beautiful place; I imagined all of them—the faces on the documents—walking among the fall trees with the gold and red beneath their feet, and finding pleasure in where they lived.

I wanted to tell my father that I was there. I remembered a time I was visiting Kraków with my husband and daughter, years after my father had visited me on my Fulbright. It was my birthday in June during the Jewish Festival. My father had always asked me for a full itinerary when I traveled, so I had given him the names of the hotels where I would be. I was amazed that at the age of 90-something, he thought of me, figured the time difference, found the phone number of the hotel, and called to wish me a happy birthday. I happened to be briefly in my hotel room when he phoned, and it felt significant to me in my search for my identity and for my feelings of displacement since childhood, that he should find me here, in his country of birth, on my birthday. That we should have this conversation from Poland where he found me felt like the opposite of displacement—it was instead acknowledgment, preservation of a past and a personal history; an integration of that history with the present; and the start of a reconciliation between us about the formerly hidden. I also recalled that we had spoken by phone from Israel when I visited there—that time on his 76th birthday. I wanted to experience that feeling again from years before in Haifa and Kraków, so I phoned my father from my Brest hotel just to tell him I was in the city of his birth. But the person on the other end of the line was not the same person who had phoned me in Kraków. My father was 100 years old in 2012, and I could see he did not have the energy to appreciate the kismet, the *bashert* of my being in his birthplace a century later. He was tired. I realized with a start that I was gradually losing him, despite his longevity and vigor. I was at once glad I had searched to know him and myself truly, but I was also sad that time seemed to have run out. I went to sleep with the window open and could hear the wind move the leaves of the trees.

Behind curtains redux
Kobrin, Belarus, 2012

It was pitch black in the early morning when Julija came to meet me in my hotel lobby. She was bundled in a white quilted jacket and warm pink scarf. Professional as earlier, she explained that Alexei's father, Maxim, the head of Brest's Jewish community, wanted to meet me and asked if he could come with us that day to Kobrin. I said it would be a pleasure. Julija said that was good because he was in the car already.

Fine, I thought, since I arrived in Brest everything had been a surprise every hour—and every surprise turned up unexpected but welcome results. Back home I was characteristically a planner, and I did not typically welcome unexpected changes. I suddenly realized that there, and when I lived in Poland in the 1980s, I was and am a different person, at least in that regard — I was open to all exigency.

Julija and I walked out into the dark, a cold wind and slight slurry of snow whipping about. I saw Alexei's car pulled up and waiting for us. As we approached the car, the back door quickly opened and a man with brisk, athletic moves sprang from the car. He was at once courtly. He took my hand, and I had a moment to think that as in Poland, he was about to bring it to his lips in the traditional greeting Polish men use when introduced to a woman for the first time. But no, instead he took my shoulders and gave me a kiss somewhere between my cheek and mouth. Even though I had known his son, Alexei, for only one day, I realized that such ready familiarity would be the last thing Alexei would display. Julija introduced us in Russian, and I had the chance to take in Maxim as she was speaking. Wearing the black leather cap I have seen on many older men in Brest, atop Maxim's head it gave an entirely different impression. On Maxim it was jaunty and youthful, and was matched with a fashionable black leather jacket cut to the waist, revealing a trim physique. My first glancing impression of his athleticism was confirmed. At some point before exiting the hotel lobby, Julija had told me that Maxim was 79 years old, and I expected a worn-down old man. Maxim was anything but worn down. I had a moment to think that Maxim seemed more vital (and more confident and presumptuous) than his son who was 49 years old. Sometime later Julija told me that Maxim had been married "a few times."

When Julija pronounced my surname in our introduction, Maxim leant forward and asked again for its pronunciation, and then a moment later, for its spelling. He inclined his ear towards Julija's words, his intelligent face scrutinizing the information. Suddenly he looked surprised, and talking rapidly to Julija, instructed her to tell me that two weeks ago there in Brest he has seen the work of the Brest-born painter, Jacob Balgley, who emigrated to Paris and died there. I was stunned. That was the Jacob Balgley my UCLA student had first found and brought to my attention; the relative about whom the book was written and shared with me by my cousin in New York; and the same relative whose original work my father and I went to see at the Armand Hammer Museum in Los Angeles years past. There he was again. Even though "big red" was overstuffed already, at the last minute I had decided to pack the book on Jacob Balgley. I could not have predicted how important that would become during my visit to Brest.

Billboard announcing Jacob Balgley's exhibition in Brest in 2012.
Courtesy Balgley Family Archive

A billboard in 2012 announcing the art exhibition of Jacob Balgley in Brest. Courtesy Balgley Family Archive

Before setting out for Kobrin, Maxim and Julija wanted me to see the famous Brest Fortress. The Imperial Russians had built it in 1833, on the site of a former Lithuanian ducal castle, and though it was partially destroyed, it was still an impressive monument. It was best known for its historic defense in World War II, when the Red Army fought against the invading Nazis in June, 1941. The Russians had no warning of the incipient attack. Nazi weaponry was nearly twice what

The Bug (pronounced Boo-g) River Among its various names, Brest had also been called "Brest nad Bugiem," "Brest on the Bug." Courtesy Balgley Family Archive

the Russians had, yet the Russian soldiers held out until July 20—without provisions and lacking water. Two thousand Russian soldiers died and about 7,000 were captured. In the 1960s the Soviets made the fortress area a memorial, naming it "Brest Hero Fortress," which included a huge sculpture named *Thirst* and another titled *Courage*. I learned that the center of the Fortress, the "Citadel," was situated on an island where the Bug River and Mukhavets River met. One of the three fortifications around the Citadel was named for the city of Kobrin, the largest of the three. The current symbol of Brest on the city's shield and flag is that fortress. It was still possible to see an inscription written by a Russian soldier scraped into the wall which translated reads: "I am dying, but I won't surrender. Farewell Motherland. 20.VII.41."

Julija and Maxim were solemn as we toured the area. Across outsized cement expanses I saw marching student soldiers. In the distance beyond the fortress, it was possible to see the refurbished Russian Orthodox churches in bright colors, their wedding cake swirls and gold adornment in surreal contrast with the devastated walls of the fortress.

I was interested, but also anxious to get to Kobrin. Current Brest is in many ways a monument to World War II, and I was looking for signs of the Jewish world that existed there before the Holocaust, if it were even possible to uncover it. I had learned that Jews were forcibly removed from Brest by order of the Russian high command on August 1, 1915. I was recalling how my father would say he was from Brest, but then switch to Kobrin. That had confused me when we discussed his early life. I knew that his mother and her family were from Kobrin. But learning that there had been an order in 1915 to expel the Jews of Brest, I realized that my father would have at that time been 3 years old, his three siblings a few years older, his father already departed in 1913 for America, and his mother on her own with the four children. It is very likely then that the family relocated to Kobrin after their expulsion from Brest. Indeed, three weeks after the Russians ordered the removal of Jews from Brest, the Austro-German army occupied the city in 1918. Apparently, some of the expelled Jews returned, but were again exiled by the Germans. When the Poles occupied Brest in 1919— after the end of World War I, Jewish traditional secular and cultural activities had returned and grown. I wonder if this had any effect on my father and his family? Again, I wondered why my father had not been enrolled in a school, but because his family left in 1920, it was perhaps too early for Jewish life to recover from the exile and occupation. A statistic showed that half of the students in general schools in Brest in 1921 were Jewish; and the Jewish population of Brest in 1921 was 15,630 out of a total of 29,460. Years after, the mayor of Brest was a Jew. It seemed that things were arguably better for the Jews under Polish rule. But I believe my grandfather was prescient in leaving in 1913—no matter about any improvements, change happened quickly, and the fate of the Jewish population was always tenuous.

We left Brest and made the short way to Kobrin on a modern roadway. Thinking about my father and his family moving from Brest to Kobrin, I reflected that I was looking for a past that was by then covered over by cement--perhaps it was not possible to see the relics of the time when my grandmother grew up and later brought her four children there.

Sign announcing entry to Kobrin with date and Christian iconography. Courtesy Balgley Family Archive

Our first stop was the Jewish cemetery in Kobrin. Snow covered the area, and the grounds were muddy and so wet that my boots sank in and I felt the icy water soak into my socks. Julija explained that "people came and took the sand and dirt" from the banks of the body of water at the perimeter of the cemetery, so that the cemetery became inundated with water. The early unseasonable snow made the ground slippery, and as I walked among the graves, the spongy earth itself felt like it could give way, as if the graves, and the people interred in them were sliding off the planet to be forgotten forever.

In this bleak black and white tableau, we saw a slight movement—a black figure in the cemetery, the only other person there. We approached him and learned that he was a rabbi from Israel. But he spoke some Russian, so Maxim and Julija were able to converse with him. He had come to visit the grave of the famous Rabbi Moshe Palliar (Polier of Kobrin, 1784–1858). I saw there was a small sign posted on the street edge of the cemetery indicating that the rabbi's grave was there. I spotted a larger sign commemorating other famous rabbis interred there. I saw the rabbi's trouser legs were soaked like mine. The atmosphere was bereft, if an atmosphere can grieve. The inscriptions were mostly unreadable; the headstones had become artifacts of nature—worn and disintegrating. I could see some Hebrew writing, but it was all disappearing. I took some photos of the more legible tombstones, thinking a friend who knew Hebrew could help me read them later. Many of my relatives were likely buried there—and who knew dating back to what century? They were there, and so was I, but we could not recognize each other—or I could not recognize them. I had a moment: did the dead recognize me?

At the Kobrin Jewish Cemetery
The engravings on the tombstone had been eroded, but it was likely my
relatives were buried here.

Bottom: first left: My gloved hand placing a stone on an unreadable grave;
at least, I had left a mark of respect. Courtesy Balgley Family Archive

We went on to the Kobrin Synagogue. Jews had lived in Kobrin from the early 1500s and there had been a synagogue, at least one and maybe more, as early as that. That one, built in the eighteenth century, was the last one in existence in Kobrin. I realized that must have been the synagogue for my grandmother and great grandparents—and possibly my father—though he had never mentioned attending one there. The snow was melting so the building seemed to be weeping itself—the guts of the structure were open in places and inside were rusted iron barrels. What would have been the arched windows were replaced with curved particle board wood panels painted white with black lines painted on to indicate panes. That gave the façade the look of a child's drawing of a house. The attempt to imitate the original windows was both disturbing and touching. Julija commented that the synagogue looked better that time than the last time she had visited there. For me, the formerly holy place looked a shambles. Like the cemetery, nature seemed to be reclaiming that once vital center.

The synagogue at Kobrin. This eighteenth-century building was probably where my great grandparents attended religious services. By 2012 the fabric of the structure was rapidly disintegrating and the beautiful original arched windows were replaced by timber boards cut to occupy the window spaces. These boards were then painted with black lines to make them look like window panes. Courtesy Balgley Family Archive

Next we went to the Kobrin Museum, which Julija had explained was important to see. We drove to the center of the town and onto an expansive platz where a large old building sat. We entered the museum, and I was surprised by its grandeur—white marble of the kind I saw at the Brest train station was underfoot. Julija was insistent about finding a particular area of the museum. I followed along, not knowing what she wanted us to see.

Moment of discovery behind curtains in the Kobrin Museum when I found family names in a list, signifying major local property owners, engraved into a marble tablet. Courtesy Balgley Family Archive

Looking around quickly, Julija found a museum employee who appeared to be in charge. In quick Russian she told him what she wanted, and he shook his head, trying to end their conversation. But she was persistent, yes, she told me, and she pushed past him, grasping my arm and leading our small group up a grand curved marble staircase. The museum fellow looked annoyed and called something after her. But she didn't appear to hear, and up we went. Again, Julija pivoted her body rapidly and looked around that space. Suddenly, aha, she had it. In a recessed marble alcove was a semi-circle covered by curtains. Curtains again. As on the train from Terespol to Brest. So much veiled and hidden. Julija pulled them back and excitedly shook her head affirmatively, and pulled me closer. She moved her hand down a list engraved into the curved marble, and then exclaimed again, pointing a finger to a spot: "Here is Balgley!" And in a moment, she also found "Slomiansky," my grandmother's maiden name.

Those names, Julija explained to me, were some of the important property owners in Kobrin. She pointed to the name inscribed in Cyrillic: first word is "Balgley," second word is the given name, "Taiba," and the last lengthy word meant "daughter of Velvel." "Taiba" would be "Tova," the Hebrew version of "Gittel" which means "good," and "Toba" in Yiddish means "dove." More astounding, at least for me, was that it was a woman who was listed as the property owner. My great grandfather's name, Ze'ev, is also known as Velvel—William—or "Wolf," but I know this "Velvel" would be another person with this name, not my great grandfather, since I knew the names of all of his children. I wished there had been dates accompanying those names to trace which Velvel Balgley that might have been, but that was not to be found. The "Slomiansky" surname of my grandmother we did not follow up on. I had read in the earliest Kobrin records that in the 1500s Jews owned many orchards. In later years one of those, I knew, had been my great grandfather, Aaron Slomiansky, who had not allowed his grandchildren to run among his apple trees when they came to say a final farewell

There was discussion then between Maxim and Julija that we should meet a couple they knew who lived in Kobrin. Julija explained to me that they were well-to-do people who established a Baptist church there. I was nonplussed and a little put off, if I had been honest. But I trusted Julija and I was ready. Thus began a strange episode.

It seemed that the couple, in their late 30s or early 40s, had been generous supporters of Jewish memory in Kobrin. We arrived at their large modern home, entirely out of place in that setting, and we were greeted warmly. The young man and woman embraced Maxim, Alexei and Julija, and I was introduced. I was told that the couple established and now cared for a memorial down the street to the Jews of Kobrin. We walked there together—it was practically in their backyard. Near to the memorial was the grave of a local Catholic priest who had assisted the Jews and was murdered by the Nazis. I saw some flowers on his tomb and an inscription honoring his heroism. Just a bit further down the road we came to an immense and new Baptist church. I am given to understand that the couple has been instrumental in establishing the church there, and that they had worked with Baptists from the United States. Maxim and Julija indicated that they were impressed.

We then went inside their home. Again, it was stuffed with amenities and all sorts of objects of a bourgeois sensibility. But stranger than all of this was the multitude of Christian and Jewish icons throughout the house. I saw a photo of the young man as an air force pilot and Julija told me he was an important officer in the Russian military. I wondered if that could explain their affluence. The wife spoke no English, but she was very sweet in the fluttering way a nervous hostess would be. He spoke English quite well, so he conversed directly with me. He was sociable, but I felt a disingenuousness. He seemed to be acting for Julija and Maxim, and when he turned to me, he was sizing me up. Something was amiss for me there. In the meantime, his wife had offered me dry socks to replace the soaking ones on my feet. Since Julija had explained to him why I had come to Kobrin, he jokingly said, "Ah, the socks of the grandfather." We laughed, and it was funny, but there was a mocking tone there, too. A fish dinner was served, but apparently it had not come out right, as the wife was unhappy. The contrast between the failed fish, and the overly ornate table setting added to the strangeness, all the window dressing of a formal table was there, even to excess, and yet there was no real substance to the meal. That was how I felt about the entire experience, and I was grateful when it was time to leave.

The day was darkening, but Julija had not faded one bit. She and Maxim had talked further and she told me that we should now go to the office of the local Brest newspaper that had been working on a project showcasing former well-known Jews from Brest. It turned out Jacob Balgley was one of these. And Maxim had been right: just two weeks before my arrival in Brest, the city had mounted an exhibition of the work of Jacob Balgley. What were the chances of that occurring so close to my one and only trip to my father's birthplace? I was just slightly too late. Again, that feeling of destiny, kismet, *bashert*—the same shiver I experienced at my grandparents' Brooklyn apartment so many years ago.

We arrived early evening to the offices of the Brest newspaper, *Brestskiy Kuryer* (Brest Courier). I was surprised we could make a visit at that hour—the sky was darkening and I was thinking that business offices would be closed. But not there, apparently. Everything was upside down or the reverse of what one expected—just like living in the old Poland.

The evening may have been upon us, but opening the door to the office we were met with bright lights and action. The office was alive and busy—everyone seemed to be expecting me and knew who I was. Plenty of attractive young people in motion at their work stopped to smile at me. I was introduced to the editor-in-chief of the newspaper, who here will remain unnamed or pseudonymnously (as are all other Belarusians I met here described): the 2020 and 2021 protests against the government in Belarus have resulted in the beatings, imprisonments and deaths of brave protestors. It would not be safe to think persons named here would be overlooked by Lukashenko's regime. The editor had the look of a classic journalist, an intellectual, hair in all directions, but handsome in his rough and ready way and with courtly manners. He struck me as old Russian nobility, one of the sort like Tolstoy, who was interested in the underdog, in this case, the Jews of Brest. He stood to greet me, friendly and open. He explained (to Julija in Russian or Belarusian, I was unsure) that they were stunned, thrilled that a relative of one of the individuals they were researching, should come to Brest—and to their office. As Julija translated this for me, the editor-in-chief continued to stand, and then looking at me over the top of his wire-rimmed glasses, he placed his hand over his heart. I could only nod my head in acknowledgment. I turned to the walls and saw that they were covered with beautiful posters for each of the individuals they had researched: I noticed, among others, Paul Krugman,

Ayn Rand, Menachem Begin—and then Jacob Balgley. I could not believe what I was seeing, what I had found—or what had found me. I came to my senses and realized I had brought with me a copy of the book on Jacob Balgley, the book my cousin had given me years before. I took it from my bookbag and handed it to the editor. He fell back in his chair, amazed, and told us that their research group had been looking for that book for ages. I told him it was theirs to keep. He said again how stunned he was that I should appear there at that time, a relative of a person from a bygone century had materialized just as they were researching Jacob's past. Julija looked at me as she had in the Brest Archive when we turned up the avalanche of information on my relatives murdered by the Nazis and again at the Kobrin Museum where my family's surnames were engraved into the marble wall. "I have had other Jewish clients from Europe and from America, but I have never experienced this sort of luck," she said. But I have to think, it is not luck, but kismet: *bashert* continues to be my constant companion. The editor made me a gift to me of the Jacob Balgley poster. He then told me that I will now go to the Gorky Library where, as he put it, "Your family tree awaits you."

By then it was nighttime, but Julija told me it was no problem, that the librarians were there and awaited us. She was indefatigable. On we went through the dark streets with Alexei at the wheel. It was so dark I could barely make out the outlines of the library's structure, but we entered a spacious lobby, burnished wood on the wall and beneath our feet, sconces and lamps emitting an amber glow. I felt like I had stepped into a scene from a Tolstoy novel. We turned into an office, large, high-ceilinged, oriental rug over the wooden floor, low-lit honey-colored lamps sat on an oversized antique desk behind which sat "Ala," the head librarian of the M. Gorky Library of Brest, who had obviously been awaiting our arrival. Like the editor, she did not speak English, and like him, she welcomed me with excitement. A samovar sat on a sideboard, and Ala offered tea to Julija and me. It was ready momentarily, and she served it to us in glasses placed in the traditional silver-handled holders meant for that purpose. We sat across from Ala in oxblood-colored leather chairs and relaxed with our tea. Yes, I thought I am in nineteenth-century Russia. Ala already knew the entire story, so she was smiling and seemed amazed in the same way that the newspaper editor was. I was treated like some sort of celebrity, and it was a bit unnerving. Ala produced the Jacob Balgley family tree, carefully hand-drawn and clear. I saw it and realized with some disappointment that it was a limited tree—it did not show Jacob's specific connection to my part of the Balgley family, but it contained enough information that I could use to research a fuller tree. I expressed my gratitude through Julija and we took our leave.

The poster that was on display in the Brestskiy Kuryer (Brest Courier)
newspaper office when I visited in 2012. It advertised the exhibition in
Brest by my Paris-based relative and artist Jacob Balgley, which had ended
just before I arrived there. I was happy to be able to give the newspaper
editor a copy of the book on Jacob Balgley by Jeanne Warnod. Courtesy
Balgley Family Archive

Another poster at the Brest newspaper office: Menachem Begin, born the same year as my father, 1912, in Brest. Courtesy Balgley Family Archive

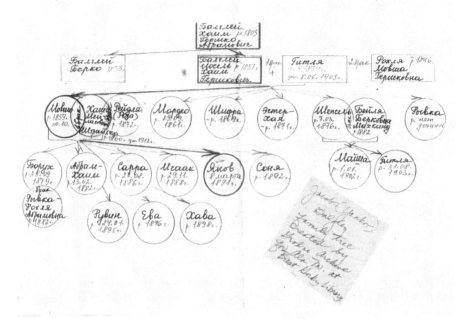

The Jacob Balgley family tree presented to me by Brest Gorky Library.
Courtesy Balgley Family Archive

I was exhausted from the momentous day which had started in the dark and ended the same way. Alexei was there waiting to drive us. I suggested we could drop Julija to her home first, but she demurred and said she had an easy bus trip home. I looked skeptically at her, again asking if we could drive her. "No, Alexei is here to drive you to your hotel now." I gave in—feeling there was nothing else to do.

Back at the Hotel Hermitage, I climbed the stairs

The nineteenth-century façade of the very comfortable Hermitage Hotel where I stayed in Brest, Belarus during my research visit in 2012. Courtesy Balgley Family Archive

to my comfortable room. I went to the window and opened it to smell the trees that sheltered the area behind the hotel. The wind caught the floor-length diaphanous drapes which ballooned around me—curtains again, but not the kind that hide. That day so many veils had been pulled back and so readily—and

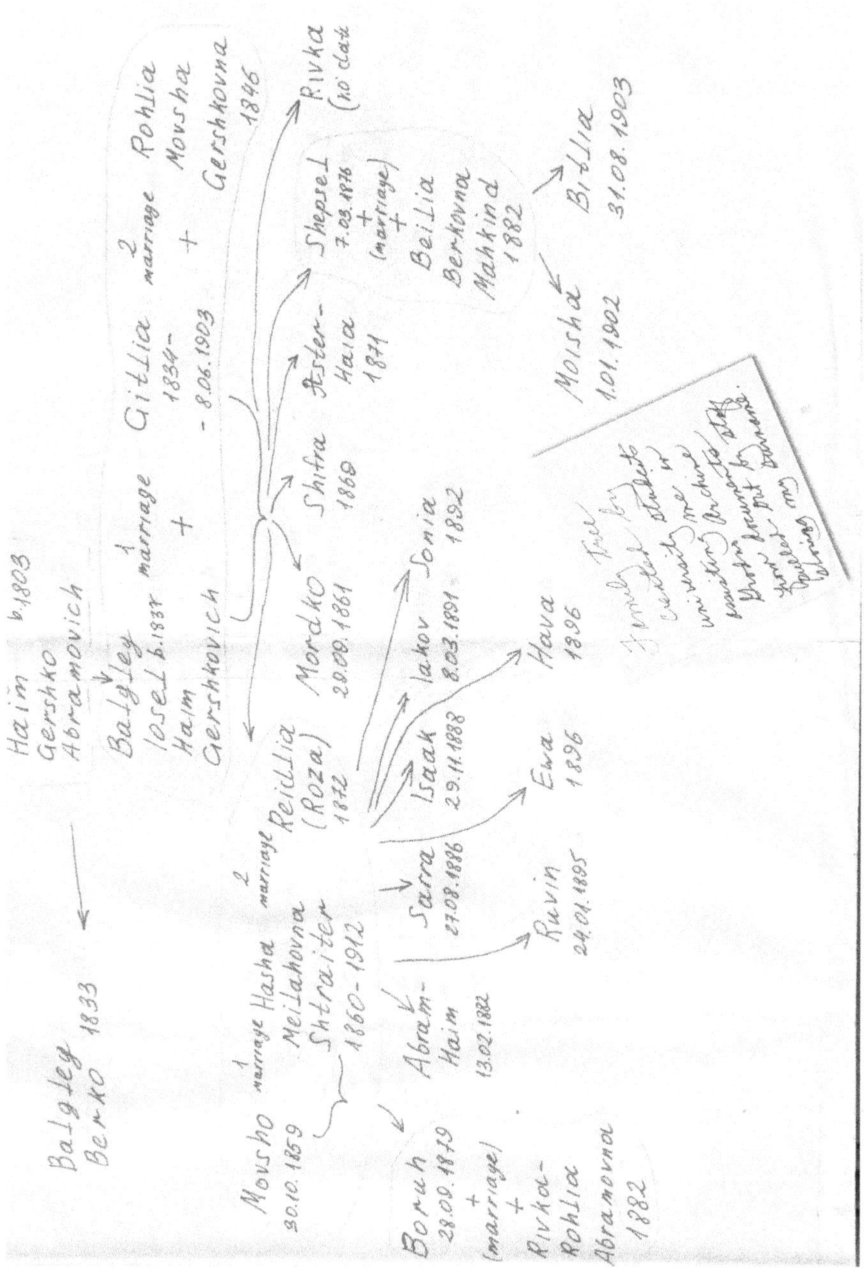

Balgley Benko 1833

Haim b.1803
Gershko
Abramovich

Balgley
Iosel b.1837 marriage
Haim
Gershkovich

Gitlia marriage 2
1834 –
– 8.06.1903

Rohlia
Movsha
Gershkovna
1846

Rivka
(no date)

Mousho 30.10.1859 marriage Hasha Meilahovna Shtraiter 1860–1912

Reidlia (Roza) 1872

Mordko 20.08.1861

Shtra 1869

Ester-Haia 1871

Shepsel 7.03.1876 + (marriage) Beilia Berkovna Mahkind 1882

Boruh 28.00.1879 + (marriage) + Rivka-Rohlia Abramovna 1882

Abram-Haim 13.02.1882

Sarra 27.08.1886

Isaak 29.11.1888

Iakov 8.03.1891

Sonia 1892

Ruvin 24.04.1895

Eva 1896

Hava 1896

Moisha 1.01.1902

Bsilia 31.08.1903

Translated version of Jacob Balgley family tree. Courtesy Balgley Family Archive

I had only been here two days. I reflected on my responsibility to remember and to record and to share what I was learning. I fell dead asleep; I did not know then that the family tree would blossom in directions I could not have imagined.

Contemporary feel of coffee house in Brest. Courtesy Balgley Family Archive

The next morning Julija and Alexei arrived a bit later. The sun was out and the gold leaves on the old trees caught the light and fluttered in the wind. Julija explained that she wanted me to see the memorial to the murdered Jews of Brest and the building that used to be the main synagogue in the city.

We first found the building which had been the main synagogue in Brest. Other synagogues had preceded this one, built in the nineteenth

Streetscape in contemporary Brest. Courtesy Balgley Family Archive

century. A brick structure, it was then a movie theatre and unrecognizable for the function it once served. Julija took me to the dark and sweating basement, however, where there was some trace of the original structure. She explained that the synagogue had once been very beautiful and originally stood taller than the churches in the city. It was thus required to be renovated so that it stood at a lower height. We departed there quickly.

We then arrived at an open area surrounded by tall trees. The granite monument there was mid-sized and had on its façade an engraved seven-branched menorah. An inscription in Hebrew and Russian indicated that it was the spot from which the Jews of Brest were marched from the Brest ghetto to the forest where they were shot over open ditches. Others had been executed at the Brest Fortress; others sent on trains for so-called "resettlement." I saw the dates of October 15–18, 1942: in those three days nearly all of the 20,000 Jews of Brest were murdered. I learned that there was a secluded place in the Bronna Góra forest nearby where those murders took place. Jews from Kobrin and other cities were brought by train to that execution place in the forest, approximately 50,000 people shot over death pits. At the base of the memorial was a colorful mosaic in the shape of the Star of David. Flowers had been strewn there even recently. Bronna Góra forest was about an hour by train from where we stood in Brest. Julija indicated the path, marked where people walked to the trains that took them to the forest. She pointed to the path; some people were walking on it. I approached it and walked by myself on it for some time. The faces of my relatives on the Ghetto Passports rose up before me. The glorious-colored leaves blew on the trees above me.[12]

The granite monument marking the spot at the beginning of the path on which the Jews of Brest were marched by Nazi troops and shot en masse in the woods outside the city. This horrific incident took place between October 15–18, 1942, when 20,000 Jewish people of all ages were murdered, and their bodies dumped in open trenches. I walked the path myself alone for a time. Courtesy Balgley Family Archive

We departed and then Julija explained that we must go to a particular state bank to pay in cash for my photocopying of documents from the Brest Archive. This had to be a specific bank, she said, and a specific window at that bank. One can only pay in cash. Alexei got us there quickly. The place was a monstrosity, huge beyond imagining, the people like insects running around inside. Julija guided me to the correct window. I handed over the cash. Alexei stood back and waited, looking on and about the massive area, at the mash of people trying against the odds to get business done there.

We returned then to the Brest archive and showed the receipt indicating that payment had been made, so that I was then allowed to take ownership of the copied documents. These were sealed and stamped. A massive stack, heavy. Then the ladies of the Brest archive softened a bit, even smiled and curtseyed slightly to Julija and me. Maybe it was because they saw that we really meant business as we had actually paid. Maybe they got people who order all sorts of fonds which they searched for, and then the people never return to actually pay for the copies. Somehow they had been won over by us. Maybe it was just the politeness of a farewell, but it seemed more than that. They seemed to care about the research I was doing, about the tragedy that lay behind my reason for wanting to recover such information. But perhaps I was reading much too much into their late-blooming friendliness. I noticed that the youngest clerk who had been so taciturn was now watering one of the many flourishing plants in the room. I had a new impression of her suddenly: she had a lousy administrative job in a totalitarian country, but found the documents searchers like me want, and we, the searchers, come and go to our foreign homes, with little or no regard for the likes of her who regularly dug out the stories of our lives. Then she could afford to smile, we were grateful to her, she saw, and we had paid. She turned from her dusty gray files to the nourishing of the plants the fronds of which stretched over the walls and up towards the ceilings—there was where her heart resided, not in providing stories of the dead, but in nurturing the living.

Julija urged me to go to Grodno. I had suspected as much, as the pre-1920 records were there. That was where my father's "metrics" would have to be, if they were anywhere. The files I had collected at the Brest archive were about my family members who did not get away, who were murdered after my father left, though a few of the records revealed emigration to Palestine or the United States, and in one case, Chaim Balgley, went to Shanghai before the Nazi invasion. I later learned that Shanghai became a destination

A well-maintained Orthodox church in Brest. Courtesy Balgley Family Archive

for European Jews who could not get entry anywhere else, and that a vital Jewish community grew there during the war years. A documentary, *Shanghai Ghetto,* chronicled the story of that community. So some of my family and other Brest Jews escaped annihilation, but not many. Julija told me that nineteen of the original Jews of Brest survived the massacre in October of 1942. But none of them were known to have returned to Brest. The 1,000 or so Jews who then lived in Brest came from the east after the war. They were not the "original Jews" of Brest, but considered transplants. I was told that was the reason the Belarusian government would not supply funds to the Jewish community to restore the disintegrating synagogues. The rationale was that those synagogues did not belong to such "newcomers." The rightful owners were dead, went the argument, and so no money was made available and the shuls decayed. Meanwhile, the Orthodox churches were freshly renovated and like new.

This was my last night in Brest. Alexei drove Julija and me back to my hotel. I invited them to come into the hotel for some time together. It had really only been three days but it felt more like three months because of the discoveries we had made. I felt like I had known both Julija and Alexei for a long time—or more accurately, that my knowing them had nothing to do with time—it was what had happened, the enormity of what has been uncovered that made me feel like we were old comrades.

The first night Julija had seen me into my hotel, we were saying goodnight, and it felt so puny to simply thank her and go up to my hotel room. So I reached out and hugged her lightly, and she seemed embarrassed and flustered by the gesture. I felt I had misjudged the cultural appropriateness and I regretted what I had done, thinking that she would find me silly, not a person to be taken seriously, a person given to hugging anyone for anything at any time. But it was too late to take it back, obviously, so I consoled myself that what I had done was sincere for me, even if considered naïve about cultural norms in Belarus.

Now it was my last night. I asked Julija and Alexei to have a drink or coffee with me in the Hermitage dining room—perhaps they could have dinner with me? No, no, they said, no dinner, but a coffee or tea perhaps. We sat in the beautiful room. Darkness had fallen outside the glass doors which formed one entire wall of the restaurant. Snow covered the trees outside. I ordered wine; Julija and Alexei ordered a coffee. I was starving but could not order food if they did not. I thought it would be a short conversation. But I was wrong. They seemed to change in the candlelight. They were not "on the job" anymore, perhaps? I had already asked after and learned about their families in passing, but then the conversation deepened. Alexei told me how his first wife had left him because even though he was a Russian officer and relatively affluent, he could not provide her with the things she wanted. He shared a photograph on his phone which showed him in his Russian uniform—an officer's—standing to attention. The photo seemed like something from another century. He was obviously proud to be a Russian officer—there was no ambivalence in the photo, and his first wife looked at him adoringly. But then he explained that he met someone later in his life and how happy they were. He showed photographs on his phone of this second wife and his daughter from his earlier marriage, the daughter now studying in Israel. He showed wedding photographs where he is dressed in traditional Russian garb—the belted muslin collarless shirt with dark trousers tucked into high boots; she is in an embroidered peasant dress. They look happy and amused, knowing and ironic about their get-ups. Ironic, yes, but Alexei told me that they learned Russian dances just before the wedding celebration, and they performed for all their friends. The party itself was held in a wooden structure in the forest. The photograph he showed of the place struck me as an idealized peasant dwelling—something Tolstoy would have approved of.

Alexei's Jewishness seemed to disappear in all this Russian ritual and costume. But then he showed a photo of himself visiting his daughter in Israel: they stand in the blinding sun on a modern patio, palm trees visible in the background. We turned to Julija who threw up her hands and comically explained that she is not modern enough to have a phone with photos—how can she show us family photos, she asks, laughing at herself.

So instead she gave us verbal pictures of her husband, also a Russian officer, of herself as a young Belarusian girl who fell in love with him, of her three daughters, one married to a Roman Catholic, one to a Russian Orthodox, and another to a Jew. She shrugged and said, "This is normal. This is how it should be."

They stayed much longer than I had expected, and I was glad. I offered drinks and dinner again, but again they demurred.

We then had the matter of payment to look after. In order to have the right amount of ruble in cash to give her, I had calculated as carefully as I could, based on what Julija had told me her salary should be. I had gotten the rubles when we went to pay for the document copies at the state bank. It turned out that she had slightly altered the charges she had originally set. Before it had been a price per day; now it was by the hour. I could appreciate that because our "days" had been from early morning to 9 p.m, certainly not a regular business day. But I had not anticipated this, and had the rubles equaling the exact amount she had initially quoted. I was happy to pay the difference. The problem was that the bus for Grodno left at 6:30 a.m. the following morning.

How would I get the additional money to her? I asked if there was a possibility that a bank would be open so early in the morning. Yes, it turned out, there could be. Julija used her cell to make a call. Afterwards, she explained that a colleague of hers from where she used to work now worked at a cash exchange window and has confirmed that the window would be open very early the next morning. We agreed that Alexei would collect me even earlier than planned so that we might go to that exchange window before I boarded the bus to Grodno. We arranged that I would provide the additional payment to Julija through Alexei. It clearly mattered to her that I provide the additional amount, and seeing that it did, it now became very important to me to pay it. I also needed to ask of Alexei what he should be paid. Always cool and casual, he shrugged like it was no big deal and in Russian told Julija, "100 dollars." She translated to me. I nodded my understanding to him. Talking payment in a setting that now seemed to be one based on friendship rather than business was a bit awkward, but I was determined to provide what they expected. The last thing I wanted to leave them with was the impression that I would take advantage of them.

Now it was time to say goodnight to her and goodbye—I would not see her in the morning—only Alexei will be taking me to the bank window and then to the Brest bus station. Now Julija's and my embrace seems entirely natural. We hugged and kissed goodbye. In just two days together, we had become fast friends. We still are.

That night I slept off and on. I knew I would have to wake in the dark—about 4 a.m.—and again, though I had set my phone alarm and left a wakeup call at the hotel desk, I trusted neither, and I could not miss that departing bus or the visit to get the cash beforehand.

It was 5 a.m. in the morning—black as midnight—when Alexei came to pick me up at the Hermitage Hotel. We arrived at Julija's former place of employment, with its bright lights in a modern looking building. This was a currency exchange, but the purpose of the rest of the building was not clear to me. In any case, the large lobby appeared open for business as if it were midday. An attractive young woman dressed smartly in business attire greeted me. She spoke very good English and knew Julija well. She accompanied Alexei and me to the cash window to be sure I had no trouble with the transaction. We did it quickly. Strange, I think, because monetary transactions had seemed so unpredictable and inexplicably complicated there up until then. I was relieved. I had brought from Ireland small mementos as gifts. I had no idea then who Julija would be, what the nature of our relationship would be, so the Irish linen handkerchief with the hand-stitched red and purple fuchsia seemed not grand enough as a gift for her. But it might have been just right in her eyes. Who could say? I wrapped the cash in the handkerchief and gave it to Alexei to give to Julija later. I handed him the hundred dollars in cash and in characteristic form, he made light of it, nodded and pocketed the money in his jeans. It was easy and not awkward to do business with him.

Then on to the Brest bus station. It continued to feel inconceivable that it was morning as it was so black and cold. Alexei had no English and I had no Russian, so up till then it was through Julija's translations that we had communicated. But then we were on our own. And it seemed funny, because we had little trouble making ourselves understood to one another. He had enough Polish to understand my elementary vocabulary, and his answers, half-Polish/half-Russian, were mostly understandable to me. We had not really needed Julija to translate for us at all. He told me about his and his wife's vacations to Austria and Germany and Bulgaria. He told me how beautiful the accommodations were. He had been to Paris, Prague, London, Vienna, Tel Aviv, among other places. He explained about plans for the future. I was thinking how this man in the earliest black and white photo I saw where he stood to attention in his Russian military uniform seemed to span centuries; at 49 years old in 2012, he had seen and been part of a dramatically changing world. I was reminded how the visitor should never assume very much about the natives of the land she visits—so much is not available to the naked eye, so much is hidden behind the curtain. Again, courtly as on our first meeting, Alexei bowed slightly and shook my hand, and between the two of us there was then true warmth.

The bus from Brest to Grodno was dated and offered no comforts. It became clear quite soon that it would be a long trip. The old bus rumbled down country roads where it picked up passengers near farms and meadows. Peasant women in heavy shoes and the traditional black-flowered scarf came aboard, along with purple-haired young women dressed in what must have been the latest fashion in Belarus. Although the distance between Brest and Grodno was only about 150 miles, the trip took about seven hours. It continued to be quite dark most of the way so it was not possible to see outside the windows; the ride felt more like a subway trip. People on board mostly slept or tried to as we lurched along the way.

Svtlana and Ivan
Grodno, Belarus, 2012

It was 1p.m. when we arrived at the Grodno bus station. Julija had done her best to arrange a guide for me there, but I then realized she was a rare gem, and I had reined in my expectations. She had told me that a particularly bright university student who speaks excellent English would be my guide in Grodno, and that he would meet my bus when it arrived.

I spotted Ivan, a young man, among the older crowd. With him was a youthful blonde woman—really a girl with a ponytail and a welcoming smile. We found each other, and I discovered that Ivan did present himself with an air of confidence and self-regard that would make him a choice for this job. He told me with an adolescent smile of superiority that both his parents were anesthesiologists, so he, unlike his fellow citizens, did not need to worry about receiving good medical care. He was about the age of the students I had in Poland, but those students had grown up in a climate of political dissent in the 1980s, and like their parents, were opposed to their regime. Belarus in 2012 was a different story. No matter the Soviet Union had fallen apart by 1991, and Belarus had regained its national identity and freedom (theoretically) from totalitarianism, this had been Russia for years, and young people there had not grown up with the fierce national identity which my Polish students had. Belarusians had been contained by the giant for a long time. That is not to say that Belarusians lacked a sense of their unique culture as distinct from a Russian one. But they did not have the sensibility that the Russians had crushed their identity, as the Poles felt. Julija was the only person who spoke openly with me about her disgust with Belarus's president Alexander Lukashenko. He was a totalitarian dictator, she told me, and I had no trouble believing it, seeing how present-day Belarus resembled communist Poland. He had been in the Soviet Army for years, and had voted against Belarus's independence from the Soviet Union. He ran the country as if it had never separated from communist Russia. I had read earlier that he arrested dissidents without trial and imprisoned them in cells with proven criminals. So when I casually asked Ivan how he felt about his government, he essentially shrugged, as if the question were not really significant, and pointed out again the prestige of his physician parents. In fact, I learned Ivan had not been specifically selected by Julija to be my guide, but that when she inquired, Ivan had been chosen by an associate of his father's. I learned that his companion was his girlfriend; she was charming in all the ways that Ivan was not: curious, modest, and, I learned, a very accomplished musician, specifically as a vocalist. When Ivan led us to his new car, explaining that it was new, Svtlana took the back seat in order to give me the front. As we drove to the Grodno Archive to begin work that afternoon, Ivan first dropped Svtlana at the university for her music classes; I asked her about her studies. When she explained her work, it became obvious that she had been studying music regularly since childhood. I asked further, and she began to explain, but Ivan made a deprecatory remark about her talent. It was supposed to be a joke, but it was not funny and revealed his need to feel superior. As we dropped her at the university, I found myself wishing she were the one who would accompany me to the archive.

Ivan drove his new car to the Grodno Archive, a formerly beautiful building of the pale yellow color one associates with old Poland and old Scandinavia. We entered the small office that was the Grodno Archive, larger than the one in Brest, but outfitted with the same classroom-type desks. There I observed the conceited Ivan grow immediately obsequious. In fairness, he was young and very likely had never been in the archive, or for that matter, acted as anyone's "guide" to his city. Julija had done her best, but he only got the job because of his parental connection. The clerks were barely attentive to him, explaining he and I would have to wait to see the archive director before we could begin any research. He seemed accustomed to that sort of treatment, and I had to think that beyond the sphere of his parents' nepotism, he was regularly exposed to this attitude like any other citizen trying to do business in the polis. He appeared to actually shrink in size, and came over to me to whisper that we would have to wait.

We waited for over an hour. I was concerned about the clock moving towards closing time, but there was nothing to be done. Finally, a clerk beckoned to him with a curled finger and said with a smirk that the director could see us.

We walked through the office door to an antique looking, wood-paneled and well-appointed office. Behind a desk, larger than the ones set for researchers in the outer office, sat the director. A middle-aged blonde, she squinted at us through a cigarette's smoke haze that hung about her head and face. Appearing already annoyed by our presence, she glanced up and exhaled. She took me in with a quick survey from head to foot, and then looked at Ivan. She began with a single phrase in Russian directed at Ivan which seemed like, "What?" He nervously tried to answer, turning at intervals to gesture towards where I stood beside and slightly behind him. Poor kid, he was doing his best, but she was not about to make this easy. At one point, she must have said something like, "What KIND of family research?" to which he replied, "*Yevrei,*" a word I did know in Russian which translates to "Jewish." At this her eyes flitted over to me where I stood, again making an appraisal and exhaling smoke. Ivan was given to understand that she could not promise my father's "metrics" from 1912 would be in her archive. Also, she told him, I would have to pay for any papers I might want to copy. This was in keeping with the Brest archive; the difference was the director was already preparing us for disappointment.

Eventually, we got down to work in the outer office, using the same process Julija and I had used in Brest--tedious copying of fond numbers from the research I had brought from Miriam Weiner's "Routes to Roots" website. The folders started appearing, but unlike the documents in Brest, these were all handwritten and of course, in Russian. The calligraphy in Cyrillic gave each page the look of a specially prepared parchment. Beautiful to behold, but impossible for me to read and a challenge even for Ivan.

Ivan found some Balgleys, but not my father or his family. The work was painstaking and slow, but I did not give up hope just then, believing that it would just take longer than at the Brest archive. Ivan kept the documents bearing my surname in a pile, and when within an hour the clerks announced the archive would be closing (there was one other researcher in the room), he returned all the folders to the clerks, asking please, that the pile be kept separate for the next day.

It was already getting dark by that time. With Lukashenko's clock set to Russia's rather than Europe's, the sun set by 5 p.m. or earlier, and the day remained black until 8 a.m. or 9 a.m. in the morning. It was then time for Ivan to deliver me to the hotel where I had made reservations by selecting one online, the Semashko Hotel.

The hotel was not nineteenth century like the archive, but instead a late 1950s ugly structure. Stepping into the Semashko Hotel lobby I found the staff reminiscent of the workers at the hotels I had stayed in at Leningrad in 1988—bored people standing around with no discernable work. They moved, unsmiling and cold, to assist me. Checked in, I learned that the way to my room was reminiscent of the tunnel at the railroad station in Terespol—up and down redundant staircases with my heavy bag—until I at last found my room. The trip had been long. I was looking for a shower, but found that there was no hot water available in the hotel just then—and maybe for days—no one knew these things, just like Poland in the 80s. I decided to go to dinner in the hotel's dining room, but found that the offerings were meager. Inexplicably, chewing gum was listed among the items on the menu.

Back in my room, I decided to email Miriam Weiner of *Routes to Roots* to tell her how her work had made my research possible and to share the information about the unhelpfulness of the staff and the records at Grodno.

A collage of the materials we were studying at the Grodno Archive with Svtlana and Ivan. This provides an idea of the variety, age, and condition of the documents bearing the Balgley name we found. Courtesy Balgley Family Archive

I thought she might have some advice or might send me in a new direction. I will never forget the circumstances under which I received an email response immediately after I sent mine. Ms. Weiner wrote from a public computer made available to people caught in the destruction wrought by Hurricane Sandy in New York. She was one of those people, and had only a limited time for her turn on the computer. Amazingly, she used part of that time to answer me. She confirmed that the officials in Belarus had been earmarked as being at best unhelpful to Jewish researchers there, and at worst, obstructionist. What I was experiencing was typical. But how atypical and heroic was the fact that Ms. Weiner answered me at all in the middle of a hurricane!

The next morning Ivan arrived to take me back to the archive. Again, it was pitch black. We arrived to find a handwritten note on the door announcing that the archive would be closed that day for maintenance. That was bad news; I only had one more day to remain in their country, and that would be the following day, a Friday. If we could not get into the archive then, there would be no other opportunity. Ivan apologized for the archive, saying that they certainly should have told us the evening before when we were there that they would be closed the following day. Of course, but I was not surprised that they failed to inform us.

In place of the archive research, then, we decided I should see Grodno. Ivan took me to the churches in the city, all Russian Orthodox save one, a Roman Catholic church. These were all well-preserved and cared for. I could not help but notice that for much of the information on these places, Ivan would turn to his phone's Wikipedia. I had to laugh—he really was not cut out for the job, but nepotism put him in that spot.

Though Ivan knew my interest lay in Jewish Grodno, he was unsure where the synagogue was located. We found it, however, and met a Mr. Jerusalem, who was supervising improvements being done on the building. It was clear it had been an impressive place that had been severely damaged and left with no one to take care of it. But this was changing with Mr. Jerusalem's efforts to raise awareness and money to renovate. The improvements that were taking place the day I visited were dramatic. Care was being taken to retain the appearance of the interior and exterior, and though there was much more to be done, what I saw revealed painstaking work. Through a doorway off the main hall of the synagogue was a small museum chronicling the history of Grodno's Jewish community. That was Mr. Jerusalem's project entirely. Although just a single room, it was freshly painted and care had been taken with the exhibits. These were primarily photographs of accomplished members of the community, all of whom had perished in the Shoah. But there were also photos of the progress of the synagogue's status from its former glory before the war, its damage during the war, and now the present ongoing project to restore it. Mr. Jerusalem took such personal pride in the exhibits, all of which had captions written in Russian and Hebrew and English. He asked me if I knew of Jewish organizations in America that would help with the costs of the synagogue. I did not believe I could give him sources he would not already know about, but I listed off the ones which might be helpful.

Mr. Jerusalem, photographed in the synagogue in Grodno when I visited there in 2012.

Once an impressive structure, the synagogue was severely damaged during World War II. Under Mr. Jerusalem's direction, the synagogue and accompanying museum were being painstakingly restored. Courtesy Balgley Family Archive

Grodno synagogue, also under renovation. Courtesy Balgley Family Archive

Interior of Grodno synagogue museum. Courtesy Balgley Family Archive

Concentration camp photo in the Grodno synagogue museum of a man whom my sister and I thought so resembled our father, Ely Balgley. Courtesy Balgley Family Archive

As I was preparing to leave the museum and synagogue with Ivan, a middle-aged man in business attire and seemingly in a rush, appeared. Dressed in an expensive black wool overcoat, and wearing a fedora, he stopped to introduce himself. Mr. Korzh was a Jewish entrepreneur in Grodno. His family had lived there for as long as he could remember and had miraculously eluded the Nazis by escaping further to the east. He was also involved with fundraising to complete the synagogue renovation, and he told me he was confident it would be completed. He explained he had been in a hurry because he was wanted at the Grodno Castle up the street where he was to meet the Israeli ambassador to Belarus. The ambassador was due within the hour to open an exhibition of photographs of Israel by recent immigrants to the country from all over the world. He immediately invited me to attend. I told Ivan if he had to end his day, I could get to the exhibition on my own. But, no, he wanted to come, and I could see that he was actually curious. Ivan, proud of his city, had not known that before the war Grodno had been 94 percent Jewish. Much of his cockiness had evaporated since we had been at the synagogue and its museum; he seemed genuinely not to have known much at all about the Jewish history of Grodno, and he was interested.

The exhibition was fascinating, in fact. Impressions of Israel from varying national perspectives by recent immigrants to the country revealed subtleties about both the places photographed and the photographers. Ivan leaned in to read the signage. I was introduced by Mr. Korzh to the Israeli ambassador; it was unusual to have an American visitor to the city.

Our day ended; Ivan returned me to my hotel and went on his way. I decided I would not try to dine again in the hotel restaurant, but would strike out on my own, walking in the dark and barely lit streets of Grodno to see if I could find a more unique spot for dinner.

Soon enough I saw an attractive restaurant which resembled a cabin in the woods, a sort of lodge, and seemed like one of a kind, rather than the state-run places. The interior was warm and welcoming, but the maître d', I quickly learned, was of the type I encountered regularly in communist Poland. I asked for a seat for one, and was told that unfortunately there was nothing available. Although the place was serving a number of parties, there were plenty of empty tables. Remembering this routine, I smiled at the host, and handed him ten dollars in cash, at which he nodded, and then immediately sat me at a nice table. The food was better, but not a great deal better than the hotel's. The price of wine was advertised in the menu by a measure I could not follow. No matter, I finally got the waiter to understand that I would like a full glass of their red wine, no matter how many ounces or milliliters. I made my way back to my hotel room over crumbled sidewalks and holes in the road. In door fronts there were many loud drunken men, the presence of which took me back to the broken alcoholic men of communist Poland, and to the words of my students at that time, "No hope; no future."

Ivan dutifully collected me the next morning to spend what would be my final day at the archive. We picked up where we had left the first day, but again the records were in calligraphic Cyrillic, and though he tried, Ivan did not have the quick eyes which Julija possessed. Halfway through the day Ivan explained that I must pay before any copies are made, a difference from the Brest archive. I gathered that the method of transacting payment will be much the same as at Brest: going to the "correct" bank; finding the "right" window; paying the amount and receiving a receipt that allows the archive to make the copies and release them to me with a seal and a stamp. But time was short, so Ivan agreed to do this for me. Neither he nor I had any idea what the cost would be, so I gave him in excess of what it could be. I waited at the archive looking at the notes Ivan has made in English. The best part of the day was that Svtlana, Ivan's girlfriend, had joined us, and she helped locate my surname in the fonds. She was more expeditious in this than Ivan had been, so we managed to gather more than we originally thought possible.

As we waited for the photocopying, I asked Svtlana where there might be a bathroom. She in turn asked a clerk, and we found one down the hall. Before we reached the door, Svtlana was already apologizing for what I would find. When I entered I saw why. The toilet, which was just a filthy hole, was elevated above the floor so that it was necessary to climb up to reach it. There were no handrails, so balance counted. It was not possible to sit down even if one wanted to, so it was necessary to hold a squat position. I saw no toilet paper. When I exited, Svtlana was blushing, embarrassed and apologizing. I avoided comment for fear of making her feel worse. I did say, though, that Belarusian women must have very strong upper thighs to manage those facilities. She readily agreed, and said that all bathrooms in public places were like that one. Ivan returned from the bank, gave me the change, and presented the receipt to the clerks. They now began the process of copying while we waited. It was clear that would take a while.

Stowed in Ivan's car was my suitcase, the ungainly "big red" now containing all the copies from the Brest archive in addition to all the documents I had brought with me to Belarus. I was leaving by bus from Grodno later that day, so I had checked out of the Semashko Hotel. The photocopying was finally accomplished, the stack of documents sealed and stamped for me to take. My bus to Warsaw was due to depart in a matter of hours, so I invited Svtlana and Ivan to have a meal with me before I left Grodno.

We three made our way to a restaurant they knew, sort of an upscale cafeteria, and we enjoyed a glass of wine together with our meal. We talked more about their future plans. Ivan had grown considerably less arrogant during my stay. I watched that evaporate out of him when he learned more than he could have imagined about his city and about both the former and continuing Jewish life there. He has been a bit chastised by accident. He had great plans for his future; he intended to become a physician like his parents, but first he said he would travel the world. Svtlana said she would graduate with honors from the music conservatory, and would continue to sing and to teach music. Now that we had stopped working, the two of them appeared so young and vulnerable. I felt a surge of affection for both of them, and wondered if those future plans would materialize. I hoped so.

It was time to go to the Grodno bus station. I had initially planned to take a train from there to Warsaw, but Ivan talked me out of it, arguing persuasively that the bus would be better. I was doubtful, but I trusted him. I admitted to myself that what Ivan might have been accustomed to might not have fitted my idea of bearable, but I was game.

Общественный приговоръ №

1877 года февраля 10 дня Нижеподписавшиеся лица евреи составляющіе Молитвенное Общество Кобринской Еврейской Синагоги состоящей въ г. Кобринъ по Пинской Улицѣ, собравшись сего числа слушали предложеніе Кобринскаго Городскаго Упрощеннаго Общественнаго Управленія отъ 31го января сего года за №206 мъ, предложено намъ на основаніи 1308, 1309 и 1310 ст. XI т. 1ч. Уст. Дух. Дѣлъ Иностр. Исповѣд. Изд. 1896 года и согласно циркуляра по Гродненскаго Губернскаго Правленія отъ 20го мая мая 1887 года за №2470, произвести выборы на должности Членовъ Молитвеннаго Правленія означенной Синагоги а именно Учёнаго, Старосты и Казначея на наступающее 3хъ лѣтіе и посудобе или между собою единогласно приговорили избрать изъ среда себя на должности Членовъ Молитвеннаго Правленія намѣ тѣ: Учёнаго Хаима Шлёмовича Леха. Старосты Мордко Машковича Мендбуха и Казначея Шая Либеровича Лейхтунга.

These documents do show the "Balgley" name, but were unreadable even by Svtlana and Ivan. Courtesy Balgley Family Archive

2

listopada   7
O.A.9/7677   Z a ś w i a d c z e n i e

    Zarząd Miejski stwierdza,że nieruchomość
położona w Brześciu nad Bugiem,przy ul.3-Maja
Nr.45 zapisana w ewidenoji nieruchomości Zarządu Miejskiego m.Brześcia nad Bugiem na imię Beł
glej Etli,zaś dzierżawcami tej nieruchomości na
okres 36 latni są:Mejerowicz Herszko i Bałglej
Fajga.-

    Powyższe wydaje się Mularowi Zelikowi,ce
lem przedłożenia odnośnym władzom sądowym w
Brześciu nad Bugiem.-

                          Za Prezydenta miasta

                          Naczelnik Wydziału
                          Ogólnego/.-
          BS.

Oryginal zaświadczenia
o. . al dn.   2 5 LIST. 1937
Podpis

Some of the documents from the Grodno Archive also indicate the Balgley name and 3-Maja property in Polish. We have moved from documents at first dating 1930, now indicating 1937. Courtesy Balgley Family Archive

As it turned out, Ivan had a work assignment at the time of my departure, so he said he would take Svtlana and me to the bus station, but would need to take his leave from us before my bus departed. When we reached the station, Ivan jumped out of the car to retrieve my suitcase, and I paid him in cash what he had quoted me earlier. His expression had been changing over the course of time I spent with him. The self-regard I had seen I now decided had more to do with bravado to hide a lack of confidence—a kind of defense against appearing ignorant or foolish or inferior to a westerner because of where he was from. By then, his face was open as he hugged me goodbye, thanking me for the time we had spent together. Svtlana and I watched him as he drove off in his late model red vehicle. She turned to me with an expression that said, "Well, that's Ivan." We smiled at one another. We talked more about her singing and I asked her if she would sing something for me. I could see she was accustomed to performing as she agreed. I suggested we find an empty area around the bus station where I could video her. She was happy to comply. We found an outside wall on the side of the station where no one seemed to be. I had asked her to sing anything she liked. Imagine my surprise when she began to sing *The Star-Spangled Banner* with great concentration and devoid of irony. Her singing was stunningly accomplished—her voice could fill any arena in the United States. Svtlana was absolutely unselfconscious when she sang. When she finished, I told her what I thought. She modestly accepted my praise, but I could see that she was a virtuoso, a serious vocalist, and expected as much from herself.

I did not unearth my father's birth record there where I was told it would be, but Svtlana's singing was the high point of my visit to Grodno, and I reflected that the dream for her future which she shared during our meal had every chance of being realized.

My bus rumbled in, a decrepit artifact. Svtlana and I embraced and held onto each other for some moments. I had fallen in love with her—her modesty combined with her talent were irresistible. With all due respect to Ivan, I was guilty of hoping she would not tarry too long with him, he who did not seem to appreciate her.

I took the first open seat as I entered the bus. The interior of the bus had the look of an old-fashioned living room. The seats were over-stuffed, dusty, dated armchairs, so fluffy they did not seem to fit in the bus. In fact, the bus itself seemed overstuffed with such seats. The impression of a parlor was completed by the curtains on the windows. Curtains again, like the ones on the train to Brest from Terespol. These were almost drapes. Once again, the dual feeling of being insulated, protected from the outside, combined with a sensation of being cut off, uninformed, disoriented, separated from the workings of the outside world—imprisoned, even entombed. Once I had sat down, I was told by a passenger boarding after I had that those were his seats. How? I was not aware of any reservations or prohibitions. I stood with a shrug, but he was undaunted and unembarrassed. But I reminded myself quickly that I was in Belarus; like communist Poland, none of that needed to make sense to me. Stepping into the narrow aisle, a pretty and smiling middle-aged woman gestured to me, indicating that there was an empty seat just next to her.

We got underway, the bus coughing and shaking. Although the distance between Grodno and Warsaw was only about 170 miles, I learned that the trip promised to take over six hours. Surprisingly, smoking was prohibited on the bus, but years of cigarette smoke had permeated the seats and curtains, so the air was stale and odorous.

With the jostling of the bus on the road, sinking into my seat, I soon slept. I was not sure how much time had passed when we reached the border with Poland. But it was dark then, and the light from the border office was so glaring it hurt the eyes. The office itself was a small glass enclosure. It was difficult to imagine how we would all pass through there. I learned we would do so in small groups, with the rest of the passengers left to stand in line in the cold night. All passengers were required to exit the bus and take their luggage with them. I was thinking about all the sealed and stamped records in my suitcase, and wondering if I would meet an obstacle there. First there was a line manned by Belarusian officers who examined our passports, I gathered, to confirm that Belarusian passengers had the proper visas to leave their country. About anyone else, a foreigner like me, I had no idea. When my turn came, I wondered if my suitcase would be opened for inspection. I had been warned in Belarus that without certain stamps on my sealed documents, they could be confiscated. I saw "big red" handed about and exhaled when it was only x-rayed, not opened. Finishing with the Belarusian exit, we were put in a line where Polish officers stood. That line was more expeditious, and soon we were all piled back on our bus.

As it turned out, I was later to learn (through the generous translation of a former student from Poland) what some of the documents written in Russian and some in Polish stated. Over fifty documents at least, there were birth and death records of my ancestors living in Brest, the earliest going back to 1806. A listed landowner was "Moshko Abelovich Balgli, aged 40, his wife Genya, also 40, and their children, a son, Gersh, aged 15, daughters Ginda aged 13,

Haya, aged 10, and Genta, aged 6. There were real estate and tax records—in 1909 Gersh Balgley owned a one-storey stone building worth 160 rubles for which he owed a tax bill of 4.48 rubles. Military records were there, as well. In 1897 Shepsel Yoselevic Balgley, in good health, literate, was drafted into the military and sent to the Kremenchug artillery division. In 1914, Itzak Moshkovich Balgley, aged 25, paid a fine of 300 rubles to exempt his brother, Yakov Balgley, from the draft, to enable Yakov to emigrate. It occurred to me that the painter Jacob Balgley born in 1891 and emigrating from Brest to Paris where he made his career as a painter, would have been 23 years of age in 1914. I suspect this was the Yakov that brother Itzak had paid for, to free him from military service. In fact, Jewish families in that period, accustomed to having their sons impressed into the czar's army, would falsify birth records, claiming a son to be a daughter, in order to hide him from the draft. The document further stated that the father of Itzak and Yakov agreed to pay the fine at the rate of 3 rubles per month. But a following document, issued on May 5, 1914, stated that permission to emigrate could not be issued until the fine of 300 rubles was paid in full. Handwritten synagogue and yeshiva records, one dated in 1890, was from the Kanelya Religious School Society, one signatory was Srul Leyb Balgley, another was Leyzor Yosele Balgley who signed in 1895. It appeared that once again records found at the Brest archive pertaining to the property at 3-go Maja Street were found there, and the story continued: a certificate dated November 25, 1937 issued by the Municipal Government in Brest indicated that the real estate at number 45 3-go Maja Street owned by Etli Balgley was rented for 36 years to Hershko and Fejga Balgley (here spelled in the Polish way as Bałglej). Interestingly, the records showed that those tenants were able to build on the property and sublet it to third parties. It seemed to me that Etli was a father helping his offspring. Again, the everyday-ness of the records was what stunned. Those people were centuries before planning the lives of their families, right up to the time, caught in the act of living, when all such plans and the families for whom they were made were erased forever.

Birth Record

Witold Wrzosinski - Avanim
To: Kathleen Balgley

Thu, May 14, 2015 at 2:09 PM

Dear Kate,

translation is enclosed. The white section is necessary, unfortunately. It covers the information about another person born on the same day and the archivists from Minsk are very concerned about us seeing even a bit of this top secret information. However, we were still able to confirm the date of birth (25th June 1912 in the Russian calendar, which equals 8th July 1912 in the Western Calendar and 23rd Tamuz 5672 in the Hebrew Calendar).

Best,
Witold

Email sent to me with my father's birth record by professional researcher in Warsaw, Witold Wrzosinki, indicating the correct date of my father's birth in Brest: July 8, 1912. Interesting that this record was finally located in Minsk, Belarus. Courtesy Balgley Family Archive

а) КНИГА ДЛЯ ЗАПИСКИ РОДИВШИХСЯ ЕВРЕЕВЪ НА 191 ГОДЪ. 67

ЧАСТЬ I-я О РОДИВШИХСЯ.

№ Мужескаго Женскаго	Кто совершалъ обрядъ обрѣзанія.	Число и мѣсяцъ рожденія и обрѣзанія. Христіанскій.	Еврейскій.	Гдѣ родился.	Состояніе отца, имена отца и матери.	Кто родился и какое ему или ей дано имя.

a) Registry Book for Jewish Births in the year 191[empty]

[Stamped page number] 67

N°		Who performed the circumcision	Day and month of circumcision		Place of birth	Social status of the father, names of parents	Who was born and what name was given
	Male	Female	Christian	Jewish			
184		Secondary Rabbi	Same as above	Same as above	City of Brest	Brest townsman Srul _Balgley_ and mother Sore-Feyge Aronovna[1]	Boy Eliya

My father's birth record finally found in the Minsk, Belarus archive by a professional researcher in Warsaw after my departure from Belarus. Courtesy Balgley Family Archive

IX

Warsaw ⚘ Okopowa Jewish Cemetery

Once we crossed the border into Poland, even without a clear view outside the window, the change from Belarus to Poland was palpable. Lights flickered on in the blackness of night, partially visible through the curtains on the bus window. I pulled back the curtain. There was something to see outside the window—it was a gift to be able to *see* at all. Though it was late at night, lights were on. The earlier blindness had lifted, and the obscurity, the unpredictability, the feeling of the lack of control over one's destiny, dissipated. One was oriented by the well-lit street, the unfettered window, the sense of knowing where one was, both literally and figuratively, the capacity to see out and beyond and on to something new. I reflected on the metaphoric veiling of my identity which sent me on that journey in the first place, and all the literal curtains and veils and walls I encountered in communist Poland and Belarus, and I was reminded of my father's answer when I asked him what he remembered most about his first days in America, "How thoughtful these people are to provide lights so we can see at night. This was my first and lasting impression."

Dorota and Agnieszka

Arriving in Warsaw in the middle of the night, I got a taxi to return to the hotel I left from—Hotel de Silva. This time I do not have to be on a train or bus at 5 a.m., so the next morning I rose in the morning light. Even though the time in Belarus was relatively brief, I had forgotten the pleasure of sunlight in the morning.

I had continued to be in regular contact with a former student from Wrocław whom I had met during my Fulbright in the 1980s. We had planned to meet in Warsaw on my return from Belarus. Dorota had studied for her Masters degree in American literature with me in Poland, and she eventually completed her doctorate in Asian-American women's literature at UCLA. To this day, she is one of two most talented students I had ever met in four decades. During the years after I finished the Fulbright and was living and teaching in California, she added significantly to my reading and understanding of Poland's nascent democracy, and the explosion of research in Poland since my departure on the heretofore unspoken of history of Polish-Jewish relations. Although I knew the subject was shrouded in Poland, I was genuinely surprised when Dorota confided to me that I was the first person who ever broached the topic in school and elsewhere of the relationship of Poles to Polish Jews before, during and after World War II. By 2012, that subject had been unburied and brought to light—the controversies over the research covered internationally. Most notably, *Neighbors: The Destruction of the Jewish Community in Jedwabne, Poland*, written by Polish-American Princeton University history professor Jan Tomasz Gross in 2001, revealed the story of how in July 1941 in the northern Polish town of Jedwabne, Poles massacred their Polish Jewish neighbors during the Nazi occupation. This convinced many Poles of their country's legacy of atrocity, and outraged others at the suggestion that unaided by the Germans, Poles would have annihilated their Jewish neighbors. Despite denials, the story was corroborated. Since then, more studies have appeared documenting Polish attacks on Polish Jews, from pogroms in the nineteenth and twentieth centuries, throughout the war, and after the war when some Jews returned to claim their property, then occupied by Poles. The research continues, and the students I had in Poland in 1988 who denied any wrongdoing on the part of Poles during World War II, today acknowledge their former ignorance and accept the reports.

Dorota and Agnieszka had arranged to pick me up at my hotel and go to the Jewish Cemetery in Warsaw. I had toured the cemetery when I lived in Poland, but this time would be different. Through my own research I had learned that at least three Balgley graves were in that cemetery. Years before, my father had told me his paternal grandfather's name was "Wolf," the Yiddish name for the Hebrew "Ze'ev." In researching a catalog of graves at Okopowa Jewish Cemetery, I found Ze'ev Balgley, born in Brest, with dates that matched the genealogical chart I had begun. Father to my grandfather Israel and his many brothers, one of whom was still living and whom I had met during my visit to New York, the "elder" Uncle Morris, and the one daughter, Aunt Beatty, whom I met at Brighton Beach, this was the tomb of my great-grandfather. I had been stunned when I found the listing, accompanied by a photograph of the grave and a number. I was excited and anxious to get to the cemetery to see this grave.

And when Dorota and Agnieszka met me at my hotel, they were anxious to take me there. A gray, drizzly fall day, we set out. It turned out that neither of them had ever visited the cemetery, and they were not fully aware of its location. That surprised me. I thought of the Okopowa Jewish Cemetery as a sort of monument in the city of Warsaw. But again, it was so recent then that Poles knew anything about the destroyed Jewish community of Poland, that even the likes of Dorota and Agnieszka, two intellectuals who knew more about Jewish life in Poland than most Poles, would not feel that the cemetery was part of their national past. Such was the continuing historical separation of Poles and Jewish Poles.

Driving in Warsaw was not a simple matter to begin with, but Agnieszka seemed to know how to handle the obstacles. She and Dorota were speaking rapidly to one another in Polish about where the Jewish Cemetery was located. They knew it was not too far from the famous Christian cemetery, *Cmentarz Powazkowski*, so we headed in that direction. I knew that the Okopowa Jewish Cemetery was very large, so I thought it could not be missable. But we did make a mistake. Parking the car, we went to the gate of another cemetery only to learn it was not the right one. Dorota and Agnieszka discussed further, and at last it seemed we had arrived on that wet Sunday at the gate of the famous Okopowa Jewish Cemetery.

Through the large double gate, we walked to the posted map. I had the document with the photograph and catalog number of my great-grandfather's grave. We managed to find the number on the map and set out.

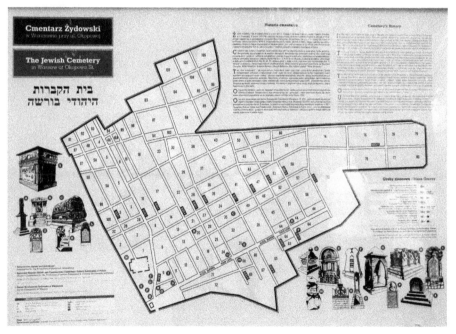

Map of the central part of Okopowa Jewish Cemetery. The cemetery extends much beyond this map. Courtesy Balgley Family Archive

Cemetery's History

IN THE LATE 14TH CENTURY, Jews came to Warsaw and settled in the Old Town between Wąski Dunaj and Piekarska Streets. In the years 1527 to 1795 Jews were not allowed to live in the city. It was not until the mid-18th century that they began to settle in the suburbs in large numbers. In 1780, they founded a cemetery in Praga. The Warsaw community established its own cemetery in 1806 outside the city ramparts, at what was then Gęsia St. and is now 49/51 Okopowa St. From its founding until 1939 about 150,000 people were buried here. The Okopowa St. cemetery covers an area of 33.4 hectares and is one of the last Jewish cemeteries in Poland which is still being used.

This "house of eternity", as the cemetery is often referred to in Hebrew, is a monument of gravestone art, of Jewish art, and Jewish presence in Warsaw. Its value as a record of Polish Jews is incalculable, because the material heritage of the Jewish community was almost totally destroyed during World War II. Among the gravestones, one can find traditional vertical slabs (matzevot) decorated with a wealth of ornaments and symbolic reliefs and covered by Hebrew inscriptions with beautifully carved letters (sections 1, 2, 8, 9 of the cemetery). Visitors can also see splendid tombs which differ in design from the traditional style (sections 10, 26, 31 and the main lane). The mausoleum of Ber Sonnenberg (section 1) with two bas-reliefs is a masterpiece. Among the sculptors who made the tombs are: Abraham Ostrzega, Feliks Rubinlicht, Henryk Stifelman, Mieczysław Lubelski, Mark Antokolski and Bolesław Syrewicz.

The styles of the tombstones and the contents of the epitaphs reflect the diversity of Warsaw's Jewish community. Among those buried here are: rabbis and tzaddikim (Hasidic leaders); leaders of secular movements like the assimilation movement, Zionism and socialism; promotors of Hebrew; Yiddish writers, journalists and actors; people prominent in Polish life: industrialists, physicians, scientists, artists, publishers, philantropists and patrons of culture. Thousands of victims who lived in the Ghetto established in Warsaw during World War II are buried here in mass graves.

On the occasion of the burial of a famous person, the funeral ceremonies were imposing with huge crowds in attendance. Such for example was the funeral of the Yiddish writer I.L. Peretz.

Until World War II, the cemetery, which included a funeral house and a synagogue, was taken care of by the burial society (Chevra Kadisha). Now the cemetery is owned by the Jewish Community of Warsaw. In 1973 it was officially recognized as a historical monument; it is under the protection of the Warsaw conservator's office. Since 1979 the appearance of the cemetery has improved thanks to the efforts of the Community. Conservation has also been done by the Citizens' Committee for the Protection of Jewish Cemeteries and Cultural Monuments in Poland, formed in 1981. The Committee collects information about the cemetery's history and the location of graves to replace, if only in part, the original archives which were destroyed during the war.

History in English from map above. Courtesy Balgley Family Archive

Top: Sculpture of Dr. Janusz Korczak, pen name for Henrik Goldszmit walking with the orphans he accompanied to the Treblinka death camp.

Bottom: Memorial gravestone to Dr. Janusz Korczak, indicating his death at Treblinka death camp. Courtesy Balgley Family Archive

But understand: this cemetery is 83 acres, the approximate size of sixty-three football fields—a city onto its own. There are other Jewish cemeteries in Warsaw, but Okopowa Jewish Cemetery is one of the few still in operation where burials continue to take place. It is also one of the largest Jewish cemeteries in Europe. Established in 1806, the cemetery has over 150,000 marked graves of the original 250,000. As we tried to manage a route to my great-grandfather's grave, I saw that there was a section of mass graves for those who died in the Warsaw Ghetto. We passed the monument to Janusz Korczak, the pen name of Henryk Goldszmit, who as a physician, teacher and author of children's books, headed the Jewish children's orphanage before and during the Nazi occupation. Though he had access to a safe haven, he went with the children when they were marched from the Ghetto to Treblinka for extermination. A well-known photograph shows the children holding hands as they walk with Dr. Korczak.

Angel in black

We gave up at the Warsaw Jewish Cemetery on Okopowa Street—in spite of the photograph I had of the tombstones which bore my surname, as well as numbers that were meant to indicate the part of the cemetery where the graves could be found. Dorota and Agnieszka were still tramping through wet leaves, but I was older, and maybe more tired, and certainly I knew short of a miracle, we lacked the tools to find those graves. The sky was gray above the golden soaked leaves covering the graves. The trees leant into one another just as the gravestones appeared to do. As the afternoon darkened, it seemed both the trees and the gravestones moved closer and closer to one another, shutting down, furling inward, the reverse of a bloom, closing off even the tiny pathways leading through the forest—a community going to sleep.

And in fact we were nearing the closing time posted on the cemetery gate: 16:00—it was just fifteen minutes before 4 p.m., even though the sky was so dark it felt already like nighttime. As a last ditch effort, I went to the woman in the kiosk inside the cemetery gate. Like all kiosks in Poland, it was nearly impossible to see the clerk—the windows were always too dark and crowded with items, the opening through which to speak too low to see a person's face on the other side. I always felt at an immediate loss when approaching kiosks—faceless boxes—to be understood and to get what I needed required face-to-face contact, gestures and expressions, and those were denied in the kiosk world. It was too easy for the voice behind the glass to get rid of you because you could not see them to make your direct appeal—their anonymity protecting them from your supplication. That kiosk was not much different.

The lady did lower her head to view me through the little opening, but she was already looking closed herself, her bored expression and tired eyes told me she was not going to be of much help. I tried anyway. In Polish: "Perhaps Madame can point me to the section number marked here?" And I held up the page with the color photograph of what I believed was my great-grandfather's tomb. Her eyes flitted for a second over the page, and then she shook her head, and pointed a finger straight up over her head. I saw the sign to which she referred—in short, it was closing time and she was finished doing business that day. I had a chance to glimpse her face: impossible to know her age, yet it was a handsome Semitic face, a face formerly pretty, but prematurely old, I thought, and I found myself wondering if she was a volunteer, or a low-paid clerk—how she came to be in this job—for love, for money? A Jew living in Warsaw in 2012? What of her family's history, her history, her story, her need to close right now to get the bus home to make dinner for her kids. We were both Jews, I thought, and wondered if she might feel some empathy with my search to find my family in that enormous cemetery. If she did, she hid it well—she was already pulling the curtain across the tiny orifice of a window.

Suddenly, a figure was walking towards the kiosk at a brisk pace. Everyone else had gone and those who remained seemed to be moving without much direction, maybe just tourists looking at the famous Warsaw Jewish Cemetery? She seemed almost an apparition at first—was this person heading towards me? A woman, dressed in a fashionable black overcoat fitted to her trim frame, silver-haired with wire-rimmed glasses, a chic leather attaché over one shoulder, and a flash of a cerulean blue scarf over the other, moved quickly towards me, as if I had summoned her, as if it were her job to find me. She only tapped me lightly on the forearm, and nodding to me, turned to the kiosk woman and spoke quickly in Polish to her. I could not follow their rapid conversation. Then the woman in black turned to me and in perfect English said, "I believe I can help you. One moment." At that point she took out a tiny cell phone and nodding to me once again, gestured to a bench near the gate where we could sit. Again, a quick dart of Polish, and she hung up, turned to me and said, "I know the person who did all the cataloging of the gravestones here; she can find those graves readily. Don't worry. She doesn't answer just now. But she will call back." I hovered between incredulity and gratitude. The "She will call back" left me wondering, but in a matter of seconds, the cell phone whirs, and now there is a brief conversation, in the middle of which, my lady in black for a second puts the phone to her shoulder, and looking at me, asks, "Can you be here tomorrow at 10 a.m.?" Ah, yes, I can do that. The phone conversation was finished, and she turned to me to say that "Alicja" would be there tomorrow at that hour to meet me.

The kiosk woman was wearily pushing the tall gates closed, so I called to Dorota and Agnieszka who, during that time, had been studying the posted cemetery map and had no idea what had transpired. My rescuer took my arm and indicated we could continue our conversation outside the cemetery gates. I introducd myself and then Dorota and Agnieszka. She nodded and produced her card for us. She herself was late, she explained, but I should have no worries, Alicja would be here and she knew what she was doing. I began to thank her, wanting to make a gesture that showed I registered her help, but she friendly, business-like, had to go. Dorota, Agnieszka and I watched her turn on her chic booted foot, and disappear down the street, hurrying all the way. We turn to one another, Who WAS that? WHAT was that? None of us had seen her earlier in the cemetery. How was she even aware of my dilemma? I had no chance to explain much to the kiosk lady. It was as if she had simply materialized for the purpose of providing me with this information and then— vanished just as quickly. Now this was the real world, whatever that means, and I did have an actual business card in my hand, so we looked up her name online, found her Facebook, and discovered among other things that she was a Warsawian Jew whose favorite periodicals, like mine, were *The New Yorker* and *The New York Review of Books*! That familiar shiver of *bashert* which had begun in my grandparents' Brooklyn apartment, found me in the forests when I lived in Poland, presented itself in the Archives of Brest and the Kobrin Museum, came over me then as I read about this angel in black.

A pink umbrella

It was raining again on Monday morning as Dorota drove me to the Warsaw Jewish Cemetery for the 10 a.m. assignation with the black angel's expert. This time Dorota knew the way without a hitch, having made our mistakes the day before. I was wondering if anyone would really be there to meet us. Our black angel had understood my needs so entirely in an instant that she seemed too good to be true. Also, my years in Poland had taught me never to rely on anything.

The rain was coming down in earnest now. The cemetery gates were open and with just a glance I had a moment to think how different the place looked in the morning: there was some odd sort of vitality in that place of the dead, like a small city where daily rhythms altered appearances. But nothing moved here, I reasoned. Still, the trees that had closed down upon our leaving the night before now seemed to have opened, if only tentatively and drowsily in the wan morning light. Among those grays and greens an impossibly oversized neon pink blossom appeared just inside the cemetery gates. The blossom pivoted towards us, its stem held by a young woman who greeted us with, "You are Kate?" I realized then that I must have been expecting a scholarly type, patined with age like the gravestones themselves. Instead, I found Alicja, 30 years old at most, a Jewish Snow White with creamy skin and dark cascading hair. The pink from her umbrella overhead had added a rose glow to her face, and rain droplets shimmered on her hair. She was the daylight version of the black angel, who, it occurs to me now, was Alicja's photo negative with her silver white hair and black coat. Alicja's English was accented but perfect. That cemetery was her workplace and home. As she guided us without hesitation to the location of my great grandfather's grave, to that needle in a haystack we had searched for the day before, she gave us the history of the cemetery.

As mentioned already, the Okopowa Street Jewish Cemetery is at least 83 acres behind a wall. Established in 1806 next to the Powazki Polish Catholic cemetery opened in 1790, Dorota and Agnieszka were not the only Poles who had never seen the Okopowa Jewish Cemetery. It seemed strange that such an historical place, one of the largest Jewish cemeteries in Europe, should not be familiar to Poles, especially local Warsawians, but that fact underscored a reality that may slip from current understanding: despite assimilation and Jewish contributions to the Polish nation, in large part, Poles and Jews lived separate from one another throughout Polish history. At its start, the cemetery was reserved for the upper strata of Jewish society. In 1913, since disagreements had surfaced over the administration of the cemetery, it was decided that the cemetery be divided into four parts: a section for the Reformed, one for state and military burials, one for the Orthodox, and one for children. By the end of World War I, the cemetery was overcrowded. As a solution, between 1918 and 1936 fourteen mounds were built over the quarter formerly reserved for children. The high wall visible today was erected in 1930.

An inescapable irony: in 1939, construction had begun on a special Mausoleum of Jews Fighting for Polish Independence, but that work stopped with the Nazi occupation of Poland. Over time, the cemetery had become a museum in a forest, if you will. Having replaced several smaller Jewish cemeteries in the city, it is today ecumenical in the best way—Orthodox and Reform are included here, along with a mass grave for victims of the Warsaw Ghetto Uprising. Famous figures are buried there, along with a memorial to the Jewish children murdered by the Nazis. Partly destroyed during the war by the Nazis, the cemetery was used as a site for mass executions and burial of victims of both the Warsaw Uprising of 1944 and the Warsaw Ghetto Uprising. After the fall of the Ghetto, the Nazis dynamited all buildings near the cemetery— including the synagogue. So it was overwhelmingly inspiring to see that the cemetery continued then, reopened after the war, and was currently taken care of by volunteer workers and the likes of Alicja, who with her team, has catalogued nearly every grave in the cemetery.

And the graves themselves were astonishing. Though Jewish law prohibited tombstones (matzevot) from being decorated with visual art, sculptor Abraham Ostrzega (1889–1942), created stunningly memorable (and controversial) works of art for several matzevot.

As we went deeper into the cemetery, the graves became older and older, like ancient ruins or maybe more like eroded natural artifacts. The huge trees sheltered us as we made our way—a canopy offering protection from the rain. Alicja guided us over the rain-soaked leaves which were so deep that once off the cemetery's main paths, it was as if we were walking on soft cushions, every shade of golden and red and amber.

The place was serenely quiet—we saw no other visitors that day. Alicja's voice was authoritative but soft; she was a professional, an expert docent,

Examples of Abraham Ostrzega's controversial matzevot at Okopowa Jewish Cemetery. Courtesy Balgley Family Archive

but there was something else to her narrative. It was personal. In her cataloguing of those graves, she had become a part of a community. She told me, "You know, people ask me, isn't it terribly depressing to work in a cemetery, among the dead and especially the murdered? But I say, 'This place is a record, but also a place of refuge where a community can finally rest beyond the reach of its tormentors. This place is about continuity.'"

I felt strangely like I was in an organic, living place—I could not explain it—maybe the feeling was akin to being in truly great museums where time disappears. For me, it was again the trees, the forest, the lush and wild vegetation, the young and old trees like families standing near to one another, the brilliant green lichen that covered the gravestones. The cemetery was anything but a sad place—it seemed more like a protest against despair: "We are here."

We reached my great grandfather's gravestone, inscribed in Hebrew. Alicja read to me: "Ze'ev Balgley born Brześć, 1858, died Warsaw, 1915." So my father never knew his grandfather, being only 3 years old when Ze'ev died. And my grandfather, Israel, having left Brześć for the United States in 1913, was not in Poland when his father died. But my father had recalled to me years before that his grandfather was called "Velvel," "Wolf," a name associated with the tribe of Benjamin, a tribe in the Bible described as a wolf, a courageous warrior. That Wolf had been buried in Warsaw, rather than Brześć, puzzled me, but then I recalled his son Herschel, brother to my grandfather, Israel, had lived in Warsaw at that time, and I realized it was to Herschel's home that my father, his siblings, and my grandmother had stopped when traveling to Le Havre to leave Europe for America. Herschel

Headstones recovered from Nazi road paving, now placed in a wall at the Okopowa Jewish cemetery. Courtesy Balgley Family Archive

My path through the Okopowa Jewish Cemetery. Leaving any main path, it was necessary to walk through a heavy thicket. Courtesy Balgley Family Archive

was grandfather to Yossi, the lovely relative in Michigan with whom I had made a connection when I went to his son's wedding in Detroit. Yossi later traveled to Warsaw and with the help of the guide I had come to know there, visited the spot where his affluent grandfather had lived in Warsaw--a beautiful house that was in the end located just at the inside of the boundary of the Warsaw Ghetto, on the famous Niska Street. There was nothing of it left now. Herschel and much of his family lost their lives there. But Herschel's son, Abba, Yossi's father, was in the Polish Army, and his story, as I related it earlier, led him to Israel where he lived on.

cemetery	Warszawa
sector	80
row	7
number	29
sex	M
surname	Bałglej
first name	
hebrew name	Zeev
fathers name	Chaim Shlomo
husbands name	
maiden name	
date of birth (m/d/y) (m/d/r)	
date of death (m/d/y) (m/d/r)	12/24/1915
additional info	żył lat 57, z Brześcia Litewskiego

The photo of my great grandfather's, Ze'ev's tombstone in the Jewish Historical Institute's archive of the graves at Okopowa Jewish Cemetery. Indicated here the city of the cemetery (Warsaw), the sector (80), the row (7), the number (29), the sex (M), his surname (spelled with the Polish "j" for "y"), Ze'ev's father's, my great great grandfather's name (Chaim Shlomo), the date of Ze'ev's death (December 24, 1915), his age at the time of death (57 years), and the city of his origin (Brest-Litovsk).
Courtesy Balgley Family Archive

cemetery	Warszawa
sector	64a
row	2
number	10
sex	F
surname	Balglej
first name	Mirjam
hebrew name	Miriam
fathers name	Yitzhak
husbands name	Dov Ber
maiden name	Frydland
date of birth (m/d/y) (m/d/r)	
date of death (m/d/y) (m/d/r)	4/28/1921
additional info	żyła lat 82

Another Balgley grave at Okopowa Jewish Cemetery: Miriam Frydland, born 1839, wife of Dov Ber Balglej; Miriam died in 1921 at the age of 82 in 1921. Courtesy Balgley Family Archive

Candle child

The story of my family unfolded before me, and I was led by a luck that felt not luck, but a destiny that was fated for me, that same feeling which overcame me as a child in my grandparents' Brooklyn apartment.

In her *In Andalusia, on the Trail of Inherited Memories*, Doreen Carvajal wrote of a "discarded identity" which found its home in a place never before visited—"the archaeological site of memory."[13] Carvajal reports on a French psychologist, Anne Ancelin Schützenberger, who worked for many years researching and developing what she named the "ancestor syndrome" a condition in which a person, as Carvajal explains, is a "link in a chain of generations, unconsciously affected by their suffering or unfinished business until [we] acknowledge the past." When my father would time and time again express his wonderment and surprise at my identification with my Jewish self, I once half-jokingly told him that his mother was returning to him in the shape of his daughter. But it was only half a joke. And I believe he felt that.

Besides this "ancestor syndrome," Carvajal tells of the research of a Dr. Darold Treffert, a psychiatrist in Wisconsin, who through his work with savants in music, mathematics and the arts, people who have suffered brain injury or dementia, excel in areas they had never learned. Treffert believes this is genetic memory, what he called "factory-installed software," that appears when "a huge reservoir of dormant knowledge" materializes after an injured brain rewires to recover. Carvajal reports, "This is possible, Treffert explains, "only through genetic memory. In the animal kingdom, we accept without question migration patterns that birds are born with which they never learned." He gives the example of the monarch butterfly which makes a trip from Canada to a 23-acre spot in Mexico, and they take three generations to get there."

Like Doreen Carvajal and her first-time journey to the once Jewish world of Andalusia, a place unknown but beckoning to her, I found myself wondering if I was not drawn to Poland like the butterflies to their "ancestral" home. Carvajal points to studies that look at whether our ancestors' memories and experiences can be inherited, a field called epigenetics, the proposition of which is that genes have memory—what our ancestors "breathed, saw and ate—can directly affect us decades later." I had not attributed my feeling of *bashert* to epigenetics, but I would not discount it, either.

Carvajal reported also on the findings of Jerusalem psychiatrist, Dina Wardi, who works with the children of Holocaust survivors. Wardi found that survivor parents "often designated certain children as 'memorial candles' who took on the mission of serving as a link to preserve the past and connect the future." I am not clear on whether Wardi believes this would be a conscious or unconscious designation of children by parents, but that ultimately is irrelevant. The point is one child in the family becomes the locus for inherited memory. Again, although I am not the immediate child of a Holocaust survivor, I find myself reflecting: Am I a "memorial candle," a "candle child" in my family? Am I fueled by genes or something else, compelled to retrieve lost memory and denied identity? One of Wardi's findings is that the children of survivors have a "compulsive ambition to achieve"—I recognized how this surely fits my siblings and me, as well as our children—my father's grandchildren.

I have been taken to my great grandfather's tomb, a needle in a haystack, located through the efforts of the Angel in Black and Alicja of the Pink Umbrella. *Bashert* or something other, I am amazed. I say my farewell to Alicja. She has told me that her surname is Goldman, so she can never hope to find her family's story, the name being too common.

Leaving the cemetery, I made my way to the Jewish Historical Institute in Warsaw, not far from the cemetery. Before going to Warsaw I worked with a genealogist there through email and even by phone from Ireland. She was one of those cool types I have known throughout my years in academia—formal, sniffy in a way that seemed to suggest that her time was too important for you to be taking much of it. But once we met in person, the air between us warmed up. She seemed to decide that I was not a stupid person after all, and that the task was intellectually interesting to her. She used her computer program to help me a bit on my family genealogy, and promised to help more later. But after I returned to the United States, her correspondence trailed off, and I never did receive from her a response to the list of relatives I sent to her. No matter, another door will open in the future.

X

The Abbey Pub 🌳 A Taste of Wisdom

Finale
Seal Beach, California 2013

It was St. Patrick's Day. There was a tradition in my family because of my mother's heritage to make a big deal out of that holiday on March 17. Although St. Patrick's Day in America is largely an opportunity and excuse for people to carouse and drink, in my family while on that day we wore green and ate corned beef and cabbage like other Americans, we also associated the day with remembering the oppression of the Irish by the British, of the Catholic Irish by the Protestant Anglo Irish, and celebrating the uniqueness of Irish wit and charm. My father once told me that the two major romances of his life were both with Irish-American women—the second one, my mother. He mused, "I've always been drawn to the Irish, and not only women; I have a special feeling for Irish men, too."

So it was St. Patrick's Day, my mother had been gone for nine years by then, and my father had spent those years living alone in a pleasant enough facility for the elderly. We, his children, and especially my older sister and her husband, who lived close by his place, saw my father regularly, and we all gathered to celebrate holidays. This day was one of those. It was a sunny, cool day in Southern California, and I knew my father would enjoy getting out. It was too difficult for him to walk then, so I took his wheelchair with us to an Irish pub I knew near the Seal Beach, California pier. It was always a bit of a physical struggle to get him from the car to the wheelchair, but we were both small people and we managed.

I pushed his wheelchair as we moved down the tree-studded street to the Abbey Pub. We laughed about how St. Patrick's Day had somehow been a touch point for our family. We could not say exactly why, except for my mother's background, but there was more to it than that, we agreed. We talked about Irish wit. I suggested it was akin to Yiddish wit. We laughed again when we recalled my Jewish grandmother's saying, "Old people should never have been born." He joked that now at 101 years of age, he could appreciate that sentiment. But he never complained. My mother never did, either. So frequently friends of mine would comment that their ailing, elderly parents would focus on their pains, and that this would be the sole topic of conversation. My parents amazed me with their forbearance: I never heard a word of complaint.

My father ordered a Heineken; I don't recall now what I had. But we sat in the Abbey Pub, an Irish bar near the beach, and relaxed with our drinks. Maybe because we were relaxed, my father brought up my official conversion to Judaism. He shook his head, and said as he had a few times before, "I wish my parents were alive to see this." A complex statement since he had separated from them over their intolerance of his out-of-faith marriage to my mother. A complex statement because he had actively hidden his Jewish identity, and I had resented him for it, but never had the guts to openly confront him on what I had seen as hypocritical, particularly in someone who had raised me to eschew any racial or religious prejudice. I often wondered if I could not bear to hurt him, somehow, without really knowing why. Even as I had disapproved, maybe I had had some kind of empathy, without understanding why. He and I had had our good moments over the years on my problem with his (and my) Jewish identity: his coming to Poland and our tears there; our time at the Armand Hammer Museum looking over the Jacob Balgley art where we both understood without a word the meaning of "there is nothing so whole as a broken Jewish heart." And he had attended my mikveh. But his return to his statement about wishing his parents were alive to see this was different than those earlier displays of a shared feeling.

I told him that day in the pub that I had confided to my rabbi that I was upset with my father because he had "turned away" from his Jewish identity. Even then, I avoided saying "hid." And I reported the rabbi's response to me: "Let it go. It was a different time and he was in a particular situation as an immigrant."

The expression on my father's face at that telling was an inward one—one looking back in time to the young person he had been and the decision he had made, maybe allowing himself now some empathy for that former self. Or perhaps judging himself through my eyes—that is to say, disapprovingly. But I also detected relief in his face—he saw that I was not judging him, not anymore, at least. I never knew if he was aware that I judged him, but maybe he knew it all along. He had given spirited speeches about how religion divides people, how it brainwashes them. But that may have been an unconscious flight from the real question—it's one thing not to believe, another to hide. But he even fought there: what is a Jew, he would ask rhetorically, and provide the answer himself, "It's not a race, it's a religious belief," adding, "Actually the term 'Jew' is imprecise—if anything, it should be "the Hebrews."

Was this self-exculpation? Possibly. But during such discussions with my father he reminded me of the author of the *Ethics*, Baruch Spinoza, the Dutch-Portuguese Jewish philosopher who was excommunicated from Amsterdam's Jewish community for his challenge to the Hebrew Bible, applying Euclidean mathematics to philosophy, and arguing that God and nature are the same thing. A determinist, Spinoza held that all events, including those we think of as consequences of our free will, are the results of previously existing causes. As Rebecca Goldstein in her *Betraying Spinoza: The Renegade Jew Who Gave us Modernity*, summarizes, "The fundamental intuition underlying Spinoza's thinking was simply this: For every fact that is true, there is a reason why it is true. There simply cannot be, for Spinoza, the inexplicably given, a fact which is a fact for no other reason than that it is a fact." [14] That the name "Spinoza" means "thorn" in Portuguese was fitting, and his community visited the harshest version of ex-communication, *"herem,"* upon him when he was 23 years old—his views, a stab into the heart of their belief. He made his living as a lens grinder, and died at 44, likely from the dust he inhaled in his work. He turned down awards that came his way, and never offered a direct riposte to the community which disowned him. As Goldstein writes:

We now recognize that his methodology for exposing the nature of reality was inspired by one of the strands that the seventeenth century's men of science were weaving into what we now refer to as the scientific method, that magnificently subtle, supple, and successful blend of mathematical deduction and empirical induction. Spinoza was keenly interested and involved in the intellectual innovations that we now look back on as constituting the birth of modern science . . . . There are contemporary physicists and cosmologists who are inspired by the Spinozist ideal of 'a theory of everything', one in which mathematics alone would determine its truth. String theorists, in particular, pursue physics almost entirely as a deductive endeavor letting their mathematics prevail over niggling questions . . . . A number of propositions that he [Spinoza] produced from out of his deductive system ... have been, centuries later, scientifically vindicated. [15]

I never knew if my father read Spinoza, but he was, in any case, a Spinozist. As a scientist, this gave him the basis of his argument against religion, generally, Judaism specifically, and provided at least one part of the defense for his denial of his Jewish identity. His argument was respectable, but for me it did not account for the veiling of his Jewish self. There were moments when I thought he was regularly testing his own ideas on this subject out loud to see if he believed them. After all, I had witnessed his outraged tears after Munich when he told my dismayed mother that if the world was like that, he did not want to live in it. I had watched him rightly throw my German-American childhood friend off his property. I saw him weep in Poland. He was not without his personal connection to Jewishness. Yet, he had not owned it, and had built up a rationale that allowed him to distance himself from it.

But all this fell away on that day, celebrating St. Patrick's Day in a Southern Californian Irish pub, when he looked at me and said, "You are a lot braver than I ever was." This, it turned out, was what he had been thinking at my mikveh. In that second, all my judgments, all the years of confusion and hurt, all the veils and curtains over things that could not be said—all these fell away. My heart rose up, and I felt tears of love ready to pour from my eyes. I wanted to speak, but my throat was choked. I waited a moment to get my voice. What I had to say in response was amazingly simple, given all the years of turmoil. I surprised myself with how simple it was: "Dad, I am not brave. It is an honor for me to be able to claim my Jewish identity—today, it is my luxurious choice. For you, everything was different."

That was all. There was no need for dialectic like we had engaged in before. No speeches on either of our parts. Both of us good at argument, clever with language, now there was an understanding that had no need to be spoken: language would only fail it. There was tenderness. And hope. We smiled at one another, thinking of the State of Israel, and saying, "The story isn't over yet."

The years I had absorbed his underlying premise that the world was not to be trusted, that intrinsic hopelessness, gave way. We were both suddenly modest in our opinions *per se*. It felt like two children who are filled with wonder and curiosity about the world, or two very old people who can take much for granted about the other's feelings without having to explain anything. Our eyes told the story of how much we agreed and felt in our hearts. Maybe my Jewish grandmother was right that "old people should never have been born," but at that moment I felt that the older I had gotten, the less I knew, and that here, perhaps, was the beginning of wisdom.

END

EPILOGUE

As I said, my father died at 102 on October 4, 2014, and yes, my three siblings were at his bedside, but I was not. Strange that I should not be there. Painful. I guess our goodbye, our closure, was 2013 at the Abbey Pub.

I had gone to Poland in the first place to learn hard truths and to rescue hope. What had I found? That generalizations residing at the end of the "good" or "evil" extremes of judgment did little to enlighten. That Roald Hoffman was right about the "tense middle," that E.M. Forster's "excursions into either realm," his "only connect the rainbow bridge" described my position. And that these were also ways of saying that in our lifetimes we will surely travel the spectrum from hope to mistrust and even to despair, that even day-to-day we will find occasion to be inspired, and then on others to be devastated. And by at last formally owning my Jewish identity, I found the fitting space as the candle child of my family.

After visiting my great grandfather's tomb in Warsaw, and the archives in Brest, I knew my family had a long history in Brest. I wanted to see if I could learn how far back this history could be traced. So when I heard nothing back from the Jewish Historical Institute for further research into the history of my family, another door did open. That door turned out to be my decision to hire a Polish genealogist. After I found my father's records in his apartment and planned my trip to Belarus, an American friend, Jeremy Borovitz, a former Peace Corps volunteer in Ukraine, referred me to Witold Wroszinski, a Polish genealogist, a reportedly expert Jewish genealogy expert. Witold himself was half-Jewish.

Sight unseen, from California, I had hired Witold to begin research on my family genealogy, and gave him all the names and family connections I had gathered from information I had learned from my father, my Uncle Morris, my Israeli relatives living in Michigan where I attended their son's wedding, and the Balgleys I had met in Israel. I now had Jacob Balgley's portion of the family tree which I had been given at the Gorky Library in Brest. It seemed possible armed with this information that Witold could learn more and piece together a family tree. It was, in any case, worth a try.

After meeting my family in New York and in Israel, I found other relatives in the United States. Again, *bashert*, unlikely coincidences led to my discoveries: my younger sister, Lisa, had learned of a Paul Balgley when she was an undergraduate at UCLA in the late 1970s. Her inquiry led her to Meredith Balgley, his sister, but no further contact ensued. However, when I began to put together the family tree, through Lisa's initial contact, I reached out to Meredith. As it turned out, coincidentally at just about this same time, my brother, Michael, a great lover of classical music, learned of a Noah Bendix-Balgley, premiere violinist and concert master of the Berlin Philharmonic. Michael's initial message to Noah fell into the hands of someone posing as Noah's agent, and only later did we learn that Noah had known nothing of Michael's attempt to reach him. When Meredith and I arranged to meet in person, my elder sister, Janie, and I met Meredith and her son, Aaron, in Los Angeles. As it turned out, Noah Bendix-Balgley was the son of Meredith, and brother to Aaron. I shared the family tree with Meredith and Aaron that day, and later Meredith hired my genealogist, Witold, to research how her branch of the family connected to what we had already discovered.

I followed up on Aunt Beatty's branch of the family. The artwork I had admired in her home at Brighton Beach had been done by her son, Willard Miranker, Professor of Computer Science at Yale, long-time research scientist at IBM, and painter. Willard had died, but had three sons, Andrew Miranker, Professor of Molecular Biophysics and Biochemistry and Professor of Chemical and Environmental Engineering at Yale; Daniel Miranker, Professor of Computer Science, Department of Computer Science at University of Texas, Austin; and Glen Miranker, Chief Technology Office for Apple. As I indicated previously, it was Andrew Miranker who sent me the painting of our great-grandparents and Beatty as a child, which his father Willard had painted from the photograph I had seen.

Later still, Meredith reported to me that a Lydia Balgley Schigimont from Cologne, Germany had read that Noah Bendix-Balgley was concert master of the Berlin Philharmonic and had contacted him. I had been looking for the connection to Jacob Balgley, and failing to find his daughter, Rachel Blanc-Balgley, who had written in the 1980s to my cousin David in New York, I looked for her son, Olivier Blanc, who would be living in Paris. Efforts to locate him were discussed, and I attempted contact with Saphir Gallery in Paris where Jacob Balgley's work was reportedly collected. Then the sudden contact after two decades of trying to find a family relative of Rachel's, daughter to painter, Jacob Balgley, out of the blue Lydia Balgley Schigimont (in Cologne, Germany) contacted Noah Bendix-Balgley, concert master of the Berlin Philharmonic, son to my American relative found "by accident," Meredith Balgley of Asheville, North Carolina) to check on family connections. Thus, as it turned out, my long search for any relatives of the painter, Jacob Balgley,

Photographed in Berlin, standing left to right: Friend of Lydia, Lydia (Balgley) Schigimont, Lydia's husband, Michael Schigimont. Seated row left to right: Lena (Balgley) Schneidermann (daughter of Lydia), Meredith Balgley, Meredith's husband Erik Bendix, Meredith and Erik's son Noah Bendix-Balgley, Shenshen Balgley, Noah and Shenshen's son, Ari Balgley. Courtesy Balgley Family Archive

Aaron Bendix-Balgley, son of Meredith Balgley and Erik Bendix, brother to Noah, pictured above. Courtesy Balgley Family Archive

whom I had known of since my teaching days at UCLA in the 1980s, and had learned more about in the book, "Balgley" by Jeanine Warnod, provided to me by my cousin, David Balgley, and whose work my father and I had gone to see at the Armand Hammer Museum in Los Angeles—it turned out that Lydia Schigimont's grandfather, Abraham, had been brother to the painter, Jacob. Lydia herself is also an accomplished painter, as is her daughter, Lena Schneidermann, who currently lives in Cologne, the latter highly conversant in English and with whom I am in regular contact. Too, Lena has now met Aaron and Noah and Meredith in Germany.

Just as I finished writing this book, Andrew Miranker contacted me, explaining his father's 3,000-plus paintings must at last find their final disposition, and offering me the painting his father had done of our great grandparents, Ze'ev and Bluma, the very same painting I had seen when I visited Aunt Beatty in the "Little Odessa" of Brighton Beach.

I had already been lucky to meet Yossi and Dorit (Balgley) Ben-Gal in Michigan, and then later in New York and California. I met their children, Nitsan and Itai, both of whom are married and have one son each.

Further research revealed Robert Balgley, CEO, Mersive Technologies, Inc. in Colorado, and his sister, Linda Balgley Shore, who lives in California. Linda, Meredith, both my sisters, Janie and Lisa, my daughter Emily, and I all were able to meet one another in Southern California. Plans are in the works for a possible Balgley family reunion of all contacts.

After I connected with Lydia she discovered Jacob Balgley's grave and his wife's grave in Paris. Courtesy Balgley Family Archive

Lydia and daughter Lena, who both live in Cologne, Germany, orginally from the Soviet Union. Courtesy Balgley Family Archive

Yossi and Dorit (Balgley) Ben-Gal, in Michigan on the occasion of their son's wedding. Courtesy Balgley Family Archive

Yossi and Dorit's son Itai, his wife Melanie, and son Ital. Courtesy Balgley Family Archive

Nitsan (Balgley) Ben-Gal, daughter of Yossi and Dorit, and sister to Itai, here pictured with her husband, John Nguyen, and their son Daniel. Courtesy Balgley Family Archive

Linda Balgley-Shore, her brother Rob Balgley, their parents Gloria and Howard Balgley. Courtesy Balgley Family Archive

Shirley (Balgley) Tainowitz and daughter Randi (Tainowitz) Borgen. Courtesy Balgley Family Archive

Daughter Emily, myself and father Ely at his 100th birthday.
Courtesy Balgley Family Archive

My parents, Ely and
Margaret with my
siblings, brother Michael,
sisters Lisa, Janie, and
myself. Courtesy Balgley
Family Archive

Los Angeles, 2015

Back in California I met Rabbi Haim Bialek, Executive Director of Jewish Renewal in Poland, who invited me to read from my writings to a group at his home in Los Angeles. Rabbi Haim has successfully led this group with trips for Americans to Poland, as well as spearheading a host of other projects to grow awareness of Jewish history and current Jewish life in Poland. At Rabbi Haim's home I was introduced to Severyn Ashkenazy, a philanthropist based in Los Angeles, born in Poland, having come to the United States after World War II, and educated in America and France. Severyn had established a center in Warsaw, *Beit Warszawa* (Warsaw House), where due to his charity, services and celebrations, offered a sense of continuity and hope to the Jewish community there. Severyn and his partner, Irina, invited me to visit in Warsaw, and in a matter of months, I went to *Beit Warszawa*. There I met members of the Jewish community of Warsaw. Maybe this could be the blossoming my father and I had alluded to in our hopeful talk at the Abbey Pub.

APPENDIX

From its very beginning, Brest had been at the epicenter of history. The fact of the city's multiple names testifies to this: first founded by the Slavs, the town is called "*Berestye*" in Kievan Rus. As early as 1019 the Russians were fighting with the Poles for control of the town when the Kievan Rus took the city from the Poles. For years to follow, Polish kings and dukes fought with Rus princes to regain the territory. A century later, Mongols invaded and destroyed the city. For three decades it was not rebuilt, at which time it became part of the Grand Duchy of Lithuania. Teutonic knights burned the outskirts of Brest in 1379, and in 1500 the entire city was destroyed by the Crimean Tatars. In the sixteenth century, the city became part of the Polish-Lithuanian Commonwealth and was renamed "*Brześć Litewski*" in Polish for Brest-Litovsk or Brest of Lithuania. Brest was continually the place where east would meet west: an historic meeting between the councils of the Roman Catholic Church and the Eastern Orthodox Church bishops in the region took place there in the late 1500s. That meeting resulted in the establishment of the Belarusian Greek Catholic Church in Belarus and the Ukrainian Greek Catholic Church in Ukraine. In 1660 a Muscovite Russian army invaded, taking the Brest castle and killing nearly 2,000 defenders along with their families. The 1700s saw the town captured by the Swedes, and in 1792 the army of the Duchy of Lithuania, an arm of the Polish army, fought the invading Russian Imperial Army. Two years later, the land between Terespol and Brest saw a battle won by the Russians over the famous Kościuszko army of Poland, and Brest became a part of Russia. This was known as the "Battle of Brest," and the Poland-Lithuanian Commonwealth was partitioned for the third time in 1795. The two earlier partitions, the first in 1772 was initiated by Prussia's Frederick the Great to prevent Austria, unhappy with the Russian Empire's expansion, from going to war. The second was in 1793, with the Poles unable to defend against Russia in 1792, terminated the Polish-Lithuanian Commonwealth. This led to the third partition in 1795 which effectively removed Poland from the map. Russia now ruled Brest, and it was in the nineteenth century under Russian rule that the Brest Fortress was built, where the Polish Royal Castle now demolished, had once stood.

So when my father was born in Brest in 1912, the city was Russian. But by 1915, during the World War I, Germany captured the city. Three years later, when my father would have been 6 years old, the historic Treaty of Brest-Litovsk was signed at the Brest Fortress, ending the war between the Quadruple Alliance (Germany, Austria-Hungary, the Ottoman Empire, and Bulgaria) and Soviet Russia. Brest then became a city of the German Empire. However, the treaty was short-lived, and later that year after Brest had been briefly part of the Belarusian Democratic Republic, Poland, now reconstituted, again took back Brest as her own.

Thus, the years of my father's childhood in this city, 1912 through to 1920, he and his family lived under the aegis of three different countries. Even as the family was preparing to depart in 1920, the Polish-Soviet War had begun, and was not ended until 1921 by the Peace of Riga, wherein Poland kept control of Brest, western Ukraine and western Belarus.

During these chaotic and violent centuries, naturally the Jewish community of Brest was affected by such changes, and its own history was certainly as dramatic. Brest has been called by several names, all of which delineate its turbulent history: as noted earlier, first, *Berestye* by the Kievan Rus who founded the town, and later *Brestye* or *Berestov*; *Brześć Litewski* (Brest of Lithuanian) when the city was part of the Lithuanian-Polish Commonwealth; in Polish, *Brześć nad Bugiem* (Brest on the Bug River); *Brest-Litowsk* in Belarusian. But for the Jews of Brest, the city went by its Yiddish name, *"Brisk"* or *"Brisk de-Lita"* (Brest of Lithuania). A type of Talmudic study initiated by Rabbi Chaim Soloveitchik of Brisk is named for the city—the "Brisker Method." In brief, this method changed the traditional holistic way of interpreting the Talmud, and instead used a more analytical or conceptual strategy which searched for precise definitions. The Brisker Method has undergone changes over time, and has been the subject for debate and controversy, but it is still practiced in yeshivahs today.

Dating from the second half of the fourteenth century, Brest had been the largest of the first five Jewish communities in Lithuania. During the fifteenth and sixteenth centuries, Jewish Brest rose to great importance as both a religious center and a mercantile center. A charter from the Polish king Casimir Jagellon in 1447 to all Jews of Poland and Lithuania indicates that Brest controlled many territories; in 1463 Casimir conferred several estates in Brest to a Jew, Levan Shalomich, and leased a number of villages to him as well. In 1472 when the property of a Jewish merchant was seized in Prussia, both secular councilors of the king, as well as the bishops of Wilno, intervened in support of the Jewish merchant. Yet, on the other hand, Alexander Jagellon, the son of Casimir in 1495 banished the Jews of Brest and other Lithuanian cities to Poland. Eight years later they were allowed to return to Brest. During the period of the banishment, Alexander had given the Brest synagogue to Brest's Christians to be used as a hospital. However, when the Jews of Brest returned, the synagogue was returned to them. In the 1500s Jews filled high offices in Brest as "Seniors," but that honor was essentially a way for the king to be assured the Jews over which the Senior ruled, would pay their taxes in full and on time. In 1576, King Stephan Bathory excused all Jews of Brest from paying taxes because of the serious losses they had incurred from fires in the region. Custom house records show that nearly all the merchandise imported from Germany and Austria through Lublin belonged to the Jews of Brest. From Germany they imported iron, paper, paint, locks, knives, mirrors, mohair, muscatel, olives, furs; from Hungary, wire; from the Silesian part of the country, ribbon, wine, velvet, pepper, sugar, raisins; and from Moravia, cloth. They exported soap, bridles, copper belts, grain and lumber.

The Jewish "Pinkes" or Archives of Lithuania indicate that in 1566 Brest had 106 Jewish house owners out of 852. The houses were small wooden dwellings, and were often homes to families of more than fourteen people. A synagogue was also a frame building until 1569, when a brick synagogue was built, and many homes were then built with brick. A wealthy mercantile city, Jewish Brest was also renown as a center for religious study. The yeshiva at Brest brought students from Italy and Germany to study with famous rabbis, scholars and Talmudists, among them Moses, the grandson of Rabbi Heshel, and Abraham ben Benjamin Ze'ev Brisker. A series of edicts from King John Casimir from 1655 through 1662, prohibited (gentiles) from building inns or selling liquor, justifying this by stating that the Brest leaseholders of the king would be harmed. The king warned that any such buildings would be confiscated; the king released Jews from military service for four years, defending this by citing how the Jews had been hurt by an invasion from Moscow. Finally, the king released the Jews of Brest from paying their creditors for three years, again arguing that the Jews had suffered losses from the Moscovite invasions. All of these edicts were in truth ways for the king to protect the benefits he incurred through his relationship with Jewish merchants and tax collectors. For the Christian citizen, then, the Jew became the target for his anger and resentment, rather than the king.

By the 1630s the friendly relations that had existed between Christians and Jews of Brest began to deteriorate. Lawsuits between Jews and Christians based on property became numerous. A more serious case indicates that a Christian murderer of a Jew was released from prison by a priest who was paid off by the murderer. Authorities removed guards from the prison to allow the murderer to escape, and those citizens who saw him flee did not assist the

Jewish community in trying to recapture him. Conflicts arose between the Jews and the Catholic and Greek Orthodox clergy. Lithuanian youth were educated by the Jesuits, and with encouragement from them, attacked and beat Jews in what was known as "*Schülergelauf*," organized assaults on Jewish persons and property. This was happening in other Polish cities during the same period.

In Kraków, students from a Jesuit Academy claiming that Jews had blasphemed their religion, invaded the Jewish quarter, killed many people and wounded others, stole over 4,000 florins, and made their victims promise not to prosecute them. Jews sometimes retaliated. Again in Brest, the rector of the Jesuit College there requested a formal protest against the Jews for what he called their hatred of Christian blood, charging that the Jews had attacked children of the city's officials with heavy clubs, and keeping for proof a club at the college.

The infamous Cossack Uprising in 1649 under General Chmielnicki against Poland entirely destroyed Brest, with over 2,000 Jews killed in the city, along with Poles, the wives and children of both murdered, palaces destroyed, wooden buildings burned and the entire city demolished. From the start of the seventeenth century, the edicts from Polish kings which had helped Jews then disappeared, and the community was held responsible for all debts. By the eighteenth century the Jewish kahals were bankrupt. Brest declined with the partitions of the Polish-Lithuanian kingdom.

The city was partially rebuilt during the second partition of Poland and Brest came into the possession of Russia. Two years later, in 1797, Brest was annexed to Lithuanian provinces, and finally in 1801, it came under the governance of Grodno. A year later, a fire destroyed much of the Jewish quarter, including five small synagogues. When in the nineteenth century, Nicholas I, Czar of Russia, built the Brest fortress, many more Jewish buildings were brought down, including the ancient synagogue. During the work on the fortress, the Jewish cemetery was destroyed, and tombstones moved to another location, where their inscriptions could not be read. The government did provide partial reparation for these losses. In 1838 a Jewish hospital was built with forty beds and a pharmacy. In 1851 a new synagogue was built and in 1877 a home for the poor was established, as well as a Jewish school for 500 pupils. In 1895 and 1901 two more fires occurred and in consequence, lives and property were lost, and the number of Jewish poor increased.

My family records, as far as back as I have currently been able to trace, date to the 1700s. I know that my Brest ancestors owned property at that time. What suffering or success they likely experienced, genealogy has not yielded. But at least it is possible to know what the conditions were in Brest before, during and after the dates I see for my ancestors.

Books known as *Yizkor* (translated literally from the Hebrew, "May God remember"), so-called "memorial books" have been created by the collective effort of Holocaust survivors from their respective home cities and towns. The Yizkor Book of Brest includes anecdotal stories from the nineteenth and twentieth centuries. In particular, the Yizkor Book tells of the expulsion of the Jews from Brest in 1915 by Nicholas II. That explained why my father and his family relocated to Kobrin, the original home town of my grandmother, Sarah Slomiansky, twenty-nine miles from Brest. Three years later after the expulsion, the Jews of Brest were allowed to return. There exists a Yizkor Book of Kobrin, as well, chronicling the rapid change of governing countries there after World War I, with the Treaty of Brest-Litovsk establishing peace between the victorious Bolshevik Russian government and the Central Powers which included Austria-Hungary, Bulgaria, the Ottoman and German Empires. The Yizkor Books of Brest-Litovsk and Kobrin demonstrate how the Jewish communities both thrived and suffered. When in 1915 the Germans defeated the Russians and took Brest and Kobrin as theirs, the Germans built Jewish schools, and replaced Russian language with Ukrainian language in the gentile schools. The Germans also provided cholera shots for the population. This explains for me why my Uncle Morris, the younger, my father's eldest brother, had told me how things improved in their towns under the Germans, remarking the irony of this. In 1918, when Poland took possession of Brest, things deteriorated. One reason cited was that Poland, having been partitioned by foreign occupation for nearly two centuries, had little experience of what democracy was. Jews were not allowed to work in the civil service, transport or state-owned monopolies. By the time my father and his family left in 1920, Poland had established a sort of state capitalism known as "etatism" which nationalized many industries, including liquor, timber and salt, all of which had been created by Jews. As the Polish government nationalized these industries all Jewish employees were dismissed. As risky and difficult as it was, my grandfather was prescient when he left his family for the United States in 1913, working for seven years with the help of HIAS (the Hebrew Immigrant Aid Society) to bring his family out of Poland in 1920.[16] HIAS had been originally established in 1881 in the United States to aid Jewish refugees. Since then, and the time the agency aided my grandfather in what in retrospect we now realize saved my father and the family from annihilation, HIAS assisted over 4,000 Vietnamese refugees, and works currently with Syrian refugees, and others regardless of national, religious or ethnic origins. To date, HIAS has resettled nearly five million people.

NOTES

1   Adrienne Rich, "Split at the Root: An Essay on Jewish Identity" in *Blood, Bread, and Poetry: Selected Prose 1979-1985,* (New York and London: W. W. Norton and Co., 1986), 100.

2   I later learned that the home my father, his mother and three siblings traveled to in Warsaw was the home of my grandfather's brother, Herschel. *Bashert* occurred once again: traveling to Israel to meet my relatives, I learned of Yossi (Balgley) Ben-Gal, an Israeli now living in Michigan. I met Yossi's mother and sister in Tel Aviv and Haifa where I was the recipient of their spectacular hospitality. Yossi's mother and daughter then led me to eventually meet Yossi and his wife, Dorit, in Michigan. As Yossi and I matched our information about the Balgley geneaology, we confirmed that his grandfather, Herschel, was a brother to my grandfather, Israel, and furthermore, that it was to Herschel's home in Warsaw that my father as a little boy accompanied by his mother and three siblings had traveled to from Brest to Warsaw. As I describe later, my father's shock at the familiarity of the house where I took my parents to stay in Warsaw when they visited me in Poland, was his recall of Herschel's house, an affluent Jewish home, reminiscent of the home where I was staying in Warsaw. Later, when Yossi and Dorit visited Warsaw, they went to the spot where Herschel's home had been on Niska Street. We all confirmed that Niska Street had been enclosed in the infamous Warsaw Ghetto, thus Herschel himself and his house were destroyed by the Nazis. However, as I relay later, Herschel's son, Abba, father to Yossi, was a soldier in the Polish Army, and had survived, like other Jewish soldiers in the well-known Anders' Polish Army, by leaving the army to remain in Israel when the troops came through the Middle East.

3   Kenneth M. Luderer, *Time to Heal: American Medical Education from the Turn of the Century to the Era of Managed Care*, (New York: Oxford University Press, 1999), 64.

4   Jan T. Gross, *Neighbors: The Destruction of the Jewish Community in Jedwabne, Poland* (Princeton University Press, 2001). Gross' book was a bombshell in the Polish community: the carefully researched story of how Poles unaided by the Nazis turned on their Jewish neighbors with whom they had lived for years, murdering them in a frenzied bloody attack. The fallout from Gross's report brought to the fore the long-buried discussion of Polish anti-Semitism, and reignited the passionate controversy over Polish complicity during the war. That controversy has not only not subsided but grown over time. At one point, the president of Poland and the president of Israel traveled to Jedwabne for a memorial service with many other notable attendees. Since the publication of *Neighbors*, the following books by Gross have appeared and continue to stoke the controversy:

      Jan T. Gross, *Fear: Anti-Semitism in Poland after Auschwitz* (Random House and Princeton University Press, 2006).

      Jan T. Gross with Irena Grudzinska Gross, *Golden Harvest* (Oxford University Press, 2012)

      Because of Gross' exposure of Polish participation in the murder of Poland's Jews, the Polish regime, the Law and Justice Party or PiS, led by President Andrzej Duda, attempted to rescind Gross's honor, the Knight's Cross of the Order of Merit, which he had been awarded for his work opposing Polish communism. It is not clear at this writing if Duda and his cohorts ever succeeded in rescinding the honor.

      After Gross's *Neighbors* was published in 2001 in the US (2000 in Poland), in

2004 this book appeared: *The Neighbors Respond: The Controversy Over the Jedwabne Massacre in Poland*, Antony Polonsky and Joanna B. Michlic, eds., (Princeton and Oxford: Princeton University Press, 2004). Thirty-three articles offering various perspectives are offered here.

5   Ela Szlufik of Research Center for History and Culture of the Jews of Poland, Jagiellonian University, Cracow, Poland, *Tikkun*, volume 3, no. 1, Letter to the Editor, p.7 and pp. 81–82. An inflamed series of letters to the editor in this issue were ignited in response to Abraham Brumberg's "Poland and the Jews" in an earlier issue of "Tikkun." Szlufik's references to him necessitate a brief resume: As the first editor of the journal, *Problems of Communism*, in the early 1950s, his analyses drew a wide audience of intellectuals and government officials. He remained the journal's editor in chief until 1970, after having made the journal a highly praised forum for analysis in the cold war period. Mr. Brumberg wrote on Eastern European subjects for *The Nation, Dissent, The New York Times, The New York Review of Books*, among other publications. His work for pieces on the situation of the Jews in Poland and the Soviet Union were widely known. Interestingly, he was born in 1926 in Tel Aviv, after his parents had fled there from Poland where his father had been a leader of the Jewish Socialist Bund. But the family returned to Poland when Brumberg was a child, and again had to flee in 1939. The family went first to Lithuania, then Japan, and finally the United States in 1941. Brumberg received a bachelor's degree in social science from the City College of New York in 1950, and a master's degree in Soviet studies from Yale in 1953.

6   Alexander Beider, *Dictionary of Jewish Surnames in the Kingdom of Poland*, (Avotaynu , 1996). Alexander Beider, *Dictionary of Jewish Surnames in the Russian Empire* (Avotaynu, 2008).

7   Jerzy Ficowski, *Bruno Schulz, Xięga Bałwochwalcza (Book of Idolatry)*, Warszawa: Wyawnictwo Interpress, 1988.

8   Roald Hoffmann, "The Tense Middle," in Jay Allison and Dan Gediman with John Gregory and Viki Merrick, eds., *This I Believe*, p.112.

9   Antoni Słonimski,"Elegy for the Little Jewish Towns" in Eva Hoffman, *Shtetl: The Life and Death of a Small Town and the World of Polish Jews*, (New York: PublicAffairs, 1997), 1.

10 This is the painting by Jacob Balgley done in 1917 on the cover of this book.

11 I had been given to understand by my Polish colleagues in the US who kindly interpreted the documents of Motel Balgley and Sara Balgley for me that these may have been "standard" applications for identity cards since their colleagues had been required to apply for identity cards in the Poland of the 1960s and 1970s. But the research from JewishGen below provides the actual story of such "Ghetto Passports": I learned that a "Brest Ghetto Passport Archive" had been established, and JewishGen, an affiliate of the Museum of Jewish Heritage had ultimately uncovered the following research: "The Brest Ghetto Passport Archive represents the first phase of the Phoenix Project, a multi-year effort, directed by John Garrard (Professor of Russian Literature at the University of Arizona) to computerize data on the Holocaust drawn primarily from newly-opened archives in the Soviet Union. The data was digitized by Phillip Hammonds, a University of Arizona graduate student, and has been re-engineered by Michael Tobias for JewishGen. Many of these archives have been microfilmed and may be studied at the United States Holocaust Memorial Museum in Washington, D.C., and at Yad Vashem in Jerusalem ... *The Brest Ghetto Passport Archive consists of documents prepared at the order of the Nazi authorities after the capture of Brest in the summer of 1941. All Jews of 14 years of age and above living in the Brest Ghetto were required to obtain and sign for identity papers, which included their names, ages, and the names and dates of birth of their parents. A photo of*

each person was taken and all those receiving these internal passports were required to sign.... These passports survived in the archives captured by advancing Soviet troops in 1944. Also captured among many other valuable documents was a ledger recording the distribution of passports and again the signature of all those receiving them." *Thus, the applications for identity cards for Motel and Sara Balgley here pictured, which required their photographs and the presence of a person to verify that they were telling the truth, were not "standard" in the least, but rather the prelude to internment in the Ghetto. In the list of Balgleys listed in the Brest Ghetto Passport Archive, we see Motel and Sara, he 14, and she 15. "By the time Brest was liberated, all the people living in the Brest Ghetto had been murdered, including many children under the age of 14. Only a very few former Jewish inhabitants of Brest survived the Nazi occupation."* Italics, my own.

12   The horrific history that this monument recorded was disturbing enough—5,000 men were executed immediately after the Nazi invasion in June 1941. The other thousands of Jews commemorated here, as the monument reads, were marched to freight trains and driven the 62 miles to the Bronna Gora woods, ordered to strip, and stand over a trench where they were shot, approximately 50,000 persons. Those who were not killed in these actions, were forced into the Brest Ghetto. But in 2019 there was a discovery of the remains of 1,214 bodies in a mass grave in Brest during an excavation for an elite apartment building in the center of the city where the Brest Ghetto had been from 1941 to 1942. Young Belarussian soldiers dug and scraped carefully for days at the site finding human bones, pieces of clothing, the remains of shoes. Bullet holes were found in the skulls, the military chief, Dmitry Kaminsky, explained, indicating that all the victims were shot in the back of the head and the bodies disinterred were lying face down. His team is trained to do such work: normally, they search for the remains of Soviet soldiers. But here they have found the skulls of teenagers, of women, and one female skeleton in particular holding the remains of an infant. BBC interviewed Mikhail Kaplan, a Jew whose family from Brest was annihilated. He explained that everyone knew of these mass murders, but after the war Stalin and his regime never spoke of them. Any post-war memorials were dedicated to "Soviet citizens" without mention of the Jews who were alone targeted for extermination. After this excavation, 120 blue caskets marked with the Star of David were buried in a local cemetery. A rabbi led a funeral service where approximately 300 people were in attendance—Israel's ambassador to Belarus was among these. Some leaders of Brest's small Jewish community criticized the symbolic funeral, wanting instead DNA tests to establish the identities of the murdered. I wonder what Balgleys might have been discovered—young Motel and Sara?
     BBC News, Sarah Rainsford, April 1, 2019
     CBS News, Caitlin O'Kane, May 23, 2019

13   Carvajal, Doreen. *The Forgetting River: A Modern Tale of Survival, Identity, and the Inquisition.* Riverhead Books, 2012.

14   Rebecca Goldstein, *Betraying Spinoza: The Renegade Jew Who Gave Us Modernity,* New York: Nextbook Schocken, 2006), pp. 9–10.

15   Goldstein, *Betraying Spinoza,* pp. 9--10.

16   Today the building that was the headquarters for HIAS from 1921 to 1965 stands at 425 Lafayette Street in New York, now the home of The Public Theatre. The Theatre holds five theater spaces and "Joe's Pub," a cabaret-like space for new performances named for Joseph Papp (born Joseph Papirofsky in June, 1921), famed theatrical producer and director. But the building was originally constructed in 1849 as a home for the East Village's lavish Astor Library. More than fifty years later the library joined the Lenox Library and the Tilden Foundation to become the New York Public Library. A beautiful architectural structure, but what was to become of it? HIAS was just coming into its own, and it hired architect Benjamin Levitan to manage alterations that would create the appropriate sort

of space HIAS would need. While Levitan was impressed by the building's original structure—elaborate iron and wood book stacks, skylights, columns, double-height spaces, vaulted ceilings—he knew that the place had to allow for the needs of HIAS. The goal of Levitan and HIAS was to create a space that was at once aesthetically welcoming, but could also accommodate freshly-arrived Jewish immigrants emergency shelter, food, place for religious practice, a "landing space" so these immigrants could begin their new lives in the city. According to a report written in 2018 by Janine Veazue of the Jewish Historical Society, "After the final structural reconstruction efforts were finished, a community bazaar was held to furnish the building, it was dedicated by President Warren G. Harding on June 5, 1920. This new HIAS location provided ample space for both the organization's executive headquarters and facilities to ease immigrans into many aspects of American life. The building's features included:

*Separate dormitories for men and women
*Two kosher kitchens—one for meat preparation and one for dairy
*A large dining room for comfortable communal, social eating
*An operating synagogue, both for those living within HIAS' walls and neighborhood residents
*Holiday celebrations, such as a yearly neighborhood Passover Seder
*Facilities for children, including donated toys and games, classrooms, and a playground

In addition to providing personal shelter and community interaction, 425 Lafayette Street also became 'base camp' for various HIAS-sponsored immigration and community services:

HIAS Immigrant Bank
The bank, which was licensed by NY State, was established in 1923 and limited itself to the receiving and transmitting of money to/from immigrants' famiies abroad. For many years, no other U.S. banks would send dollars abroad.

Citizenship Services
The HIAS offices were open every Sunday in order to accommodate those who were not able to apply for citizenship applicatons during the week. HIAS office staff also prepared Affadavits of Support and led citizenship clsses for clients during these extra weekend hours.

Ellis Island Services
HIAS set up satellite offices at Ellis Island in order to offer personal and immediate aid to those arriving in New York, those who were in danger of being deported back home, and those requiring other forms of legal aid.

In honor of HIAS' work and how they turned one building into a place of hope for thousands of Jewish migrants, a plaque is affixed to the outside of 425 Lafayette Street. It reads:

> ## THIS PLAQUE IS DEDICATED TO
> ## HIAS, THE HEBREW IMMIGRANT AID SOCIETY,
> ## WHICH OCCUPIED THIS BUILDING FROM
> ## 1921 TO 1965.
>
> AS THE INTERNATIONAL MIGRATION AGENCY OF THE AMERICAN JEWISH COMMUNITY, HIAS' WORK, PROVIDING RESCUE AND REFUGE FOR ENDANGERED AND PERSECUTED PEOPLE OF ALL FAITHS AND BACKGROUNDS AROUND THE WORLD, CONTINUES TO THIS DAY.
>
> FOUNDED IN 1881, HIAS HAS RESCUED MORE THAN 4,500,000 MEN, WOMEN, AND CHILDREN, INCLUDING MEMBERS OF ALMOST EVERY JEWISH FAMILY IN AMERICA. TENS OF THOUSANDS OF THESE REFUGEES AND MIGRANTS WERE SHELTERED AND FED IN THIS BUILDING BEFORE THEY ENTERED THE MAINSTREAM OF LIFE IN THIS GREAT NATION.

"This plaque is dedication to HIAS, the Hebrew Immigrant Aid Society, which occupied this building from 1921 to 1965.

As the International Migration Agency of the American Jewiswh Community, HIAS' work, roviding rescue and refuge for endangered nd persecuted people of all faiths and backgrounds around the world, continues to this day. Founded in 1881, HIAS has rescued more than 4,500,000 men, women and children, including members of almost every Jewish family in America. Tens of thousands of these refugees and migrants were sheltered and fed in this building before they entered the minstream of life in this great nation."

Bibliography

Abramsky, Chimen, Maciej Jachimczyk, Antony Polonsky, eds. *The Jews in Poland.* Basil Blackwell Limited, Oxford, 1986.

Agursky, Mikhail, et al. *From Under the Rubble.* Translated by Michael Scammell, Little, Brown and Company, 1975.

Allison, Jay, and Dan Gediman, editors. *This I Believe II: More Personal Philosophies of Remarkable Men and Women.* Henry Holt and Company, 2008.

Antler, Joyce, ed. *America and I: Short Stories by American Jewish Women Writers.* Beacon Press, Boston, 1990.

Arendt, Hannah. *Antisemitism: Part One of the Origins of Totalitarianism.* Harcourt, Brace, Jovanovich, New York, 1951.

---. *On Revolution.* Penguin Books, Limited, New York, 1965.

Arendt, Hannah. *Totalitarianism: Part Three of the Origins of Totalitarianism.* Harcourt, Brace, Jovanovich, New York, 1951.

Ascherson, Neal. *The Struggles for Poland.* Random House, 1987.

Ash, Timothy Garton. *The Polish Revolution: Solidarity.* Vintage Books, 1985.

Baker, Cynthia M. *Jew.* Rutgers University Press, New Brunswick, New Jersey, and London, 2017.

Baker, Russell, et al. *Inventing the Truth: The Art and Craft of Memoir.* Edited by William Zinsser, Houghton Mifflin Company, 1995.

Barańczak, Stanislaw, editor. *The Polish Review: XXXV, ser. 1.* Polish Institute of Arts and Sciences of America, 1990.

Bar-Itszhak Ḥaya. *Jewish Poland: Legends of Origin.* Wayne State University Press, 2001.

Behar, Ruth. *An Island Called Home: Returning to Jewish Cuba.* Rutgers University Press, New Brunswick, New Jersey, and London, 2007.

---. *Letters from Cuba.* Nancy Paulsen Books, an imprint of Penguin Random House, New York, 2020.

---. *Lucky Broken Girl.* Puffin Book, an imprint of Penguin Random House, 2017.

---. *The Vulnerable Observer: Anthropology that Breaks Your Heart.* Beacon Press, Boston, 1996.

---. *Traveling Heavy: A Memoir in Between Journeys.* Duke University Press, Durham and London, 2013.

Beinart, Peter. *The Crisis of Zionism.* Times Books Henry Holt and Company, 2012.

Bellow, Saul. *To Jerusalem and Back: A Personal Account.* Viking Books, New York, 1976.

Berger, Alan. *Crisis and Covenant: The Holocaust in American Jewish Fiction.* State University of New York, Albany, 1985.

Biale, David. *Power and Powerlessness in Jewish History.* Schocken Books, 1987.

Binyon, Michael. *Life in Russia.* Berkeley Books, 1985.

Brodski, Josif. *Proces.* Wydawn, 1989.

Brodsky, Joseph. *Less Than One: Selected Essays.* Farrar, Straus & Giroux, 1986.

Cahill, Thomas. *The Gifts of the Jews: How a Tribe of Desert Nomads Changed the Way Everyone Thinks and Feels.* Nan A. Talese/Anchor Books, 1998

Cain, Betty Swanson. *American from Sweden: The Story of A.V. Swanson.* Southern Illinois University Press, 1987.

Carroll, James. *Constantine's Sword: The Church and the Jews: A History.* Houghton Mifflin, Boston, 2001.

Catholic Teaching on the Shoah: Implementing the Holy See's We Remember. United States Catholic Conference, 2001.

Cherry, Shai. *Coherent Judaism: Constructive Theology, Creation & Halakhah.* Academic Studies Press, Brookline, MA., 2020.

---. *Torah Through Time: Understanding Bible Commentary From the Rabbinic Period to Modern Times.* The Jewish Publication Society, 2007.

Cohen, Rich. *Tough Jews.* Vintage Books, 1999.

---. *The Avengers: A Jewish War Story.* Vintage Books, New York, 2000.

Curry, Jane Leftwich, editor. *The Black Book of Polish Censorship.* Vintage Books, 1984.

Czerniawski, Adam. *Scenes From a Disturbed Childhood.* Serpent's Tail, 1991.

Davies, Norman. *God's Playground: A History of Poland; The Origins to 1795, Vol I.* Oxford University Press, 1982.

---. *God's Playground: A History of Poland, Vol II, 1795 to the Present.* Columbia University Press, New York, 1982.

---. *Heart of Europe: A Short History of Poland.* Oxford University Press, 1986.

Dawidowicz, Lucy S. *From That Place and Time: A Memoir, 1938-1947.* W. W. Norton & Company, 1989.

Diamant, Anita. *The Red Tent.* Picador, 1997.

Dillard, Annie. *For the Time Being.* Alfred A. Knopf, 1999.

---. *Living by Fiction.* Harper and Row, New York, 1982.

---. *The Writing Life.* Harper & Row, 1989.

Dillard, Annie, and Cort Conley, editors. *Modern American Memoirs.* HarperPerennial, 1996.

Dobroszycki, Lucjan, and Barbara Kirshenblatt-Gimblett. *Image Before My Eyes: A Photographic History of Jewish Life in Poland Before the Holocaust.* Schocken Books, 1977.

Duda, Eugeniusz. *From the History and Culture of Jews in Cracow: Guide to the Permanent Exhibition in the Old Synagogue.* Historical Museum of Cracow.

Engelking, Barbara. Translated by Jerzy Michalowicz. *Such a Beautiful Sunny Day: Jews Seeking Refuge in the Polish Countryside, 1942-1945.* Yad Vashem Publications, 2016.

Englander, Nathan. *What We Talk When We Talk About Anne Frank.* Alfred A. Knopf, 2012.

Epstein, Helen. *Where She Came From: A Daughter's Search for Her Mother's History.* Plume, 1998.

Epstein, Lawrence J. *At the Edge of a Dream: The Story of Jewish Immigrants on New York's Lower East Side 1880-1920.* Jossey-Bass, 2007.

Fabrègues Jean. *Edith Stein: Philosopher, Carmelite Nun, Holocaust Martyr.* St. Paul Books & Media, 1993.

Falkowska, Maria. *Translated by E.* Kulawiec

Fast, Howard. *The Jews: Story of a People.* Ibooks, 2006.

Ficowski, Jerzy, and Bruno Schulz. *Xięga Bałwochwalcza.* Interpress Publishers, 1988.

Foer, Jonathan Safran. *Everything Is Illuminated.* HarperPerennial, 2003.

Forster, E. M. *Howards End.* Vintage Books, 1921.

Frazier, Ian. *Family.* HarperPerennial, 1995.

Gibbons, Reginald, editor. *TriQuarterly 57: A Window on Poland, Vol I.* 1983.

Gillon, Adam, and Ludwik Krzyzanowski, editors. *1964. Introduction to Modern Polish Literature: An Anthology of Fiction and Poetry.* Hippocrene Books, 1982.

Gimbel, Steve. *Einstein's Jewish Science: Physics at the Intersection of Politics and Religion.* Johns Hopkins University Press, Baltimore, 1968.

Ginzburg, Natalia. *Family Sayings.* Seaver Books, 1986.

Głowacka, Dorota, and Joanna Zylinska, editors. *Imaginary Neighbors: Mediating Polish-Jewish Relations After the Holocaust.* University of Nebraska Press, 2007.

Gold, Ben-Zion. *The Life of Jews in Poland before the Holocaust: A Memoir.* University of Nebraska Press, Lincoln and London, 2007.

Gold, Michael. *Jews Without Money, 1930.* Carroll & Graf Publishers, 2004.

Goldberg, David J., and John D. Rayner. *The Jewish People: Their History and Religion.* Penguin Books, 1989.

Goldstein, Rebecca. *Betraying Spinoza: The Renegade Jew Who Gave Us Modernity.* Schocken Books, 2006.

Gopnik, Adam. *Through the Children's Gate: A Home in New York.* Vintage Books, A Division of Random House, Inc., New York, 2007.

Gornick, Vivian. *Fierce Attachments: A Memoir, 1987.* Farrar, Straus and Giroux, 2005.

---. *The Situation and the Story: The Art of Personal Narrative.* Farrar, Straus and Giroux, 2001.

Grass, Günter. *Peeling the Onion: A Memoir.* Translated by Michael Henry Heim, Harcourt, 2007.

Green, Arthur. *Radical Judaism.* Yale University Press, New Haven and London, 2010.

Gronowicz, Antoni. *Polish Profiles: The Land, the People and Their History.* L.awrence Hill & Company, 1976.

Gross, Jan Tomasz. *Fear: Anti-Semitism in Poland After Auschwitz.* Random House, 2006.

---. *Golden Harvest.* Oxford University Press, 2012.

Hampl, Patricia. *A Romantic Education.* W.W. Norton & Company, 1999.

Havel, Vaclav. *Largo Desolato: A Play in Seven Scenes.* Grove Press, 1985.

Heller, Celia S. *On the Edge of Destruction: Jews of Poland Between the Two World Wars.* Schocken Books, 1980.

Hertz, Aleksander. *The Jews in Polish Culture.* Northwestern University Press, Evanston, 1988.

Heschel, Abraham Joshua. *God in Search of Man: A Philosophy of Judaism.* Farrar, Straus, Giroux, New York, 1976.

---. *Man is Not Alone.* Farrar, Straus, Giroux, New York, 1976.

Hoffman, Adina and Peter Cole. *Sacred Trash: The Lost and Found World of the Cairo Geniza.* Schocken Books, New York, 2011.

Hoffman, Alice. *The World That We Knew.* Simon and Schuster, New York, 2019.

Hoffman, Eva. *Lost in Translation: A Life in a New Language.* E.P. Dutton, 1989.

---. *Shtetl: The Life and Death of a Small Town and the World of Polish Jews.* PublicAffairs, 2007.

Howard, Maureen. *Facts of Life.* Penguin Books, 1980.

Howe, Irving, ed. *Jewish American Stories.* New American Library, New York, 1977.

---. *World of Our Fathers: The Journey of the East European Jews to America and the Life They Found and Made.* New York University Press, New York, 1976.

Inchausti, Robert. *The Ignorant Perfection of Ordinary People.* State University of New York Press, 1991.

Jacoby, Susan. *Half-Jew: A Daughter's Search for Her Family's Buried Past.* Scribner, 2000.

Jahn, Gary R., editor. *Slavic and East European Journal, Vol. 35 No. 3.* 1991.

Jasienica, Paweł. *Jagiellonian Poland.* Translated by Alexander Jordan, American Institute of Polish Culture, 1978.

Judt, Tony. *The Memory Chalet.* The Penguin Press, 2010.

Jütte, Robert. *The Jewish Body: A History, trans.* Elizabeth Bredeck, University of Pennsylvania Press, Philadelphia, 2021.

Kates, Judith A., and Gail Twersky Reimer, editors. *Reading Ruth: Contemporary Women Reclaim a Sacred Story.* Ballantine Books, 1994.

Kazin, Alfred. *A Lifetime Burning in Every Moment.* HarperCollins Publishers, 1996.

---. *A Walker in the City.* Harcourt Books, 1979.

Korbonski, Stefan. *The Jews and the Poles in World War II.* Hippocrene Books, 1989.

---. *The Polish Underground State: A Guide to the Underground 1939-1945.* Translated by Marta Erdman, Hippocrene Books, 1981.

Korczak, Janusz. *The Warsaw Ghetto Memoirs of Janusz Korczak.* Translated by Edwin P. Kulawiec, University Press of America, 1978.

Kościuszko, Jefferson. *Correspondence.* Edited by Bogdan Grzeloński, Interpress Publishers, 1978.

Kott, Jan, editor. *Four Decades of Polish Essays.* Northwestern University Press, 1990.

Kovner, Abba, et al., editors. *Beth Hatefutsoth: The Nahum Goldmann Museum of the Jewish Diaspora.* Fourth Printing, 1985.

Kriwaczek, Paul. *Yiddish Civilisation: The Rise and Fall of a Forgotten Nation.* Vintage Books, New York, 2005.

Kroszczor, Henryk, and Henryk Zimler. *Cmentarz Żydowski W Warszawie.* Warszawa, 1983.

Kubar, Zofia S. *Double Identity: A Memoir.* Hill and Wang, 1989.

Kuncewicz, Maria, editor. *The Modern Polish Mind: An Anthology.* Little, Brown and Company, 1962.

Lanzmann, Claude. *Shoah: An Oral History of the Holocaust.* Pantheon Books, 1985.

Lehrer, Erica and Michael Meng, eds. *Jewish Space in Contemporary Poland.* Indiana University Press, Bloomington and Indianapolis, 2015.

Levi, Primo. *The Periodic Table, 1984.* Translated by Raymond Rosenthal, Everyman's Library, 1995.

Lewin, Abraham. *A Cup of Tears.* Edited by Antony Polonsky, Basil Blackwell, 1989.

Lewin, Isaac. *The Jewish Community in Poland.* The Polish Institute of Arts and Sciences of America Books, 1985.

Limmer, Ruth. *Journey Around My Room: The Autobiography of Louise Bogan.* Penguin Books, 1981.

Liulevicius, Vejas Gabriel. *A History of Eastern Europe.* The Great Courses, 2015.

Luderer, Kenneth M. *Time to Heal: American Medical Education from the Turn of the Century to the Era of Managed Care.* Oxford University Press, 1999.

Lukas, Richard C., editor. *Out of the Inferno: Poles Remember the Holocaust.* University Press of Kentucky, 1989.

Mairs, Nancy. *Carnal Acts.* HarperCollins Publishers, 1990.

---. *Plain Text: Essays.* The University of Arizona Press, 1986.

Mendelsohn, Daniel Adam. *The Lost: A Search for Six of Six Million.* HarperPerennial, 2007.

Metzker, Isaac, editor. *A Bintel Brief: Sixty Years of Letters from the Lower East Side to the Jewish Daily Forward.* Schocken Books, 1971.

Michlic, Joanna B., and Antony Polonsky, editors. *The Neighbors Respond: The Controversy Over the Jedwabne Massacre in Poland.* Princeton University Press, 2004.

Milosz, Czeslaw. *The Captive Mind, 1953.* Penguin Books, 1980.

---. *The Seizure of Power.* Translated by Celina Wieniewska, Farrar, Straus and Giroux , 1982.

---. *A Year of the Hunter.* Translated by Madeline G Levine, Farrar, Straus and Giroux, 1994.

Miłosz, Czesław, ed. *Postwar Polish Poetry.* University of California Press, Berkeley, 1983.

Morris, Benny. *Righteous Victims: A History of the Zionist-Arab Conflict, 1881-2001.* Vintage Books, 2001.

Mosbacher, Eric, translator. *Ferdydurke, 1961.* Edited by Philip Roth, Penguin Books, 1986.

Mur, Jan. *A Prisoner of Poland: Martial Law, 1981-1982.* Harcourt, Brace, Jovanovich, New York, 1984.

Murphy, Cullen. *God's Jury: The Inquisition and the Making of the Modern World.* Houghton Mifflin Harcourt, 2012.

Museum Narodowe We Wrocławiu: Zbiory i Wystawy. Wrocław, 1983.

Neiman, Susan. *Learning from the Germans: Confronting Race and the Memory of Evil.* Farrar, Straus and Giroux, 2019.

Potok, Chaim. *Wanderings: Chaim Potok's History of the Jews.* Fawcett Crest, 1980.

Rahden, Till. *Jews and Other Germans: Civil Society, Religious Diversity and Urban Politics in Breslau, 1860-1925.* Translated by Marcus Brainard, The University of Wisconsin Press, 2008.

Rendell, Kenneth W., and Samantha Heywood. *The Power of Anti-Semitism; The March to the Holocaust 1919-1939.* Museum of World War II, 2016.

Rich, Adrienne. *Blood, Bread, and Poetry: Selected Prose 1979-1985.* W. W. Norton and Co., New York and London, 1986.

Rich, Adrienne. *Diving Into the Wreck: Poems 1971-1972, W.W.* Norton and Co., New York and London, 1973.

Rodriguez, Richard. *Brown: The Last Discovery of America.* Penguin Books, 2002.

Roiphe, Anne. *Generation Without Memory: A Jewish Journey in Christian America.* Summit Books, New York, 1981.

Roth, Henry. *Mercy of a Rude Stream: A Star Shines Over Mt. Morris Park.* Picador, 1994.

Roth, Joseph. *The Wandering Jews.* Translated by Michael Hoffman, W. W. Norton & Company, 2001.

Rudner, Lawrence. *The Magic We Do Here.* Houghton Mifflin Company, 1988.

Sagajllo, Witold. *The Man in the Middle.* Hippocrene Books, New York, 1985.

Sakowska, Ruta, et al. *The Warsaw Ghetto.* Interpress Publishers, 1987.

Salsitz, Norman. *A Jewish Boyhood in Poland: Remembering Kolbuszowa.* Syracuse University Press, 1992.

Sarton, May. *Journal of a Solitude, 1973.* Norton & Company, 1977.

Sartre, Jean-Paul. *Anti-Semite and Jew.* Schocken Books, New York, 1965.

Schama, Simon. *Landscape and Memory.* Vintage Books, 1996.

Schlink, Bernhard. *Guilt About the Past.* University of Queensland Press, 2009.

Scholl, Inge. *The White Rose: Munich 1942-1943, 1970.* Translated by Arthur R. Schultz, Wesleyan University Press, 1983.

Silberman, Charles E. *A Certain People: American Jews and Their Lives Today.* Summit Books, 1985.

Simon, Kate. *Bronx Primitive: Portraits in a Childhood.* Harper & Row, 1982.

Singer, Isaac Bashevis. *Love and Exile: An Autobiographical Trilogy.* Farrar, Straus, Giroux, New York, 1984.

Slezkine, Yuri. *The Jewish Century.* Princeton University Press, 2004.

Snyder, Timothy. *Bloodlands: Europe Between Hitler and Stalin.* Basic Books, New York, 2012.

Soto, Gary, editor. *California Childhood: Recollections and Stories of the Golden State.* Creative Arts Books Company, 1988.

Steiner, Jean-François. *Treblinka, 1966.* Translated by Helen Weaver, New American Library, 1979.

Steinman, Louise. *The Crooked Mirror: A Memoir of Polish-Jewish Reconciliation.* Beacon Press, 2013.

Steven, Stewart. *The Poles.* Macmillan Publishing Company, 1982.

Szpilman, Władysław. *The Pianist: The Extraordinary True Story of One Man's Survival in Warsaw, 1939-1945.* Picador, New York, 1999.

Tóibín, Colm. *The Sign of the Cross: Travels in Catholic Europe.* Random House, New York, 1994.

Topolski, Jerzy. *An Outline History of Poland.* Translated by Olgierd Wojtasiewicz, Interpress Publishers, 1986.

Twain, Mark. *Concerning the Jews.* Running Press, 1985.

Vital, David. *A People Apart: A Political History of the Jews in Europe 1789-1939*. Oxford University Press, 1999.

Wałęsa, Lech. *A Way of Hope*. Henry Holt and Company, 1987.

Wardi, Dina. *Memorial Candles: Children of the Holocaust*. Translated by Naomi Goldblum, Routledge, 1992.

Waterford, Helen. *Commitment to the Dead: One Woman's Journey Toward Understanding*. Renaissance House Publishers, 1987.

Wedel, Janine. *The Private Poland*. Facts On File Publications, 1986.

Weschler, Lawrence. *The Passion of Poland: From Solidarity Through the State of War*. Pantheon Books, 1984.

---. *Vermeer in Bosnia: Selected Writings*. Vintage Books, 2005.

Wex, Michael. *Born to Kvetch: Yiddish Language and Culture in All of Its Moods*. HarperPerennial, 2006.

White, E.B. *Here is New York*. Harper and Bros., New York, 1949.

Wiesel, Elie. *Dawn*. Bantam Books, Toronto, et al, 1960.

---. *Night*. Bantam Books, Toronto, et al, 1960.

---. *Souls on Fire*. Summit Books, New York, 1972.

Wisse, Ruth R. *The Modern Jewish Canon: A Journey Through Language and Culture*. The Free Press, 2000.

. *Yizkor Book of Brest-Litovsk – Volume II, Encyclopedia of the Jewish Diaspora.*.

. *Yizkor Book of Kobrin; The Scroll of Life and Destruction*. Eds. Betzalel Shwartz and Israel Chaim, Bil(e)tzki, Tel Aviv, 1951.

Zinsser, William. *Writing About Your Life: A Journey Into the Past*. Da Capo Press, 2004.

Acknowledgements

A book like this spanning time and space includes so many people to thank. Typically, the author's acknowledgements end with a personal thanks to a partner. But mine has to begin there: call it *bashert* that led me to meet the artist, John David Ratajkowski, in the late 70's, a painter who had been to Poland during martial law in1981, barely escaping with the paintings he was exhibiting at that time in Warsaw. While my entire life had been involved with the subject of my Jewish identity, it was meeting John that determined me to go to Poland. This was 1984 when we went to Poland together. During that visit it was the utter absence of discussion of Polish Jewry, the disturbing silence on the subject, and the implied taboo of even speaking about this annihilated community so significant to Poland's history, that made me know I had to return on my own. I applied for and won the Fulbright award to teach American literature to Polish university students.

The Fulbright years (1987-1989) when I lived and taught first at universities in Silesia and then in Wrocław offer a veritable cast of Polish friends and colleagues who made my two years in that country such a full and unforgettable experience. From the taxi driver, Dziedzic, and his wife, Hania, in Sosnowiec, who without their generosity and care I'm not convinced I would have arrived to my classes on time; to colleagues Jurek and his wife Ewa, who welcomed me into their home from the very first, and became fast and enduring friends; to Pani Zofia in Warsaw who treated me like her absent beloved daughter; to the Sieniawska-Kania family in Łazy who shared more than one of their family holidays with me, and who understanding my drive to learn about the history of the Jewish community in Poland, introduced me to their lifelong friend, Dr. Danuta Havel, a Polish Jewish survivor of the Shoah. Dr. Havel gave me firsthand views of living as a Jew in pre and post-war Poland.

In Wrocław, my second year assignment, it is to my brilliant and welcoming MA students, that I owe the biggest debt of gratitude. They made the teaching a delight, and often guided me through the machinations of government-imposed difficulties. Piotr, for example, on day one of class, showed me an underground (literally and figuratively) copy center where I could get the papers I needed reproduced for my students. Dominika, the most gifted student

I ever had in my career to date, whether in the US or Europe, advised me on so many matters concerned with just managing to figure out how to live everyday life. The friendship of colleagues at the Institute in Wrocław, Dorota, Bożena and her husband, Krzysztof, and her brother, Romek, provided a social life for me that was wonderfully warm and a break from the hard work of teaching and living in Poland

In Israel, the welcoming hospitality of my never before met relatives, Mira and Itzhak Shpilman and their children; Rachel, Ron, Ze'ev and their family, who spelled their name "Balgaly", all embraced me and fêted me with genuine affection. The American journalist living in Israel, Mike Tannenbaum, made it possible to find and meet my family there by seeking them out before my arrival—many thanks.

In Brest, Belarus, (please note that in order to protect my friends in Belarus from governmental retribution, I have necessarily used pseudonyms), my indefatigable guide, Julija, so dedicated to my quest that she never gave up: because of her devotion, I found records of my lost family, needles in a haystack that the less committed would never have found. We became lifelong friends in three days. Our driver in Brest, Alexei, delivered us expeditiously to every odd place we needed to go and on time. He was invested in my search, it was clear. Alexei's father, Maxim, the nominal head of Brest's Jewish community, recalled my surname, and connected it to Jacob Balgley, the painter who had lived in Brest and died in Paris in 1934: just two weeks before my arrival to Brest, there had been an exhibition of Jacob Balgley's paintings. To my friend, Staszek, with whom I disagree on most things Polish and Jewish, thank you for figuring out the labyrinthine path from Warsaw to Brest—that train timetable was confounding even to a Pole. You got me there. And once in Grodno, Belarus, among the dusty archives and endless obstacles to research, the work of Miriam Weiner, creator of "Routes to Roots", who stood in a line for computer use during Hurricane Sandy and answered my cry for help, you are the definition of *mensch*.

For the creating of this book, when it was in the gestational phase, my friend, the teacher and writer, Kay Allgire, Ph.D., not only spent hours talking with me about the possible ways this story could be told, but also because I hadn't enough room in my home office to accommodate the scores of boxes of files I had created for the book, she graciously made room in her own home for me to store them. At this stage, John, by now my husband, listened to and talked with me about what I wanted this book to be. Our daughter, Emily Ratajkowski, gave me perspectives and ideas about my story that proved fresh and essential.

But before writing could even begin, a veritable library of files of my research, dozens of boxes shipped by me from Poland filled with stacks of my notes, photographs, pamiątka (the Polish term for "keepsake"), this last a heuristic for recollection, all these mountains of boxes had to be unpacked and organized in some fashion. Thank you to teacher Tim Roberts who provided me with student assistants, Elise Echeverria, Marisa Youmans, Taylor Rudman. These young people dug in with enthusiasm and intelligence, and over one hundred binders were produced organized by subject. I now had pay dirt: the writing could begin.

I want to thank the generous readers of my early drafts: my supportive siblings, Michael J. Balgley, Jane M. Davis, and Elise M. Balgley; trusted friends and colleagues, Karen Romero, Patricia Demory, Jim McElroy, Marcia Appelbaum Caulkins, Elizabeth Fowler Ross, Merrie Sasaki, and again, Kay Allgire. And once the draft was refined, it went to Dermott Barrett in Dublin, Ireland, a gifted reader and respondent who provided a valuable European perspective on the book.

Without the talent and dedication of IT genius, Mike Gates, this project could not have proceeded. Working page by page, Mike designed layout for the many photographs and documents I include in the book for posterity sake. His patience with and cheerful reactions to my tech naivete were endless—his mark is truly on this book.

The wiley and wise guidance of Jennifer McCord led me through the labyrinth of self-publishing—and Rudy Ramos, designer extraordinaire, provided final design for the book—many thanks for your care and patience. Thank you, too, to Gelila Yoseph, for her wonderful design work for the cover, and to Erica Putis for creating the book's website, handling copyright permissions, and myriad other matters I could not have resolved!

Every quotation mark and comma had to be vetted: this painstaking review was led by Kay Allgire. I owe an inestimable debt of gratitude to her for her generosity with her time and expertise. Any punctuation errors in the book are mine, not hers!

To the hugely talented team at Studio West in San Diego: Colin Tedeschi, Brian Keim and David Martinez for professionalism rarely seen—you made the creation of my audiobook enjoyable and interesting—gratitude and admiration.

To my dear friend, Karen Romero, who performed the Preface to my book for the audiobook, you've been such a stalwart supporter from the start, my heartfelt gratitude.

A special debt of thanks to Rabbi Haim Beliak of *Beit Polska*, Jewish Renewal in Poland, in Los Angeles who was the first to take a special interest in my book, inviting me to present to a select group of Jewish scholars, professors and philanthropists at his home, and who continued to create opportunities for the public to learn about my book. It was at Rabbi Beliak's home where I met philanthropist, Severyn Ashkenazy, who encouraged me in my research. When I returned to Poland to continue research, warm thanks to Severyn and Irina sayn-Wittgenstein who opened their home to me in Kazimierz Dolny and to their center, *Beit Warszawa*, where I attended services and met many of the Jewish community in Warsaw.

To Witold Wrzosinski, genealogist in Warsaw, who researched the Balgley family back to the 1600's in Brest; and to Alijca Goldman/ Mroczkowska of the Jewish Historical Institute in Warsaw, who met me at the Okopowa Jewish Cemetery and led me without hesitation through the rain to my great- grandfather's grave—I am indebted to your work and your help with my project.

Gratitude to Anita Lanner, my dear friend in San Diego, a hidden child and survivor, who invited me to her Havurot group at her home to present my writing-in-progress, and to the La Jolla JCC who sponsored my project's presentation there.

To my reviewers: Rabbi Shai Cherry, scholar and author, who was my teacher and friend from the start of my journey to adoption; to the late Professor Mike Rose, a wonderful writer and teacher and friend from UCLA; to Robert (Larry) Inchausti, my colleague and friend at Cal Poly, whose own writing and research in part inspired me to take on this project; to Professor Steven Marx, another Cal Poly colleague, close friend, and author whose perspective as a child of Jewish parents who fled Germany provided a particularly honest and insightful response to my book; to Louise Steinman, author of a marvelous book, *The Crooked Mirror*, to which mine may be a prequel, who became a friend and a generous supporter; to Professor Cezar Ornatowski, scholar and friend, who brought his own unique perspective as a citizen of Poland to his review; to Ruth Behar, author of *An Island Called Home: Returning to Jewish Cuba* and many other books and film; to Professor Alain Cohen, whose double expertise in literature and psychoanalysis brought an original perspective to his reading of my book—warm gratitude for your time and praise..

The extended family I discovered by dint of research for this book is a joy that is unparalleled: Shirley Balgley Tainowitz and her daughter Randi Borgen, schlepped me all over Brooklyn and beyond to my father's old haunts and to meet the eldest surviving Balgleys, Aunt Beattie and Uncle Morris, my grandfather's siblings, and to the other Uncle Morris, my father's estranged brother, who embraced me as his niece. Meredith Balgley, her husband, Erik Bendix, their son, Aaron came to San Diego to meet me; their other son, Noah

Bendix-Balgley, concertmaster of the Berlin Philharmonic made time to meet me at his concert in Los Angeles; artists Lena Schneiderman and her mother Lydia Schigimont of Cologne, descendants of the very same Jacob Balgley, the painter I had early on learned about, both gifted painters themselves, are dear friends, though as yet only virtually due to Covid.

A special debt of thanks with affection to Yossi and Dorit Ben-Gal, their children Itai and Nitsan, who again, like needles in a haystack, I was able to find, befriend, and benefit from all the help they provided in putting together our family tree.

Gratitude that can almost not be put into words to Professor Dominika Ferens, the self-same former student who helped me survive during my Fulbright; that person who has remained a friend for all the decades since that time; and who now as Professor at the Institute of English Philology at Wrocław University in Poland, composed the Preface to this book at a time when she had several doctoral dissertations to direct; her own writing deadlines to meet; and preparation as keynote speaker at an upcoming conference. Dominika remains my ideal as a writer, critic, thinker, teacher, human being.

To oncologist Dr. Anuj Mahindra and the team of nurses in the chemo ward, thank you for taking care of me, keeping me alive, so I can enjoy my good fortune in the love of these people here mentioned.

Kathleen Balgley
June 2022

About the Author

Kathleen A. Balgley, Ph.D. in literature from University of California, San Diego, was during her four-decade academic career tenured Associate Professor of English at California State University, San Luis Obispo; Lecturer at UCLA Writing Program; and Associate Director of Writing at UCSD's Sixth College. Recipient of numerous awards, she received, among others, a grant from the California Council of the Humanities for her project on Roma culture and history, another from the California Literature Project, and was awarded a Fulbright Professorship to communist Poland two years before the fall of the Berlin Wall (1987-1989). Her essays and reviews have appeared in the United States and Poland.

Author Kathleen A. Balgley at the grave of her great-grandfather, Ze'ev (Velvel or "Little Wolf") Balgley (1859-1916) at the Okopowa Jewish Cemetery in Warsaw, Poland

CPSIA information can be obtained
at www.ICGtesting.com
Printed in the USA
LVHW041220200523
747578LV00001B/2